UNDER FIRE

U.S. Military Restrictions on the Media From Grenada to the Persian Gulf

Jacqueline E. Sharkey

THE CENTER FOR PUBLIC INTEGRITY

1910 K Street, N.W., Suite 802
Washington, D.C. 20006
(202) 223-0299

The Center for Public Integrity is an independent, non-profit organization examining public service and ethics-related issues in Washington with a unique approach combining the substantive study of government and in-depth journalism. The Center is funded by foundations, corporations, labor unions, individuals and revenue from news organizations.

Special thanks to the **Deer Creek Foundation** and the **J. Roderick MacArthur Foundation**, which provided specific funding for this project.

This Center study and the views expressed herein are those of the author. What is written here does not necessarily reflect the views of individual members of The Center for Public Integrity Board of Directors or the Advisory Board.

Copyright © 1991 THE CENTER FOR PUBLIC INTEGRITY. All rights reserved. No part of this publication may be reproduced or used in any form or by any means, electronic or mechanical, including photocopying, recording, or by any information storage or retrieval system, without the written permission of The Center for Public Integrity.

ISBN 0-962-90123-7

A popular government without popular information, or the means of acquiring it, is but a prologue to a farce or a tragedy, or, perhaps both.

James Madison

Jacqueline E. Sharkey is one of this country's preeminent international investigative journalists. During the past eight years, her investigative reporting from Central America has won several national awards, including an Overseas Press Club Citation for Excellence, a Society of Professional Journalists Distinguished Service Award, an Investigative Reporters and Editors Award, and the Sidney Hillman Foundation Award. Her articles on U.S. policy in the region, which appeared in *Common Cause Magazine*, helped lay the foundation for an investigation of Col. Oliver North's private contra network by a Senate Foreign Relations subcommittee, and were used by investigators for the Iran-contra congressional committees. Sharkey, a University of Arizona journalism professor, is a former *Washington Post* copy editor, and was a Fulbright fellow in Colombia. She has B.A. and M.A. degrees in journalism from the University of Arizona, and a master's degree in the study of law from Yale Law School.

Researchers in Washington, Miami and Arizona assisted Sharkey. They include:

Christine Stavem, chief researcher for the project, is Senior Associate at the Center for Public Integrity in Washington, and a graduate of the University of Arizona.

James R. Callard, an adjunct professor at Fort Lewis College, is doing research for his doctoral dissertation. An officer and pilot in the Air Force Reserve, he was deployed to Saudi Arabia during Operation Desert Storm.

Elizabeth Baker teaches media communications at Pima Community College and is a graduate student at the University of Arizona.

Elizabeth Hannan has a master's degree in journalism from the University of Arizona. Her graduate work included award-winning research on U.S. media coverage of the Grenada invasion.

Beth Hawkins is completing a master's degree in journalism at the University of Arizona and worked as a stringer in Central America for the *Los Angeles Times*.

Donine S. Henshaw has a bachelor's degree in radio-television from the University of Arizona and is a journalist working in Tucson.

Kenny Langone has a master's degree in journalism from the University of Arizona and is a freelance reporter and photographer based in Tucson.

Sue Mullin is a freelance writer and researcher in Miami who has worked extensively in Central America. Her stories have appeared in *USA Today* and *The Orange County Register*.

K. J. Scotta has a bachelor's degree in fine arts from the University of Arizona and is a reporter for the *Tucson Citizen*.

William H. Wing, a professor of physics and optical sciences at the University of Arizona, served as scientific and technical consultant for this study, and provided invaluable editorial assistance.

Maggy Zanger, who has a master's degree in the study of law from Yale Law School, is an investigative reporter who has worked in Central America and the Middle East.

Jean Cobb, who edited the study, for the past year has been Senior Editor at the Center, and until recently was Associate Editor of *Common Cause Magazine*. In 1988, she won the Investigative Reporters and Editors Award for outstanding investigative journalism. In 1989, articles on campaign finance by Cobb and other magazine staffers received the Society of Professional Journalists Award for public service.

Charles Lewis is the founder and Executive Director of the Center for Public Integrity. For 11 years, he did investigative reporting at ABC News and CBS News, most recently as a producer for the program, *60 Minutes*.

TABLE OF CONTENTS

Chapters

I	Executive Summary	1
II	The Military-Media Relationship	7
III	Pentagon Information-Management Techniques	23
IV	Issues Raised by Media Restrictions	31
V	The Vietnam War	39
VI	The Falklands/Malvinas War	61
VII	The Invasion of Grenada	67
VIII	The Invasion of Panama	91
IX	The War in the Gulf	107
X	Conclusions and Recommendations	157
	Endnotes	173

Appendices

A.   Department of Defense Principles of Information

B.   The Sidle Panel Report

C.   Review of Panama Pool Deployment — December 1989 (The Hoffman Report)

D.   Media Ground Rules and Guidelines for Operation Desert Shield and Operation Desert Storm

EXECUTIVE SUMMARY

The recent war in the Persian Gulf has been perceived as a major triumph for U.S. military forces and foreign policy. Victory parades have made front-page news, Gen. H. Norman Schwarzkopf has become a new national hero, and President George Bush has received some of the highest public opinion ratings in history. But one aspect of the conflict has received less attention. The Gulf War included unprecedented restrictions on the press by the military, and an extensive campaign by the White House and the Pentagon to influence public opinion by presenting Americans with carefully controlled images and information concerning the conflict and the issues surrounding the Bush administration's decision to use U.S. troops to resolve the crisis. The result was a defeat for the First Amendment guarantee of press freedom and the public's right to independent information about the political decisions that can lead to U.S. military involvement abroad, and the ramifications of such involvement.

This study examines the controversies surrounding restrictions on the media during the Gulf War and two major U.S. offensive military operations in the 1980s: the invasions of Grenada and Panama.

Major Findings

Extensive research about military restrictions on the press and the political factors that have contributed to these restrictions during the past 10 years reveals a disturbing pattern of escalating control over media access to information on and off the battlefield. The evidence shows that, increasingly, information about Defense Department activities is being restricted or manipulated not for national security purposes, but for political purposes — to protect the image and priorities of the Defense Department and its civilian leaders, including the President, who is the Commander-in-Chief of the Armed Forces.

This pattern is not simply a clash of mentalities between the military and the media. Many crucial decisions about information policies have been made by civilian leaders in the Pentagon and the White House over the objections of military officers who have fought hard to maintain journalists' access to the field and Armed Forces personnel, and have worked around the clock during operations to assist reporters' and photographers' efforts to present independent information to the American people.

The techniques used by the government to limit and shape news coverage — which have included prohibiting access to military operations and releasing misleading data about U.S. successes and casualties — bring up issues that go far beyond the obvious need to balance military secrecy requirements with the public's right to know. This information-control program has distorted accounts of what occurred during the military operations in Grenada, Panama and the Persian Gulf, has led to false perceptions about the operations' short- and long-term impact on these regions and on U.S. policy, and has threatened the historical record.

Research for this Center REPORT, prepared during the past twelve months, has included examining dozens of books and articles by military officers and civilian

Pentagon officials that discuss the relationship between the Defense Department and the press; analyzing thousands of pages of U.S. military documents; reviewing dozens of U.S. and British legal documents; reviewing hundreds of articles by journalists, academics and policy analysts in the United States and Great Britain; viewing hundreds of hours of television coverage and public affairs programs featuring speakers on all sides of the debate; studying transcripts of briefings and news conferences by White House, Pentagon and State Department officials; and interviewing dozens of people who served as military officers, Pentagon officials or journalists during World War II, Korea, Vietnam, and the three operations in question. Material used in this study has been restricted as much as possible to primary documents and first-person accounts.

Evidence Relating to the Gulf War

In the months following Operation Desert Storm, considerable evidence has emerged that the news-management strategy used by the Bush administration was designed not to enable the American people to make an objective evaluation of the events leading up to the conflict and the conduct of the war itself, but to promote public support for predetermined agendas, such as access to oil and support for controversial weapons systems.

Highlights of this evidence include:

• Congressional testimony by a former Pentagon official that the Defense Department "doctored" statistics about the success rates of weapons systems in the Gulf to increase public support for the war and congressional support for additional weapons funding.[1]

• Congressional testimony by a former Pentagon adviser that the Patriot missiles were not as effective as the Defense Department claimed, and that they may have caused more damage than they prevented.[2]

• Statements by Air Force Chief of Staff Gen. Merrill A. McPeak which indicate that Pentagon videos depicting laser-guided bombs hitting their targets with surgical precision — which were shown repeatedly on the networks and Cable News Network — presented a distorted view of the air war. At a postwar briefing, McPeak released statistics showing that such bombs represented 8.8 percent of the ordnance dropped by U.S. forces on Iraq. The remaining 91.2 percent of the 84,200 tons of bombs dropped by the United States during the conflict were "dumb" bombs that had no precision guidance systems.[3]

• Statements indicating that Pentagon briefer Lt. Gen. Thomas Kelly's claims during the first week of the war that bombing missions had an 80 percent success rate[4] were misleading. After repeated questioning by reporters, Defense Department officials clarified that "success" meant a plane had taken off, released its ordnance in the area of the target, and returned to its base.[5] Gen. McPeak admitted during his postwar briefing that during the first 10 days of the air war, the weather was so bad that coalition pilots could not even see 40 percent of their primary targets.[6] Lt.

Gen. Kelly later said the problem resulted from a "policy change" about how the term "success rate" should be defined.[7]

• Evidence that private video firms interested in producing Gulf War programs that would present the U.S. military effort in a positive light were allowed greater access to the field than journalists. Quantum Diversified, a Minneapolis firm that wanted to make a video featuring the National Guard, spent eight days photographing selected units in the Gulf in October 1990. At the time, reporters sometimes waited weeks to spend brief periods of time with specific military units. The itinerary for Quantum Diversified — which received technical assistance for the video from NFL Films — was set up with the consent of U.S. Central Command and the help of Pentagon officials, including the Office of the Assistant Secretary of Defense for Public Affairs (OASD/PA).[8] When Quantum Diversified wanted to shoot additional footage in March, Pentagon officials again arranged space on a military flight, and Central Command sent a message to Army, Air Force, Marine and Navy officials stating the crew had theater clearance. Maj. Robert Dunlap of the National Guard Bureau's Public Affairs Office in the Pentagon said the Defense Department was happy to help because Quantum Diversified wasn't a "fly-by-night" operation that would "put out a bunch of bad news stories."[9]

• Indications that the Pentagon was unwilling to disclose what it knew about the likelihood of civilian casualties caused by U.S. and allied bombing. During Pentagon briefings, officials repeatedly stressed that U.S. planes were avoiding civilian targets, but little was said or asked about the long-range effects that the bombing of Iraq's infrastructure would have on the civilian population. A report prepared in May 1991 by a Harvard study team predicted that 170,000 Iraqi children would die within the next year as a result of the effects of the Gulf crisis. One principal reason was that coalition bombing destroyed health and sanitation facilities, and agricultural production.[10] A United Nations report said that thousands of Iraqis would die because of the "near-apocalyptic" conditions created by the bombing, and indicated that children and the elderly were especially at risk.[11]

• Evidence that while Defense Department personnel were complaining about the numbers of journalists from large media organizations who were sent to cover Operation Desert Shield, the Pentagon was providing transportation, escorts and special access to the battlefield for more than 150 reporters from smaller cities and towns so they could produce "Hi, Mom" stories about local troops stationed in Saudi Arabia. Most of the resulting coverage was highly supportive of the Defense Department's actions.

• Evidence of a wider effort by the Bush administration to shape public opinion about the long-term effects of the Gulf War. A Jan. 25, 1991 Department of Energy memo ordered DOE contractors and personnel working in DOE facilities to "immediately *discontinue* any further discussion of war related research and issues with the media until further notice." [Emphasis is DOE's.] The memo provided a script instructing personnel to tell reporters who wanted information on the environmental consequences of the war to state that "predictions remain speculative, and do not warrant any further comment at this time."[12]

• Evidence of a sophisticated public relations campaign by private organizations and foreign groups to build support for White House policies in the Gulf. In August 1990, Hill and Knowlton — a PR firm whose President and Chief Operating Officer of Public Affairs, Worldwide is Craig Fuller, Vice President Bush's Chief of Staff from 1985 to 1989 — was hired by representatives of the Kuwaiti government to help sell the American people on the need for U.S. military intervention. Hill and Knowlton's President and Chief Executive Officer, USA, Robert Dilenschneider, said in a speech that the firm's job was "to build support behind the President."[13] One way it did this, Dilenschneider said, was by providing the media, which were "controlled by the Department of Defense very effectively," with "the kind of information that would enable them to get their job done."[14] Hill and Knowlton was paid more than $10 million for its efforts.[15]

• Indications that Bush administration officials were acting from political motivations when they decided to bar the media from Dover (Del.) Air Force Base during the arrival of caskets carrying troops killed in the Gulf War. During the 1989 U.S. invasion of Panama, two networks and CNN showed split-screen live coverage of President Bush joking with reporters before a press conference as the bodies of U.S. soldiers killed in the fighting arrived simultaneously at Dover. The President said at a later press conference that the coverage made him look callous, and had prompted negative letters to the White House.[16]

The Falklands Model of Press Control During Wartime

The current system of media restrictions and information control is the latest refinement in a Pentagon and White House policy that has been evolving for more than 25 years.

The Vietnam War provided the impetus for the system's development. Many military officers believed that the United States lost the war because negative media coverage turned the American people against the conflict. In the late 1970s, Pentagon officials began searching for a new model for dealing with the press. They found one in Great Britain, where the Thatcher government had strictly controlled the media during the 1982 war with Argentina over the Falkland Islands. The fact that the Pentagon was interested in this model of press control had chilling overtones, because Great Britain still retains some of the press restrictions that led the Founding Fathers to adopt the First Amendment guarantee of press freedom.

One article written for a U.S. Naval War College publication outlined the lessons that the Pentagon could learn from the Falklands model. To maintain public support for a war, the article said, a government should sanitize the visual images of war; control media access to military theaters; censor information that could upset readers or viewers; and exclude journalists who would not write favorable stories. The Pentagon used all these techniques to one extent or another during subsequent wars.[17]

Grenada

The 1983 invasion of Grenada gave the Pentagon its first opportunity to try these news-management techniques. Pentagon personnel, with the knowledge and approval of the White House, barred journalists during the first two days of fighting. Reporters who tried to reach the island by boat were detained by U.S. forces and held *in communicado*. Journalists who tried to fly in were "buzzed" by a Navy jet and turned back for fear of being shot down. Nearly all the news that the American people received during the first two days was from U.S. government sources. White House and Pentagon personnel reported that the conflict had been enormously successful and, in the words of Defense Secretary Caspar Weinberger, "extremely skillfully done."

In fact, the operation had been planned in great haste, and the first day's fighting had been a near-disaster for U.S. troops and a potential embarrassment for Pentagon leaders. For example, military officers did not know the location of many of the U.S. medical students they supposedly had come to save; U.S. troops were confused about the actual identity of the enemy and were supplied with tourist maps instead of strategic military maps; and more than a dozen innocent people were killed when U.S. forces accidentally bombed a mental hospital after mistaking it for a military installation.

Panama

Evidence indicates that many media restrictions in Panama were politically based. For example, Defense Secretary Richard B. Cheney decided to make sure the DOD media pool would arrive too late to cover the early hours of Operation Just Cause after President Bush twice questioned pool members' abilities to maintain operational security.[18] After the journalists arrived they were restricted to a U.S. base for several hours, listening to a lecture on Panamanian history and watching CNN television reports from the Pentagon to keep up on the progress of the war.

During the first several days, pool reporters were plagued by transportation and equipment shortages. Battlefield logistics were so confused that one plane carrying journalists was in danger of being shot down by U.S. forces.

During White House and Pentagon briefings about the invasion, officials misled reporters about U.S. casualties from friendly fire and low-altitude parachute jumps. Military officers deliberately concealed the fact that the controversial Stealth aircraft, which Cheney had praised for its "pinpoint accuracy" during the invasion, actually had missed both its targets by about 100 yards.[19]

The Media's Failings

The media bear some of the responsibility for the increased restrictions on wartime coverage. Although journalists have complained for years about the restrictions, they have presented no effective opposition, and have frequently allowed themselves to be co-opted by the Pentagon and the White House.

For example, the press complained about being confined to pools during the Gulf War, journalists fought among themselves for pool slots and turned in colleagues who tried to work outside the pool system. They presented no alternative that provided comprehensive answers for military officers' concerns about operational security and troop safety.

The media also failed to contribute sufficiently to public debate about the foreign policy issues that led to U.S. military involvement abroad. For example, before Operation Desert Shield began last August, few media reported regularly on the political, economic and historical factors that were influencing U.S. policy toward Iraq and Kuwait. Such stories, if run in a timely manner, might have had an important effect on public opinion and sparked a sharper congressional debate over U.S. military intervention.

Instead of developing a respectful but adversarial relationship with the Pentagon, many members of the press have become dependent on the military for visuals and information. For example, although reporters were physically prevented from watching and filming much of the fighting during the invasions of Grenada and Panama, the television networks showed hours of dramatic — and sometimes misleading — Defense Department footage. A similar situation developed in the Gulf, where the most exciting visuals during the air war were the Pentagon's carefully selected videos of precision-guided bombs demolishing their targets.

Some journalists believe that the lack of initiative displayed by many reporters covering the Gulf War was the media's single greatest failure, and will hurt future efforts to redefine the relationship between the Pentagon and the press.

The sad truth is that while reporters and editors complained about media restrictions, in the end many of them presented precisely the data and images that the White House and the Defense Department wanted the press to pass along to the American people. □

THE MILITARY-MEDIA RELATIONSHIP

It is the policy of the Department of Defense to make available timely and accurate information so that the public, Congress, and the news media may assess and understand the facts about national security and defense strategy.

Principles of Information[1]
Defense Secretary Richard Cheney

Retired Army Col. David H. Hackworth was angry. Now a military correspondent, Hackworth had served in Korea and Vietnam during a 25-year military career and had earned 110 medals, making him America's most-decorated living soldier. During the Gulf War, Hackworth was in Saudi Arabia covering the conflict for *Newsweek*, but was having difficulty getting access to troops and information through official Pentagon channels. He put in 21 requests to visit specific military units; none was granted. Frustrated, he got in his four-wheel-drive vehicle and went looking for units on his own.[2]

The soldiers he interviewed were eager to talk about their experiences, but since Hackworth was conducting interviews without the military's permission and without an escort, he risked being detained by U.S. or Saudi officials. While the troops succeeded in hiding him from unfriendly military officers, Hackworth wasn't as lucky on the road. As he and *Newsweek* photographer Mark Peters drove along after visiting one unit, Peters took a picture through the car window. Nearby U.S. troops, acting under orders, fixed bayonets and charged the journalists.[3]

"I had more guns pointed at me by Americans or Saudis who were into controlling the press than in all my years of actual combat," Hackworth wrote in *Newsweek*. "We didn't have the freedom of movement to make an independent assessment of what the military is all about."[4]

Like Hackworth, many journalists covering Operation Desert Storm often were denied access to the field and to military personnel. Pentagon officials said these restrictions were necessary to safeguard operational secrecy and troop safety. Gen. Colin Powell, Chairman of the Joint Chiefs of Staff, told the National Newspaper Association after the war that "the sole purpose" of the restrictions was "to protect the lives of the men and women who are entrusted to our care — and nothing else."[5]

But many journalists and policy analysts — including those with extensive military experience — disagreed. The scope of the restrictions "clearly went beyond the bounds of military secrecy and operational security. It clearly had a chilling effect on frank discourse with the troops," said *Chicago Tribune* military affairs correspondent David Evans, who spent 20 years in the Marine Corps, including three as a Defense Department analyst.[6]

The dissenters maintained that overzealous press restrictions in the Gulf led, in Hackworth's words, to a "sanitized" and "distorted" picture of the war that served neither the American people nor the country's long-range goals, and threatened the media's ability to perform their Constitutional role of informing the public.[7]

Hackworth's and other journalists' frustrations in covering the Gulf War illustrate the fundamental tensions between the military and the media — tensions that have been increasing during the past three decades. They also illustrate the split within the military itself about the responsibilities of the press in wartime. Some of the most articulate critics of the media restrictions in the Gulf are former military personnel who now work as journalists. They include such respected officers as retired Army Col. Harry G. Summers Jr., an Army War College instructor and author of a well-received book on military strategy, who has worked as an analyst for NBC News and now is a *Los Angeles Times* columnist.

The debate about the relationship between the Defense Department and the media often is portrayed as a conflict between national security and press freedom. But also at issue are the political consequences of going to war and the desire by political leaders to gain public support for their decision. This means that the definition of national security frequently is based on political as well as military factors. Since the nation was founded, efforts to control information about U.S. military activities have been directed by the White House as well as by the Armed Forces. For these reasons, the parameters of the debate about the Pentagon-press relationship can be understood only by examining the sometimes conflicting roles of the military, the media and the presidency, and the ways in which the Constitution has bound together these institutions, even as it has set them apart.

The Philosophical Foundation of the Relationship

The conflict between the military and the media is summarized in one phrase written by 19th-century military philosopher Carl von Clausewitz: "war is an instrument of policy."[8]

Clausewitz, whose classic work *On War* laid the foundation for the principles of contemporary warfare, wrote that "war is only a branch of political activity,"[9] and that the objectives of war are politically based. The exact nature of these objectives — and the price a nation might be willing to pay to achieve them — are formulated not by a country's military leaders, but by its political leaders.[10]

To wage war successfully, those leaders need the support of the people, and must convince them that the objectives are worth the price, Clausewitz wrote. Victory depends upon the relationships among a "trinity" comprising the government, the military and the people.[11]

The Founding Fathers, anticipating Clausewitz's writing by nearly 50 years, wanted to give the American people as much control as possible over decisions about going to war by giving them a voice in both political and military affairs. In his book, Col. Summers uses the Vietnam War as a paradigm for analyzing the relationships among the U.S. civilian leaders, the Pentagon and the public.[12]

"The Founding Fathers deliberately rejected the idea of an 18th century-type Army answerable only to the Executive," Summers stated in his book. "They wrote into the Constitution specific safeguards to ensure the people's control of the military."[13] One safeguard was to name as Commander-in-Chief of the Armed Forces the President, who would stand for election every four years. Another was to delegate the power to declare war only to Congress, whose members would reflect the differing views of the electorate. A third was to support the First Amendment, which would give an institution outside government — the press — the ability to provide the American people with independent information about their political and military institutions, and the people who led them.

The First Amendment enables the press to link the public, the White House and the military while remaining independent of each, Summers wrote in a May 1986 article for *Military Review*.[14] However, the media's responsibility is to the public. The task of informing the American people about their institutions gives the press power and legitimacy under the Constitution. This task is especially important when the public must evaluate controversial policies and plans, such as those involving the commitment of U.S. troops abroad. If the media are to fulfill their watchdog role, they must provide not only information that military and civilian leaders want to communicate to the American people, but also objective information that journalists have gathered from their own observations and research on and off the battlefield. This sometimes puts the media in an adversarial relationship with the government and military. But it is the only way to provide the public with the broadest range of fact and opinion, and to enable the American people to make informed judgments about the decision to go to war.

It also is one way to ensure that the American Army remains a people's army, as the Founding Fathers intended. This relationship between the Pentagon and the public is continually ratified as new members of the U.S. Armed Forces — unlike those in many countries — take an oath to support not the President or any other political leader, but the Constitution, and the principles it espouses, including government by the people and for the people. Military men and women take great pride in this responsibility. On the 200th anniversary of the Constitution, Gen. Schwarzkopf took his troops outside at 6 a.m. to renew their oath to that document in a ceremony that brought tears to the eyes of those who participated.[15]

The relationship between the military and the American people has had profound effects on Pentagon and White House policies. When a President has sent U.S. troops overseas without formulating concrete political objectives and securing a mandate from the public — as Lyndon B. Johnson did during the Vietnam War — his public approval ratings have declined. Support for the military as an institution also has eroded. After the direct U.S. military role in Southeast Asia had ended, Army Chief of Staff Gen. Fred C. Weyand, who supervised the withdrawal of U.S. troops from Vietnam in 1973, wrote the following:

> Vietnam was a reaffirmation of the peculiar relationship between the American Army and the American people. The American Army really is a people's Army in the sense that it belongs to the American people, who take a jealous and proprietary interest in its involvement. When the Army is committed the American people are committed, when the American people lose their commitment it is futile to try to keep the Army committed. In the final analysis, the American Army is not so much an arm on the Executive Branch as it is an arm of the American people.[16]

The primary link between the American people and the military is the press. The media are responsible for maintaining the connection between citizens and soldiers, especially during military operations.[17] Peter Braestrup, a Korean War veteran and former *Washington Post* bureau chief in Saigon during the Vietnam War, wrote that when the media provide objective information from the battlefield, they act as "one of the checks and balances that sustains the confidence of the American people in their political system and armed forces."[18]

The importance of the media's function in wartime is one reason why the White House and the Pentagon have tried to control what the press has said about military operations. Civilian and military leaders believe that if they can control journalists' perceptions, they can control public perceptions.

During the Vietnam conflict, the White House took an extraordinary step to do this. In 1967, President Johnson and Defense Secretary Robert McNamara prevailed upon the Pentagon high command to join a public relations campaign to convince the American people that the war was going well.[19] Many high-ranking military officers were horrified at this effort to draw them into politics. Johnson was noted for being isolated from his Pentagon advisers, some of whom had opposed escalating the war without clear-cut military and political objectives, and without a declaration of war from Congress.[20] Now the President was trying to involve them in what essentially was a political campaign to sell the war to the public. These officers were appalled when Gen. William C. Westmoreland, the commander of U.S. forces in Vietnam, returned to the United States to give speeches about how well the war was going. As Clark Clifford — an adviser to President Johnson who later became Defense Secretary — wrote years later, the decisions to politicize the military and have Westmoreland make such speeches were "grievous errors in both tactics and judgment."[21]

The involvement of the military in the political aspects of the war damaged the relationship between the Pentagon and the people in a way that had serious consequences. Westmoreland lost credibility with the public and the press. So did the military as an institution, especially as casualties mounted and Westmoreland's predictions that U.S. troops would be coming home gave way to requests that more American soldiers be sent to Vietnam.[22]

Anti-war sentiment increased along with the body count.[23] This had happened in previous wars, but dissenters had directed their anger primarily at the White House. Now protesters also made the military a target. U.S. troops were berated even though for years they were sent into battle by the Commander-in-Chief acting with the approval of Congress, which had given President Johnson great latitude to act unilaterally by passing the Gulf of Tonkin Resolution in 1964. As Col. Summers pointed out, this was "a dangerous position for both the Army and for the Republic."[24] He wrote:

> By attacking the *executors* of U.S. Vietnam policy rather than the *makers* of that policy, the protesters were striking at the very heart of our democratic system — the civilian control of the military. [Emphasis is Summers'.][25]

The nation weathered the Vietnam crisis, and the White House and the Pentagon learned several important lessons. The first was that it was a mistake to go to war without clearly stated political goals and public support. The second was that public support might be easier to obtain if media coverage could be controlled more effectively. Many U.S. military officers were convinced that negative stories about the war had turned the American people against the conflict.[26] They clung to this belief even after military historians and analysts demonstrated that it was the lack of political leadership and the increasing casualty rate — not press coverage — that led to reduced support for the war.[27] During the ensuing years, this belief had a profound impact on the evolution of the relationship between the Pentagon and the press, exacerbating the tensions that already existed between them.

Differences Between the Military and Media Cultures

Several inherent factors have created problems in the military-media relationship. One is the nature of the institutions themselves. Although the Armed Forces are an army of the people, they also are part of the political system. Former Air Force Chief of Staff Gen. Michael J. Dugan wrote in a May 1991 article in *The New York Times* that "military organizations are agents of their government, subject to all the external constraints that come with a political process. . . ."[28] The Armed Forces' Commander-in-Chief is the President, who holds the highest political office in the land. Their programs and priorities are approved by Congress through budget proceedings that are highly politicized. As Braestrup has pointed out in *Battle Lines*, a monograph on the military-media relationship, senior officers are "deeply involved in bureaucratic politics," trying to protect their budget share and their careers.[29] They must "pay heed to the mood of Congress, the predilections of the White House and the secretary of defense."[30]

The media are observers of the political system. Their job is to inform the public about political processes, including those involving the military. Journalists provide the public with information and opinions about White House and congressional activities, such as debates over whether a specific Pentagon weapons system should be funded. This information, in turn, affects voters' decisions about whom to elect as the President, and as members of Congress. Military officers are wary of the media, because negative stories "may be exploited by rival services or by critics of the military on Capitol Hill, and they always tend to cause distress within the Pentagon," according to Braestrup.[31]

Other factors that contribute to the problems between the Defense Department and the press are the differences in their institutional cultures. The Pentagon is a large, bureaucratic organization whose ideals emphasize duty, honor and country. Members of the military work in a hierarchy and have a clearly defined career path. They may disagree with superiors, but after making their arguments known they must carry out orders. To succeed, a person must be a team player.[32]

The media are a maze of independent organizations, ranging from television news operations employing thousands to weekly newspapers with a half-dozen staffers. The media are businesses. Their values are shaped by First Amendment responsibilities and by the interests and needs of owners, stockholders, viewers or readers. Competition among journalists is a driving force, and individual initiative is highly valued.[33]

Gen. Dugan summarized the differences in his *New York Times* article:

> Institutionally the military and the media are both "mission oriented" and in public service, yet their missions appear to be antithetical. Military organizations are . . . a hierarchical bureaucracy. The media organizational structure is slimmer, quicker and flatter, with a preference for facts and views that promote, if not create, conflict.
>
> Culturally, the military is remote from the mainstream of society and its members live in a subculture with inherent barriers to external communications. There are different words, different use of the same words, different living conditions, expectations, self images and more.[34]

These different priorities and working styles create friction between the Pentagon and the press. In a 1986 poll of 105 Army War College students, 51 percent of respondents expressed a negative or very negative attitude toward the media, and 89.2 percent agreed with the decision to ban the media from the initial stages of the Grenada invasion.[35] Respondents said they believed that military-media conflicts were caused by factors such as a "lack of understanding by both sides," and "basic difference[s] in aims, goals and personal (individual) values."[36] The problems worsen during wartime, as the military and the media try to fulfill their distinct Constitutional mandates.

On the battlefield, according to Braestrup, a commander must:

> . . . know the capabilities of his men and their equipment, act decisively on insufficient information, carry out the mission . . . in the organized chaos of battle. . . . he must prevail over the foe while losing as few men as possible, and killing as few civilians as possible. Failure means not only personal disgrace but the futile deaths of his men and possibly the defeat of his country.[37]

Into this milieu step the journalists, charged with informing the American people about events on the battlefield. They must tell the stories of individual soldiers and engagements. They also must put the conflict into a larger perspective, providing information that will enable the public to evaluate the human, political and economic costs of the war, thus ensuring that the country's civilian and military leaders will be held accountable.

The differing roles of the military and the media inevitably lead to confrontations. Successfully waging a war requires operational secrecy, yet secrets are anathema to journalists, who need as much information as possible to ensure that their stories are written in a truthful and accurate context. However, compromises between the two institutions are possible. Journalists acknowledge the need for operational security, and have worked hard to maintain it. The vast majority of security breaches that occurred during the Vietnam War and later conflicts resulted from journalists' inexperience or conflicting guidance from Pentagon officials about what types of information should not be released.[38]

The more intractable issues arise when national security becomes a rationale for controlling information based not on military concerns but on political considerations. Where that line should be drawn is at the heart of the conflict between the Pentagon and the press, has deeply divided military officers, and has created dissension among their civilian leaders.

History of the Relationship

Controversy about the media's coverage of military operations — and official attempts to control it — is older than the country itself. Historian William M. Hammond wrote in a 1989 article for a U.S. Army War College publication that in order to sustain the faith of the colonists, George Washington sometimes exaggerated battlefield successes when he was leading the Continental Army against the British.[39] Both Union and Confederate officers complained bitterly that media coverage of the Civil War affected troop morale and public opinion, spurring President Abraham Lincoln to authorize the suppression of numerous small and large newspapers across the country for security violations.[40] However, the Civil War also led some military officers to equate the First Amendment guarantee of press freedom with the public's right to know. After the war, in a book entitled *The Military Policy of the United States*, Brevet Maj. Gen. Emory Upton wrote:

> The people who, under the war powers of the Constitution, surrender their liberties and give up their lives and property have a right to know why our wars are unnecessarily prolonged. They have a right to know whether disasters have been brought about through the neglect and ignorance of Congress, which is intrusted [sic] with the power to raise and support armies, or through military incompetency.[41]

During the late 19th and 20th centuries, the relationship between the military and the media fluctuated. World War I was marked by animosity, but considerable freedom of access to troops in the field.[42] During World War II, which had a great deal of popular support, the relationship between the media and the military improved.[43] The Korean War became extremely unpopular, but the military did not blame this on news coverage.[44] It was the Vietnam War that marked a modern-day turning point in the relationship between the Pentagon and the press, and the conflict left a bitter legacy of antagonism and distrust between the two institutions.

The military-media relationship began to deteriorate during the early years of the war, when the country's civilian leaders wanted stringent press restrictions in order to control public opinion about the conflict.[45]

This resulted in a tremendous split among military officers. Some went along with the wishes of the White House. Pentagon personnel in Saigon staged what became known as the Five O'Clock Follies, briefings in which optimistic reports about the war's progress were given. Others became First Amendment heroes, passionately defending the media's responsibility to report the truth about the war. They argued that the press should operate only under voluntary written ground rules that spelled out what information should not be released to protect operational security. One such defender of the public's right to know was Col. Winant Sidle, who was charged with writing a strict censorship plan. Sidle spent months on the plan, and purposely made it so complex it was impossible to implement.[46]

This schism among military officers about the role of the press was dramatized by the Pentagon Papers case. In 1971, a disillusioned former Marine and Defense Department analyst, Daniel Ellsberg, gave *The New York Times* copies of government documents that showed that White House and Pentagon officials had lied to the press and the American people, and that thousands of lives had been lost in Southeast Asia because of misguided U.S. policies.

The Nixon administration went to court to prevent the *Times* and other media from printing excerpts from the Pentagon Papers, arguing that their publication would violate national security. However, many of the documents were historical, and others contained information that already had been printed in the media and scholarly journals. It was widely believed that the White House wanted to prevent publication not for military reasons but for political reasons, because the Papers showed a long pattern of deception by the country's civilian and military leaders.

The Supreme Court ruled against the government, strongly reaffirming the media's obligation to monitor the reasons for going to war, and the consequences. In his opinion, Justice Hugo Black wrote:

> In the First Amendment the Founding Fathers gave the free press the protection it must have to fulfill its essential role in our democracy. The press was to serve the governed, not the governors. . . . And paramount among the responsibilities of a free press is the duty to prevent any part of the government from deceiving the people and sending them off to distant lands to die of foreign fevers and foreign shot and shell.[47]

Although the Pentagon Papers case vindicated the judgment of some military officers, the conflict left others bitter. Despite evidence to the contrary, they believed that the press, with its increasingly critical view of the conflict, was a major reason that the United States had lost the war. As these Vietnam veterans rose to power in the Pentagon, they began looking for ways to control coverage of future conflicts. In the early 1980s they found the British government's stringent information-control program, which restricted media access to information and fostered widespread popular support for the Falklands War.[48]

The Pentagon's adoption of British news-management techniques coincided with a far-reaching program by the Reagan administration to control the flow of other types of information to the public. White House officials tried to weaken the Freedom of Information Act, passed in the wake of the Watergate scandal. They proposed giving lie detector tests to government officials suspected of leaking information to the press, and wanted employees with security clearances to sign lifetime agreements barring them from writing about their work.[49]

According to documents uncovered during the Iran-contra investigation and other congressional probes, the National Security Council and the CIA formulated plans to hire public relations firms to increase public support for Reagan's Central American policies, which included financing the contras' efforts to overthrow Nicaragua's leftist Sandinista government.[50]

The President also stepped up his anti-communist rhetoric, pointing to Nicaragua and Grenada as potential threats to the hemisphere. When White House officials began discussing a preemptive strike in Grenada in 1983, the military commanders they consulted had little use for the press.[51] The idea to exclude the press from the initial stages of the invasion quickly gained support. Top officials, including White House Chief of Staff James A. Baker III, decided not to tell White House Press Secretary Larry Speakes about the operation so he would be convincing when he told the press — as he did the night before the operation — that talk of a U.S. invasion of Grenada was "preposterous."[52]

The press was barred from the island for two days, until President Reagan had given a victory speech that talked of the operation as a spectacular victory carried out with surgical precision.[53] Information about the poor planning that led to unnecessary U.S. and Grenadian casualties eventually emerged, but stories about these problems received much less play than the original articles quoting the President and Defense Secretary about how flawless the operation had been. Public opinion did not change significantly over the long term,[54] and the White House and the Pentagon learned that controlling the initial information from the battlefield meant controlling public perceptions.

The Evolution of the Current Relationship

The decision to bar the media from the invasion was not uniformly applauded in the Pentagon. Some high-level military officers were appalled that the restrictions went far beyond what was necessary to protect national security. Congress and the media also strongly criticized the Defense Department, and a House of Representatives subcommittee held hearings.[55]

In response to the backlash, Joint Chiefs of Staff Chairman Gen. John W. Vessey Jr. asked Maj. Gen. Sidle, who had retired, to convene a panel of experts to re-evaluate the military-media relationship. The report was to be definitive, and was to mark the beginning of a new era in Pentagon-press relations.[56] Meanwhile, Defense Secretary Weinberger issued the Principles of Information on Dec. 1, 1983, committing the Pentagon to an information policy that would ensure maximum media access to information about military operations. Although the Principles are only guidelines, they reflect the content and spirit of regulations established by the different branches of the Armed Forces.[57]

Sidle initially wanted media representatives and military personnel to serve on the panel, but major organizations — including the American Newspaper Publishers Association (ANPA), the American Society of Newspaper Editors (ASNE), the National Association of Broadcasters (NAB) and the Radio-Television News Directors Association (RTNDA) — and their individual members said it would be inappropriate for media personnel to serve on a government panel.[58]

Other editors and reporters thought such participation might compromise the media's freedom to cover Pentagon activities as they thought best. Journalist Ron Dorfman wrote:

> If the government and the media negotiate rules for the coverage of secret military and paramilitary operations, we move a giant step toward acceptance of covert action as a flag draped pillar of national security deserving of the same solicitous consideration and press accorded the planning of D-Day. . . . The political objective is to force the press back onto the national — i.e., presidential — team, and the very creation of the Sidle commission puts the administration at fourth down, goal to go.[59]

Media personnel did provide written and oral presentations to the panel, fearing that if they did not participate, they would be left in a weaker position in future dealings with the White House and the Pentagon. Meanwhile, Sidle asked retired journalists (including some who had covered Vietnam) and representatives of journalism schools who were knowledgeable about military-media relations to serve on the panel.

The panel's report was released Aug. 23, 1984, nearly 10 months after the invasion. It provided the blueprint for the evolution of the military-media relationship during the ensuing seven years, and was based on this Statement of Principle:

> The American people must be informed about United States military operations and this information can best be provided through both the news media and the Government. Therefore, the panel believes it is essential that the U.S. news media cover U.S. military operations to the maximum degree possible consistent with mission security and the safety of U.S. forces.[60]

The report stressed that an adversarial relationship between the media and the military was "healthy," and that the American people needed to get information from both military officials and independent reporters.[61] The report added that the public would best be served if the military and the media developed a sense of mutual respect, and recommended that the press be neither "a lap dog nor an attack dog but, rather, a watchdog" over the activities of the Pentagon.[62]

The Sidle Report offered eight major recommendations. Perhaps the most important called for the establishment of a "pool system" of reporting. The system was designed to ensure that reporters would be present during the initial stages of military operations. Under the system, the Defense Department is supposed to provide a group or "pool" of reporters representing print and broadcast media access to military units from the start of an operation. These journalists then share their information with colleagues who remain behind the lines.

The Sidle Panel said that a pool should be used when it was "the only feasible means of furnishing the media with early access to an operation," and added that:

> planning should provide for the largest possible press pool that is practical and minimize the length of time the pool will be necessary before "full coverage" is feasible.[63]

During the past eight years, the pool system has become highly controversial. It was a bitter point of contention during Operation Desert Storm, when the military used pools for virtually the entire conflict. Reporters trying to work outside the pool system were detained. Journalists complained to military personnel that restricting coverage to pool reports violated the recommendations of the Sidle Panel, but in fact, the panel gave the military a great deal of latitude concerning the pool system.

For example, the panel stated that "full coverage" appeared to be a relative term, and that some media who testified before the panel had agreed that such coverage "might be limited in cases where security, logistics, and the size of the operation created limitations that would not permit any and all bona fide reporters to cover an event."[64] The Sidle Panel agreed that limitations on full coverage "would have to be decided on a case-by-case basis."[65] The report also made it clear that although the media should be consulted, the military must make the final decisions about the size of the pool, and where and when it should be deployed.[66]

Another major recommendation of the report was that "a basic tenet governing media access to military operations should be voluntary compliance by the media with security guidelines or ground rules."[67] The report stated that the media wanted such guidelines and ground rules to be similar to those used during the Vietnam War, and to foreclose the possibility of formal censorship.[68] This became another major issue during the Gulf War, when guidelines and ground rules were supplemented with security reviews of all copy and visuals.

Other major recommendations of the report were that public affairs planning be conducted concurrently with operations planning, that sufficient communications and transportation facilities be provided for journalists, and that qualified military personnel be assigned to assist correspondents. Finally, the report recommended that military public affairs and media personnel meet on a regular basis, and that additional public affairs instruction be provided for the military.

The panel did not address several issues. It provided no critique of the treatment of the media during the Grenada invasion, because Sidle had been instructed to look toward future operations. However, Sidle remarked wryly that if the panel's recommendations had been in place during Grenada, there might have been no need for a Sidle Panel.[69] The report also did not openly state that the First Amendment requires that the press be allowed on the battlefield; some panel members felt this was an issue that should be settled by the courts.[70]

Many military and media personnel believed that the Sidle Panel Report provided a good foundation for future discussions, and would ensure that the press never again would be excluded completely from the battlefield.

One of the first major efforts to implement the report's recommendations involved setting up a permanent national media pool that would be responsible for covering the initial phases of future military operations. The pool would include print and broadcast journalists, and membership would rotate on a regular basis.

From 1984 to 1987, the DOD national media pool covered various military exercises in the United States and Central America. The pool's first experience with an actual military operation came in 1987, when it was sent to the Persian Gulf to cover U.S. Navy efforts to protect Kuwaiti ships threatened during the Iran-Iraq war.[71] In a March 1989 article in *Parameters — U.S. Army War College Quarterly*, one Pentagon public affairs officer proclaimed the pool deployment a success. Reporters had observed security guidelines, had worked well with military escorts, and despite some delays in transmitting copy, generally were pleased with resulting coverage.[72] However, an earlier article in *Columbia Journalism Review* by reporter Mark Thompson had not been as positive, and presaged many of the problems that journalists later encountered during the Gulf crisis after Iraq invaded Kuwait. Thompson pointed to long delays in releasing copy, and reviewers making arbitrary changes in words or phrases to protect the image of the military, not operational security.[73] For example, one officer refused to transmit stories until references to officers drinking beer had been deleted.[74]

The next time the United States went to war, during the 1989 invasion of Panama, the pool system worked poorly. White House and civilian leaders in the Pentagon used the pool to restrict media access, not promote it, as the Sidle Panel had intended.[75]

A discussion of how the Bush administration manipulated the pool is contained in a critique of the Defense Department's media operation in Panama written for the Pentagon by Fred S. Hoffman, a former Associated Press reporter and DOD official. Hoffman stated that in the week before the invasion, President Bush and Vice President Dan Quayle both told Defense Secretary Cheney that they doubted that the pool could maintain operational security, but were leaving final decisions about the pool up to him.[76]

On the evening before the invasion, Cheney and Assistant Secretary of Defense for Public Affairs Pete Williams deliberately called out the pool so late that journalists missed the first hours of the attack.[77] Cheney later told Hoffman his decision was prompted by a need to maintain "maximum security possible to avoid compromising the operation and to preserve the element of surprise."[78] He acknowledged the conflict between operational security and the Defense Department's commitment to ensure that reporters covered the earliest phases of military operations.[79]

Hoffman defended the record of journalists — especially pool journalists — in protecting operational security while strongly criticizing Cheney's "secrecy-driven decision" to send the pool so late that journalists produced "stories and pictures of essentially secondary value."[80]

Cheney later tried to justify his actions, saying "the pool was created for this kind of situation," but Hoffman replied that "Cheney was misinformed," and had misconstrued the Sidle Report.[81] "The Pentagon pool was established to enable U.S. news personnel to report the earliest possible action in a U.S. military operation *in a remote area where there was no other American press presence.* [Emphasis is Hoffman's.] Panama did not fit that description," Hoffman stated.[82] He added:

> This illustrates how the perception of the pool's purpose has become skewed since it was established in the wake of the Pentagon's ill-advised denial of news reporting access to battles on the Caribbean island of Grenada in 1983.[83]

Another indication that sending the pool late was done for political, not military, reasons was that Pentagon military leaders played no part in the decision to delay the journalists, according to Hoffman.[84] Gen. Powell told Hoffman that he was "left out of the pattern," and that "the final judgement [sic] was made in the Oval Office."[85] Powell said he discussed pool decisions "in only the most general terms" with Cheney, and left day-to-day decisions to Williams.[86]

Hoffman concluded his report with more than a dozen recommendations, many of which reiterated those formulated by the Sidle Panel. Hoffman also called on Cheney to sign and reissue the Principles of Information, which the Defense Secretary agreed to do.[87]

Hoffman's recommendations were not fully implemented, however, and when the Bush administration initiated the U.S. military buildup in the Persian Gulf in August 1990, disputes between the Pentagon and the press began anew. The DOD national media pool covered the first weeks of Operation Desert Shield because the Saudi Arabian government initially was very slow in issuing visas to individual reporters. Pool members said they generally were pleased with their coverage, and the efforts of public affairs officers to facilitate the flow of information.[88]

The pool was disbanded after the Saudi government began issuing visas to numerous individual journalists. However, open coverage was not permitted. Journalists were escorted to specified military units in groups (technically they were not pools, because reporters were filing for their own media, and did not have to share material). The number of groups that went out each day was limited, because the Pentagon did not provide DOD public affairs personnel in the Gulf with sufficient support staff, communications facilities or vehicles to handle the hundreds of journalists in the Gulf.[89] Reporters who tried to work outside the pool system were ejected from military units, and some who wrote critical stories said they were denied access to military personnel.[90]

Meanwhile, DOD public affairs officers said in telephone interviews for this study that they were overwhelmed by the number of journalists who showed up to cover Operation Desert Shield, a number of whom knew nothing about the military.[91] They added that open coverage could not be permitted because it was unsafe to allow journalists to travel alone in the desert, and field commanders could not cope with dozens of reporters and photographers dropping in on their units.[92]

The conflict between the military and the media escalated after the air war began in January 1991. Pool coverage was instituted, and the number of pool slots was so limited that many journalists were left sitting at the Dhahran International Hotel in Saudi Arabia. Reporters trying to operate outside the pool system were detained.[93] Pool visits were arranged by the Pentagon's Joint Information Bureau (JIB) in Dhahran, and pools were accompanied by military escorts. All copy, photographs and video were subject to security review before being released. In a telephone interview, Col. Bill Mulvey, Director of the Dhahran JIB, emphasized that Defense Department officials in Washington and Saudi Arabia had spent many hours meeting with bureau chiefs, editors and reporters to work out a system that would accommodate as many journalists as possible without overwhelming field commanders.[94] Bureau chiefs angrily responded that the system had been thrust upon them by the Pentagon.

Media executives inundated the Pentagon and Congress with complaints. The Senate Governmental Affairs Committee held hearings on the issue on Feb. 20, 1991. Witnesses included Pete Williams, journalists such as Walter Cronkite and Pulitzer Prize winners Malcolm Browne and Sydney Schanberg, former military officers such as Col. Summers, and the authors of the Sidle and Hoffman reports.

All the former military personnel criticized the restrictions, saying they went beyond what was necessary. Sidle said pools were needed because of the number of journalists in the Gulf, but added that reporters and photographers should be allowed to move more freely after they arrived at the unit they were scheduled to visit.[95] He also recommended that security reviews be replaced by a ground rule system similar to the one used in Vietnam, where journalists who broke the rules could lose their accreditation.[96] Summers, who was working as an NBC commentator, said he thought the pool restrictions on the press were "dumb," and that "reporters ought to have total freedom to see all that we are doing, realizing that transmission might have to be delayed for security reasons."[97] Hoffman called for an end both to pools and the security reviews, and, like Sidle, called for the type of ground rule system used in Vietnam.[98] All three wanted a renewed dialogue between the two institutions to resolve these issues.

After the hearings, the Pentagon opened more pool slots in Saudi Arabia, but any goodwill was lost when DOD officials declared a news blackout during the opening hours of the ground war. After the conflict was over, pool reporters complained bitterly about delays in getting their copy back; some stories never arrived. Military public affairs officers in Dhahran said bad weather had grounded planes they had hoped to use, and that a lack of communications equipment had also hampered media operations.[99]

In the months since the war ended, resentments have continued to simmer. In June, publishers and executives of 17 news organizations sent Defense Secretary Cheney a letter detailing problems with the restrictions, stating, "we believe it is imperative that the Gulf war not serve as a model for future coverage."[100] The letter included a Statement of Principles for coverage of future operations that called for independent reporting to be "the principal means of coverage."[101] The Statement also called for an end to security reviews, and for better communications and transportation facilities.[102] The letter requested a meeting with Cheney, but within a week of sending the letter, some executives were disagreeing among themselves about what to ask for at such a meeting.[103]

In the meantime, Cheney and other Pentagon officials expressed great satisfaction with news coverage of the Gulf War. Assistant Secretary of Defense for Public Affairs Pete Williams declared that "the press gave the American people the best war coverage they ever had."[104]

Many journalists disagreed, including some who had spent months fighting the restrictions in court. More than a dozen media organizations and writers, including two Pulitzer Prize winners, had gone to federal court on Jan. 10, 1991, shortly before Desert Storm began, to file a suit against Defense Department officials and President George Bush. The suit charged that the media restrictions violated First and Fifth Amendment rights, and were based on political, not military, considerations.[105]

Throughout the war and the early weeks of the ceasefire, the plaintiffs had submitted evidence supporting their position. In April 1991, Judge Leonard Sand dismissed the case, ruling that it had become moot since the war had ended, but he said the journalists had raised serious and disturbing questions that needed to be addressed.[106] Among those questions were the following:

- To what extent should the military be involved in the political decisions that provide the foundation for military operations?

- To what extent may — or should — the military try to shape public opinion about these operations and the political factors that underlie them?

- What type of information does the public need to make informed decisions about U.S. policies and military operations, and the civilian and military leaders who design them and carry them out?

- Who should control the access to — and dissemination of — that information?

- What are the limits to the public's right to know about the political, economic and social costs of military activities and the policies that drive them?

- How should the line be drawn between information that military officials should censor for national security reasons and information that Pentagon and White House officials want to censor for political reasons? Who should draw that line?

- What responsibilities should govern the media's relationship with the Defense Department, and its civilian and military leaders?

These are some of the questions that will be examined in succeeding chapters.

□

PENTAGON INFORMATION-MANAGEMENT TECHNIQUES

Information will be made fully and readily available consistent with statutory requirements unless its release is precluded by current and valid security classification.

Principles of Information
Defense Secretary Richard Cheney

Many of the information-control techniques used by the Pentagon and the White House during the past eight years have been patterned after the British government's model of press control instituted during the 1982 war with Argentina over the Falkland/Malvinas Islands. This model is based on the concept of pre-censorship, which entails restricting media access to military operations and information. Ironically, British officials formulated these controls after studying the U.S. government's media ground rules for the Vietnam War, and the press coverage of the conflict.[1] British military officers in the early 1980s spoke openly about avoiding the mistakes their Pentagon counterparts had made in not trying to control the content and tone of stories about military operations in Southeast Asia.[2]

The Pentagon's adoption of the underlying philosophy of the Falklands model — which the Defense Department first employed with the approval of the White House during the Grenada invasion — was a chilling development. It meant that U.S. civilian and military leaders had decided to handle First Amendment issues by using a foreign model of information control from a country that does not have the tradition of press freedom embodied in the U.S. Constitution.

Britain historically has had much stricter press controls than the United States. In the 17th century, the British government required anyone in the colonies who wanted to publish a newspaper to apply for an official license. Publishers working without a license risked having their newspapers confiscated.[3] The government also forbade publication of stories that cast officials in an unfavorable light. Journalists who criticized the government faced criminal prosecution.[4] In a landmark 18th-century libel case brought by British officials, New York publisher John Peter Zenger was jailed after printing true stories about corruption in the colonial governor's office. A jury acquitted Zenger. This case later was cited by colonial leaders as a reason for adopting the First Amendment, with its guarantee of press freedom.[5]

In the 1980s, when the Falklands model was formulated, Britain still had a system of criminal penalties — including jail terms — for journalists who revealed any official information before the government authorized its disclosure. Journalists could be put on trial even if their stories were factually correct, revealed government deception or corruption, and did not affect national security.[6] During the Falklands conflict, government officials said they believed the role of the press was not to provide independent information about the conflict, but to help British officials "in leading and steadying public opinion in times of national stress or crisis."[7]

In following the British lead, the Pentagon and White House have formulated pre-censorship restrictions that are supposed to do much more than protect military operations and personnel. The restrictions are part of an effort by the U.S. military and its civilian leaders to control public opinion.

The news-management techniques used by the Pentagon and the White House in the 1980s and '90s include the following:

- **Limiting physical access to the battlefield**

In Grenada, journalists were barred from the island during the first 48 hours of fighting. During the Panama invasion, Defense Secretary Cheney deliberately delayed deploying the DOD national media pool so the journalists would miss the initial hours of the conflict.[8] Even after the journalists arrived in Panama, they were kept on a U.S. base for hours because transportation was not available. During the Gulf War, only pool reporters or journalists participating in the Pentagon's Hometown Program were allowed to visit U.S. military units.[9]

- **Having military officers control the agenda for pool reporters**

In Grenada, these officers — called "escorts" — forbade the first groups of journalists from going to areas the military did not consider safe. During the Panama operation, the military refused to take journalists to areas of Panama City that they considered "too dangerous," and barred journalists from a U.S. hospital where wounded soldiers were being treated.[10] In the Persian Gulf, journalists sometimes were not allowed to spend time with military units, even if field commanders wanted reporters to stay.[11]

- **Discouraging military personnel from talking with journalists who were not in Pentagon-sanctioned press pools or groups**

In Panama, some troops told reporters they were not allowed to speak with them.[12] One female officer said she was told that her career would be endangered if she continued speaking with reporters.[13] Pentagon public affairs officers later admitted some field commanders were confused by "conflicting guidance" from the Pentagon concerning how to deal with the media.[14] In the Persian Gulf, military personnel were told not to allow reporters who were not part of the Pentagon's press operation to spend time with their units. One unit commander, who told *New York Times* reporter James LeMoyne that he thought this restriction was uncalled for, was ordered several hours later to dismiss LeMoyne from the unit's camp because the reporter was operating outside the DOD media organization.[15]

- **Harassing and detaining journalists working outside the Pentagon's media operations**

During the first 48 hours of the Grenada invasion, when journalists were barred from the island, reporters who arrived on a rented boat were taken to the *U.S.S. Guam* and initially were not allowed to communicate with their newspapers. In Panama, journalists who were not pool members were confined to U.S. military bases for more than 24 hours on the grounds that the streets were not safe.[16] U.S.

military police in the Persian Gulf said they had been given "highest priority" orders to stop journalists who were not traveling with pools.[17] *Time* photographer Wesley Bocxe was blindfolded, searched and held by U.S. forces for more than 30 hours.[18] Reporters from The Associated Press and *The Washington Post* were also detained or threatened with detention, as were photographers from U.S., British and French news agencies.[19]

- **Arranging and monitoring interviews between pool members and military personnel**

In Panama, a story that military public affairs officers said inaccurately portrayed women in combat led to a recommendation that a public affairs officer be present during all interviews between reporters and U.S. troops during future operations.[20] In the Persian Gulf, reporters were criticized for talking with soldiers in lunch lines if their escorts were not present.[21] Some escorts interrupted interviews if they thought questions or answers were inappropriate.[22] One soldier in the Gulf was so afraid to talk with Scripps Howard reporter Peter Copeland in front of the escort that he secretly slipped the correspondent a note about problems he was having in his unit.[23]

- **Criticizing military personnel who made negative comments about U.S. policy**

In the Persian Gulf, some reporters said troops they had talked with later had been subjected to questioning about their views. *New York Times* reporter LeMoyne wrote a story in the fall that quoted several soldiers questioning President Bush's decision to send U.S. troops to the region. After the story appeared, the soldiers quoted in the article wrote a letter criticizing it. Military officials denied LeMoyne's requests to return to the unit to ascertain why the men had changed their minds. Later, LeMoyne was told by one officer that after the article had appeared, "all hell broke loose," and the troops' commanders had demanded explanations for the soldiers' critical comments.[24]

- **Requiring that all pool stories, photographs and video be subjected to a security review**

During the Gulf crisis, most journalists did not object to military reviewers looking at their material to ensure that information in their stories and visuals would not compromise operational security or troop safety. But security reviews in the Persian Gulf sometimes went far beyond their stated objective. Perhaps the most well-publicized case involved the description of U.S. pilots returning from sorties. A reviewer changed *Detroit Free Press* reporter Frank Bruni's adjective from "giddy" to "proud."[25]

Another problem was that reviewers sometimes delayed copy so long the stories became stale. An article that *New York Times* reporter Malcolm Browne wrote about the Stealth was held up for more than 24 hours after the reviewer in the Gulf sent it to the Stealth's home base in Nevada so officials there could review it.[26]

- **Threatening to cancel trips and interviews for pool reporters who wrote stories that criticized the military**

LeMoyne reported that last fall, when he was trying to schedule an interview with Gen. Schwarzkopf, a Pentagon public affairs person called him periodically to report on his chances of getting the interview. The officer said the interview request probably would be denied if LeMoyne wrote too many critical stories. After LeMoyne wrote his article quoting U.S. soldiers questioning President Bush's Middle East policy, the interview was canceled. At the same time, almost all print reporters were denied permission to visit Army units for six weeks, on the grounds that commanding officers believed there had been too many "critical" stories. When LeMoyne interviewed Schwarzkopf later, the general apologized for the cancellation and assured LeMoyne that it had not resulted from his story.[27]

- **Concealing information that would be embarrassing to the U.S. government**

In Grenada, the Pentagon hid the fact that U.S. planes had bombed a mental hospital after mistaking it for a military installation.[28] In Panama, the Pentagon did not correct its earlier claim to reporters that Noriega had 50 kilos of cocaine in his freezer after lab tests showed that the white powder was really flour, corn meal and lard.[29] In the Persian Gulf, U.S. officials saturated media briefings with images of precision bombing, and did not show reporters videos of bombs that missed their targets.

- **Misleading the media about U.S. military mistakes**

Defense Secretary Weinberger called the Grenada invasion an unqualified success despite the fact that the Pentagon's slipshod planning resulted in the deaths of U.S. paratroopers who were dropped into unexpectedly heavy artillery fire.[30] During the fighting in Panama, Lt. Gen. Thomas Kelly stated unequivocally that he knew of "no casualties that occurred" during a low-altitude parachute jump in which several U.S. troops were in fact killed, and dozens injured. Kelly later said he had no information about these casualties at the time.[31] After the Gulf conflict, Air Force Chief of Staff Gen. McPeak said U.S. forces "made some mistakes about what we bombed," but refused to elaborate, saying his recommendation that errors be disclosed "got turned around, quite frankly."[32]

- **Misleading the media about U.S. military successes**

During the Grenada conflict, Weinberger announced that U.S. forces had rescued 600 U.S. students studying at a medical school on the island in an operation that was "extremely skillfully done."[33] In fact, Schwarzkopf, the U.S. combat leader responsible for evacuating the students, had not been told that the medical school had two campuses. He had arrived at the first, thinking his job had been completed, only to be told by students that hundreds of their classmates were at another location. Schwarzkopf had to improvise another operation to evacuate the second group of Americans.[34] After the Panama invasion, Pentagon spokesman Pete Williams insisted for weeks that the Stealth bombers, performing in combat for the first time, had "precisely hit their targets."³⁵ A later investigation, prompted by a *New York Times* article, found that both had missed their targets.³⁶ During the Gulf conflict, the Pentagon released numerous videos of precision-guided ordnance demolishing their targets while leaving surrounding areas untouched. Reporters did not learn until after the war that fewer than 9 percent of the bombs dropped on Iraq had precision mechanisms, and that thousands of tons of bombs had missed their targets altogether.³⁷

- **Restricting access to areas and events that might result in coverage of U.S. casualties**

In Grenada and Panama, reporters were prevented from covering anything during the initial stages of those invasions, when casualties were highest. During the Gulf War, reporters were denied access to Dover Air Force base, when the bodies of U.S. servicemen and women killed in the conflict arrived for transshipment home. Similar restrictions continued months after the Gulf War was over. The Associated Press reported that journalists were barred from a military camp in Kuwait after a July 11, 1991 explosion there injured more than 50 U.S. soldiers. Twelve days later, three American troops were killed in another explosion at the camp.³⁸

- **Minimizing discussion of civilian casualties**

Some human rights organizations believed that the Defense Department had underestimated the number of civilian casualties resulting from the invasion of Panama, and that more civilians had been killed than Panamanian military personnel.³⁹ Defense Department officials insisted for months that their best estimate was that 314 Panamanian troops had been killed, and 202 civilians. After a year of controversy, the U.S. Southern Command issued a fact sheet stating that the Panamanian coroner's office had identified 65 military and 157 civilian remains. Another 50 bodies had not yet been identified, and 75 reports of missing persons had not been resolved.⁴⁰ In the Persian Gulf, Pentagon officials avoided the issue, saying they could not provide accurate estimates about civilian deaths. President Bush contended that the United States had no argument with the Iraqi people, and insisted that "our air strikes were the most effective yet humane in the history of warfare."⁴¹ After the war, human rights organizations estimated that between 5,000 and 15,000 Iraqi civilians had been killed, and that nearly 200,000 — mostly children and the elderly — could be expected to die within a year, principally because medical, sanitation and agricultural facilities had been destroyed by U.S. and coalition bombing.⁴² These figures did not include the tens of thousands of Shiites and Kurds killed during their rebellions against Iraqi leader Saddam Hussein after the ceasefire.

- **Minimizing discussion of enemy military casualties**

During the Vietnam War, the enemy body count was used by U.S. officials as an indicator of the war's progress. Many military officials, under pressure from the White House to present the impression that the war was being won, inflated or made up body counts. The practice became a symbol of U.S. duplicity. Since then, the Defense Department has de-emphasized body counts. Gen. Schwarzkopf —

who has admitted he lied about enemy casualties during the Vietnam conflict[43] — was reluctant to discuss the body count during Grenada, and refused to do so during the Gulf War. "Body count means nothing — absolutely nothing — and all it is is a wild guess that misleads people about what is going on," he told a reporter in Riyadh, Saudi Arabia, during a Jan. 30, 1991 press briefing.[44] The Defense Department refused to estimate how many Iraqi soldiers were killed in the fighting[45] until a public interest group filed a Freedom of Information Act request. In response, the Defense Intelligence Agency estimated that approximately 100,000 Iraqi troops had been killed and 300,000 wounded, with an "error factor of 50% or higher."[46]

- **Replacing body counts with "weapons counts"**

During the Gulf War, Defense Department officials wanted the media to concentrate on the number of weapons and facilities U.S. forces had destroyed rather than the number of people who had died. Pentagon officials in Saudi Arabia and Washington gave reporters detailed statistics about the number of Iraqi planes, tanks, armored personnel carriers, artillery pieces, Scud missile launchers, runways and bridges the allies had destroyed or immobilized each day. These statistics were widely reported in the media, with the networks, newspapers and magazines working up elaborate charts and graphs that showed how successful U.S. and allied forces had been. "The statistics went very well with all the Pentagon footage showing bridges and buildings being blown up," said one U.S. reporter. "We could keep score, like it was a living-room video game."[47] Meanwhile, estimates of enemy casualties were conspicuous by their absence.

- **Sanitizing the image of war by manipulating the language**

Throughout the Gulf War, Pentagon briefers referred to U.S. war dead as "KIA," (killed in action). Enemy soldiers who died in battle were "attrited." Civilian casualties were part of "collateral damage." Only enemy aircraft and tanks were "killed." Targets such as bridges, which also had civilian uses, were "serviced."[48]

These abbreviations and expressions served, in the words of Col. Hackworth, to present an "antiseptic" and "bloodless" picture of combat[49] that he and other current and former military officers interviewed for this study found disturbing.

- **Sanitizing the image of war by controlling visuals**

In Grenada, the Pentagon controlled both negative and positive images. News photographers were kept off the island for two days, so the Defense Department did not have to worry about photographs of U.S. casualties. Meanwhile, Defense Department cameramen shot essentially casualty-free footage that the Pentagon gave to the networks. During the crucial first two days of the operation, the American public did not see a single image of the invasion that had not been supplied by the Pentagon.

In the Persian Gulf, the Pentagon had great control over visual images because the first month of the conflict involved an air war. Photographers were limited to pictures of planes being serviced, taking off and landing. By the time carefully selected footage from the U.S. planes' gun-cameras was released — showing laser-guided bombs hitting their targets with incredible precision — U.S. journalists were so starved for pictures from the front that several actually cheered.

- **Using the media to fine-tune public opinion about the war**

During the first few days of the Gulf air war, military officials talked of how well the war was going, saying parts of the Republican Guard had been "decimated" and that U.S. sorties had had an 80 percent success rate.[50] After a week of overwhelmingly positive coverage, the Pentagon became worried about public expectations, and decided to do what Pete Williams later called "euphoria control."[51] Defense Secretary Cheney chided the media for raising expectations, neglecting to mention that the information and statistics in the stories had been supplied by the military.[52]

For weeks before the ground war began, the Pentagon had been releasing bloodless footage of U.S. bombs destroying their targets. As the time for a ground assault approached, military personnel became concerned that the public might not accept the high casualties many of them feared would occur, and tried to prepare the American people for higher body counts by rejecting the antiseptic image of war that they had created. In an appearance before the Senate Armed Services Committee shortly before the ground assault, Joint Chiefs of Staff Chairman Gen. Powell warned the committee that "Ground combat is nasty business. It is not nice and sanitized and clean as a video game, such as nice gun-camera footage."[53]

In all three conflicts, Pentagon and White House officials justified the restrictions by saying public opinion polls showed that the American people supported them. The press was portrayed as being unreasonable in asking for more information than the public wanted. As Schwarzkopf said after the Gulf War, the public has a right to know, but the media ought to ask the public how much it wanted to know.[54] Such a rationale is antithetical to a democratic system, which requires that the press be able to provide the public with what it needs to know in the long term as well as what it wants to know in the short term.

However, polls do indicate that the press has not made a compelling case for its side of the debate. A January 1991 poll conducted by the Times Mirror Center for the People & the Press showed 79 percent of the respondents thought the military restrictions on news reports during the conflict were a "good idea." That number had increased to 83 percent by the time a follow-up poll was done in March 1991.[55] Furthermore, the poll found a shift in public attitudes toward censorship. Since 1985, Times Mirror has been asking the American public to evaluate the relative importance of censorship for the sake of national security when it conflicts with the news media's ability to report stories that journalists believe are in the national interest. The March 1991 Times Mirror report stated:

> Each time this question has been previously asked, the public was either evenly divided on the issue or came down clearly on the side of the media. The current survey finds a nearly two to one majority feeling that military censorship is more important than the media's ability to report important news![56]

The fact that a large majority of the American people support a concept which distorts the flow of independent information that is essential in a democracy is cause for alarm. It raises important issues about the ways in which military restrictions on the media have affected the perceptions of, and relationships among, the country's political leadership, the Pentagon and the public. □

ISSUES RAISED BY MEDIA RESTRICTIONS

Information will be withheld only when disclosure would adversely affect national security or threaten the safety or privacy of the men and women of the Armed Forces.

Principles of Information
Defense Secretary Richard Cheney

The President serves not only as the country's Commander-in-Chief of the Armed Forces, but also as the nation's highest elected official. When a President calls for U.S. military intervention on foreign soil, not only are the country's military interests at stake, but the President's political interests as well. The evidence indicates that during the past 10 years, restrictions on the media's access to information during wartime have been developed not only by the Pentagon, but also by the White House. Some of these restrictions go beyond what is necessary to ensure operational security, and appear to have been designed primarily to control public perceptions of — and public debate about — American military operations.

One person who thinks the restrictions have gone too far is retired Rear Adm. Eugene J. Carroll Jr., a veteran of Korea and Vietnam, who is Deputy Director of the Center for Defense Information, a private research organization founded by former military officers to study defense issues. In an interview for this study, Carroll said that during the Gulf War, "the whole pipeline of information flow was politically oriented."[1] The admiral, who was Director of U.S. Operations in Europe and the Middle East under Gen. Alexander Haig in the late 1970s, said the Pentagon used news-management techniques in the Gulf "to put the Commander-in-Chief in the best possible light. He was always presented as a wise, forceful, positive leader" who was using the U.S. Armed Forces "for the good of humankind."[2]

Col. Hackworth concurred, saying he expects to see images of the post-Gulf War victory parades showing up in President Bush's re-election campaign ads in the fall of 1992.[3]

War as an Instrument of Politics

The issue of politically based media restrictions has become increasingly important during the past decade, as the Reagan and Bush administrations repeatedly have used so-called "limited" offensive wars to pursue foreign policy goals. The United States has been involved in three such wars in the past eight years, two of them within a 13-month period. These kinds of wars increasingly are becoming an accepted way of advancing the White House foreign-policy agenda. For this reason — and because public support for civilian leaders tends to rise sharply during short-term military operations — it is important for Americans to be fully informed about the circumstances leading to any decision to commit U.S. troops overseas, and about the ramifications of that decision at home and abroad.

Limited wars with low casualties for the winning side tend to dampen criticism of national leaders and to boost their ratings. The Falklands victory is thought to have saved British Prime Minister Margaret Thatcher's career in 1982.[4] The Grenada invasion in 1983 deflected criticism of President Reagan arising from the truck-bombing deaths of more than 200 U.S. Marines in Lebanon just days earlier, and actually increased his popularity.[5] The invasion of Panama muted discussion about President Bush's indecisiveness, as well as his earlier dealings with Panamanian Gen. Manuel Antonio Noriega during Bush's term as CIA Director in the mid-1970s, and as head of the U.S. drug war in the mid-1980s.[6]

Some policy analysts say the public relations aspects of these victories tend to be transitory, lasting only a few weeks or months.[7] The effects, however, can be significant. During the 1984 presidential campaign, *The New York Times* analyzed national polls of younger voters and found that many supported Reagan because of his image of strength and success, which was bolstered by the Grenada invasion.[8] These responses were ironic, because many U.S. allies — including Great Britain, still basking in its victory in the Falklands conflict — condemned the invasion as unjustified and a violation of international law.[9]

Many military experts — including Gen. Schwarzkopf, who was Army adviser to the commander of the U.S. invasion force on Grenada — agreed that some aspects of the operation were poorly planned, resulting in unnecessary U.S. and Grenadian casualties.[10] The American people did not see any of this, however, because journalists were barred from the island until the fighting was almost over. The news releases and visuals provided by the Reagan administration as a substitute for independent coverage were rigorously edited to present the operation as an impressive success.

This type of news management carries an inherent danger for the military, according to Peter Braestrup. "The credibility of military operations will erode if journalists and the public believe that deceptions, secrecy or press curbs in war zones are being employed not for security reasons but to serve the needs of domestic politics or bureaucratic self-protection," he wrote in a 1985 background paper on the military-media relationship.[11]

Pre-censoring Public Perceptions

The most disturbing element of the restrictions developed during the past decade has been pre-censorship, which entails limiting access to the theater of operations and the troops. By contrast, post-censorship allows comparatively freer access to the battlefield, but imposes strict controls on the information that journalists can send from the field. The distinction is important, because under post-censorship regulations, reporters and photographers can be full witnesses to military operations. Having journalists on the scene ensures that the public eventually will get an independent account of the action. If journalists are not able to use the material they have gathered immediately because of operational security, they nevertheless will have seen and recorded the events firsthand, and can provide their accounts to the public later.

These independent accounts can be crucial in helping the American people assess the impact of going to war and the wisdom of the civilian leaders who made the decision to do so. By contrast, when this information is controlled and disseminated by the Pentagon or the White House, the voters lose their ability to make well-founded judgments about the policies and the performance of their elected leaders. Such practices undermine the foundation of the First Amendment, which the Founding Fathers wrote because of their experience with British press restrictions, which included censorship and criminal penalties for journalists who wrote articles critical of government officials.[12] These penalties, which included lengthy jail sentences, were imposed even if the articles were true. In fact, British law was based on the idea that "the greater the truth, the greater the crime."[13] The First Amendment was a response to this and was based on two ideals:

• An informed electorate was essential for a democratic government;

• The electorate must be able to receive their information from an institution outside the government.

Attorney Floyd Abrams, a specialist in First Amendment law, summarized this position in a statement during House Judiciary Committee hearings on media restrictions imposed during the Grenada invasion:

> . . . if the public does not have information, it cannot play a meaningful role in the formulation of policy. When information is suppressed by the government, legally guaranteed freedoms to think and to speak become meaningless.[14]

The integrity of the U.S. policy-making process is also at issue. Many government officials in the legislative and executive branches rely on information provided by newspapers, magazines and broadcast news programs. If the media are prevented from preparing accurate and comprehensive reports, government officials will be basing decisions — including decisions about war and peace — on distorted or incomplete information.

Monitoring the Military

Open media coverage also helps the Defense Department by providing independent and objective information that military officials themselves use when preparing evaluations of the performance of troops, field commanders and weapons systems, according to Maj. Gen. Sidle, Col. Summers and other former and current Pentagon officials.

In an article for *Military Review*, Col. Summers pointed out that during the Vietnam War, when field commanders were prohibited by their superiors from briefing the Joint Chiefs of Staff about what was really happening in-country, the media remained the only conduit for objective data about the conflict.[15]

Historian William M. Hammond of the Army Center of Military History provides another example in his book *United States Army in Vietnam — Public Affairs: The Military and the Media, 1962-68*.[16] Hammond chides the media for not having pursued reports about malfunctions in the M-16 rifle. Problems with the rifle resulted in the deaths or injuries of dozens of U.S. troops during the Vietnam conflict. Army officers, including Col. Hackworth, had tried to work through the system to get problems with the rifle rectified.[17] One reason these officers did not succeed was that the news media — responding to the Pentagon's pleas that they be more supportive of the military effort — ignored the story for months, according to Dr. Hammond. He wrote:

> That the news media failed to make much of the issue may have worked to the detriment of U.S. forces in South Vietnam, if only because the lack of an outcry allowed deficiencies in maintenance and support for the weapon to go uncorrected.[18]

The Gulf War provided another concrete example of how the media can assist the military. *St. Louis Post-Dispatch* reporter Lawrence O'Rourke was assigned to a medical pool. Early in the war he filed a story about one of the first casualties, describing how the wounded soldier had lain on the ground for more than two hours before being evacuated. As a result of the article, the military reexamined and changed procedures to provide for faster evacuation.[19]

The Influence of Public Relations

Another issue that arose during the Gulf crisis concerned the ability of foreign governments to manipulate American public and congressional opinion regarding U.S. policy. After Iraq invaded Kuwait, representatives of the Kuwaiti government hired Hill and Knowlton — a public relations firm whose executives include former Reagan and Bush administration officials — to convince Congress and the American people of the necessity for U.S. military intervention in the Gulf. Throughout the fall, Hill and Knowlton sent video news releases (VNRs) to hundreds of television stations that outlined the plight of Kuwait and urged Americans to support President Bush's policies. In an April 1991 speech, Robert Dilenschneider, Hill and Knowlton President and Chief Executive Officer, USA, estimated that more than 30 million Americans had seen one VNR, and more than 60 million had seen another.[20]

Hill and Knowlton also monitored congressional activities regarding the Gulf crisis, and provided information kits to House and Senate members. Ultimately, Congress voted to authorize President Bush to use military force to expel Iraqi troops from Kuwait.[21]

Hill and Knowlton was not the only firm working for Kuwait. An examination of Justice Department foreign agent registration forms found that several other firms, including Neill and Company and Pintak/Brown International, were hired by representatives of Kuwait.[22] The Neill firm was hired to provide advice and information on U.S. congressional actions relating to the administration's policy in the Gulf, and to "consult from time to time with members of Congress and other officials of the Government of the United States on issues and legislation" pertinent to Kuwait.[23]

These activities have outraged some members of Congress. "I resent that on an issue that should be decided by information from experts, so much is being spent to influence me and the American public," Rep. James A. Hayes (D-La.) told a *Washington Post* reporter in December 1990.[24]

Kuwait's success in promoting support for U.S. military intervention in the Gulf is ironic in light of the origins of the U.S. law designed to monitor these activities. Congress passed the Foreign Agents Registration Act (FARA) in 1938, after federal investigators discovered that two U.S. public relations firms were clandestinely disseminating propaganda for the Nazis.[25] At the time, Europe appeared headed for a war, and Congress was concerned that the German government would use U.S. firms to influence public opinion about whether the United States should enter the conflict.[26]

FARA requires that U.S. firms or individuals file foreign agents' registration forms with the Justice Department within 10 days after agreeing to act on behalf of a foreign government or group, and to file copies of any political propaganda within 48 hours of disseminating it.[27] The law is designed for the "protection of the integrity of our Government's decision-making process,"[28] but Republican and Democratic members of Congress and the General Accounting Office (GAO), the investigative arm of Congress, have stated that FARA is "plagued with loopholes" and poorly enforced.[29] Congressional hearings on strengthening FARA are under way, and a bill to close loopholes has been introduced in the House,[30] but some policy analysts are not sure this will remedy the problems. The Justice Department has been unwilling to enforce the current law vigorously,[31] and the proposed legislation does not address the issue of possible conflicts of interest among former high-level federal officials who represent foreign governments or organizations. A GAO official told a Senate committee in September 1990 that 76 former officeholders — including 18 White House officials and 22 other Executive Branch officials — had gone to work for foreign interests during fiscal years 1980-85.[32] Questions about the propriety of this situation arose during the Gulf War, because one of Hill and Knowlton's top executives for worldwide public affairs is Craig Fuller, Vice President Bush's former chief of staff.

Distorting History

In the long term, the historical record may be the final casualty of the government's information-control policies. In testimony before the Senate Governmental Affairs Committee in February 1991 about media restrictions in the Gulf, CBS special correspondent Walter Cronkite pointed out that news reports are drafts of history, and that journalists must be present if the record is to be accurate. Cronkite stated:

> History begins to be distorted with every second that passes after it occurs. . . . [Witnesses] refine the story, to make a better story. . . . So it's very important to get the first impressions. . . . It's essential to be there when it happens.[33]

When journalists are denied sufficient access to the battlefield and the troops, they cannot prepare the objective, independent accounts that are crucial if future historians and researchers are to put events and issues into proper perspective, and government officials are to make informed decisions. If news reports of war are based principally on information controlled and disseminated by the government, they reflect not reality, but an official version of events.

Gen. Powell, in a speech to newspaper executives after the war, assured them that the historical record of the Gulf War was intact. "Every fact about Operation Desert Shield and Desert Storm will eventually come to the light of day," he said. "Historians will search and dig. After time, nothing will be hidden. Even classified information has a lifetime and is ultimately available. In America, secrets are not buried . . . ."[34]

Despite this reassuring rhetoric, there is no guarantee that all the facts about the Gulf War will ever be known, much less that they will be revealed in a timely manner that would contribute to public discussion. The ramifications of a distorted and delayed historical record are made clear in *A Peace to End All Peace — The Fall of the Ottoman Empire and the Creation of the Modern Middle East*, by David Fromkin.[35] The book details how British, French and Russian policies in the Middle East after World War I set the stage for the current Gulf crisis. The volume was widely praised as the crisis intensified, and sold well. Many readers wondered why such an important work — which provides a fresh perspective on events in the Gulf — was not written decades earlier. The reason, according to the author, is that "hitherto secret official documents" had only recently been made available to researchers. According to the author, the documents showed that:

> Russian and French official accounts of what they were doing in the Middle East at that time, were, not unnaturally, works of propaganda; British official accounts — and even the later memoirs of the officials concerned — were untruthful too. British officials who played a major role in the making of these decisions provided a version of events that was, at best, edited and, at worst, fictitious.[36]

Historians wonder what would have happened if the book *had* been written 70 years ago, when policy makers might have changed the course of events. If government officials and the public had had the information in Fromkin's book during the 1920s, perhaps there would have been no Gulf War in the 1990s. Likewise, will policy makers and scholars today have to wait 70 years to see crucial documents and learn the full extent of what occurred during the Gulf War?

Despite Powell's promise, this idea is not far-fetched. Several organizations of American historians have been fighting the State Department over its refusal to discuss stringent declassification policies and practices.[37] Historians maintain that the Department's overzealous concern for secrecy has led officials to refuse to declassify documents — many of them decades old — that should have been available to scholars, and has threatened the accuracy of the historical record. The chairman of the Advisory Committee on Historical Diplomatic Documentation, which consults with the Department regarding preparation of volumes of the historical series, *Foreign Relations of the United States*, resigned in 1989 in protest of these policies.[38]

In an August 1990 newsletter, Bradford Perkins, the Organization of American Historian's delegate to the Advisory Committee and its acting chairman, illustrated the seriousness of the situation by pointing out that these were major deletions in a volume about U.S. relations with Iran:

> For the committee, the problem was starkly revealed during discussion of the recently published volume, *Iran 1951-54*. An expert in the field who reviewed this volume for the committee concluded that, because of extensive deletions, the volume presented not only a woefully incomplete but even an entirely misleading account of events surrounding the ouster of [Iranian Premier] Mohammed Mosadeq [by a CIA-supported coup that put Shah Reza Pahlavi back in power in 1953]. Since the general picture is already well known, (and the CIA representative in Iran has published his memoirs, presumably with the Agency's concurrence), the committee fears that excessive deference may have been paid to security considerations. It regrets the lack of access to classified materials that might lay these fears to rest.[39]

Historians are concerned that documents relating to U.S. involvement in Grenada, Panama and the Persian Gulf might be hidden or altered in the same way as the documents concerning Iran. If this occurs, then by the time the truth emerges, it will be too late to affect the course of contemporary events.

Paul Finkelman, a law professor and historian who is a former Chair of the Committee on Access to Documents and Open Information of the Organization of American Historians, said in an interview that in future decades, historians may well discover all the relevant details of these military operations. The question is whether these discoveries "will come out in time to be meaningful for the development of public policy, or simply meaningful for a larger understanding of distant historical events."[40] □

THE VIETNAM WAR

A free flow of general and military information will be made available, without censorship or propaganda, to the men and women of the Armed Forces and their dependents.

Principles of Information
Defense Secretary Richard Cheney

Memories of Vietnam have affected every successive U.S. military action, from the invasion of Grenada to the Persian Gulf War. During Operation Desert Storm, President Bush vowed repeatedly that the conflict would not be similar to the "long, drawn-out agony of Vietnam," a war that killed or wounded some 350,000 Americans and millions of Vietnamese, dragged on for more than a decade, lost the support of the American people, resulted in a U.S. president's decision not to seek reelection, and ended with an American withdrawal from the battlefield.[1]

Military leaders were equally determined that the U.S. Armed Forces would not endure another such experience. Both top U.S. military leaders during the Gulf War, Gen. Colin Powell, Chairman of the Joint Chiefs of Staff, and Gen. H. Norman Schwarzkopf, head of Central Command, first experienced warfare in Vietnam. Schwarzkopf, who served two tours of duty in what he called the "terrible, horrible war" in Southeast Asia,[2] has described his experiences there as a turning point in his life. He told one magazine reporter, "I measure everything in my life from Vietnam,"[3] and said to another, "We all carry scars from Vietnam, and those scars will never go away."[4]

One reason the conflict in Southeast Asia had such a lasting impact on the American people and their institutions was that it altered the relationships among Clausewitz's "remarkable trinity" of the government, the military and the public.[5] It also resulted in a deep bitterness toward the U.S. media, the institution that links the elements of that trinity. The Pentagon and the press talk of the lessons they learned in Vietnam, but many of these "lessons" are, in fact, myths that have increased the inherent tensions between the military and the media, and have undermined their ability to carry out their respective Constitutional roles.

The Military's Myths About the Vietnam War

Many military officers believe that one of the most important lessons to be learned from Vietnam is that negative media coverage loses wars. These officers became convinced that if they could find a better way to control press access to information about a conflict, they could control public perceptions about — and support for — U.S. military operations. This belief has persisted despite research by military analysts and historians that have shown that casualties and confusion about U.S. goals in Southeast Asia — not media coverage — led the public to turn against the war.

The lesson that these officers seem to have overlooked is that the politically based media restrictions which the Pentagon supported during the Vietnam War worked against the military's own objectives, on and off the battlefield. In some cases the restrictions led to the suppression of field commanders' negative assessments about the progress of the war. In other cases, these policies resulted in increased U.S. casualties.

The White House decision to use politically based information strategies to shape news and public opinion deeply divided military personnel. Many U.S. officers believed that these policies, which went beyond what was needed to protect operational security and troop safety, compromised the U.S. military's Constitutional role as a nonpolitical national security force. They also were concerned that White House insistence on presenting a positive image of the progress of the war had led to a policy of ignoring or suppressing pessimistic reports from the battlefield, a decision which distorted the very information that White House leaders used to make policy and Pentagon officers depended upon to draw up battle plans.

This situation resulted in one of the greatest ironies concerning the myths about the military-media relationship in Vietnam. Far from despising the press, some of the most experienced U.S. military officers sought out reporters they respected in order to get the truth about the war before Congress, the American people, and their own leaders in the Pentagon.[6]

Journalists' Myths About the Vietnam War

Journalists have their own illusions about the Vietnam War. They remember it as a conflict in which reporters had relatively free access to the battlefield and operated under voluntary guidelines. During the Persian Gulf War, journalists continually called for a return to the media policies that the Pentagon used during the conflict in Southeast Asia, arguing that these policies allowed more complete and accurate coverage. Journalists have forgotten that many techniques used in the Gulf War — such as restricting access to military bases and requiring that reporters be accompanied by a military escort — also were used at times in Vietnam.[7] Many of these techniques did not succeed as well as they did in subsequent wars for several reasons, including the fact that the war lasted for years, giving full-time correspondents time to develop excellent sources within the U.S. military and diplomatic communities in South Vietnam. In addition, many parts of the country were connected by road, so journalists could reach some military facilities fairly easily. Nevertheless, the restrictions tried during the Vietnam War set the stage for what happened in future conflicts.

Journalists also have overlooked the fact that they were co-opted by an extensive campaign by the White House, State Department and Pentagon to manipulate information about the war for political purposes. Most reporters presented the U.S. point of view in their stories, even in news analysis pieces criticizing American policies. However, some of the information journalists received from military briefers in Saigon was edited or altered by U.S. officials so that it would present an optimistic picture of the conflict. Historian William M. Hammond's book on the military-media relationship in South Vietnam from 1962 to 1968, prepared for the Army Center of Military History, has numerous examples of Pentagon and State Department personnel misleading reporters about issues such as the combat role of U.S. advisers in the early days of the conflict, the extent of U.S. involvement in the fighting in

Laos and incompetence among South Vietnamese military officers. This made accurate reporting extremely difficult, whether a reporter had access to the battlefield or not. In many cases, even well-intentioned journalists misinformed the public and Congress about the war.

The Real Lessons of Vietnam

As a result of their distorted memories about coverage of the conflict, the military and the media have forgotten one of the most important lessons of the Vietnam War: that the politically based information policies instituted by the White House and the Pentagon had tragic consequences for all concerned.

Perhaps more than any previous 20th-century conflict, the war in Vietnam illustrated how political factors influence military restrictions on media coverage, and undermine both national security and the military's duty to protect the Constitution. Current disagreements among military officers about the role of the media during wartime and the effects of media coverage on public opinion reflect the angry debates that took place in the White House, the Pentagon and the Military Assistance Command, Vietnam (MACV) during the conflict in Southeast Asia. The way in which those debates unfolded, and their intensity, offer an eerie preview of the bitter exchanges between military and media personnel during successive conflicts, including the Persian Gulf War.

Background on Media Restrictions and War Coverage

In 1961, President John F. Kennedy decided that Southeast Asia was crucial to U.S. national security interests. During the next two years he sent thousands of U.S. military advisers to assist the South Vietnamese Armed Forces, who were trying to end an insurgency inspired by North Vietnam and its supporters in the South, the Viet Cong.[8] As the number of advisers and their involvement in combat increased, the Kennedy and Johnson administrations tried to minimize the importance of the U.S. military presence by promoting the notion that the United States was playing only a supporting role in the conflict. From the beginning, U.S. officials were concerned that they would lose support for their policies if the public and Congress learned the full extent of U.S. involvement in Southeast Asia. Information policies were designed not only to protect military operations and troop safety, but also to safeguard the political agenda and public opinion ratings of the President.

In his book, Dr. Hammond explained the White House rationale:

> By limiting the American public's knowledge of what was happening in South Vietnam, it would help to defuse any adverse domestic reaction to U.S. risk-taking in Southeast Asia . . . . The American people . . . seemed little interested in a foreign war. If enthusiasm for the conflict in South Vietnam began to fade because of negative reporting in the press, the American effort to defeat Communist aggression in Southeast Asia would also begin to slip and might even fail for lack of support. A low profile, achieved through restraints on the press at the scene of conflict and designed to sustain the American public's support for the war, seemed a safer course.[9]

Media restrictions designed to prevent "frivolous, thoughtless criticism" of the South Vietnamese government and the U.S. role in the conflict were in place by early 1962 — nearly three years before U.S. combat forces were sent to South Vietnam.[10] The groundwork for these restrictions was laid out in a joint message from the Defense Department, State Department and United States Information Agency (USIA) known as Cable 1006, which ordered military officials in Vietnam to ensure that journalists did not go on military operations that might result in news stories that were unfavorable toward U.S. policy.[11]

Efforts must be made, the directive stated, to emphasize the South Vietnamese role in the war because "it is not . . . in our interest . . . to have stories indicating that Americans are leading and directing combat missions against the Viet Cong." The cable stressed the need for U.S. military and civilian officials to be able to operate without interference from journalists.[12]

The directive "prompted the U.S. mission in Saigon to persist in the practice of excessive classification to a degree that denied newsmen access to whole segments of the war," according to Dr. Hammond.[13]

Another restriction that harmed the military's credibility with the media involved State Department and Pentagon orders prohibiting military briefers from talking about South Vietnamese matters unless the information that they presented had been cleared by the South Vietnamese government.[14] If the government wanted information about a battle withheld, MACV spokesmen were obliged to go along.[15] The inability of military public affairs officers to correct mistaken impressions and misinformation further eroded journalists' trust.[16]

Perhaps the most damaging practice in the early years of the conflict was the White House and Pentagon decision to conceal the extent of the U.S. role in the war in Southeast Asia. Military briefers were under orders to restrict information about the use of napalm. They could not acknowledge that U.S. pilots were flying combat missions for the South Vietnamese Air Force at a time when the United States officially had only an advisory role.[17] At one point, U.S. officials tried to keep reporters from finding out about the pilots' combat missions by denying journalists permission to visit the Bien Hoa Air Base, where U.S. airmen lived. Reporters uncovered the truth as the number of sorties climbed above 1,000 per month and casualties from these operations included U.S. pilots.[18]

By mid-1962, the few U.S. correspondents stationed in Saigon were furious about U.S. restrictions on information. Pulitzer Prize winner Homer Bigart, a *New York Times* correspondent, wrote that American officials who leaked information critical of the South Vietnamese government were "tracked down" and ordered not to talk with journalists.[19] He added that "correspondents who send gloomy dispatches are apt to be upbraided for lack of patriotism."[20] David Halberstam, a young *Times* correspondent who later would win his own Pulitzer for his reporting from Vietnam, wrote:

> [U.S. military officers] feel they are being muzzled by the South Vietnamese government with the support of the United States . . . . American officers serving in the field and flying helicopters believe that

Americans at home have too little knowledge and understanding of what is going on in Vietnam.[21]

Military officials, under enormous pressure from the White House to help maintain public support for the war, vacillated about information policies. They believed that they should be open with the media, yet they thought a positive image of the war was important for motivating the South Vietnamese government and troops. They also feared that a drop in public or congressional support would curtail the troop deployments, materiel and logistical support they needed to prosecute a war effectively. Ultimately, many military officials bowed to the political pressure.

For example, in November 1962, Gen. Paul D. Harkins, commander of U.S. forces in South Vietnam, issued a memo telling U.S. officers in the field to be "sincere and truthful" with reporters and not to use "security as an excuse" to avoid discussing unclassified matters.[22] Meanwhile, he pressured his advisers for impressive enemy body counts that he could present to the media, and rejected officers' pessimistic assessments of the capabilities of the South Vietnamese military and the progress of the war.[23]

Meanwhile, the few journalists covering the war listened to the advisers that Gen. Harkins and other officials ignored. As a result, the assessments of the war presented by reporters such as Halberstam and Jacques Nevard of *The New York Times* were "closer to the truth" than Defense Secretary Robert McNamara's, according to Dr. Hammond.[24] He wrote:

> The two reporters had based their conclusions on the practical, concrete testimony of American advisers at the scene of the action. McNamara, on the other hand, placed great store in statistics which, although useful as indicators of enemy activity, failed to grasp the basically political, human essence of the war.[25]

A War of Statistics

One reason that McNamara turned to statistics was that the United States was not fighting a conventional war, so traditional measures of military success — such as the amount of land won from the enemy — were not especially meaningful. The most important statistic during the Vietnam conflict was the enemy body count, which Col. David Hackworth, who spent years leading troops in the field in South Vietnam, estimated was exaggerated by 20 to 25 percent.[26] The emphasis on body counts "weakened the moral fiber of the officer corps" by "making everyone a bounty hunter and a liar," Col. Hackworth wrote in *About Face*.[27] Officers added civilians to enemy body counts or simply made them up, according to Hackworth and other Armed Forces personnel.[28] In his book, Col. Hackworth recalled that one battalion commander, desperate to hide the fact that an operation had failed, asked an officer for the number of his college football jersey. "Eighty-six," the officer said. "Great body count!" the battalion commander replied.[29]

Gen. Schwarzkopf admitted in an interview after the Gulf War that he had lied about body counts in South Vietnam because of pressure from his superiors. He told *Life* magazine reporter Michael Ryan:

Body count was a lie . . . . I was forced to participate in that lie. Many times people would call me up on the radio after a battle and say, "What was your body count?" I'd say, "I don't know what the body count was." They'd say, "Well, make one up. We have to report a body count." So eventually, just to get them off your back, you'd say, "O.K., the body count was two-fifty."[30]

The inflated body counts caused problems within the very institutions that promoted them. In the end, these statistics became part of the Pentagon's files, causing confusion about the very figures the White House and Pentagon were trying to use to develop battle plans to win the war.[31] In his book, Dr. Hammond discussed events of October 1967, three months before the Tet offensive. At that time, the Defense Department's Office of Systems Analysis questioned the MACV body counts and the optimistic statements about the progress of the war based on those counts. DOD analysts in Washington found that although MACV officials said 55,000 enemy troops had been killed in action in 1966, only 19,500 could be accounted for. The analysts said the "degree of probable delusion" revealed by this discrepancy was cause for national concern. Gen. Westmoreland disputed the findings, but dispatched teams to major headquarters in South Vietnam to monitor the body count. He later declared that their findings upheld his view that the count by and large was honest.[32]

The Battle of Ap Bac

During those early years, military-media relations reached a low point after the battle of Ap Bac in January 1963. South Vietnamese forces, accompanied by U.S. advisers, surrounded a company of Viet Cong, but made numerous mistakes and allowed the enemy to escape. The South Vietnamese took heavy losses and three U.S. advisers were killed. After the fighting, two U.S. Army officers and two reporters, including Neil Sheehan of United Press International, were almost killed when a South Vietnamese commander decided to fake a counterattack on Ap Bac so he could tell his superiors he had tried to regroup. He had his men fire dozens of artillery shells at the town. No enemy were in the area, but the shells killed several South Vietnamese soldiers, wounded 12, and narrowly missed U.S. military men and the journalists.[33]

U.S. advisers complained bitterly to reporters about the incompetence of South Vietnamese forces and their lack of fighting spirit. When the stories broke, Gen. Harkins tried to save face for the U.S. and South Vietnamese governments by calling the Ap Bac battle a victory.[34]

Dr. Hammond stated that Ap Bac was a turning point for many journalists, who became convinced that U.S. military and civilian spokesmen were lying to them continually.[35]

The battle of Ap Bac also was a turning point for some military officers. Men such as Army Lt. Col. John Paul Vann, the adviser of the South Vietnamese forces at Ap Bac who became perhaps the most respected U.S. official in South Vietnam, began talking more openly with reporters as they saw their efforts to inform the Pentagon of problems in the field ignored or suppressed.[36]

Clark Clifford, a Johnson administration adviser who succeeded McNamara as Secretary of Defense, wrote that U.S. officials in Saigon and Washington made a grave error in dismissing stories written during this time. He stated:

> One area we failed to investigate during those early years of the American buildup was the growing gap between the optimistic reports of progress that were coming in through the official chain of command and the increasingly skeptical reporting by some of the journalists covering the war . . . . Even though those skeptical reports were based in part on the views of many junior American officers serving as advisers to the South Vietnamese Army, the Administration viewed the reports as a public-relations nuisance rather than as something that needed to be looked at carefully . . . . It was a serious oversight on our part.[37]

Congress Holds Hearings on News Coverage

In the months after Ap Bac, some members of Congress became increasingly concerned about the difference between official reports about how well the war was going and stories written by reporters in the field. They also took note of reporters' complaints about being denied access to operations and personnel.

In May 1963, a House Government Operations subcommittee held hearings on news restrictions and coverage of the Vietnam conflict.[38] Assistant Secretary of State for Far Eastern Affairs Roger Hilsman told lawmakers that many problems regarding the suppression of news resulted not from U.S. policies, but from those of the South Vietnamese government, which did not "understand the free American press."[39] He said U.S. information policies were based on the principle that it was "essential that the American people have available the fullest possible picture of what is happening in Vietnam and our role there . . . . reporters should be given the widest possible access to news and information on Vietnam."[40]

Less than a year later, the death of Air Force Capt. Edwin Gerald "Jerry" Shank called the truthfulness of Hilsman's statements into question.

The Shank Letters

Capt. Shank was a U.S. adviser killed during a battle in South Vietnam in early 1964. Shank had written numerous letters to family members about the war, and they released them in March to the *Indianapolis News*.[41] What Shank had to say was damning:

> What gets me the most is that they won't tell you people what we do over here. I bet you that anyone you talk to does not know that American pilots fight this war. We — me and my buddies — do everything. The Vietnamese "students" we have on board are airmen basics. The only reason they are on board is in case we crash there is one American "adviser" and one Vietnamese "student." They're stupid, ignorant, sacrificial lambs, and . . . . a menace to have on board.[42]

Within weeks, major media had picked up the story. Readers, viewers and members of Congress were outraged at being misled about the U.S. role in the conflict. Relatives of U.S. soldiers and airmen killed in South Vietnam bought a full-page ad in the *Washington Star* listing the names of the 127 Americans killed in the conflict since 1961 and charging the Defense Department with concealing other casualties.[43] Maine Republican Sen. Margaret Chase Smith commented in May 1964 that "there is a genuine need, a desperate need, for the American people to be told the truth on the Vietnamese war. They are not getting the facts from their government."[44] Three months later, the situation in the Gulf of Tonkin underscored the importance of Sen. Smith's statements.

The Gulf of Tonkin Incident

In August 1964, the Johnson administration announced that U.S. ships had been attacked twice by North Vietnam without provocation. This information galvanized public opinion behind the conflict. Lawmakers passed the Gulf of Tonkin Resolution, which granted the President broad powers to "take all necessary measures to repel an armed attack against the forces of the United States and to prevent further aggression" in South Vietnam.[45] The Resolution had broad support among the media, the public and Congress. Even members of Congress who had grave doubts about the war, such as Sen. Richard Russell (D-Ga.), voted for the measure because, as Russell said, "Our national honor is at stake."[46] The only lawmakers who refused to back the Resolution were two Democratic senators, Wayne Morse of Oregon and Ernest Gruening of Alaska. Sen. Morse objected that Congress did not know enough about what had happened in the Gulf of Tonkin, and said the Resolution would draw the United States deeper into a war that would cost thousands of lives with no assurance of victory.[47] His statements were prophetic. President Johnson used the Resolution to escalate U.S. involvement in the war. Seven months later, in March 1965, the President sent the first U.S. combat forces to South Vietnam.

Later, discrepancies arose concerning what had happened in the Gulf of Tonkin, including the fact that the second reported North Vietnamese attack probably never had occurred, and that top U.S. officials were well aware of this at the time President Johnson made his nationally televised comments about the need to retaliate against North Vietnam.[48]

Lawmakers and journalists were furious that the White House had misled them about the incidents, and that the Johnson administration's information-control policies had contributed to Congress' decision to grant the President the power to escalate the conflict in Southeast Asia unilaterally. The news media in Washington and Saigon were embarrassed that they had unquestioningly accepted the Johnson administration's version of events (the U.S. Navy's official film on Tonkin was narrated by NBC's Chet Huntley),[49] and had failed to follow up on stories written by the few reporters who had examined documents and interviewed crew members of the U.S. ships involved in the Gulf of Tonkin episode.[50]

Information Control Revisited

Ironically, as the President was pushing for passage of the Gulf of Tonkin Resolution in the summer of 1964, State Department, USIA and Pentagon officials were trying to restore U.S. credibility with the press in Saigon by revamping MACV information policies.

This effort, led in part by USIA Director Carl Rowan, had begun in the wake of the controversy engendered by the Shank letters. Rowan said new policies had to be developed "to wipe out the several directives now on the books which some military information officers interpret as requiring them to lie."[51] He recommended that Barry Zorthian be placed in charge of the entire U.S. public affairs program in Saigon. State Department officials agreed with these recommendations, and charged Zorthian with developing policies that would promote "maximum candor and disclosure consistent with the requirements of security."[52]

Under Zorthian's leadership, public affairs officers were encouraged to be more open with the press, and received more training about the situation in Southeast Asia before being sent overseas. Journalists were given more assistance with transportation to the field. Sometimes only a small group of journalists would be allowed to visit a particular base, especially when transportation to a remote base was difficult or a field commander could accommodate only a limited number of journalists for a particular operation. But this caused few complaints, because journalists had so much access to other areas of the field.[53] Correspondents could get rides on military vehicles and aircraft, and by 1966 the military had daily scheduled flights for journalists from Saigon to eight major areas in South Vietnam.[54]

However, the emphasis of the new public affairs effort was still to get more positive stories in the media that would, in Dr. Hammond's words, help "prepare a climate in the United States receptive to the official point of view."[55] To accomplish this, MACV officials arranged press visits to sites that they thought would encourage favorable stories about the U.S. presence in South Vietnam.[56] They also designed the prototype of the Hometown Program used in the Gulf War, flying over dozens of stateside reporters and editors to South Vietnam for quick, supervised visits to the front.[57] These trips quickly became controversial. Assistant Secretary of Defense for Public Affairs Arthur Sylvester told the Senate Foreign Relations Committee during 1966 hearings on U.S. news policies in Vietnam that the tours were designed "to help assure a balanced output of on-the-scene news,"[58] but Sen. Joseph S. Clark (D-Penn.) countered that journalists who accepted such trips were "trained seals" who "wrote what they were told."[59] Journalist Malcolm Browne, who was stationed in Saigon and won a Pulitzer Prize for his reporting from Southeast Asia, said the trips were nothing more than "junkets" designed to manipulate journalists' impressions about the success of U.S. efforts in South Vietnam.[60]

Relations between U.S. officials and the press did improve under Zorthian's leadership, but problems persisted. After U.S. combat forces began arriving in March 1965, and U.S. involvement and casualties escalated, the Johnson administration's obsession with controlling public and congressional perceptions increased.

The Johnson Administration Monitors News Coverage

Johnson administration officials "questioned every news story that threatened the low profile it sought" in Vietnam, and became "agitated every time unfavorable news appeared," Dr. Hammond wrote.[61]

The U.S. government's attitude about the role of the media was illustrated by Assistant Secretary of Defense Arthur Sylvester's 1965 comment to Saigon correspondents that in time of war, journalists had an obligation to become the "handmaiden" of government. When reporters pressed him about the credibility of U.S. spokesmen, Sylvester said, "Look, if you think any American official is going to tell you the truth you're stupid."[62]

By early 1965, Gen. Westmoreland had received signals that "the president himself was becoming increasingly concerned about the U.S. mission's failure to keep the Saigon correspondents under control," according to Dr. Hammond.[63] In August, frustrated by negative stories about the war, Gen. Westmoreland — who had made an effort to be more open to journalists than his predecessor had been — sent a cable to his deputy saying he was unhappy about "distorted and unfavorable publicity," and the fact that the MACV Chief of Information was "not exercising [the] controls available to him in that the press is apparently allowed to free-wheel as they please."[64]

As a result of these pressures — and despite the best efforts of public affairs officers who fought for press access to the field and truthful disclosure — access to information about the war continued to be restricted for political purposes in Washington and Saigon.

For example, new efforts were made to limit officers' comments to journalists.[65] In 1965, the Assistant Secretary of Defense for Public Affairs ordered officers to limit reporters' access to information that might embarrass the military or increase discussion of the war.[66] Meanwhile, Adm. Ulysses S. Grant Sharp, the Commander-in-Chief, Pacific, told the Joint Chiefs of Staff he would try to help reduce the number of critical stories by instructing commanders to "avoid statements which add fuel to the already burning fire."[67] In 1966, Adm. Sharp refused MACV public affairs officers' requests that he relax restrictions on information about cluster bombs, partly because he was "concerned that what he considered emotional topics might fuel antiwar sentiment in the United States," Dr. Hammond wrote.[68]

Briefings Mislead Military Officers and U.S. Officials

During this time, military briefers in South Vietnam continued providing a falsely optimistic picture of the war that misled not only some journalists, but also Pentagon and White House officials.

Col. Hackworth recalled a briefing at which U.S. officers called a November 1966 operation a decisive U.S. victory that had resulted in high enemy casualties. These officers had presented this same information to Gen. Westmoreland and Gen. Earle G. Wheeler, Chairman of the Joint Chiefs of Staff. When Col. Hackworth later talked to U.S. soldiers who had participated in the battle, he found that "there was almost no correlation" between the laudatory briefing and what U.S. troops were saying actually had happened in the field. In fact, the Americans had been "chewed up and spat out" by the North Vietnamese Army, Col. Hackworth wrote, and the information presented to the U.S. commanders was "rah-rah bullshit."[69]

In his memoirs, Clark Clifford, President Johnson's adviser and Defense Secretary, explained the effects of these optimistic briefings on his decisions about U.S. policy in Southeast Asia:

> . . . I was influenced, starting in 1966, by a steady stream of optimistic briefings coming from the military, the White House, and even the CIA . . . . I read messages from the Embassy in Saigon that described in glowing terms the steady strengthening of the South Vietnamese government . . . . Later, when I began to take a firsthand look at the situation, I discovered that much of the information from the Embassy and the military command in Saigon was either inaccurate or irrelevant . . . . I had no idea how inaccurate those official reports were until I made a trip to Southeast Asia in the late summer of 1967. Until then, I had . . . accepted them as accurate, and I had supported the military requests for more troops as the best way to end the war quickly.[70]

Problems facing military and government officials who were trying to communicate the truth about the situation in Vietnam were compounded by White House and State Department demands that MACV and the American Embassy present the South Vietnamese government and military in the best possible light. U.S. officials feared that negative press coverage of the South Vietnamese would affect public support for the war.

Col. Henry A. Shockley, a former Chief of Intelligence Collection in Vietnam, told the House Select Committee on Intelligence during hearings in December 1975 that there was a restriction against collecting information on the South Vietnamese Armed Forces, despite numerous reports from U.S. field commanders about South Vietnamese officers' corruption, incompetence and unwillingness to fight the North Vietnamese and the Viet Cong. Shockley added that U.S. policy makers purposely suppressed information regarding South Vietnamese shortcomings because they were concerned that reporters would learn about it.[71]

This attitude — and the fact that poor battlefield decisions by South Vietnamese officers resulted in the deaths of American soldiers — infuriated U.S. field commanders. Col. Hackworth wrote in his book that "criticism of our ally was forbidden," and that by 1969 — four years after U.S. combat forces had arrived in South Vietnam — American officials still had not addressed problems with the South Vietnamese Armed Forces.[72] Col. Hackworth wrote that corruption was so pervasive that the only way he could get one South Vietnamese commander to go into battle was by promising to provide a U.S. helicopter to fly the officer's wife to Saigon for a shopping trip.[73] Yet U.S. officers who had confronted the Defense Department with the inadequacies of the South Vietnamese Armed Forces had been silenced.[74] Col. Hackworth himself had spent months in fruitless efforts to get the Pentagon high command to pay attention to his pessimistic reports.[75] As a result, he began providing reporters he trusted with information and documents concerning problems in the field. As the situation continued to deteriorate, Col. Hackworth —

who had won more than 100 medals during his military career — decided to take the story of the U.S. soldiers in the field directly to the public, and to retire from the Army. He appeared on ABC's "Issues and Answers" in June 1971, while he was still in South Vietnam. After the program was aired, U.S. soldiers cheered him for telling the truth.[76]

The U.S. Government Considers Censorship

As the U.S. role in South Vietnam escalated, the Johnson administration considered setting up a system of formal military censorship several times. One reason was that Defense Secretary McNamara was upset that reporters were filing detailed stories about troop deployments and operations. Although these stories had little effect on military security, McNamara believed that they "seriously compromised policy and decision-making."[77] Administration officials also were concerned about the political impact of stories that predicted an increased U.S. combat role and criticized the South Vietnamese government and Armed Forces. Gen. Westmoreland thought that the "maximum candor" policy should be modified "in view of [the] changed nature of military activities."[78]

After months of discussion, the idea of establishing a system for censorship was rejected. Military public affairs officers had argued against such a system on several grounds. Journalists had an excellent record of observing the ground rules and protecting operational security, so censorship could not be justified on that basis. Some officers also were uncomfortable with imposing censorship when Congress had never declared war. Some also believed censorship would prevent journalists from fulfilling their Constitutional responsibility to inform the public about the war. In addition, any censorship program would have to be carried out in conjunction with the South Vietnamese government, whose repressive press policies already had caused problems for U.S. officials. Pentagon officers also believed that censorship could turn congressional and public opinion against the administration because it violated American values.[79]

Col. Summers summarized the argument in *On Strategy*:

> Imposition of total censorship would not only jeopardize the very basis of American society but would also sever the link between the American people and their military. The ultimate price could well be higher than any advantages that might accrue through improved U.S. strategic security.[80]

Nevertheless, Pentagon public affairs chief Sylvester at one point ordered Winant Sidle, a colonel working with MACV at the time, to write up a censorship plan. Col. Sidle purposely made the plan so complex and detailed that it could never be implemented.[81]

MACV Moves to Control the Visual Images of War

After giving up on censorship, U.S. officials turned to additional voluntary measures to control news coverage. MACV officials, worried that graphic images of the war would erode public support, held a series of meetings with television journalists in Saigon in 1966 and warned reporters and photographers that if complaints about footage of the dead and wounded arose, field commanders would not allow TV photographers to accompany the troops. Pentagon officials met with representatives of the three networks and several newsfilm companies to emphasize that editors should be selective when choosing what footage to broadcast. The news media, whose executives also were concerned that ratings might be hurt by film that was too realistic, agreed to a series of guidelines that limited what they would show on the air. The result, according to Dr. Hammond, was that the American people rarely saw realistic combat footage.[82] Hammond wrote:

> . . . most of what the public saw bore little resemblance to the mayhem critics of the press presume . . . . In fact, the action scenes from any episode of the popular television dramas "Gunsmoke" and "Kojak," carefully paced and filmed for effect, were probably more brutal than all but a few of the most explicit films from Vietnam.[83]

In 1967, MACV took another step to limit the impact of television by requiring that each television reporter be accompanied by an escort, who was to act as a "qualified military observer," Dr. Hammond wrote.[84] Gen. Westmoreland believed that many negative news stories resulted from unthinking soldiers acting improperly on camera or making disparaging remarks. He believed neither would occur if an escort were present.[85]

In addition, the Defense Department sent its own teams of photographers to Vietnam, to supply film and still photographs to media outlets that could not afford to send their own correspondents.[86] According to Assistant Secretary of Defense Sylvester, these photographers had supplied more than 640 still photographs and more than 150 television news reports about the war to U.S. media by August 1966.[87]

The Military Becomes Involved in a Public Relations Campaign

In 1967, the Johnson administration decided to use another tactic to ensure favorable coverage: public relations appearances by high-ranking military officials to promote U.S. policy. At first, the high command resisted. Gen. Westmoreland turned down several requests, then made a trip in April 1967, hoping it would suffice. But by the fall, with the prospect that U.S. troop levels would be nearly 400,000 by year's end, the White House became increasingly concerned about public opinion. Gen. Westmoreland agreed to make another trip in November. The visit would be justified on the grounds that he would participate in discussions about how the United States could maximize military success in the ensuing months, but as Dr. Hammond pointed out, the trip had another effect:

> . . . there appears to have been little doubt in military circles that the general was participating in a major public relations initiative. His presence in Washington created opportunities not only to promote the theme of progress in the war but also to attack critics of the administration's war policies and to bolster the president's sagging standing in the polls.[88]

Gen. Westmoreland's decision to become involved in the political aspects of the war upset many military officers, and eroded his credibility with the public and the press.[89] The situation was exacerbated by the fact that during his visit — two months before the Tet offensive — he made a series of statements about how well the war was going, stressing that U.S. forces were wearing down the North Vietnamese and their supporters. Westmoreland told a National Press Club audience:

> . . . the enemy has not won a major battle in more than a year. In general, he can fight his large forces only at the edges of his sanctuaries . . . . His guerrilla force is declining at a steady rate. Morale problems are developing within his ranks.[90]

Ten weeks later, tens of thousands of North Vietnamese and Viet Cong troops launched coordinated attacks on military and civilian targets throughout South Vietnam. In the ensuing months, as the American people saw U.S. casualty figures rise and new requests being made for additional American troops in South Vietnam, they began losing faith in their military leaders.[91]

The Tet Offensive, 1968

The consequences of an information-control program based on presenting a false image that the war was going well became shockingly apparent when the Viet Cong launched the Tet offensive in late January 1968. The offensive, which lasted for weeks, caught the media, Congress and the public by surprise. Although Gen. Westmoreland had warned that an enemy attack was imminent, neither the media nor Congress had been briefed about how extensive it might be. The relentless optimism of the Johnson administration and the military high command in Saigon had not prepared them for the thousands of troops who descended on South Vietnamese cities and towns.

In the ensuing years, the media have been criticized for portraying the Tet offensive as a victory for the North, when in fact it was a defeat, inflicting very heavy losses on the Viet Cong. Military officers who are critical of U.S. media coverage of the conflict point to the Tet coverage as one of the major reasons the American people turned against the war.[92]

This interpretation, however, oversimplifies a very complex situation, according to military analysts and historians.[93] For example, public opinion polls showed that news coverage of Tet did not immediately erode U.S. support for the war. The percentage of Americans who backed the U.S. war effort actually increased after the Tet offensive had begun, according to Dr. Hammond and other analysts.[94] The percentage of Americans who considered themselves hawks rose from 56 percent in January 1968 to 61 percent by early February, according to the Gallup organization. The number of Americans who expressed confidence in U.S. military policies in South Vietnam rose from 61 percent in December 1967 to 74 percent in February 1968. Seventy-one percent of respondents wanted to continue the bombing of North Vietnam, an increase of 8 percentage points from the previous October.[95]

What the United States *did* lose during Tet was the illusion, maintained continuously by the White House, the State Department and the Pentagon, that the war was going well. Former Johnson adviser Clark Clifford, nominated to succeed Robert McNamara as Defense Secretary just weeks before the beginning of Tet, wrote in a 1991 magazine article based on his memoirs that the offensive "made a mockery of what the American military had told the public about the war, and devastated Administration credibility." He said the "size and scope" of the offensive and the high U.S. casualties, not news coverage, helped turn public opinion against the war in the long run.[96]

Although media coverage did not alter public opinion about the war at the time of the offensive, it did affect interactions between Congress and the White House, according to Peter Braestrup, a former Marine and *Washington Post* bureau chief in Saigon, whose book *Big Story* is a definitive analysis of Tet news coverage. Braestrup wrote that in the wake of the Tet offensive, Washington-based reporters, whose stories usually faithfully reproduced White House policy statements, waited for President Johnson to provide a clear, definite story line. His inability to do so, coupled with articles from Saigon that contradicted the optimistic picture of the war that the U.S. government previously had presented, created an opportunity for congressional and other antiwar leaders to make their views heard. Doubts about the President's war policy could be presented at a time when the media and the public were open to opposing points of view, and the President was less able to extract a high political cost for perceived disloyalty.[97]

Dr. Hammond stated that the President's inability to formulate a decisive course of action after Tet was a major reason why U.S. support for the war began to decline in the months following the offensive. Citing polling data from *Big Story*, he wrote:

> The lack of any effort by Johnson to marshal public opinion in his favor also affected the American public's mood of aggressiveness, which likewise began to drain away. By the end of March the percentage of those expressing confidence in U.S. military policies in South Vietnam had fallen precipitously from 74 percent to 54 percent.[98]

The man who had based his foreign policy on controlling public opinion eventually was overcome by it. Johnson never fully recovered the initiative, his approval ratings fell, and in March 1968, he decided not to run for reelection. Vice President Hubert Humphrey, saddled with Johnson's policies and image, lost the presidency to Richard Nixon, who promised to pursue peace negotiations vigorously. More than four more years would pass before the last U.S. troops were withdrawn from South Vietnam, in March 1973.

The Order of Battle Controversy

The effects of the U.S. government's information-control policies involved another major issue: allegations that the Pentagon high command had lowered estimates of enemy troop strength because military officials believed that if the news media published the true numbers, Congress and the American people would stop supporting the war. These allegations, if true, were extremely serious, because they meant that Pentagon officials may well have increased U.S. casualties, because battle plans based on the altered figures would have been doomed to fail.

The allegations, raised in U.S. military and intelligence circles in the mid-1960s, did not become widely known until after U.S. involvement in the war had ended, when a CIA analyst named Samuel A. Adams, who had spent years analyzing Viet Cong troop strength, wrote an article that appeared in the May 1975 issue of *Harper's* magazine.[99] In the article — which had been cleared by the CIA[100] — Adams detailed how his 1966 analysis of captured enemy documents led him to believe that the United States had seriously erred in preparing the official order of battle, the U.S. military's estimate of enemy troop strength. The Pentagon had estimated troop strength at 270,000. Adams believed the number was closer to 500,000. He wrote:

> It was important because the planners running the war in those days used statistics as a basis for everything they did, and the most important figure of all was the size of the enemy army . . . . If the Vietcong Army suddenly doubled in size, our whole statistical system would collapse. We'd be fighting a war twice as big as the one we thought we were fighting . . . . the addition of 200,000 troops to the enemy order of battle meant that somebody had to find an extra 600,000 troops for our side.[101]

During the next seven years, Adams fought vainly to have his estimates accepted by the Pentagon. The CIA and some military officers initially supported his finding that the enemy order of battle was too low, but in subsequent meetings decided to use figures presented by MACV, which continued to estimate the order of battle at less than 300,000. In the *Harper's* article, Adams said he had been told by one military officer that an estimate above 300,000 was not politically acceptable. One way the military kept the number down was by excluding categories of Viet Cong supporters from its official order of battle. For example, as estimates of some categories of enemy forces increased, the Pentagon removed groups of village-level Viet Cong supporters — such as the civilian Self-Defense and Secret Self-Defense units — from the order of battle.[102]

Adams blamed the heavy U.S. losses during the January 1968 Tet offensive partly on the Pentagon's and CIA's refusal to acknowledge that the order of battle was much higher than the numbers they had presented, an argument that officials of those agencies continue to deny today.[103]

Adams' story sparked angry and heated denials from government officials at the time. In a letter to *Harper's*, James C. Graham, a former member of the Board of National Intelligence Estimates, said the article "presents a distorted picture of the CIA's analytical effort on Vietnam." He added that Adams' methodology — especially his reliance on captured documents whose timeliness, accuracy and statistical validity had been questioned — often "raised more questions than it answered."[104]

In September 1975, the House Select Committee on Intelligence held wide-ranging hearings on U.S. intelligence operations, which included testimony about alleged intelligence failures regarding the Tet offensive. Adams was their first witness.

He repeated his criticisms, and this time quoted from telegrams and memoranda from the White House, the military high command and the CIA. Some of the documents had never been made public. They included an Aug. 20, 1967 cable sent from Gen. Creighton Abrams, Deputy Commander of U.S. forces in South Vietnam, to Joint Chiefs of Staff Chairman Gen. Wheeler. The cable said that the higher enemy troop-strength estimates being discussed at that time were "in sharp contrast to the current overall strength figure of about 299,000 given to the press here." Abrams argued for dropping two categories of Viet Cong to keep down the estimate because he feared press reaction, Adams testified. "We have been projecting an image of success over recent months," the cable continued. If the higher numbers became public, "all available caveats and explanations will not prevent the press from drawing an erroneous and gloomy conclusion." The cable added, "All those who have an incorrect view of the war will be reinforced and the task will be more difficult."[105]

Adams' testimony was strongly denied by other witnesses, including Lt. Gen. Daniel O. Graham, former head of the MACV Current Intelligence and Estimates Division. He countered that the Tet offensive itself proved Adams' figures were wrong. "Had the Allied forces been attacked by a half million or more troops, one would have to give some credence to Mr. Adams. Since that was not the case, he should be given no credence," Lt. Gen. Graham told the committee.[106]

He also defended Gen. Abrams' cable, saying the general was "attempting to prevent phony figures — that is Adams' figures — from being entered into Washington-level documents describing armed strength of the enemy."[107]

Lt. Gen. Graham defended Gen. Abrams' decision to eliminate the Self-Defense and Secret Self-Defense units from the enemy order of battle, agreeing with the assessment that "these forces contain a sizable number of women and old people" who had "almost no military capability."[108]

Another witness, U.S. Army intelligence officer Richard G. McArthur, supported Adams. He told the committee that his superiors cut his estimate of enemy guerrilla forces from about 80,000 to about 40,000 in 1968. McArthur testified that when he protested, the chief of the Order of Battle Section told him, "Lie a little, Mac, lie a little."[109]

Some members of Congress also questioned whether the U.S. military had underestimated enemy troop strength. Rep. Robert McClory (R-Ill.), a member of the House Intelligence Committee, said during the 1975 hearings that he had visited Vietnam during the fall of 1965 — more than three years before the Tet offensive — and had met with Gen. Westmoreland. Rep. McClory recalled what the general had told him:

> He reported to me the number of troops that were coming across the border from North Vietnam and the number that we were killing as soon as they came across the border. He was able, in very simplistic terms, to explain to me that the war was going to end just about a year after my visit there in October 1965.
>
> Apparently, a lot of troops appeared from other places, and the war dragged on for about 10 years — or actually 7 or 8 years after that.[110]

Gen. Westmoreland responded to these allegations in a December 1975 letter to Intelligence Committee member Rep. Dale Milford (D-Texas). He wrote:

> I categorically deny, as others before me, that there was an effort by military intelligence to deliberately downgrade estimates of Vietcong (VC) strengths in order to portray the VC as weaker than they actually were.[111]

Gen. Westmoreland said the revised estimate of enemy strength released in November 1967 — which had dropped the Self-Defense and Secret Self-Defense forces from the order of battle — "reflected the views of the military intelligence staffs in Saigon and Hawaii, CIA, and the Pentagon."[112] He said these forces "could not be considered a part of the Communist Military Threat" and "possessed no offensive capability."[113] He wrote:

> I can state with certainty that adoption of these figures would have created false and misleading impressions by the news media. Our concern was to keep the record straight, not be a part[y] to misleading the American public as to the true enemy situation.[114]

But some military commanders disagreed with Gen. Westmoreland's assessment of the capabilities of civilian Viet Cong supporters. These supporters were responsible for making and setting many of the mines and booby traps that killed thousands of U.S. troops and wounded thousands more, according to military officers.[115]

In his 1990 book, *About Face*, Col. Hackworth wrote that mines and booby traps were "responsible for probably 50 percent of all U.S. casualties in Vietnam . . . ."[116] Hackworth stated:

> There were just so many incidents — seemingly hundreds of them — that involved civilian VC sympathizers. A particularly bad one . . . occurred before I arrived, when three VC sympathizers in the form of teenage girls selling Coca-Cola were responsible for an ambush that led to serious casualties.[117]

The House Select Committee on Intelligence itself came to believe that political factors affected the enemy order of battle. This assessment is in the committee's January 1976 final report — which the House voted not to release until the Executive Branch had done a security review of the document because of the detailed discussion of intelligence matters.[118] The report was leaked to *The Village Voice*, which ran excerpts in February 1976. In the report, the committee said that U.S. officials had a "degraded image of the enemy" that resulted in part because the disputes over the order of battle "created false perceptions of the enemy U.S. forces faced, and prevented measurement of changes in enemy strength over time."[119] The committee added that "pressure from policy-making officials to produce positive intelligence indicators reinforced erroneous assessments of allied progress and enemy capabilities . . . . In the context of the period it appears that considerable pressure was placed on the Intelligence Community to generate numbers, less out of tactical necessity than for political purposes."[120]

The Military's Myths Persist

In the years since U.S. involvement in the Vietnam conflict ended, the country has been trying to come to terms with the ways in which the war changed the relationships among the President, the public, the Pentagon and the press.

The war continues to affect the military-media relationship, with many officers insisting that news coverage was primarily responsible for the loss of public support for the war. This belief has persisted despite studies by military analysts and academics that have shown that media coverage did not turn the American people against the conflict. Instead, the high number of U.S. casualties and confusion about the goals of the war led the public to lose confidence in the U.S. role in the conflict.[121] In his February 1991 testimony about Gulf War media restrictions, Col. Summers stated:

> . . . blaming the media for the loss of the Vietnam War was wrong. The media, and television in particular, is good at showing the cost of the war. But [the] cost of anything only has meaning in relation to value . . . . It was not the news media, which reported the price, that lost the war. It was the government which, especially in the case of President Lyndon B. Johnson, deliberately failed to establish its value.[122]

Dr. Hammond agreed with that assessment, and pointed out that an analysis of years of polling data showed that public opinion fell 15 points every time casualties increased by a factor of 10.[123]

Analyses of Vietnam coverage also debunk another myth: that most of the coverage was negative. As Col. Summers wrote in his book, *On Strategy*:

> There is a tendency in the military to blame our problems with public support on the media. This is too easy an answer . . . . the majority of on-the-scene reporting from Vietnam was factual — that is, the reporters honestly reported what they had seen firsthand.[124]

Retired Army Maj. Gen. Sidle, who worked in public affairs for MACV in Saigon, said during an interview for this study:

> The bad news always got passed along and always was remembered, and the good news nobody bothered to pass along and then was not remembered . . . . when you look at the actual coverage, it wasn't all that bad. I used to think they [journalists] did a lousy job myself until I got back to the States and looked at some of it.[125]

Dr. Hammond pointed out in an article for *Reviews in American History* that until the 1968 Tet offensive, most journalists covering the war implicitly accepted the U.S. government's rationale for the American role in the Southeast Asia conflict. He wrote:

> . . . the great bulk of war reporting by American correspondents reproduced the official point of view.
>
> Reporters during the early years of the war, for example, criticized U.S. tactics and strategy but never argued about the wisdom of the American presence in South Vietnam.[126]

Neil Sheehan, who served in the U.S. Army and later covered the Vietnam conflict for UPI and *The New York Times*, confirmed this view in his book *A Bright Shining Lie*. He wrote that in the early 1960s, American reporters shared the military's "sense of commitment" to the war.[127] He stated:

> Our ideological prism and cultural biases were in no way different. We regarded the conflict as our war too. We believed in what our government said it was trying to accomplish in Vietnam, and we wanted our country to win this war. . . .[128]

Another criticism made by military officers is that television made the conflict a "living room war" whose nightly combat scenes resulted in the loss of public support for U.S. military operations in Southeast Asia. Marine Corps Maj. Cass D. Howell expressed the feelings of many officers when he wrote in a 1987 article in *Military Review*:

> The power and impact of television was *the* deciding factor in turning American public opinion from one of supporting the U.S. defense of South Vietnam to one of opposing it. [Emphasis is Maj. Howell's.][129]

Dr. Hammond and military analysts have stated repeatedly that this is untrue. Dr. Hammond has written that research has shown that of about 2,300 reports from South Vietnam aired on evening television news programs, no more than 76 "showed anything approaching true violence — heavy fighting, incoming small arms and artillery fire, [soldiers who had been] killed and wounded within view."[130]

Dr. John E. Mueller, whose book *War, Presidents and Public Opinion* is considered the definitive analysis of polling data regarding the Vietnam War, wrote that the data do not support the conclusion that "largely uncensored day-by-day television coverage of the war and its brutalities made a profound impression on public attitudes." He stated:

> [The data] clearly show that whatever impact television had, it was not enough to reduce support for the war below the levels attained by the Korean War, when television was in its infancy, until casualty levels had far surpassed those of the earlier war.[131]

Dr. Mueller also found that media coverage of anti-Vietnam War protests actually may have *increased* support for the war because some segments of the public had such a low opinion of protesters. Without such coverage, he said, the war might have been even less popular.[132]

Another persistent myth about press coverage is that reporters frequently violated operational security and endangered the lives of the troops. Pentagon officials and military historians and officers repeatedly have refuted this. Barry Zorthian told the Senate Governmental Affairs Committee during the 1991 hearings that security violations by the media were "not a major issue" during the Vietnam conflict.[133] Maj. Gen. Sidle told the committee that the military "had to suspend accreditation to nine reporters [for security violations] . . . out of several thousand" who covered the war.[134] Some of the more serious violations were committed by correspondents for foreign media, and some were inadvertent. Maj. Gen. Sidle said two of the most glaring violations involved an aerial photograph of the U.S. base at Khe Sanh taken by a reporter for a Japanese newspaper, and a story about an upcoming U.S. offensive inadvertently printed by a U.S. newspaper while a news embargo was in effect.[135] Dr. Hammond pointed out in his book that another violation that angered MACV officials, a UPI story stating that the Khe Sanh base would be used for future offensive sweeps, resulted from an on-the-record interview with the Marine Corps commander in South Vietnam, "an indiscretion on the part of the general rather than the reporter."[136]

Maj. Gen. Sidle admitted, however, that despite all the evidence that the overwhelming majority of coverage in Southeast Asia was accurate, fair and did not compromise military security, the Armed Forces "still have generals and admirals who hate the press, and that's a problem."[137]

Zorthian stated that the myths about media coverage have had a profound impact on the development of more restrictive Pentagon information policies in the years since the Vietnam War. He told a National Press Club forum in March 1991 that "it doesn't really matter" what the truth is about the coverage of Vietnam. "The important thing is the perception," he said.[138]

Zorthian testified during the 1991 Senate hearings that the Gulf War restrictions suggested

> that the military has decided that one of the "mistakes" of Vietnam it is determined not to repeat is the unrestricted movement and coverage by the media in that period which it believes led to a distorted picture of the Vietnam War for the American public. Accordingly, the military has established the current restrictions on the movement and coverage by correspondents to . . . project instead a picture of the war which will be controlled and based largely on official sources.[139]

Consequences of the Military's Myths About News Coverage

One of the most troubling aspects of the military's continuing misperceptions about press coverage of Vietnam is that they have overshadowed a crucial reality about the politically based White House and Pentagon information policies used during Vietnam: those policies contributed to the deaths of U.S. troops. Col. Hackworth pointed out in *About Face* that field commanders were under so much pressure to produce body counts that they sometimes stopped fighting in order to send soldiers out to count casualties. Some of these men were killed while counting the dead.[140]

In his book on the military-media relationship during the conflict, Dr. Hammond pointed out that U.S. government pressure on the media to support America's military role in South Vietnam was one reason journalists did not follow up on reports about problems with the M-16 rifle, a weapon that Col. Hackworth characterized as "the worst infantry weapon ever forced upon America's fighting men,"[141] and whose malfunctions killed and injured U.S. troops.[142]

Allegations that U.S. military officials lowered the enemy order of battle because they feared stories about the true figures would hurt congressional and public support for the war raised additional concerns about how information policies might have affected U.S. troops.

The Military and the Media Forget a Crucial Lesson

In focusing on the misperception that news coverage turned the American people against the war, U.S. military leaders have forgotten that political censorship has a corrosive effect on democracy, and on the military itself. Information-control policies designed to protect not military security but presidential approval ratings undermined the military's promise to defend the Constitution, including the right of the American people to receive unbiased, independent accounts of military conflicts, so they can pass judgment on the civilian and military leaders who took them to war. These policies also damaged the credibility of the military with Congress, which believed it had been misled about such events as the Gulf of Tonkin incidents, and with the American people.

Despite evidence to the contrary published in the years since Vietnam, many military officers have remained convinced that the U.S. news media turned the public against the war. A typical opinion was expressed by Maj. Howell in his 1987 *Military Review* article:

> In retrospect, it is easy to see that the unlimited and often biased reporting of the Vietnam War severely limited the military's prosecution of it by undermining public support for the cause. It is not a possibility but a probability that this will occur again should the United States go to the defense of another ally.[143]

Thus the lesson of Vietnam, for officials such as Maj. Howell, was not that politically based information control in a democracy at war is a failed idea, but that the principle must be applied with greater diligence in future wars.

In the wake of the Vietnam War, the conflict that provided White House and Pentagon officials with a new model for information control and media management was Britain's war with Argentina over the Falkland Islands in 1982. □

THE FALKLANDS/MALVINAS WAR

Information will not be classified or otherwise withheld to protect the government from criticism or embarrassment.

Principles of Information
Defense Secretary Richard Cheney

American media coverage of the Vietnam War had a major influence on how British officials dealt with the press during the Falklands conflict.[1] Jim Meacham — a U.S. officer in Vietnam who became a military affairs correspondent for the British news magazine *The Economist* and wrote about the war from London — said officials in the Thatcher government repeatedly told him, "This is why you Americans lost the Vietnam War, because you had a free press."[2]

Executives of the London-based Independent Television News (ITN) — which later supplied excellent footage of the Persian Gulf War to U.S. news operations, including CNN — said it seemed that "the Vietnam analogy was a spectre constantly stalking the Falklands decision-makers and was invoked privately by the military as an object lesson in how not to deal with the media."[3]

Maj.Gen. Sir Jeremy Moore, one of the British commanders during the Falklands conflict, said that the "gory pictures" shown on television in the 1960s and '70s "brought forcefully home to me the problem that the Americans had during the Vietnam conflict."[4] Brig. F. G. Caldwell, Director of Defence Operations, Plans, and Supplies at the British Ministry of Defence (MoD), said at a Royal United Services Institute seminar that Vietnam offered valuable lessons about controlling the media. For example, Caldwell said, if the British went to war, "We would have to start saying to ourselves, 'Are we going to let television cameras loose on the battlefield?'"[5]

The answer was, only if the visual images could be strictly controlled by the military. This became a major part of the government's news-management program, and access to video footage of the Falklands conflict was highly restricted and heavily censored. After the conflict was over, military officials told the House of Commons Defence Committee, which was investigating media coverage, that they were pleased that so little visual coverage of the war was shown. "Thank heavens we did not have unpleasant scenes shown," said Brig. Tony Wilson, commanding officer of 5 Brigade.[6]

The Falklands/Malvinas war began in April 1982. After years of arguing about who had a better claim to the South Atlantic Islands, Argentina took over the city of Port Stanley after a three-hour battle with the British Royal Marines.

The incident set off a wave of outrage in Great Britain, and Prime Minister Margaret Thatcher quickly announced that the Royal Navy would sail for the South Atlantic.

Military and MoD personnel had very definite ideas about what information the public should have. Their philosophy was based on the idea that "information is a weapon of war,"[7] and that what people saw, heard and read should be shaped in such as a way as to support the British position.[8] This meant that bad news, such as casualty figures, would be delayed or minimized, and that graphic combat photographs would not be permitted.

These news-management techniques had the support of civilian officials in the Thatcher government and in Parliament. In their December 1982 report on Falklands media coverage, members of the House of Commons Defence Committee wrote that by using a broad definition of operational security, military and civilian leaders could justify manipulating the news during wartime to ensure favorable public opinion:

> There is another view of operational security according to which, in addition to the negative function of preventing the disclosure of information prejudicial to military operations, there is a more positive function: the furtherance of the war effort through public relations, if practicable.[9]

From the beginning, several factors enabled the British government to exercise what the House of Commons Defence Committee called "absolute control" over broadcast and print coverage of the conflict.[10]

The first was geographic; the Falklands were about 8,000 miles from Great Britain and 300 miles from Argentina, and were far from well-traveled air and sea lanes. The only way journalists could get to the Falklands was to travel with the troops. Once there, they were dependent on the military to get them from the ships to the battlefield and back.

This situation enabled the Thatcher government to control the number of correspondents who would cover the war, as well as where they went and what they saw. Royal Navy officials, who initially wanted *no* journalists on board, finally consented to take 29 members of the British press. No representatives of foreign media were allowed.[11] The Royal Air Force took no journalists, and allowed neither reporters nor photographers to travel to the base they used on Ascension Island, which is in the South Atlantic near the equator, and about halfway between London and the Falklands.

Although British officials insisted that they had little influence over which reporters and photographers were selected by the news media to cover the conflict, many of the journalists chosen wholeheartedly supported Great Britain's decision to go to war. Max Hastings of the London *Standard*, whose father was a noted World War II correspondent, wrote, "Most of us decided before landing [in the Falklands] that our role was simply to report as sympathetically as possible what the British forces are doing here today."[12]

A second factor that enabled the British government to control press coverage was that all journalistic dispatches had to be sent through military channels, because technical problems with broadcasting from the South Atlantic precluded journalists from using their own satellite facilities. Reporters and photographers were totally dependent upon the goodwill of naval officers to send their material back to London.[13]

To ensure that no sensitive information was transmitted back to Great Britain, the activities of journalists on each ship were monitored by a military officer who also censored their copy. After stories reached London, they went through a second set of censors before being released.[14]

Information provided by the correspondents on the Navy ships was supplemented by Ministry of Defence briefings in London.

These factors enabled the British to set up an extremely effective news-management system that depended primarily on pre-censorship, but included post-censorship security reviews to filter information that the Ministry of Defence did not want the public to learn.

This system also enabled the military to control visual images of the war. For example, when Britain's HMS *Sheffield* was hit by an Exocet missile on May 4, 1982, British officials refused to fly a news photographer to the site for three days — until one of the Navy commanders needed pictures for his own assessment.[15] When a casualty from the *Sheffield* was buried at sea from the quarter-deck of another ship on which correspondents were stationed, television reporters were not allowed near the scene. The public affairs escort said, "It wouldn't be decent to film it."[16] Later, when ITN correspondent Michael Nicholson challenged the escorts' handling of the *Sheffield* affair, public affairs officer Graham Hammond said, "You must have been told you couldn't report bad news before you left [London]. You knew when you came you were expected to do a 1940 propaganda job."[17]

Another tactic the British government used to control the image of the war was to give the military responsibility for shipping news video back to London. It took more than two weeks for the pictures of the *Sheffield* incident to reach Great Britain.[18] Other trips took as long as 23 days by sea,[19] delays which British television executives charged were deliberate.

When video arrived in London, MoD Army and Navy officers again gave footage a security review. In his book about the Falklands conflict, Robert Harris wrote that BBC executives thought much of the material the MoD wanted to cut was for political, not military, reasons. BBC officials told Harris:

> . . . the [MoD] officers "appeared not to be fully briefed and differed in their attitudes to their task." Enraged editors found censorship going far beyond security and straying into questions of "taste" and "tone." The BBC was told not to use a picture of a body in a bag, not to use the phrase "horribly burned," not to show a pilot confessing, jokingly, that he had been "scared fartless" on one mission. "Clearance," rather than emotive words like "censorship" or "vetting," was the Ministry's euphemism for this extraordinary process.[20]

The images that appeared on British TV and in British newspapers — weeks after the events occurred — principally involved guns firing, planes taking off and landing, and officers conferring, much like the footage that would later come out of Grenada, Panama and the Persian Gulf.

Audio reports also underwent censorship that sometimes seemed dominated by political considerations. One reporter described an Argentine air attack on British ships at Bluff Cove, during which more than 50 British troops were killed, as a "day of extraordinary heroism." The story was quickly cleared. Another talked of the attack as a "setback," and included the sentence, "Other survivors came off unhurt but badly shaken after hearing the cries of men trapped below." That story was held up until the sentence was cut, by which time the BBC and ITN had used a more "up-beat" version.[21]

Some reporters, such as ITN's Michael Nicholson, were so disgusted with the security review process that they decided to put the word "censored" at the top of their dispatches, only to have their escorts tell them such a practice would not be allowed. When Peter Archer of the British Press Association telexed a memorandum to his boss saying that his reports were being censored, the word "censored" in the telex was censored.[22]

In addition to censorship, government officials and conservative newspapers attacked media that adopted a neutral tone or tried to present information from Argentine officials.[23] After BBC commentator Peter Snow compared British and Argentine versions of different events in the war (and stated that the British version appeared more accurate), a conservative member of Parliament, John Page, said Snow's comments were "totally offensive and almost treasonable."[24] Several days later Prime Minister Thatcher echoed Page's complaint, stating that "many people feel that the case for our country is not being put with sufficient vigor on certain — I do not say all — BBC programs."[25] Rupert Murdoch's London newspaper, the *Sun*, accused Snow of being one of the "traitors in our midst."[26]

Other conservative spokesmen joined the attack. One accused reporters of "reporting live propaganda out of Buenos Aires," and added, "I believe it to be a travesty of the role of the journalist to swallow handouts and report what is provided at face value. . . . I believe one must exercise one's judgment and not allow oneself to become a vehicle for propaganda and misleading information."[27]

Yet the media were expected to report what the Thatcher government provided at face value, including misinformation and disinformation released by the British military. When asked whether deceiving the press or deceiving the public through the press was reasonable on grounds of operational security or morale, Sir Terence Lewin, Chief of the Defence Staff, answered:

> I do not see it as deceiving the press or the public; I see it as deceiving the enemy. What I am trying to do is to win. Anything I can do to help me win is fair as far as I'm concerned, and I would have thought that that was what the Government and the public and the media would want, too, provided the outcome was the one we were all after.[28]

After the war Sir Terence said correspondents had been "most helpful with our deception plans."[29]

British media who protested this philosophy got little support from the House of Commons Defence Committee Report on press restrictions during the Falklands War. The report concluded that "misinformation is not a practice which should be deplored in time of conflict unless its use can be shown to be counterproductive in terms of ultimate operational success."[30] The report also stated:

Many principles, supposedly regarded as sacred and absolute within the media, are applied in a less rigid and categorical way by the public as a whole when it is judging its Government's conduct of a war. In our judgment the public is, in general, quite ready to tolerate being misled to some extent if the enemy is also misled, thereby contributing to the success of the campaign.[31]

Examples of misinformation and disinformation abounded during the Falklands campaign. On April 21, 1982, members of the Special Air Service (SAS) were landed on a glacier on South Georgia Island to begin a campaign to recapture the island from the Argentines. By the next morning they were trapped in a blizzard with 100 mph winds. Two of three helicopters that went to rescue the troops crashed; the pilot of the third managed to rescue all 13 SAS troops and the four helicopter crew members.[32]

MoD officials, who assumed there had been no survivors and worried that news about casualties would have a negative effect on public opinion and the House of Commons, denied that the incident had occurred. On April 24, 1982, MoD spokesman Ian McDonald — who had promised the London press corps never to tell "an untruth" — responded to reporters' queries by stating, "The task force has not landed anywhere."[33]

When South Georgia was recaptured the next day, the operation was presented as a flawless campaign resulting in an effortless victory. In her statement to the House of Commons, the Prime Minister made no mention of the SAS difficulties during their initial aborted landing.[34] The news that two helicopters had crashed during the incident did not emerge until three weeks later, when a letter that a serviceman wrote home made its way to the British press.[35]

McDonald later justified his initial response by saying that the SAS patrol wasn't the "task force."[36]

Another controversial incident involved the British sinking of the Argentine ship *General Belgrano* on May 2, 1982, which killed more than 350 Argentine troops. At the time, the Thatcher government said that the ship had been sailing toward the British fleet in a threatening manner. After the war was over, Clive Ponting, a Ministry of Defence official, sent a member of Parliament documents which showed that the government had lied. In fact, the *General Belgrano* had been sailing away from the British fleet for half a day when it was attacked.[37]

After the British media printed this information, Ponting was arrested and tried in 1985 under Britain's Official Secrets Act of 1911, which forbade government officials from making public any documents or information that the British government wanted to keep confidential.[38] A jury refused to convict him.

Back in the United States, military officers closely analyzed the way in which their British counterparts handled the press during the Falklands War, and U.S. military journals carried numerous articles about what the Pentagon could learn from news-management techniques used by the Thatcher government. One article, written for the *Naval War College Review* by Navy Lt. Cmdr. Arthur A. Humphries in 1983, reads like a primer for future Pentagon actions, although the author has said the article was simply an analysis of the British public affairs plan, not a specific set of suggestions for the Defense Department.[39] The article outlined several lessons from the Falklands which could help sway public opinion during a potentially unpopular war:

- To maintain popular support for a war, your side must not be seen as ruthless barbarians;

- If you don't want to erode the public's confidence in the government's war aims, then you cannot allow that public's sons to be wounded or maimed right in front of them via their TV sets at home;

- You must, therefore, control correspondents' access to the fighting;

- You must invoke censorship in order to halt aid to both the known and the suspected enemies;

- You must rally aid in the form of patriotism at home and in the battle zone but not to the extent of repeated triumphalism;

- You must tell your side of the story first, at least for psychological advantage, causing the enemy to play catch-up politically, with resultant strategic effect;

- To generate aid, and confuse at least the domestic detractors, report the truth about the enemy and let the enemy defectors tell their horror story;

- Finally, in order to affect or help assure "favorable objectivity," you must be able to exclude certain correspondents from the battle zone.[40]

The first opportunity for the Pentagon to implement these principles came in October 1983, less than a year after the article appeared, when the Reagan administration decided to invade Grenada. Two U.S. officers reportedly told a CBS News correspondent during the Grenada affair, "We learned a lesson from the British in the Falklands."[41] □

THE INVASION OF GRENADA

The provisions of the Freedom of Information Act will be supported in both letter and spirit.

Principles of Information
Defense Secretary Richard Cheney

U.S. officials had been closely monitoring events on Grenada, a member of the British Commonwealth, since 1979, when leftist leaders of the New Jewel Movement ousted Prime Minister Eric Gairy. The Prime Minister — known for his repression of political opponents and his belief in witchcraft and astral projection — was informed that he had been overthrown during a trip to New York City to address the United Nations on the subject of UFOs.[1]

The man who took charge after the overthrow was London-trained lawyer Maurice Bishop, who became Prime Minister. Bishop's party, the New Jewel Movement, was nationalist, and his economic philosophy was based on democratic socialism. His principal goals included educating the populace and improving the economy of Grenada, where per capita income was less than $500 per year.[2] Bishop accepted aid from Cuba and the Soviet Union and began constructing an airport at Point Salines that he said would be capable of accepting jetliner traffic, thereby increasing the tourist trade.

Bishop also made overtures to Washington. Grenada's main link with the United States was through hundreds of U.S. students who attended a U.S.-run medical school on the island. The school had been started by U.S. entrepreneur Charles Modica, and its top administrators were Americans. The school employed a number of Grenadians, and was important to the country's economy. After deposing Gairy, Bishop visited school officials to assure them that the new government hoped to maintain good relations.

Bishop's efforts to deal with the U.S. government were less successful. Reagan administration officials disliked his contacts with the Soviet Union and Cuba, and thought Grenada might become a fortified military outpost for those countries, and a staging area for subversion in the Caribbean and Latin America. The new Grenadian airport increased the administration's suspicions. Although the facility was being built partly with assistance from Western Europe, it was being constructed with the help of Cuban workers, and Reagan officials were convinced that it would be used primarily for military purposes.[3]

The Crisis Escalates

As hostile signals from the United States increased, Bishop visited Washington in the spring of 1983, hoping to convince the White House that his government was not a regional security threat. President Reagan, Vice President Bush and Secretary of State George Shultz refused to meet with Bishop. With the help of several Senators, including Republican Lowell Weicker of Connecticut, Bishop did succeed in speaking with lower-level U.S. officials. The Senators supported Bishop's efforts to forge closer ties to the United States, but no one was able to change the administration's antagonistic stance.[4]

In mid-October 1983, Bishop was put under house arrest by a more leftist faction of the New Jewel Movement led by Deputy Prime Minister Bernard Coard and Army Gen. Hudson Austin.

A few days later, on Oct. 19, 1983, Bishop supporters freed the deposed prime minister from jail. As he walked through the capital of St. George's, he was met by a welcoming crowd. The military fired on them, killing more than a dozen people. Bishop ordered his supporters to surrender, and most of the crowd was allowed to return home, but Bishop and several high-ranking supporters were executed. The government, under military control, declared a shoot-to-kill curfew, closed the airport, forbid foreign journalists to enter the country and arrested Alister Hughes, a correspondent for a Caribbean news agency who also worked for Time and had criticized the new government.

Despite the crackdown, officials were quick to reassure medical school personnel that students were not in danger, and that they wanted the school to remain open.[5] The new government also told the United States and Caribbean nations that the violence was over, the government would be turned over to civilians in a matter of weeks, and U.S. citizens and other foreigners were safe. The United States dismissed these assurances as "not worth two cents, because we didn't trust them," according to White House spokesman Larry Speakes.[6]

Events on Grenada also alarmed Cuba, which denounced the killing of Bishop and expressed concerns that the United States would use the situation as an excuse to move into Grenada.[7] In fact, the Reagan administration had discussed military intervention at an Oct. 20, 1983 meeting of U.S. national security advisers chaired by Vice President George Bush. One rationale for intervention was the possible need to evacuate U.S. medical students and other personnel.[8] After the meeting, the Reagan administration diverted U.S. ships carrying troops to Lebanon toward Grenada in case they were needed for what one State Department official later called a "nonpermissive evacuation" of the island.[9]

Reagan administration officials also wanted an additional rationale for intervention that might have a better legal foundation. They were happy to respond on Oct. 21, when several leaders of the Organization of Eastern Caribbean States (OECS), after some prompting by U.S. officials in the region, joined the leaders of Barbados and Dominica and issued a formal call for U.S. assistance to counter what they said they perceived as Grenada's increasing instability and militarism.[10]

Talk of an impending invasion began circulating in the Caribbean, with regional leaders who opposed U.S. intervention leaking information about possible scenarios. Grenada's military leaders continued diplomatic efforts with the United States and Caribbean nations to resolve the situation.[11]

Gen. Austin met with medical school Vice Chancellor Geoffrey Bourne to assure him of the students' safety and ask for assistance in helping Grenada return to parliamentary democracy. U.S.-based personnel affiliated with the medical school — including Peter Bourne, who had been a White House official during the Carter administration — later said they tried to contact the State Department to inform them that the students were not in danger, but found that Reagan administration officials "just weren't interested."[12]

The Washington Post reported that U.S. Ambassador to Barbados Milan Bish contacted medical school officials and asked them to make a televised plea for U.S. intervention "to protect the medical students."[13] Peter Bourne said officials turned down the request. Bish later denied making it, saying he had only discussed the students' safety with school personnel.[14]

In the meantime, medical students assured their families that they felt safe, and parents of some medical students met in New York City and sent a telegram to President Reagan urging him not to take "precipitous action" in Grenada.[15]

The White House and Pentagon Outflank the Press

From Oct. 20 until the invasion five days later, stories from Washington reflected the administration's wish to minimize discussion of military intervention. *New York Times* reporter B. Drummond Ayres Jr. filed a story from Washington on Oct. 21 stating that a Defense Department official had said the United States viewed the situation on Grenada as nonthreatening, and had sent ships toward the island as a precautionary measure.[16]

A *Washington Post* story filed on Oct. 22 cited two presidential aides saying that the U.S. ships had been sent to the area only to protect Americans if necessary, and that no invasion was planned.[17] The story quoted another unnamed administration official as saying the Pentagon had been "dusting off contingency plans" for an invasion, but added that a Pentagon official had denied this.[18]

Stories from the Caribbean, however, were filled with speculation about possible U.S. intervention. Because of Grenada's ban on foreign journalists, many U.S. reporters were working out of Bridgetown, the capital of Barbados, which is about 150 miles northeast of Grenada. A United Press International story from Bridgetown on Oct. 22 said Grenada's leaders were warning of an imminent invasion.[19]

An Oct. 23 *New York Times* story from Bridgetown reported U.S. officials' claims that the ships' deployment toward Grenada was a precautionary measure.[20] It quoted Gen. Austin as saying the island's airport would reopen on Oct. 24, and reported that the government radio station on Grenada was calling the U.S. claim that American citizens might be in danger "an excuse for a U.S. invasion."[21]

At the time these articles were published, White House and Defense Department officials had in fact been actively considering an invasion for several days.[22] Their planning on Sunday, Oct. 23, was interrupted by horrifying news from Lebanon: a truck bomb had destroyed a Beirut building occupied by a U.S. Marine peacekeeping force, killing more than 200 U.S. troops. That evening, Reagan made what Secretary of State George Shultz described as "a tentative decision" to invade Grenada based on the analysis by OECS leaders and presidential advisers that a "very uncertain and violent situation" existed that was "threatening to our citizens."[23] The invasion would be known as Operation Urgent Fury.

During the planning, Pentagon and White House officials agreed that the media would be excluded from the invasion, and that the White House press office would not be told about the operation in advance.[24]

The decision to ban the press reflected the abiding dislike that many military commanders had for the media in the wake of Vietnam, and their belief that if media access had been more tightly controlled, the coverage would have been more positive. The Chairman of the Joint Chiefs of Staff, Gen. John Vessey Jr., was known to have admired the way the British controlled media coverage during the Falklands War.[25] One White House official said Gen. Vessey believed that "If you get the newspeople into this, you lose support of public opinion."[26] Vice Adm. Joseph Metcalf III, who would lead the Joint Task Force during Urgent Fury, and Deputy Joint Task Force Commander Maj. Gen. H. Norman Schwarzkopf were known to harbor resentments about media coverage during the Vietnam War.

Former Marine and *Washington Post* staffer Peter Braestrup, now Senior Editor at the Library of Congress, said the actions were unparalleled in recent times. In *Battle Lines*, he wrote:

> . . . the government's failure, at the outset, to allow an independent flow of information to the public about a major military operation was unprecedented in modern American history. . . . In World War II, Korea, Vietnam, and lesser military engagements, civilian authorities saw to it that, in keeping with our tradition as an open society, reasonable provision was made for journalists in war zones. There was tacit agreement between the military and the media that the president, in his role as commander-in-chief, and his civilian subordinates assumed responsibility for media policy as for the war effort as a whole. Civilian authority did not defer, as it did in Grenada, to the commander in the field.[27]

The United States Prepares for War

At 2 a.m. Monday, Oct. 24, a note from Gen. Austin arrived at the U.S. Embassy in Barbados. It reiterated his guarantee of the safety of U.S. citizens, and promised to return the country to a civilian government within two weeks. The note made little impression on U.S. officials, and at 6 p.m. that evening, President Reagan signed the order to invade.[28]

Several Washington reporters were told by longtime sources that an invasion was imminent. CBS White House correspondent Bill Plante asked White House spokesman Larry Speakes whether the information was correct. Speakes talked with White House Deputy Press Secretary Robert Sims, who specialized in foreign affairs. Sims told Speakes that Deputy National Security Adviser Rear Adm. John Poindexter had said the idea was "preposterous."[29]

Speakes passed the word to Plante, who in turn told reporters in New York and Washington, who stopped pursuing the story.[30]

"There wasn't much debate about it," Plante is quoted as saying in Mark Hertsgaard's book, *On Bended Knee — The Press and the Reagan Presidency.* "There are unwritten rules concerning the qualifiers and statements made by White House spokesmen. And with that much of a knockdown, there wasn't much choice. Given the normal rules of the game, you have to assume they're not lying," Plante said.[31]

The Battle Between the Military and Media Begins

The operation began about 5 a.m. on Oct. 25, and initially involved 1,900 U.S. Army and Marine Corps troops, accompanied by forces from several Caribbean nations and supported by the U.S. Navy and Air Force.[32] The battle plan was to have the Army take control of the airport under construction at Point Salines, and then proceed to the medical school to evacuate the American students. The Marines would assault the island's other airport, while U.S. and Caribbean forces would attack various military sites.[33]

In a short statement that day, President Reagan said the invasion had been undertaken to protect "innocent lives" and "to help in the restoration of democratic institutions in Grenada."[34]

"We are determined not to make an already bad situation worse and increase the risks our citizens faced," Reagan said.[35]

But that is exactly what the United States had done, according to Charles Modica, the chancellor of the medical school. Speaking at a news conference from the school's Bay Shore, Long Island, office, Modica said the president had "acted on the wrong advice" in ordering the invasion. "I think the students are in more danger," as a result, he said.[36]

An editor at United Press International — which had been in touch with medical students and their families in the United States by phone for days — agreed with Modica, saying students had told the news service they had not been harassed by Grenadian troops.[37]

The next day, after an extensive briefing by the administration, Modica changed his mind. He told reporters, "There were many factors unknown to me," including the fact that "the people I was dealing with were not the only leaders in Grenada," and that students might not have been allowed to leave the island.[38]

Independent verification of the students' situation was impossible, because the U.S. military had barred the media from covering the invasion. No reporters would be allowed on the island for two days.

The Washington press corps, already angry that they had been misled concerning the start of the invasion, became even more furious after hearing about the press ban. White House briefings became bitter and contentious, especially after Speakes refused to provide details about last-minute efforts by the Grenadian government to talk with U.S. officials about how Americans on the island would be safeguarded.[39] When asked whether the Reagan administration's policy was to tell the truth on a selective basis, Speakes replied, "The policy of the White House is to tell the truth."[40]

Speakes and other White House spokesmen also said they had not been lying when they had told reporters an invasion had not been planned. Senior administration officials such as Chief of Staff James A. Baker III had decided not to tell them about the invasion until 6 a.m. on Oct. 25, an hour after Operation Urgent Fury had started.[41]

Behind the scenes, however, Speakes sent an angry memo to Baker, White House Deputy Chief of Staff Michael Deaver and White House counselor Edwin Meese III, complaining about being misled and stating that "the credibility of the Reagan administration is at stake."[42] Les Janka, Deputy Press Secretary for Foreign Affairs, resigned after writing a letter saying his credibility had been "perhaps irreparably" destroyed.[43]

The White House Explains Its Philosophy of Information

At an Oct. 26, 1983 press conference with Joint Chiefs of Staff Chairman Gen. Vessey, Defense Secretary Weinberger affirmed that military leaders had decided not to allow the media to witness the invasion, and that President Reagan and other White House advisers had agreed. Weinberger said he "wouldn't ever dream of overriding" a commander's decision,[44] and that journalists would be allowed on the island "as soon as the commanders notify us that it is appropriate."[45]

Weinberger's comments stunned the media and members of Congress, who thought this policy had grave implications for the Constitutional principle of a civilian-controlled military. *The New York Times* said in an editorial:

> What a perversion of the idea of civilian control of the military. If some general does not understand the big principle at stake here, then civilian commanders — like the Secretary of Defense — surely should. The principle is not hard to grasp. It's not a case of accommodating a few hundred reporters or their employers. It's a case of responsibility to 235 million Americans who depend on those reporters. The public needs to know what its Government is doing, the more so when it commits troops to an expedition whose wisdom is debated so heatedly.[46]

When the White House press corps insisted that Speakes take their demand that journalists be allowed on Grenada directly to the President, Reagan backed up Weinberger, saying reporters would be allowed on the island when the Defense Department decided it was safe enough.[47]

The safety of journalists was one of the first rationales offered for excluding the media from the island. At the Oct. 26 press conference with Gen. Vessey, Weinberger said the press ban was instituted because military officers were not able to guarantee "any kind of safety" to anyone.[48]

This met with derision from members of the media and Congress. Sen. Nancy Kassebaum (R-Kan.) pointed out that reporters had worked "under far worse" conditions in Lebanon — where hundreds of Marines had just been killed in a bombing attack.[49] CBS newsman Walter Cronkite responded to the allegations about protecting media personnel by saying, "For heaven's sake, journalists have been going into unsafe places from time immemorial to get the story."[50] Cronkite said the administration's news blackout set a "terribly dangerous precedent, an impossible precedent."[51]

Gen. Vessey said at the press conference that military secrecy was another reason for excluding the media. "We were going in there very quickly and we needed to have surprise in order to have it be successful," he told reporters.[52]

Journalists also found fault with this because the U.S. and Caribbean press had been running stories about a possible invasion of Grenada for days, and the Grenadian government radio had provided daily reports of events leading up to the operation.[53]

In addition, reporters had an excellent record of maintaining operational security in previous wars. Jerry W. Friedheim — Executive Vice President of the American Newspaper Publishers Association, who had been an Assistant Secretary of Defense for Public Affairs during part of the Vietnam War — was especially angry. He reminded administration officials that journalists and military officers had long "been able to find ways to provide both troop security and the flow of information that an open society demands," and implied that the White House and Pentagon decision to exclude the media was an insult to military officers in Vietnam who had fought for journalists' access because they regarded it as their duty to "help a free press serve a free society."[54]

Washington Post Managing Editor Howard Simons agreed that reporters would have maintained operational security. "If somebody had come to me and said, 'You can't report this until the operation is secure,' I would have said, 'Fine.'"[55]

Another rationale presented by the administration was that invasion planning had been so rushed there had not been time to formulate a public affairs plan. Several military officers interviewed on background for this study said this was untrue.[56]

Perhaps a more honest assessment of the Pentagon's decision was given by Vice Adm. Metcalf, the Joint Task Force Commander for the Grenada operation. He told reporters on Barbados, "I'm down here to take an island. I don't need you running around and getting in the way."[57]

The Military Wins Initial Skirmishes With the Press

Metcalf seemed willing to go to great lengths to accomplish that. After the press restrictions had been eased, Metcalf asked journalists at an Oct. 29 press conference, "Any of you guys coming in on press boats? Well, I know how to stop those press boats. We've been shooting at them."[58]

Journalists assumed Metcalf was joking, even though reporters who had tried to reach the island during the press ban had been threatened by the U.S. military. ABC correspondent Josh Mankiewicz, who had hired a fishing boat, turned back after a U.S. destroyer cut across the boat's bow. "I got a good look at that gun on the foredeck and decided that we were simply outclassed," Mankiewicz said. "I know *force majeure* when I see it."[59]

Two ABC staffers who had hired another boat, correspondent Steve Shepard and producer Tim Ross, were forced back by a Navy plane. "This Navy jet came over and made a couple of runs at us," Ross said. "First it just waggled its wings. Then it made a lateral pass. Finally it opened the bomb doors, and the pilot dropped a buoy about 30 feet ahead of us just to show what else he could drop and how close he could drop it."[60]

A CBS correspondent chartered a plane in Barbados and taped some distant aerial shots of the island and naval activity before a U.S. jet fighter chased off his plane.[61]

Four journalists who did reach Grenada were held *in communicado* by Adm. Metcalf. These journalists — Edward Cody of *The Washington Post*, Don Bohning of the *Miami Herald*, Morris Thompson of *Newsday* and a British reporter — were part of a group of seven who had left Barbados the day before the invasion, anticipating U.S. military intervention. They hopscotched by plane and boat across several small islands, and finally set out for Grenada from Carriacou, about five hours away, in a wooden fishing boat named the *Odin C.*, for the Norse god of war.⁶² As they approached Grenada and heard the roar of explosives, the boat's captain wanted to stop, but the journalists urged him on after hearing radio reports on the Voice of America's Caribbean frequency that U.S. forces had control of the harbor in the Grenadian capital of St. George's.⁶³

When the journalists landed at the harbor shortly after noon on Oct. 25, about 7½ hours after the invasion had begun, they were astonished to find not the Marines, but Grenadian troops in charge. They were escorted to a nearby fire station, where they spent the day listening to radio reports that the war was over,⁶⁴ while at the same time hearing "chatter from a 50-caliber machine gun nested several buildings away and the dry crackle of AK-47 bursts."⁶⁵ It wasn't the only misleading radio transmission the journalists were to hear. *Time* correspondent Bernard Diederich later wrote:

> . . . nothing the radio reported matched what was happening on the ground. As we sat literally on Fort Rupert's doorstep, Radio Trinidad broadcast a war communique from U.S. sources describing how U.S. Marines were storming the fort, although only lizards were stirring on the ancient battlements before us. With the first bombardment in the morning, the garrison had fled, leaving one dead comrade behind.⁶⁶

In the afternoon the journalists asked to leave the station to file stories from the nearby telex office, but the Grenadians would not let them leave without a military escort. After dark a member of the People's Revolutionary Army showed up and agreed to escort them, but by that time, telex and telephone lines were dead.⁶⁷

The soldier then offered to take them to a hotel. The journalists chose the St. James, near Fort Rupert. By morning the city was silent. They passed some looted shops, then found a Marine unit set up in a park. A Marine platoon leader checked their identification, smiled and asked for help. "We just got here last night," he told *Washington Post* reporter Cody. "Can you please tell us what the fuck is going on?"⁶⁸

Later that day the journalists asked a Marine officer whether he could arrange a helicopter ride to a Navy ship so the reporters could try to file their copy. Two hours later, Cody, Bohning, Thompson and a British journalist flew off for the *Guam*. The other three journalists, including *Time* correspondent Diederich, decided to stay on Grenada. Diederich wanted to look for Alister Hughes, the *Time* stringer who had been arrested.⁶⁹

When the journalists arrived on the *Guam*, they were not allowed to file their stories or even communicate with their news organizations, which had not heard from them in more than 48 hours. The reporters were watched continually, even as they slept, and were "more or less captives of the U.S. Navy," Bohning said.⁷⁰

Metcalf dispatched an officer to tell the journalists that they couldn't file stories because shipboard communications were tied up with military messages, but agreed he would try to get a message to one newspaper so editors would know the reporters were safe.

The Washington Post later reported that White House Deputy Chief of Staff Deaver and a senior Pentagon official had told the newspaper that Cody and the other reporters had been evacuated to the *Guam* for their own safety after they had wandered into a firefight.[71]

Meanwhile, the journalists asked to ride on one of the frequent military flights to Barbados, so they could use the phone, or to Grenada. They were put on a helicopter bound for the Point Salines airport, then removed just before takeoff. Metcalf explained he didn't want to send civilians back into a high-risk area. Cody later wrote, "It was not clear whether he meant Grenada as a whole, where we had just spent two days, or Point Salines," which was under U.S. control.[72]

The next day, Metcalf said reporters could go to Barbados or could accompany the Marines back to Grenada, where "an operation" was planned against the last defenders at Fort Frederick. The reporters elected to go with the Marines. When they arrived on Grenada, *Time* correspondent Diederich told them the fort had been undefended since the previous afternoon.[73]

Days later, Metcalf told Bohning and Cody during a telephone conversation that he had deliberately kept them on the *Guam* to prevent them from filing firsthand accounts of the invasion.[74] Metcalf said he was "following orders" from Washington to hold the reporters, but provided no other details.[75]

During the time the three American journalists were held on the *Guam*, Diederich had continued his tour of the island. He found Fort Frederick deserted, and later saw a barefoot woman in a long brown dress as she walked in the other direction through the rubble of a St. George's street. When he asked whether she was all right, the woman turned, exposing the open front of her dress, and laughed. She had been a patient in a mental hospital that the U.S. military had bombed by mistake, killing more than a dozen patients. Others, like herself, had wandered off into the city.[76]

At sunset, Diederich set off for Richmond Hill prison to try to look for Hughes. The guards had fled, and the prisoners were in the process of breaking the locks off the doors. Diederich found his colleague unharmed. As they prepared to leave, the journalists warned other prisoners to remain where they were, fearing that U.S. forces might mistake their prison uniforms for Grenadian military garb and shoot. Diederich and Hughes promised to notify U.S. officials of the prisoners' situation. Later that evening they found a Marine commander and told him what had occurred.[77]

Twenty-four hours later, after Diederich had flown to Barbados to file his story, he was astounded to hear a radio report that Marines were storming Richmond Hill prison and encountering fierce resistance from Cuban defenders. Diederich had not seen a single Cuban anywhere near the prison the previous day.[78] He wrote in an article for *Worldview* in July 1984:

> Reality was the first casualty of the Grenada "war," and there was something strangely Orwellian about the whole affair — as if "1984" had arrived early.[79]

Diederich later found out that radio reports were being disseminated by U.S. Army psychological operations forces. The commander of Army psy-ops confirmed that Diederich and his colleagues had picked up one of the early reports from the psy-ops station the morning of the invasion, when they heard that U.S. forces controlled the harbor.[80] Diederich wrote that the reports had a major effect:

> Psy-ops had a field day. Its reports were picked up and disseminated throughout the world. There was no competition. . . .The ban [on journalists] was bad enough but, in presenting its case, the administration strained credulity with a strong case of misinformation.[81]

Without any media on the scene, however, the veracity of these reports went unchallenged.

The Media Fight Back, and Surrender

In an article in *Armed Forces Journal International*, Les Janka, who had resigned after being misled about the invasion, wrote that the administration's decisions to exclude press officers from pre-invasion planning and to deny or delay media access to Grenada were "serious breach[es] of constitutional responsibility," and that President Reagan had "abdicated a vital political responsibility" by not allowing the American people to receive objective information about the operation.[82]

Janka — who previously had served as Deputy Assistant Secretary of Defense for Near Eastern Affairs — stated that if administration public affairs officers had been involved in the pre-invasion planning, they could have designated a "small pool of press writers and photographers" to go with the invasion task force after agreeing to guidelines about reporting embargoes. He pointed out that PAOs had used this technique occasionally in Vietnam, with great success.[83] "With such an arrangement, the American people could have received objective reporting on the first day of the operation with no compromise of military security or mission effectiveness," Janka wrote.[84] Instead, the administration had tried to make the public reliant upon government-supplied news, an action that was "as unacceptable as it is un-American," Janka stated.[85]

White House officials disagreed. Baker defended his decision to go along with military leaders' suggestions that the media be excluded from the invasion, and said he would do the same thing again if the United States were involved in another "commando raid" like the one on Grenada.[86] He also said he had not told anyone in the White House to tell a lie. "I never, ever ordered anyone to lie to the press," Hertsgaard quoted Baker as saying in his book *On Bended Knee*. "I might have told [Poindexter] not to tell the press office about it. That's different."[87]

As the invasion wore on, media executives and editors stepped up their protests. The American Society of Newspaper Editors complained that the news blackout went "beyond the normal limits of military censorship."[88] The American Newspaper Publishers Association released a letter saying the administration's decision to ban the press was "unprecedented and intolerable."[89] *New York Times* Managing Editor Seymour Topping said, "We have strenuously protested to the White House and the Defense Department about the lack of access. . . . We also are disturbed by the paucity of details about the operation released by the Pentagon at a time when the

American people require all the facts to make judgments about the actions of our government."[90]

Television executives also protested. CBS President Edward Joyce sent a letter on Oct. 25 to Weinberger that stated:

> I wish to protest in the strongest possible terms the position of the Defense Department in restricting CBS News' access to the Island of Grenada.
>
> I would also like to protest the attitude expressed by your Public Affairs office as indicated in the statements of Colonel Robert O'Brien and Lt. Colonel Leon DeLorme today to our correspondent Bill Lynch that "we learned a lesson from the British in the Falklands." To use the censorship by the British as an example to be followed by the United States in this military operation is baffling to me and deeply disturbing because it refutes the principles of the First Amendment of the United States Constitution.[91]

Despite their protests, newspaper and network executives undercut their arguments by filling news holes and newscasts with words and images produced by the White House and the Defense Department. The front pages of establishment newspapers were filled with White House and military pronouncements about how well the invasion was going and how it occurred "just in time."[92] Dissenting points of view were relegated much less play, and less space. For example, British Prime Minister Margaret Thatcher's hostile reaction to the invasion was given only perfunctory coverage, despite the fact Grenada was a member of the British Commonwealth, and Thatcher herself had enthusiastically taken England to war over the Falklands only 18 months before.

Few media covered Connecticut Republican Sen. Lowell Weicker's angry denunciation of the invasion. Sen. Weicker found the praise for the administration's "swift and effective" action regarding Grenada repugnant. He told the Senate on Oct. 28, 1983:

> Now, if you want swift and effective action, that should have been taken in June of this year when Maurice Bishop was alive and in this country seeking the assistance of the United States to effect a rapprochement between his government and this Government. That would have been swift and effective action to protect not only the lives of American citizens in Grenada, but also the lives of American citizens which will be sacrificed in the future if we continue to substitute rhetoric for a meaningful dialog.[93]

Sen. Weicker said the Reagan administration's refusal to open serious discussions with Bishop about a rapprochement was a direct cause of the current crisis because it sent Bishop back to Grenada "empty-handed," and led the Grenadian military to believe he was ineffective.[94]

Few initial stories about the invasion presented the U.S. action in this type of historical perspective, partly because many reporters were not well-versed on the history of U.S.-Grenadian relations. Few stories citing administration statements about how well the operation was going carried disclaimers, despite the administration's misinformation about the start of the operation.[95]

The Media Present the Official Pictures

Newspapers and networks used not only information, but visuals supplied by the Pentagon. Most early video footage showed scenes such as weapons caches found on Grenada and Cuban prisoners, but very little fighting.[96] It projected the image that the invasion, as Adm. Metcalf said later, "was going to be a marvelous, sterile operation."[97]

Some of the Defense Department video was shown by the networks after President Reagan's nationally televised address on Oct. 28, 1983 about the "brilliant campaign" the Armed Forces had waged on Grenada.[98] Earlier that day, the Defense Department had flown a small pool of journalists to Grenada with a military escort, and the networks had hoped to use that material. But the journalists' plane was held up on Grenada by small arms fire, so only the DOD footage was available.[99]

One executive described the Pentagon videos as "lifeless and nondescript" with "no fighting at all."[100] *Washington Post* TV critic Tom Shales characterized it as mostly "American students smiling, blowing kisses and flashing the 'V' sign as they were escorted off the island under military protection. It looked like a bunch of kids coming home from camp."[101] Nevertheless, all the networks used the pictures. NBC anchor Tom Brokaw, who later said the video was "the most benign kind of footage," introduced it after warning viewers that the administration had "tightly controlled" news coverage of Grenada.[102] CBS anchor Dan Rather told the audience that the footage had been "shot by the Army and censored by the Army," and the words "Cleared by Defense Dept. censors" were superimposed over the video. Afterward, Rather twice repeated that the government had censored the footage.[103] Robert Frye of ABC said network news personnel were "very concerned about the control — to use a polite word — that the administration has decided to exert on the coverage."[104]

When news executives later saw the pool footage, which had been shot while news photographers were under military escort, they weren't much happier. The videos included shots of weapons caches and prisoners of war. ABC correspondent Richard Threlkeld said journalists had gotten only "a worm's eye view" of what was happening on Grenada,[105] while a network news producer pronounced the footage "garbage."[106]

News photographers got better footage at home. On Wednesday, Oct. 26, the day after the invasion began, the first medical school students evacuated from Grenada arrived in the United States and provided the most lasting images of the conflict as some of them knelt and kissed the ground after getting off the plane.[107]

"I've been a dove all my life," said Jeff Geller of Woodbridge, N.Y., one of the students who kissed the tarmac. "I just can't believe how well those [Army] Rangers came down and saved us."[108]

There was no question the students had been in danger. Mary Ellen Guido of Manhassett, Long Island, said the back wall of one dormitory room had been blown out by a shell.[109] Philip Underwood of Patchogue, Long Island, said a bullet had crashed through his dormitory room door.[110] Steven Piccard of Dearborn, Mich., said, "There was a bullet in a friend of mine's pillow, and one went through the room right next to me."[111] Some students said they had been afraid of being taken hostage by Grenadians.[112]

What had occurred to some students, however, was that much of that danger had resulted from the U.S. invasion itself. Their views got little notice initially. For example, a Page 1 story about the returning students in *The New York Times* on Oct. 27, 1983 made passing reference to these dissenting views, but provided no follow-up. A Page 1 story in *The Washington Post* did not mention such views at all, although a story the previous day on Page 11 had been entitled, "Americans in Grenada, calling home, say they were safe before invasion."[113] Early coverage of the students' return was overwhelmed by their genuine happiness in being out of the war zone.

This first-day coverage of the students' return was crucial to public opinion. As *New York Times* reporter Robert D. McFadden pointed out, the U.S. ban on reporters in Grenada meant that "the accounts by returning American students were the first nongovernment reports on the situation."[114] At the time the students were arriving on Oct. 26, journalists Cody, Bohning and Thompson were being held *in communicado* by Adm. Metcalf on the *Guam*.

By the next day, Oct. 28, the doubts that some returning students had about the wisdom of the invasion were getting more play,[115] but by that time, public opinion was well established. Pictures of the students kissing the ground had dominated network newscasts and the front pages of most major newspapers, and their impact was difficult to overestimate. *New York Times* reporter Francis X. Clines wrote:

> In the world of images where this city's politicians so often seek confirmation, that was the equivalent of the flag raising on Iwo Jima. "That was a climactic moment of the week," said David R. Gergen, the President's director of communications.[116]

Another *Times* reporter, Hedrick Smith, wrote that the interest that Congress had displayed in questioning the legality of the invasion or whether Americans really had been in danger had "faded after pictures were published of returning students kissing American soil. . . ."[117]

The President's Popularity Increases

The President's public opinion ratings soared in the ensuing weeks. During the previous summer and fall, public opinion about Reagan's handling of foreign affairs had been declining. A *Washington Post*-ABC News poll in August 1983 had shown that 42 percent of those surveyed disapproved of his performance in that area. In a poll in late September 1983, 50 percent disapproved.[118]

The September poll showed the President trailing two contenders for the Democratic presidential nomination. He was behind Walter F. Mondale, 46 to 48 percent, and Ohio Sen. John Glenn, 42 to 52 percent, according to a sampling of registered voters.[119]

A *Washington Post*-ABC News poll taken before the President's Oct. 27, 1983 speech showed that 52 percent of Americans favored the invasion, while 37 percent opposed it. After the speech, 65 percent approved and 27 percent opposed the operation.[120]

An *ABC Nightline* poll on Oct. 28 regarding whether the United States should have invaded Grenada drew more than 560,000 callers, who approved of the operation by an 8-to-1 margin.[121]

The president's ratings continued rising after the invasion ended. A *Washington Post*-ABC News poll in early November found 71 percent of respondents approved of the Grenada invasion, and 63 percent approved of his overall performance — his highest rating since 1981.[122] Reagan now led the Democratic presidential challengers. The survey showed him ahead of Mondale by 50 to 44 percent, and leading Glenn by 48 to 45 percent.[123] Two *New York Times* polls also showed his ratings increasing.[124]

Although the polls fluctuated during the next year, Grenada continued to be regarded as a great foreign policy success, and was mentioned by voters in the fall of 1984 as one reason they wanted to reelect Reagan as president.[125]

The White House and Pentagon Change Tactics

In the wake of the favorable polls following his Oct. 27, 1983 speech, the White House increased public relations efforts at home and eased media restrictions on Grenada. White House officials decided, in the words of *Washington Post* reporter David Hoffman, "that Reagan should respond in a way that would minimize the potential political problems for him of war and death."[126] This seemed especially important because although the polls showed increased support for the President and the Grenada operation, they also showed many Americans were concerned that the president might lead the country into war.[127]

One of the first things Reagan did during this public relations campaign was to start calling Operation Urgent Fury a "rescue mission," and to excoriate the media for calling it an "invasion," a term he himself had used the previous week.[128]

On Friday, Oct. 28, as President Reagan was preparing for his customary weekend departure for Camp David, White House aides lined up 200 staff members to say goodbye.[129] Many waved flags, and one speechwriter held aloft a poster with the words "Your Finest Hour" written on it. The phrase apparently was a reference to words used by British Prime Minister Winston Churchill during World War II in a June 1940 speech to the House of Commons.[130] *Washington Post* reporter Lou Cannon described the scene and the President's upbeat mood this way:

> At the end of a week in which the United States counted more military casualties than at any time since the worst fighting of the Vietnam war, Reagan demonstrated this optimism in a carefully staged ceremony that was reminiscent of a triumphant political campaign.[131]

. . . He went down the entire rope line, shaking hands with many people and repeatedly smiling and waving.[132]

White House aides decided that in keeping with this positive mood, the President would not travel to Dover Air Force Base in Delaware, where the bodies of the Marines killed in Lebanon and the U.S. military casualties from Grenada were arriving, and ceremonies were being held to honor the dead.[133]

The week after the invasion, hundreds of the medical students evacuated from Grenada and members of the Armed Forces who participated in the operation came to the White House for a welcome-home celebration on the South Lawn. Journalists, who usually must stand in cordoned-off areas during White House events, were welcome to mingle with the guests, who waved flags, listened to military music, and praised the President and the Armed Forces.[134] The President spoke warmly of the "heroic rescue," and told the students, "What you saw 10 days ago was patriotism."[135]

Some journalists thought the event was an obvious ploy for airtime and newspaper space, but many editors gave it excellent play, running it on evening newscasts and front pages. "I'm bitter about how we in the media continually let ourselves be manipulated by the White House," said one reporter interviewed for this study, who asked not to be identified. "Some of us gave that staged welcome-home event as much play as the stories about the administration keeping us out of Grenada."[136]

By the time the White House party was held, the Pentagon had lifted all media restrictions. The Defense Department had started flying small groups of journalists from Barbados — where more than 300 reporters and photographers had gathered to wait for a chance to cover the invasion — to Grenada on Oct. 27, 1983, 2½ days after Urgent Fury had started. On the day the medical students and military personnel were preparing to go to the White House for the welcome-home ceremony, the Defense Department was flying its last group of journalists to the island.

The Defense Department Organizes Pools

The Pentagon's public affairs operation was run by Navy Cmdr. Ron Wildermuth, who had been Deputy Public Affairs Officer for Adm. Wesley McDonald, the Unified Commander for the Grenada operation. Wildermuth said in an interview for this study that public affairs officers — except for the PAO for the Joint Chiefs of Staff — were completely cut out of the planning for Urgent Fury.[137] Wildermuth was given the job of preparing a public affairs plan after the operation had begun, and encountered the dilemma faced by many military PAOs. He had to work within restrictions set by Adm. Metcalf and other commanders, who did not like the press, while trying to convince them to ease those restrictions. Meanwhile, he had to facilitate coverage for the media, which was angry, resentful and mistrustful. One experienced PAO interviewed on background for this study described being in this position as "worse than being between Scylla and Charybdis."[138]

Wildermuth arrived on Barbados on the morning of the 27th, and went to the U.S. Embassy to find out how many media he could take to the island, a decision he believes Adm. Metcalf made.[139] Wildermuth then went to the Barbados airport to set up the Joint Information Bureau and organize the first pool. He was greeted by more than 300 angry and anxious journalists, some of whom were so intent on talking with the PAOs that they were crawling over the airport's interior walls — which did not go all the way to the ceiling — in an effort to get to the officers.[140]

Wildermuth and his staff of about a dozen people told the media they could take 15 journalists to Grenada. The PAOs wanted to take representatives of network TV, the wire services, print media and radio. Wildermuth left it up to the journalists to choose who would go. They had problems deciding, "but they worked through it," Wildermuth said. "We just said, 'Look, the plane's going to leave at such and such a time. If you can't figure it out, then nobody goes.' And they were able to figure it out."[141] The U.S. and Caribbean journalists chosen for the pool started their trip about noon.[142]

Pool members went over for the day and were accompanied by military escorts. The pool stayed together throughout the itinerary that Wildermuth and other officers had put together: visit U.S. Army commanders, see warehouses where weapons had been found, see POWs, interview students being evacuated, look at places where the action had unfolded.[143]

The second-day pool, which had 27 members, followed much the same routine. By the third day, three pools totaling 182 journalists went to Grenada.[144] There was only one security violation: a freelance photographer working for *Newsweek* broke away from the pool and stayed on the island, leading to a temporary ban of *Newsweek* personnel from the pool.[145]

The pool trips satisfied almost no one. They were "insufficient, much too short and too limited in scope," said *Los Angeles Times* Foreign Editor Alvin Shuster.[146] *Wall Street Journal* reporter Thomas E. Ricks complained that pool members saw the same things day after day.[147]

Journalists who remained behind at the Barbados airport were so outraged and desperate for news that they became "crazed," according to *Washington Post* reporter Phil McCombs.[148] Their frantic efforts to get information or a spot in the pool resulted in "a madhouse, a frustrating mob scene."[149] Wildermuth asked for Metcalf's headquarters to fly a briefing officer from Grenada to Barbados to provide daily updates for the press, and for a direct communications links with the on-scene commander. Neither request was acted upon.[150]

Adm. Metcalf met with the press on Oct. 29, and made contradictory statements. He said he was the journalists' "best friend," then made a joke about shooting at them.[151] After the press conference, Wildermuth met with the admiral to press for open coverage. When Metcalf said adequate lodging and transportation were not available, Wildermuth said the journalists would find their own, and such considerations were not reasons to limit press access. Metcalf finally agreed to open coverage, which began on Oct. 31. By that time, the operation was nearly over.[152]

The Media Discover Military Mistakes

In the weeks following Urgent Fury, reporters began discovering how badly they had been misled by White House and Pentagon officials. Rather than the smooth operation the Pentagon had projected, the invasion had been poorly planned and resulted in higher-than-necessary casualties. But the White House and Defense Department had shaped public opinion by using many of the same techniques they later would use in the Gulf War: replacing body counts with weapons counts, and refusing to estimate enemy or civilian casualties.

The White House and Pentagon shaped public opinion about Grenada by disseminating misinformation and misleading statements about the following issues:

- **The rationale for the invasion**

President Reagan had justified the invasion on Oct. 25, 1983 with the phrase, "American lives are at stake."[153] But some medical school officials and students questioned the rationale from the beginning.

Medical school Vice Chancellor Geoffrey Bourne — who lived on Grenada and supported Operation Urgent Fury's foreign-policy goals — said the invasion had not been necessary to protect students' lives.[154] In an interview with *The Washington Post* after the operation had been completed, Bourne said that Gen. Austin had been stabilizing the situation on the island after the violence of Oct. 19, 1983, and had ordered soldiers to protect and even assist the students. An informal poll at the time showed 90 percent of the students wanted to stay.[155]

That changed after two U.S. envoys visited the school on Oct. 22, 1983, Bourne said. Although the diplomats had come to ask how many students wanted to leave and did not urge the students to return to the United States, they made it clear that the U.S. government thought that was the wisest course, Bourne said. After the invasion started, students' hesitation vanished. "Nearly all of them wanted to go home to Mama," Bourne said.[156]

Some students said they had been frightened by the gunfire and bombing caused by the U.S. intervention. Student Joseph Panicali said:

> I was scared that it was, it was a [sic] unstable situation, that I would get hurt. But . . . . even when the invasion started, no one was touched by the Grenadian people. In fact, it was, we saw one near-miss of a student getting hurt and that was by an errant U.S. bomb. . . .[157]

Student Lucy Painter, who waited in her house with 28 others for four days before she was evacuated, said:

> I think the key question isn't, "Were we in danger or not after the Americans came in?" I think we were. I mean, whether it was by, because somebody might have taken us hostage, or whether it was that one of the errant U.S. bombs might have accidentally killed us or machine-gun fire. The question is whether the Americans, our country, put us in more danger by invading.[158]

Sen. Sam Nunn (D-Ga.), chairman of the Senate Armed Services Committee, also thought the Reagan administration had endangered the medical students by using them as the principal invasion rationale, especially in light of the problems the U.S. military later had in evacuating the students. He said:

> . . . if the Grenada government and military forces had decided they wanted to execute those students that were the primary focus of the mission, the way we carried out that rescue mission or invasion would have allowed them to do so, had they chosen to. In other words, the invasion itself could have dismally failed if our adversary had chosen to execute those students. . . .[159]

- **The evacuation of the medical students**

Defense Secretary Weinberger described the evacuation as "extremely skillfully done."[160] In reality, the operation ran into serious problems, principally because of faulty intelligence. Deputy Joint Task Force Commander Schwarzkopf, who was going to lead the evacuation effort, found his men facing heavier-than-expected fire as they prepared to parachute into the Point Salines airport. Years later, Schwarzkopf described what happened on PBS *Frontline*:

> You have to visualize literally a cone of tracer fire, green tracer fire, coming up into the air. Uh, C-130 aircraft flying in directly underneath this cone of tracer fire, paratroopers dropping in the air and then being shot at, in the air, from all sides on the ground. I, I can't recall any combat operations that the United [States] has ever been involved in that was, that could have been any more intense than that, and that's probably the most intense type of combat that we've ever been involved in.[161]

Schwarzkopf's troops managed to secure the airport and move on to the True Blue campus of the medical school. When Schwarzkopf and his troops arrived there, students told them that most of their colleagues were at another campus. Schwarzkopf had been told the school had only one campus. He told *Frontline*:

> I was shocked. Stunned. There's no other word for it. I mean, you know, you know, the Rangers burst in the door, sort of — if it had been a Hollywood movie, it would have kind of gone like this: The Rangers woulda broke through the door and said, "Ta da, we're here, you're rescued." And the students said, "Yeah, but what about the rest of us," you know. And the Rangers said, "What do you mean about the rest of us?" And they say, "Oh, we're the small campus. They're all located someplace else." I mean, you can imagine the shock.[162]

By nightfall, when the evacuation was to have been completed, efforts were under way to reach the second campus, but progress was slow because "the terrain is terrible, the heat is terrible," Schwarzkopf said.[163] Finally he improvised, sending helicopters in from the *Guam* to evacuate more than 200 students at the second campus.[164] Even then, hundreds more students were waiting in other places. It took four days to reach some of them.[165]

- **Problems with operational planning**

President Reagan called Urgent Fury a "brilliant campaign."[166] Some troops sent to Grenada disagreed. Planning had been done so quickly that many soldiers had no idea what they were fighting for or who the enemy was. One U.S. soldier on the island asked *Washington Post* reporter Edward Cody, "Is the Grenadan Army on our side or theirs?"[167]

The result was that troops were confused and demoralized. Scott Custer, a member of the 82nd Airborne, later told PBS *Frontline* that after the Airborne arrived at Point Salines, commanding officers "didn't know where we were going or what we were going to do."[168] The operation was so disorganized that "We didn't actually know what we were fighting for and that, that would have helped out a lot. . . . When your senior officer doesn't know what you're doing, your morale drops pretty low."[169]

Another indication of the poor planning was the fact that some troops were given tourist maps. One had been published five years earlier by the Grenada Tourist Board.[170]

The Defense Department mapping agency had not been notified about the need for maps until the day of the invasion for operational security reasons.[171] By the time the maps were delivered on Grenada, the fighting was nearly over.[172]

After the operation was over, the Pentagon officers denied they had to rely on tourist maps. At a briefing with Gen. Schwarzkopf, Lt. Col. Wesley Taylor, an Army Rangers commander, unfurled a 5-foot-long British map.[173] However, Custer said:

> . . . any type of support fire that we would need from artillery or whatnot, you need to have a grid coordinate to precisely land that shell. Otherwise, there's a chance of making some of us the casualties of our own actions. Well, they handed us these tourist maps and we had no way to direct anything from these maps. They had points of interest, which is fine if I was on a seven-day vacation and I wanted to see the Grand Answer [sic] Harbor or go visit the Windsor Estate Nutmeg Plantation, that've been great. But if I gotta call in for artillery fire, I'm like, well, "just direct at three hundred meters left of this point of interest we have here on the map."[174]

- **Civilian casualties**

In a late-afternoon press conference on Oct. 26, 1983, 36 hours after the invasion started, Defense Secretary Caspar Weinberger said he had no information on civilian casualties.[175] As late as Oct. 30, White House and Defense Department personnel were talking about how the Armed Forces had used "surgical care" and "limited force" when taking control of key sites on Grenada.[176]

But reporters learned that during the first day of the invasion, U.S. forces mistakenly had bombed a mental hospital, killing more than a dozen people. Pentagon officials said they had not learned about the incident until days later, and blamed this on the "fog of war." But retired Navy Rear Adm. Eugene Carroll of the Center for Defense Information said in an interview for this study that such a fog would have lasted less than 24 hours.[177]

On Oct. 31, 1983, six days after the invasion, the Pentagon released an official statement about the attack, saying that U.S. forces had called in an air strike in the Fort Frederick area, not realizing a hospital was nearby. Armed Forces officials learned about the incident when they picked up ham radio reports saying a hospital had been hit, the statement added.[178]

- **Enemy casualties**

For more than a week after the operation had ended, White House and Pentagon officials insisted they could not provide accurate estimates of enemy casualties. They initially told reporters that field officers had been told not to waste radio time relaying such information. After the fighting ended, they said so many bodies had been buried that a reliable estimate no longer was possible.[179] White House spokesman Larry Speakes told reporters he had heard that "there is a religious custom that the Grenadians bury their dead very soon after they die." Most Grenadians are Roman Catholics or Anglicans, and often waited days for funerals. Speakes later admitted the custom "may not be religious."[180]

At a Nov. 8, 1983 briefing, Gen. Schwarzkopf said estimates had not been provided because there had been a "deliberate decision not to focus on body counts."[181]

"We went through all that during the Vietnam War, and it got to be a gruesome operation," Schwarzkopf said.[182]

Schwarzkopf went on to say that "rough estimates" showed that 160 Grenadian soldiers and 71 Cubans had been killed during the invasion.[183] The Pentagon immediately disavowed those figures, saying they had come from field commanders, and that no casualty figures had been "validated" or "officially reported." The Pentagon said they were certain of only 59 enemy soldiers who had been killed.[184]

The contradictory figures led *Washington Post* reporters Rick Atkinson and Fred Hiatt to write in a Nov. 12, 1983 story:

> Almost three weeks after the invasion of Grenada, Pentagon officials say with certainty that U.S. forces captured 300 shotguns, 24,768 flares and 5,615,682 rounds of ammunition, among other things on a long and precisely detailed inventory.
>
> These same officials, however, say they still have no idea how many civilians or enemy soldiers were killed or wounded in the fighting that cost 18 American lives.[185]

The Media Get Embroiled in a Ratings War

Reporting about these controversies made little difference to President Reagan's ratings in opinion polls, but it appeared to help the media's. A *Washington Post*-ABC News poll taken during the first two days of the invasion showed Americans were about equally split concerning the government's media controls. Forty-seven percent said the government was trying to control reports out of Grenada more than it should, while 45 percent said the administration was not exerting excessive control.[186]

But according to a national Harris survey done several months after the Grenada operation, the media's standing had improved further. A Jan. 29, 1984 story in *The Washington Post* stated that the Harris poll showed that 65 percent of respondents believed that reporters should have been allowed to accompany U.S. troops invading Grenada. Sixty-three percent thought not allowing at least a small group of reporters to witness that type of operation would tempt a president or the military to conceal mistakes and casualties. Eighty-three percent of those surveyed by the Harris organization agreed that in a free country, a basic freedom is the right to know about important events, especially when the lives of U.S. soldiers are involved, and 53 percent thought the country was better off because Vietnam had been so thoroughly covered.[187]

Nevertheless, when John Chancellor said in a commentary on *NBC Nightly News* that "The American government is doing whatever it wants to, without any representative of the American public watching what it is doing," the network received 500 letters and phone calls, which supported the press ban 5 to 1.[188] One angry viewer wrote, "What do you think we elected Reagan for? It's damn sure you were never elected."[189] ABC anchor Peter Jennings said 99 percent of his mail supported the exclusion.[190] When CBS anchor Dan Rather told viewers the Pentagon had "censored" the film the network had just shown of the invasion, the CBS switchboard was inundated with callers, some of whom charged the network and Rather with being "unpatriotic."[191] CNN's Daniel Schorr, noting that four-fifths of callers to the network's call-in shows favored the news restrictions, said, "A startling lesson of the Grenada invasion episode is that the news media arguing the public's right to know, found themselves without general public support."[192]

The print media fared no better. When editors of the trade publication *Editor and Publisher* surveyed about a dozen daily newspapers, they found letters to the editor running 3 to 1 in favor of the Pentagon restrictions.[193] *Time* received 225 letters, which favored the press ban 8 to 1.[194]

One explanation for the difference between the polls and the experiences of individual media and journalists was that people will write or call to express their opinions only when they feel deeply about a subject.[195] *Time* writer William A. Henry III thought the dispute over barring the press in Grenada "seemed to uncork a pent-up public hostility" toward the press.[196] In an article titled, "Journalism under fire," Henry said many people who had written to news media about the Grenada restrictions held a "deep, far-ranging resentment of the press."[197] *New York Times* Editorial Page Editor Max Frankel stated, "The most astounding thing about the Grenada situation was the quick, facile assumption by some of the public that the press wanted to get in, not to witness the invasion on behalf of the people, but to sabotage it."[198]

The White House and Pentagon seized on the anecdotal evidence. A Defense Department spokesman responded to a query from a *Washington Post* reporter with the statement, "I guess most of the people think I don't have to tell you a damn thing."[199] When a *Los Angeles Times* journalist asked White House Chief of Staff Baker about the news blackout on Grenada, he said, "a large majority of the American people support it."[200] The polls showed that this was untrue, but unfortunately, many people believed Baker was right.

The Media Look for Support

The media did not get a great deal of support from Congress, either. After some initial criticism of the press ban, many lawmakers became silent when it became evident the President's decision to invade Grenada was a popular one.

On Oct. 29, 1983, the Senate adopted an amendment to a pending debt limit bill declaring that "restrictions imposed upon the press shall cease."[201] A House subcommittee held hearings on news restrictions during Grenada as part of a series of hearings on national security and civil liberties.[202] Media executives submitted written and oral testimony, warning of the dangers of allowing the Pentagon to set a precedent for barring media access to military operations.

CBS President Edward Joyce wrote:

> I am seriously concerned that we may indeed be witnessing the dawn of a new era of censorship, of manipulation of the press, of considering the media the handmaiden of government to spoon feed the public with Government-approved information. . . . I am concerned that such action will be taken again and again, whenever a Government wishes to keep the public in the dark.[203]

Lessons Learned by White House and Military Officials

Civilian and military leaders learned some important lessons from Grenada. One was that first impressions can be lasting if a war doesn't go on too long or result in high U.S. casualties; although statements made by Speakes, Weinberger and other officials later were revealed to have been untrue, this had little effect on public consciousness about the invasion.

A second major lesson was that the media could not put up an effective defense if the government decided to bar them from the battlefield. As loudly as the networks complained, they still ran the Pentagon footage of the first days of the war, because that was the only video they had. Not one of the networks refused to run the footage — which showed none of the problems encountered on the ground — as a protest. The print media similarly fell in line, printing the Reagan administration's version of events. There were some disclaimers that the information was coming from the federal government and that reporters could not present independent corroboration, but the vast majority of the copy was devoted to presenting the official story. When the media found they could not rely on other branches of government — Congress or the courts — to provide solid support for their First Amendment claims, the White House perception that the Pentagon could prevent journalists from covering battlefield activities with few negative repercussions was strengthened further.

The American people — not having seen U.S. troops or Grenadian mental patients killed, or witnessed the confusion of American soldiers as they tried to adapt tourist maps to the battlefield — thought of the invasion as an unqualified success, and supported it.

The Pentagon Takes the Initiative

The most significant action regarding the media was taken by the Pentagon itself, when Joint Chiefs of Staff Chairman Gen. Vessey, anxious to get past the press-ban controversy (which had divided many military officers), asked retired Army Maj. Gen. Sidle to prepare a report that was to provide a new foundation for the military-media relationship.[204]

Braestrup and other policy analysts found it disturbing that it was military, not civilian, leaders who had initiated the most significant official examination of the Pentagon media policies regarding Grenada.[205] Braestrup wrote:

> The secretary of defense . . . has yet to give unequivocal support to the notion that information policy is a civilian responsibility and not one that can be delegated, as it was during the Grenada invasion, to military commanders. . . . The basic question to be posed is: "How can we get them in?" not "How can we keep them out?"[206]

The Sidle Panel Report, released in August 1984, was endorsed by the press and the Pentagon, which promised to implement recommendations to initiate public affairs and operational planning simultaneously, to establish a national media pool, to rely on voluntary ground rules, to provide more transportation and communications facilities for wartime media efforts, to schedule meetings between military and media representatives, and to provide additional public affairs training for military personnel.

Some journalists believed the thrust of the Sidle Panel recommendations was misguided. Craig R. Whitney, Assistant Managing Editor of *The New York Times* and a member of the Twentieth Century Fund Task Force on the Military and the Media, stated:

> We should urge the military to be more open and forthright in its information policies, not to enumerate more restrictive measures, such as "pools" and ground rules. Civilian authorities should make it clear to the military chain of command that its duty is not to hedge in correspondents with restraints, but to be as informative as possible.[207]

After the Sidle Report was released, Wildermuth, who after Grenada became a Joints Chiefs of Staff public affairs officer, rewrote the Pentagon's basic public affairs document to incorporate the Report's recommendations.[208]

However, events during the U.S. invasion of Panama in December 1989 showed that White House and Pentagon leaders had not fully accepted the Sidle Panel's call for a military-media relationship based on respect and cooperation, and had not complied with some of the report's most important recommendations. □

THE INVASION OF PANAMA

The Assistant Secretary of Defense for Public Affairs has the primary responsibility for carrying out this commitment [to provide timely and accurate information to the public, Congress and the media].

Principles of Information
Defense Secretary Richard Cheney

When Gen. Manuel Antonio Noriega took control of the Panamanian government in 1983, U.S. officials were pleased. As court documents later revealed, Noriega had been working for the United States as an intelligence resource since at least 1958, when he was a cadet at a military academy in Peru.[1]

Since the mid-1970s, U.S. officials had had concrete evidence that Noriega had been involved in narcotics activities, but the Central Intelligence Agency kept Noriega on the payroll until 1986 because he was considered a valuable intelligence asset.[2] U.S. payments to Noriega came to light earlier this year in federal court in Miami, as U.S. prosecutors prepared to bring Noriega — who surrendered in January 1990 after the U.S. invasion of Panama — to trial on drug-trafficking charges. During pre-trial proceedings, the prosecutors filed a financial report showing that the United States had paid the Panamanian general a total of about $300,000 in cash and gifts over the years. Noriega's lawyers said government agencies, principally the CIA, had paid him millions of dollars.[3]

The trial preparations were the culmination of legal actions that began in 1988. So much evidence was produced about Noriega's activities that two Florida grand juries handed down drug trafficking and money laundering indictments against the Panamanian general. The indictments, obtained in February 1988 by U.S. Justice Department attorneys over the objections of some federal officials, were extremely embarrassing to the Reagan administration, which was running a much-publicized "war on drugs" under the direction of Vice President George Bush. The Vice President's spokesman told reporters Bush had not had "certain knowledge" of Noriega's narcotics involvement until shortly before the indictments. This assertion was contradicted by Norman Bailey, a former Special Assistant to President Reagan for National Security Affairs and a former Director of Planning for the National Security Council staff.[4] Bailey told the House Select Committee on Narcotics Abuse and Control in March 1988 that there had been "not a smoking gun, but a 21-cannon barrage of evidence" about Noriega's drug trafficking and money laundering that dated back to the mid-1970s, when Bush was CIA director.[5] Bailey said the only way a U.S. official could have been unaware of Noriega's activities was to have "willfully ignored" the "overwhelming evidence."[6]

Bailey and other officials who served during the Reagan administration told congressional committees in the spring of 1988 that although the CIA wanted to ignore Noriega's narcotics involvement because Agency personnel believed he was providing important information and services to the United States, in reality the

Panamanian general gave the U.S. very little. Francis McNeil, former Senior Deputy Assistant Secretary of State for Intelligence and Research, told a Senate subcommittee that Noriega "didn't help. He seemed to follow the rule of promising us anything but giving us a kind of political Arpège."[7]

After the 1988 indictments, the United States tried to pressure Noriega into stepping down. The Reagan administration instituted economic sanctions against Panama, but they had little effect on Noriega. U.S. officials also sent signals to political opposition groups and the Panamanian Defense Forces (PDF) that they would support efforts to overthrow the general, but Panamanian political leaders were frightened and demoralized. In the summer of 1987, they had pleaded for U.S. military intervention when thousands of Panamanians had demonstrated against Noriega, demanding his ouster. The demonstrations began after a Noriega associate had stated publicly that the general was involved in drug trafficking and had ordered the assassination of popular political reformer Hugo Spadafora, whose headless body had been found stuffed in a U.S. mail sack near the Costa Rican-Panamanian border. At the time, the Reagan administration still regarded the general as an ally and intelligence asset, and refused to act against him, even after opposition leaders were beaten, exiled and jailed. The opposition was still trying to regroup 12 months later, and responded to U.S. calls for an uprising with bitterness and rage.

The situation deteriorated during 1989. Street violence marred the presidential election campaign, which pitted Noriega's hand-picked candidate, Carlos Duque, against Guillermo Endara. After international observers announced that the opposition appeared to have won the May 7 balloting by a margin of more than 2-to-1, Noriega had the election nullified. Efforts to mediate the dispute failed, and Noriega had another associate, Francisco Rodríguez, installed as head of a provisional government that would rule for at least six months before new elections would be considered.

The Bush administration continued sending signals to the Panamanian military that a *coup* attempt would be welcomed, and the Defense Department began planning for a possible U.S. invasion.

In October 1989, a group of PDF officers attempted to overthrow Noriega. The White House knew about the plot, but was not enthusiastic, reportedly because *coup* leaders' primary motivation seemed to be a desire to gain control over more of the PDF's finances. When the *coup* attempt began on Oct. 3, the Pentagon allowed U.S. troops to block strategic roads, but gave no other support. The rebellion failed, and several of its leaders were executed. Afterward, Defense Secretary Cheney said the revolt had not been worth risking American lives.[8]

Bush and Cheney were heavily criticized in Congress and many newspapers for not supporting the attempted *coup*. Editorial writers wondered whether the president, who had been plagued by "the wimp factor" during the 1988 presidential campaign, lacked the resolve to deal effectively with foreign policy issues.

Tensions in Panama rose throughout the fall. In November, White House and military officials stepped up planning for a U.S. invasion. The planning included discussions of how media coverage should be handled.[9] Events in mid-December provided a rationale for military action. One U.S. officer was killed and a Panamanian soldier was wounded in confrontations between PDF and U.S. soldiers in the streets of Panama City. Noriega announced that conditions were equivalent to a state of war with the United States. A decision was made in the White House to begin the invasion — which would be dubbed Operation Just Cause — shortly after midnight on Dec. 20.[10]

Informing the Media

A description of the Pentagon's public affairs program during the invasion is contained in two documents prepared after the operation: the U.S. Southern Command (SouthCom) Public Affairs After Action Report, prepared by SouthCom personnel in Panama City, and the Review of Panama Pool Deployment, an analysis prepared at the Pentagon's request by Fred S. Hoffman, a former newsman and Pentagon official.

Both reports show that Cheney and Williams made crucial decisions that prevented the media from adequately covering the operation. These decisions involved denying the media access to the battlefield during the first hours of the operation; not providing the media with sufficient transportation or communication facilities; and providing reporters with a sanitized view of the invasion that included misinformation.

One major controversy involved the decision to send the Washington-based DOD national media pool to Panama rather than organizing a pool of journalists based in Panama City to cover the early stages of Operation Just Cause, as SouthCom public affairs officers had wanted. "The DOD media pool was unnecessary because of sufficient resident press," Col. Ronald T. Sconyers, SouthCom Director of Public Affairs, wrote in his after-action report.[11]

Cheney and Williams wanted to use the DOD pool because "we were accustomed to it" and pool members "knew the ground rules," Williams told Hoffman.[12] Cheney later said he had a "desire to avoid being criticized for not using it."[13] President Bush and Vice President Dan Quayle expressed concern about whether the pool could keep the operation a secret,[14] but left final decisions about the pool to the Defense Secretary. Cheney, "with full knowledge" of the implications, authorized Williams to call pool members so late that they would miss the early hours of the invasion.[15]

According to the Hoffman Report, the military had no role in delaying the pool.[16] The decision to restrict media coverage of the initial phases of the operation was made entirely by Cheney and Williams — civilian Pentagon leaders who have not served in the military.

Another controversial decision made by these two officials was to delay informing SouthCom public affairs officers that they were not going to use a local pool until 5 p.m. on Dec. 19, just eight hours before the invasion began. Sconyers and other officers scrambled to set up facilities and make logistical preparations, but there "was little time to fully prepare," according to the SouthCom after-action report.[17]

Williams began notifying the DOD pool members at 7:30 p.m. on Dec. 19 that an operation was imminent. He had trouble locating some pool members, who were at Christmas festivities.

On Dec. 20, shortly before 1 a.m. Eastern Standard Time, the U.S. invasion of Panama began. Airborne troops backed by Stealth aircraft launched an attack on strategic PDF facilities such as the barracks at Rio Hato, where soldiers who had helped Noriega fight the October *coup* attempt were located. Other forces moved to protect the Panama Canal and take control of other strategic sites in and around Panama City. As the invasion began, reporters were en route from Andrews Air Force Base near Washington, D.C.; they did not arrive until after 5 a.m., more than four hours after the start of operations.

The pool landed at Howard Air Force Base in Panama, then was moved by helicopter to Fort Clayton. The journalists wanted to go into the field immediately, but transportation was not available. Instead, the pool members were taken to a holding room. "We watched television, we got a cup of coffee. We actually watched a Bush news conference," said *Dallas Morning News* reporter Kevin Merida. "We were right there with the viewer watching CNN."[18]

SouthCom personnel arranged for reporters to cover events on the base while they awaited transportation. The public affairs officers had wanted to have newly inaugurated President Endara on hand to make his first appearance before the press, but Endara refused to have his media debut take place on a U.S. military base.[19] SouthCom then arranged for a briefing by the U.S. chargé d'affaires, who told reporters about the history of Panama.[20]

This inauspicious beginning for the DOD pool was a harbinger of things to come. The next two days were nightmares for the pool reporters and the SouthCom public affairs personnel, some of whom literally worked day and night trying to assist the journalists. Public affairs planning had been so hasty that helicopters and other vehicles assigned to reporters were commandeered for military use. The journalists were not allowed to leave the base on their own, and sometimes were reduced to watching hours of television reports from Washington.

After they got into the field with their public affairs escorts, they encountered additional problems. Battlefield logistics were so confused that one plane carrying journalists was "suspected of being PDF for a short time," and could have been shot down by other U.S. aircraft.[21] Commanders in the field had not been briefed about the journalists' arrival or the public affairs policies. Some refused to talk to journalists; others said they had been ordered not to. Reporters initially were not allowed to talk with wounded GIs, while photographers were told not to take pictures of damaged helicopters or the closed caskets of U.S. soldiers who had died in combat.[22]

Back at media headquarters, journalists found that trying to transmit copy "was a nightmare," according to pool member Kathy Lewis of the *Houston Post*.[23] The Pentagon fax machine that was to receive the copy and send it to news organizations malfunctioned, making stories incomprehensible. When Pentagon staffers tried to call the media center in Panama City, the calls were misdirected to another office or the phones went unanswered. It was hours before reporters even knew their copy had to be re-sent. Meanwhile, furious bureau chiefs were calling the Defense Department demanding to know where the pool reports were.[24]

Photographers also had a difficult time. As they tried to transmit pictures to the United States over the phone, Panamanian operators broke in on the lines, ruining the transmission. Reuters photographer Tim Aubry estimated it took 10 hours to send six to eight photos; it should have taken less than two.[25]

SouthCom public affairs officials tried to obtain additional facilities, but were hampered by numerous catch-all jobs, such as dealing with a request by the White Castle corporation for help in delivering 10,000 hamburgers to U.S. troops.[26]

The situation worsened when "pressure from Washington" to allow more reporters and photographers to enter Panama led SouthCom to open Howard Air Force base to chartered planes carrying journalists.[27] More than 300 newsmen and newswomen flew in on Dec. 21 and 22, only to be confined to military facilities because SouthCom officials thought the sporadic, ongoing fighting made it too dangerous for journalists to leave.[28] Reporters, some of whom had covered numerous wars, were outraged. Meanwhile, SouthCom "could not logistically or administratively support such a [large] group,"[29] and was unable to provide sufficient food or housing for the journalists, some of whom slept on the floor. "You might as well go home," one frustrated public affairs officer told the journalists.[30] Many did, flying back to the United States with little to show for the trip. By the time the others got into the field, the war was largely over.

In Washington, Williams said he regretted the problems that the pool was encountering. On Dec. 22, newspapers quoted him as saying that the problems were due to the "incompetence" of military officials. At a briefing later that day, Williams insisted he had been referring to his own incompetence, and had nothing but admiration for the job being done by military officers.[31]

In fact, Williams had not informed top military officials about problems with the pool. Joint Chiefs of Staff Chairman Gen. Powell said after the invasion that he "didn't have a single clue" about the difficulties until journalists told him about it in Washington on the second day of the war.[32]

Misinforming the Media

Logistical obstacles were not the only ones encountered by journalists. Misinformation supplied during U.S. briefings in Panama and Washington was another serious problem. The briefings gave a false, overly positive view of events in the field, and concealed U.S. mistakes and casualties. The truth did not emerge until weeks or months later. Once again, the stories reporting these false statements got much less media play than the misinformation.

Misleading information was given to reporters about these major issues:

- **Deaths and injuries resulting from friendly fire**

During the first days of the invasion, the Pentagon and the White House insisted no U.S. troops had been killed or wounded by friendly fire. For example, at a late-afternoon Pentagon press briefing on Dec. 20, Lt. Gen. Thomas Kelly — Director of Operations for the Joint Staff, who later led Defense Department briefers during the Gulf War — told reporters there had been no friendly fire casualties.[33] The next morning, more than 30 hours after the invasion had begun, the point was reiterated by presidential spokesman Marlin Fitzwater.[34] At the same time, Pentagon and White House officials repeatedly told reporters that the military operation had been, in Defense Secretary Cheney's words, "a thoroughly professional job that was done at minimum cost in terms of casualties."[35]

Six months later, the truth began to emerge when *Newsweek* magazine ran an investigative article in June 1990 revealing that friendly fire had killed or wounded more than a dozen U.S. troops. Williams said that as a result of reporters' questions about the *Newsweek* piece, the Pentagon had investigated and found that two U.S. soldiers had been killed by friendly fire during fighting near the PDF barracks in Rio Hato, where U.S. paratroopers had been dropped during the first minutes of the invasion. A third soldier might have been killed by friendly fire during a battle for the international airport outside Panama City, but the situation was unclear, he said. In addition, Williams said 15 U.S. troops had been wounded by friendly fire, and another 21 might have been, but it was impossible to verify because PDF troops also used U.S. weapons.[36]

Reporters who covered the Pentagon were enraged that, even in response to direct questions, the Defense Department had not disclosed the casualties during the invasion.

At a June 19 Pentagon briefing, one reporter charged the Defense Department with deliberately misleading reporters.

"There were a lot of questions after the invasion and questions from us asking for [an] account of how these things broke down. And there never was any response until this [*Newsweek*] report came out," the reporter said at the briefing.

"I don't know what you expect me to say in response," DOD spokesman Williams said. "Obviously, six months is not — is — does seem a little long."[37]

During the same briefing, a reporter asked whether the Secretary of Defense had known about the friendly fire casualties. "The Secretary, the Chairman [of the Joint Chiefs of Staff] and the President" all knew, Williams replied.

"How come we didn't?" the reporter asked.

"That's a good question," Williams responded. "I'm not sure that I totally know the answer to that one, but obviously we need to do better."[38]

- **Casualties resulting from parachute jumps during the invasion**

During the initial hours of Operation Just Cause, the responsibility for taking control of the PDF Rio Hato facility and the international airport belonged primarily to the paratroopers of Task Force Red. Hundreds of soldiers jumped at Rio Hato onto targets from altitudes as low as 400 feet. Military officials interviewed for this report told the Center that the Pentagon expects at least a 10 percent injury rate for such jumps, and additional casualties during the ensuing fighting. The actual number of deaths and injuries also depends on whether enemy soldiers anticipate the paratroopers' arrival.

The Rio Hato air drop occurred shortly before 1 a.m. Prior to the jump, two Stealth aircraft dropped two 2,000-lb. bombs into a field near the PDF barracks. Pentagon officials told reporters the bombs were supposed to "stun and confuse and frighten" the PDF troops.[39] Williams told reporters at a briefing that because of the Stealth bombing, Rio Hato "was not a 'hot' landing zone, meaning that they [U.S. forces] did not meet with resistance when they landed."[40]

U.S. paratroopers and their officers later told a different story. They said some Panamanian soldiers were panicked and disoriented, but others fired on U.S. forces.

Col. William Kernan, who led the airborne assault, was quoted in the *Los Angeles Times* on Jan. 7 as saying the PDF put up "fierce" initial resistance.[41]

Meanwhile, the Task Force Red contingents that carried out a low-altitude drop at the airport met less intense PDF resistance.[42] Military officers interviewed for this study said that reports about injuries and deaths are sent up the chain of command as soon as possible, and that the Pentagon should have had the information by the afternoon of Dec. 20.

In response to questions during a late-afternoon Dec. 20 briefing — more than 15 hours after the air assault began — Kelly told reporters, "I know of no casualties that occurred as a result of the air drop."[43] When pressed on the issue later in the briefing, Kelly remained vague:

> Q: Could you give us a little better breakdown on the casualties? We heard earlier firefights at the Comandancia. Was it also at Rio Hato?
>
> Gen. Kelly: Firefights went on here at Rio Hato. We sent our troops in well-armed and superbly trained. And I know that sounds like bragging, but that's just the truth; they were.[44]

The next day, more than 30 hours after the drop, Kelly still was not forthright about casualties. When he gave reporters a task-force breakdown on how many troops had been killed, he omitted any mention of Task Force Red. Kelly said in an interview for this study that he did not have information about such casualties at that time. "I will guarantee you that I never, ever, ever told a lie," he said.[45]

It wasn't until days later that reporters began uncovering the truth. Military doctors in the United States told journalists more than 80 soldiers had sustained injuries in the low-altitude air assault.[46] "It was the worst collection of fractures I'd ever seen in my life," Dr. William Burner told *Newsday*.[47] Pentagon officials prevented reporters from talking to injured soldiers being treated at a facility in San Antonio, Texas, for more than three days, on the grounds that such interviews would not be "in good taste," and that soldiers might unwittingly provide confidential information about the invasion.[48]

Meanwhile, some officers in Panama began to speak bitterly about the Stealth bombing at Rio Hato, which they contended had alerted the PDF to the U.S. forces' arrival.

Lt. Gen. Carl Stiner, U.S. combat commander in Panama, told reporters weeks later that one American paratrooper was shot dead while standing in the jump door of his plane.[49]

In an interview for this study, another officer said, "If you're doing a night air drop, you're doing it to surprise the enemy. If you drop bombs, you do it to kill the enemy, not to wake him up so he can shoot at you."[50]

Williams later admitted that the bombs may have been "something of a calling card," but insisted the mission had been successful.[51] Cheney agreed.[52] They maintained this position even after the full story of the Stealth's performance emerged.

- **The performance of the Stealth aircraft**

The Rio Hato bombing run was the F-117 Stealth's first combat mission. At the time, the Stealth was controversial because of its cost — more than $100 million per plane — and doubts about its capabilities. Military officials said privately that the plane was used in the invasion of Panama to show Congress its capabilities before the next round of budget hearings on Pentagon aircraft and weapons systems.

Questions arose almost immediately about whether the bombs dropped by the Stealth had hit the intended targets. Some officers told journalists that the bombs were supposed to fall on the PDF barracks, not the field beside them. Others contended that Pentagon planners initially had targeted the barracks, but decided to target two specific areas of the nearby field instead after DOD officials said they wanted to leave the barracks intact. The Stealth bombs then missed these alternative targets by a wide margin, the officers said.

At a Dec. 26 briefing, Williams emphatically denied that the Stealth had not been accurate. "The F-117 bombs precisely hit their targets," he said. "They did not miss."[53]

He later explained that early plans called for the bombs to hit the PDF facility, but the plans were changed because "the new government was going to use these same barracks for its forces" and hoped to "use many of these same soldiers for service."[54] Planners decided to have the bombs fall on designated areas in the nearby field instead. Cheney, who had inspected the Rio Hato site by helicopter while visiting the troops over Christmas, reiterated at a January 1990 briefing that the planes had hit their targets with "pinpoint accuracy."[55]

An April 4, 1990 *New York Times* article quoted unnamed Pentagon officials who — after being shown photographs of the site by reporter Michael Gordon — said one Stealth bomb had missed its target by hundreds of yards.[56]

At an April 10 briefing, Williams admitted that one of the bombs was "way off target," and that neither he nor Cheney had known this until they had seen Gordon's photographs. Cheney had "asked the Air Force for an explanation, and he's confident he'll get one," Williams said. He added that he did not believe there had been "any intent to mislead the Secretary."[57]

Williams insisted that Cheney still believed the Stealth had done "what it was supposed to do." When an astonished reporter asked how Williams could say that when the mission "was a 50 percent failure at best," Williams replied that the bombs apparently had missed because of pilot error — not because of a problem with the plane — and still had succeeded in making a great deal of noise and frightening the PDF troops.[58]

Williams and Cheney maintained that the Stealth mission had been successful even after a report by the Air Force Inspector General showed that *both* bombs had missed their targets. *The New York Times* said in July 1990 that the report, which was classified, stated that flawed planning had led to confusion about the targets and to inadequate pilot training, and that Gen. Robert D. Russ, the chief of the Tactical Air Command, had failed to tell his superiors that the Stealth bombs had missed their targets.[59] In response, Russ issued a statement saying, "There is always some confusion in the reporting of any military operation, and I didn't want to add to it . . . . it is evident that more detail should have been forwarded."[60]

Nevertheless, Williams said Cheney continued to believe that Air Force officials had not tried to mislead him, and that the Stealth had completed its mission.[61]

This position was reiterated by Gen. Merrill A. McPeak, who was appointed Air Force Chief of Staff in the fall of 1990. In a speech at the Air Force Association's National Symposium last fall about the need for the military to deal with the media from a position of integrity, McPeak discussed the Stealth episode. He said early statements that the bombs had hit their targets were true but incomplete; they had hit the field, but had missed the specific areas they were supposed to strike. The incident made it look as if "the Air Force had slanted the initial reports for its own purposes," he said. This contributed to "the appearance" of an integrity problem, the general admitted, but he remained convinced that "we [in the Air Force] do not have an integrity problem."[62]

However, the Stealth incident appears to be a direct violation of Air Force public affairs policies, which state:

> Under no circumstances will disinformation activities, or activities intended to misinform or deny releaseable [sic] information to the American public, be condoned. Such actions, in the context of public affairs, are inconsistent with the values of our nation and will not be practiced.[63]

Ironically, the news stories and subsequent Pentagon inquiries helped improve the performance of the Stealth and its pilots, and the plane later was used extensively in the air war in the Gulf.

- **Civilian casualties**

At Pentagon briefings through much of 1990, U.S. spokesmen estimated that 202 civilians and 314 military personnel had died as a result of the invasion. When U.S. and Panamanian human rights organizations began saying that the number of civilian deaths was higher, many reporters remained sympathetic to the problems that SouthCom personnel faced in trying to arrive at an accurate civilian body count. The SouthCom after-action report talked of how military personnel were trying to define the word "civilian" in light of the fact that many people fighting for Noriega were members of the Dignity Battalions, a civilian militia whose members may have been dressed in street clothes. The report also pointed out that it sometimes was impossible to ascertain whether a person had been killed by U.S. troops, PDF troops or Panamanian business owners trying to protect their property from looters.[64]

Sympathy began to fade several months later, after representatives of international human rights organizations completed reports that supported the assertions that civilian deaths had been underestimated. Several groups believed that the number of military deaths had been overestimated, and that more civilians than military personnel had been killed during Just Cause. Two Panamanian human rights organizations alleged that many civilians had been buried in unmarked mass graves.[65]

SouthCom issued a fact sheet about the body count on Dec. 14, 1990, and revised it Jan. 3, 1991. SouthCom stated that the Institute of Legal Medicine, Panama's coroner's office, had identified 65 military and 157 civilian remains. Fifty bodies had not been identified or categorized as military or civilian. The Institute also had

75 unresolved reports of missing persons. SouthCom then presented a combined body count, stating that the Institute's figures "suggest a range of between 272 confirmed dead and a maximum of 347 possible deaths (military and civilian)."[66]

The fact sheet said there were no undiscovered mass graves in Panama. SouthCom temporarily had interred 28 Panamanians in individual graves for health and sanitation purposes on Dec. 21, 1989, according to the fact sheet. The remains had been disinterred and turned over to the Panamanian government a week later for identification and final disposition. Panamanian authorities had interred 123 casualties in a common grave in a Panama City cemetery because of health concerns, and "some U.S. assistance was rendered in order to ensure that remains were afforded proper respect," the fact sheet said. Another 18 persons had been buried in a common grave in a cemetery in Colón, eight of whom had died as a result of the invasion. These casualties had been included in the Institute's January 1991 figures, according to the fact sheet.[67]

SouthCom stated that it was "impossible to determine exactly how many died as a direct result of the military action," that there still were "difficulties in distinguishing between civilian and military remains," and that issues surrounding the body count "may ultimately escape complete resolution."[68]

In an effort to help settle some of the controversy, Rep. Charles Rangel (D-N.Y.) asked shortly after the invasion to see videotapes taken by U.S. planes during the fighting. He believed that the videos would enable U.S. officials and reporters to estimate the number of civilians who had been killed. For nearly a year, the Pentagon refused to supply them, until Rangel wrote an angry op-ed piece that appeared in *The New York Times* on Dec. 20, 1990 about the Pentagon's stonewalling. Military officials then turned over some video footage, but it was so fuzzy that Rangel's staff could not ascertain what had happened.[69]

- **Noriega's alleged cocaine stash**

Two days after the invasion, when Gen. Noriega was still at large, U.S. officials took reporters to one of his residences. They opened a freezer to display plastic bags full of a white, powdery substance that they said was cocaine. Gen. Maxwell Thurman, the head of SouthCom, later confirmed that U.S. troops had found cocaine in the freezer. Lt. Gen. Kelly, the Pentagon briefer, said the cocaine weighed "50 kilos," or about 110 pounds,[70] news which made the front pages of many U.S. newspapers.

In late January, reporters began asking Defense Department officials about the cocaine after hearing rumors that the powder was not a drug after all. DOD officials vacillated. First they admitted the substance wasn't cocaine. Then several Pentagon sources, some of whom spoke on condition of anonymity, told reporters that the substance was used in voodoo rituals, and was designed to cast a spell on President Bush and members of Congress.[71] Finally, Williams admitted that the substance was not cocaine, but "farina, corn meal and lard,"[72] which are used to make tamales.

Pentagon officials insisted that no attempt had been made to mislead the media. DOD spokesman Bob Hall said the officer on the scene who had told reporters that the U.S. military had found a cocaine stash was inexperienced but "thought it was cocaine."[73] Neither he nor Williams explained why Gen. Thurman later had confirmed the soldier's statement. Williams indicated that the Pentagon had not known that the powder was not a narcotic until it had been tested, but did not say why the Pentagon had not corrected its mistake until pressed by reporters.[74]

Even experienced journalists were demonstrably upset by the cocaine story, and the misleading information presented by the Pentagon about other issues. *Miami Herald* reporter Andres Oppenheimer, who has covered Latin America for years, said he was embarrassed about having based stories on "sloppy, bad, erroneous and maybe intentionally wrong information" released by the Pentagon, and wished he had put more disclaimers in his articles.[75]

However, Oppenheimer and other journalists also were critical of the media for having printed such data without checking further. "Most of the U.S. press did not apply the same standards of reporting to [derogatory statements about] Noriega that they would normally use regarding a Miami city official or a New York mayor or a president of the United States," Oppenheimer said.[76]

One news medium did present innovative coverage during Operation Just Cause. In the first days of the invasion the Cable News Network aired a telephone number that Panama residents could call to report what was happening in their neighborhoods.[77]

The response was astounding — and revealing. CNN received hundreds of calls. Panamanians provided vivid descriptions of what was happening outside their windows that were every bit as dramatic as the descriptions that Bernard Shaw, John Holliman and Peter Arnett provided CNN of the bombing of Baghdad during the first night of the Persian Gulf War 13 months later. Residents described frightened civilians running to escape gunfire, and fighting in the streets. The picture presented by Panama City residents was in sharp contrast with the Pentagon's presentation of a well-coordinated operation designed to minimize damage to neighborhoods. It also gave Pentagon public affairs officers a graphic example of the image-control problems they would have if live television coverage were permitted from the battlefield.[78]

"The White House and Pentagon were on TV insisting that we'd won, that everything was under control, and we were just mopping up. But viewers in Panama would call to say that the fighting was going on in their front yard by the rose bushes," CNN executive Ed Turner said.[79]

As CNN provided this original coverage, its crews in Panama remained frustrated with their lack of access to news situations. Arnett, who had won a Pulitzer for his reporting in Vietnam, shook his head about the Pentagon's restrictions on journalists and told another newsman, "They got away with it again."

Members of the pool became so resigned to logistical problems that they coined two slogans: "Semper tardis" ("Always late," a takeoff on the Marine Corps motto "Semper fidelis") and "If it's news today it's news to us."[80]

"We took anything they sent our way — any crumb. We should have said, 'We don't want that. That's not news,'" Associated Press correspondent Steven Komarow said during a Cable-Satellite Public Affairs Network (C-SPAN) program about Operation Just Cause.[81]

SouthCom personnel acknowledged that lack of transportation and communications facilities were problems that the Pentagon should have foreseen, but maintained that problems also were created by the journalists themselves. The SouthCom after-action report pointed out that some journalists in the pool "were not experienced in military operations."[82] One reporter arrived wearing a tie, suspenders and a baseball cap. The report stated that a ground commander presented with reporters "dressed more for softball than field operations" might understandably consider the journalists too much of a risk to take along on a mission.[83]

Television journalists also presented special problems. The NBC team flew into Howard Air Force Base with more than 200 people and 30,000 pounds of equipment; unloading took more than four hours, and required the help of military personnel who were pulled from other duties.[84]

The special treatment that SouthCom public affairs personnel accorded one prominent broadcast journalist irritated military personnel and journalists alike. Both the after-action report and the Hoffman Report specifically mentioned ABC reporter Sam Donaldson.[85]

The reports apparently refer to an incident on Dec. 21, the day after the invasion started, when Donaldson, reporter Judd Rose and an ABC crew arrived at a U.S. base in Panama. They landed at 5 p.m., five hours before Donaldson was scheduled to present a report for PrimeTime Live. At that time, many pool reporters were having difficulties getting interviews and transportation. Nevertheless, according to Donaldson's own account, the ABC anchor called the U.S. embassy and arranged to interview the U.S. Ambassador there.[86] Col. Sconyers, SouthCom public affairs director, put Donaldson and his crew in a jeep and accompanied them to the embassy, with the crew shooting street footage along the way. When the interview was over, Donaldson was driven back to the base, where the crew had set up transmission equipment. He filed his report live at 10 p.m. and flew out early the next morning.[87]

Pool reporters and other journalists who had been confined to the base were enraged about the facilities and access that Donaldson had been provided. However, the Hoffman Report said Sconyers and his deputy indicated there was pressure from Washington to give Donaldson such treatment.[88]

Controlling Official Embarrassment

Another incident that led to problems between U.S. officials and the media was the decision by ABC, CBS and CNN on Dec. 21 to use a split screen showing simultaneous live coverage of President Bush's press conference about the invasion next to scenes of the return of the bodies of servicemen killed in Panama to Dover Air Force Base in Delaware. The President was shown bantering with reporters as the solemn ceremony at Dover progressed.

The White House was furious; spokesman Marlin Fitzwater called the action "outrageous and unfair."[89] Initially, media executives defended the decision. An ABC spokeswoman said, "We thought it was perfectly justified when he was talking about casualties."[90] Several news executives remarked that they were surprised at the president's light tone, and pointed out that the Dover ceremonies had been scheduled before the White House press appearance.[91]

At his Jan. 5, 1990 press conference, Bush asked that the networks inform him if they were going to use such a technique so he could "stop the proceedings." The

President said the White House had received "a lot of mail" from viewers who "thought their president, at a solemn moment like that, didn't give a damn. And I do, I do."[92] ABC News President Roone Arledge said through a spokesman that he agreed with Bush's complaint, reversing the network's previous position. CBS News President David Burke released a statement saying the network "understands President Bush's sensitivity," but added:

> CBS News had planned live coverage of the arrival ceremony long before the White House announced the press appearance [of President Bush] . . . . It was our judgment that we had the responsibility to broadcast live a brief portion of the arrival ceremony.[93]

CNN also stood by its decision to use the split screen.[94] One year later, after Operation Desert Storm began, the Bush administration barred journalists from Dover when the war dead arrived.

Another disagreement between U.S. officials and the press that may have had an impact later on Desert Storm media restrictions involved a newspaper story that SouthCom believed was inaccurate. The controversy began when reporters pressed public affairs officers for access to military women in the field. A number of female officers belonged to units that were in danger of being exposed to enemy fire. Many of these women were uncomfortable with repeated requests for interviews, because the media attention was creating tension in their units. SouthCom tried to ameliorate the situation by arranging a Jan. 1, 1990 press conference at which reporters could interview several women. One was Capt. Linda Bray, commander of an MP unit.

On Jan. 2, 1990, a story by Scripps Howard News Service correspondent Peter Copeland appeared in *The Washington Times*, a conservative newspaper in the nation's capital. Copeland reported that Bray and her unit had faced down 40 "heavily armed troops" in trying to secure one facility in Panama City, and later had found three dead enemy soldiers there.[95]

Copeland's story caused a "feeding frenzy" of media interest in Bray, according to the SouthCom after-action report.[96] Dozens of reporters demanded more information about the mission.[97]

Parts of Copeland's story were inaccurate, according to the after-action report. Bray and her unit had found no bodies, and Bray did not know how many troops her unit had faced during the action, the report said. When SouthCom officials asked Copeland about the story, he told them it was based on an interview he had conducted with Bray when he had met her in the field. Bray said she had a list of reporters with whom she had spoken, but could not recall speaking to Copeland, the report stated.[98]

When Copeland was asked about the after-action report during an interview for this study, he said he had talked with Bray and members of her unit *before* the press conference, and that a Pentagon official later had acknowledged that the story he had written was correct.[99] When Bray was interviewed for this study, she said the SouthCom statements about what had occurred during her unit's actions in Panama were correct, but she wanted to provide more context. Copeland had interviewed her, she said, but she could not remember the date.[100] She added that Copeland was wrong about the heavily armed troops and the bodies, but might have been given incorrect details about what had happened from other members of her unit.[101]

However, as a result of the controversy, SouthCom's after-action report recommended that during future operations, escorts should be present during all media interviews with military personnel. It stated:

> An interview should not be conducted without going through the proper PA [public affairs] channels, i.e., the Media Center, and without a PA representative present.[102]

This SouthCom recommendation calling for a more restrictive stance regarding the media was based not on concerns about operational security or troop safety, but on a dispute about accuracy. The incident involved information that was not a military secret, but could be expected to contribute to ongoing political controversy about whether women in the military should be allowed into situations that might involve hostile fire. Establishing media restrictions based on these criteria appears to go beyond the letter and the spirit of the Pentagon's guidelines. For example, Air Force public affairs policies state:

> Because the news media must be selective in their coverage, and often assume the role of government's skeptical observer or adversary, they may filter information in ways which can cause imbalance or inaccuracies. Nevertheless, Air Force media relations programs must be open and responsive within the bounds of national security, not withholding information simply because it is embarrassing to the Air Force.[103]

Despite such guidelines, the Bray incident may have reinforced Pentagon perceptions that a strict escort system — such as the type used during the Gulf War — was a necessity.

Post-invasion Criticism

Many of the other recommendations in the SouthCom and Hoffman reports focus not on problems caused by the media but on problems caused by the office of the Assistant Secretary of Defense for Public Affairs, which was responsible for organizing and coordinating the public affairs operation.

Hoffman severely criticized Williams, stating that the Assistant Secretary's lack of planning and acquiescence to Cheney's "excessive concern for secrecy" was largely responsible for the problems that journalists and SouthCom encountered.[104]

Hoffman also dismissed Pentagon and White House statements that media restrictions had been motivated by concerns for operational secrecy and journalists' safety. During previous national media pool deployments, "hundreds of newsmen and newswomen demonstrated that they could be trusted to respect essential ground rules, including operational security," the report stated. Safety considerations also "should not have been allowed to limit the pool's reporting opportunities. Newsmen and women cover wars at their own risk."[105]

The report ends with 17 recommendations calling for, among other things, additional public affairs planning; a policy directive from the Secretary of Defense detailing his support for the DOD national media pool and his insistence that other Pentagon officials support it; and better transportation and communication facilities for pool operations. Hoffman also called on Cheney to reissue and reaffirm support for the Principles of Information formulated by the Defense Department in the wake of criticism about the way the media had been handled during the Grenada invasion.

The SouthCom after-action report stated that dedicated transportation and communications facilities were essential, as were additional public affairs officers. "Six personnel cannot adequately support 500+ correspondents and maintain 24 hour operations at two locations," the report said.[106] The report recommended that PAOs be well-versed in current operations, and that extensive briefings be held daily for reporters.

"If DOD is going to assemble these [media pool] teams and ship them out, ground assets must be made available to support them," the report stated.[107]

An opportunity to implement these recommendations came sooner than many military officers expected. Less than seven months after Operation Just Cause ended, Operation Desert Shield began. □

THE WAR IN THE GULF

The Department's obligation to provide the public with information on its major programs may require detailed public affairs planning and coordination within the Department and with other government agencies.

Principles of Information
Defense Secretary Richard Cheney

Throughout July 1990, tensions between Kuwait and Iraq escalated. Iraqi leader Saddam Hussein charged the Kuwaiti government with flooding the international market with low-cost oil, costing Iraq billions of dollars in revenues. He also accused the Kuwaitis of taking too much oil from the Rumaila oil field along the disputed border between the two countries and demanded compensation. Kuwaiti officials retorted that Iraq's charges were unfounded. They said Saddam Hussein was trying to get Kuwait and other nations that had provided Iraq with assistance during its eight-year war with Iran to waive any right to repayment. On July 31, 1990, representatives of the two countries met in Saudi Arabia to try to resolve their differences, but the meeting broke up after acrimonious exchanges. On Aug. 1, Iraq invaded Kuwait, and within 24 hours, Hussein's troops had established control over the country.[1]

Following the invasion, President Bush issued statements condemning Iraq's "naked aggression," and calling for an unconditional withdrawal of Iraqi troops.[2] Noting that the United States received "close to 50 percent of our energy requirements" from the Middle East, the President said, "We remain committed to take whatever steps are necessary to defend our longstanding vital interests in the Gulf."[3]

On Aug. 2, President Bush initiated economic sanctions against Iraq. The United Nations took similar action four days later. The President also sent Defense Secretary Richard Cheney to Saudi Arabia, Kuwait's western neighbor and one of the most stable U.S. allies in the region. Saudi King Fahd accepted Cheney's offer to send U.S. troops to his country in hopes of deterring a possible Iraqi attack.

Operation Desert Shield Begins

On Aug. 6, President Bush ordered the deployment of the first U.S. forces to Saudi Arabia for Operation Desert Shield. In a nationwide address two days later, Bush emphasized that U.S. troops were being sent to Saudi Arabia in a "wholly defensive" role. His rhetoric made it clear, however, that he was keeping other options open. The President compared Iraq's takeover of Kuwait with the Nazi blitzkrieg in Europe in the 1930s, and Saddam Hussein with Adolf Hitler.[4] He warned that "a line has been drawn in the sand," and that anything less than an Iraqi withdrawal was unacceptable.[5]

Polls indicated strong initial support for the President's actions. For example, a *New York Times* poll showed that 74 percent of Americans approved of his decision.[6] However, some polls suggested that Americans felt what *Times* writer Michael Oreskes called "an undercurrent of anxiety and skepticism" that resulted from memories of the Vietnam War. Respondents who feared that President Bush's decision would lead the country into a lengthy war were less supportive of the U.S. deployment.[7] In addition, 4 in 10 respondents believed that the President had not clearly explained why U.S. troops had been sent to Saudi Arabia.[8]

On Aug. 7, the first troops left the United States for Saudi Arabia. Although this marked the beginning of what would become the largest U.S. military operation since the Vietnam War, not a single journalist accompanied the American forces. The Pentagon had not activated the press pool, and individual journalists had not been able to obtain Saudi visas.

News executives, editors and reporters were outraged that another troop deployment was taking place with no journalists accompanying the troops. A *New York Times* story, recalling that the pool had missed the initial stages of the invasion of Panama, noted:

> For the second time in eight months, American troops today headed into a foreign military operation without the special contingent of reporters and photographers that the Pentagon has pledged to summon when United States forces are sent abroad.[9]

At a press conference the next day, President Bush, who in 1989 had questioned the ability of the DOD national media pool to protect operational security before the Panama invasion, indicated that he was not disturbed by the absence of news media. "I'm glad that . . . many forces could be moved with not too much advance warning [to Iraq], and with not too much, therefore, risk to Saudi Arabia or to these troops," he said.[10] He dismissed journalists' complaints about being left behind, saying, "there's plenty of reporters in Saudi Arabia right now."[11]

That was not the case. At the time, not a single U.S. reporter was in Saudi Arabia. The country historically has controlled its press and not allowed Western journalists to spend much time there.

Journalists Complain About Lack of Access

When angry reporters pressed Defense Secretary Cheney about why the pool had not been activated, he said jokingly, "It's Pete's fault," referring to Assistant Secretary of Defense for Public Affairs Pete Williams.[12]

Williams said that he wasn't sure the DOD national media pool should be sent to Saudi Arabia because "We are not going in there the same way we went into Panama."[13] In addition, Desert Shield did not involve two of the "essential elements" that triggered deployment of the pool — combat and the need to preserve secrecy before an operation began.[14]

Cheney and Williams also said that the Saudi government's reluctance to admit reporters was a major obstacle to sending U.S. journalists, including pool reporters, to the Gulf. They said they were trying to convince the Saudis to change their policy and admit U.S. media personnel.[15]

Some journalists, however, were skeptical of the Pentagon's efforts. *Los Angeles Times* Washington Bureau Chief Jack Nelson stated in an Aug. 9 *Washington Post* story:

> I don't buy [the Defense Department's] rationale, just as I don't buy the rationale that they didn't mean to lock up our pool in Panama. It was carefully orchestrated by the Defense Department to keep us from getting in and reporting the realities of what happened there. They made a big thing after Panama saying they would correct it and they haven't.[16]

Journalists were not the only ones critical of the DOD decision to exclude reporters from the early stages of the deployment. Fred S. Hoffman, who had criticized Cheney and Williams in his report on the Pentagon's news operations during the invasion of Panama, told the Senate Governmental Affairs Committee during February 1991 hearings on media restrictions in the Gulf:

> In my view, the national media pool should have been sent to Saudi Arabia with the first deploying U.S. troops last August. But it wasn't.
>
> The circumstances for using the pool were just right then — U.S. troops were moving into a remote area; there were few, if any, American news personnel on the ground in Saudi Arabia at the time and there was the potential for fighting.[17]

News executives and reporters also wondered why the pool or another group of U.S. reporters had not been taken to U.S. Navy ships operating in or bound for the Middle East. They reminded the Pentagon that pool reporters had accompanied these ships when the U.S. escorted Kuwaiti ships endangered by the Iran-Iraq war in 1987. Williams said he would try to get reporters on ships "as soon as possible."[18]

Meanwhile, news executives met with Saudi Embassy officials, seeking permission to send staffers to the Gulf kingdom. Editors also told Pentagon officials that it was in the Bush administration's best interests to ensure that U.S. reporters reached the scene quickly, especially in light of the public's mixed reaction to the U.S. deployments. In an Aug. 10, 1990 *New York Times* piece, Executive Editor Max Frankel stated:

> A major military exercise cannot succeed without the sustained support and understanding of the American people, and it will not long be supported or understood without extensive and close-up news reporting.[19]

The DOD National Media Pool Arrives in the Gulf

The Defense Department eventually obtained Saudi visas for the 17 members of the DOD national media pool, which was deployed on Aug. 12, five days after the first troop deployment. After stopping in Tampa, Fla., where pool members received a briefing from Gen. H. Norman Schwarzkopf, the journalists arrived in Dhahran, Saudi Arabia, on Aug. 13.

The pool was accompanied by several military personnel under the supervision of Navy Capt. Mike Sherman, an experienced public affairs officer who had spent part of his childhood in Saudi Arabia, where his father worked for an oil company. In an interview for this study, Capt. Sherman said Williams left the details of the media operation to his discretion. The only specific guidance he received were the DOD pool rules and instructions from Williams to "take the news media out and show them what we're doing."[20]

Capt. Sherman set up the Pentagon's Joint Information Bureau (JIB) in the Dhahran International Hotel. His operation would be responsible for helping journalists cover the activities of military units in the field in the coming months. Another JIB, at Central Command in Riyadh, would provide military briefings and information about the buildup for reporters.

Capt. Sherman equipped the JIB with one computer that he borrowed from the hotel's chef, and another that he got from the marketing manager. He obtained a fax and a copier from other military units. Aside from the need for more equipment, he faced several other serious problems. There were no foreign news bureaus in Saudi Arabia, and no infrastructure to handle the influx of U.S. and other international media. In a series of meetings with Saudi officials, Capt. Sherman worked out an arrangement for the Saudis to provide accreditation for journalists. The U.S. military would register media personnel, provide ground rules, and ask correspondents to sign a form agreeing to abide by these rules.[21]

The DOD media pool worked in Saudi Arabia for two weeks, and members praised the access and cooperation they received. Capt. Sherman and his personnel "were doing a hell of a job," CNN reporter Carl Rochelle told a National Press Club forum after the war.[22] "If you could see it, if you could find it, you could do it."[23] However, Rochelle pointed out, there were some things "we couldn't find," and the resulting friction presaged the future problems that would confront journalists and JIB personnel. Pool members never were granted access to crews of F-117s or B-52s. They submitted repeated requests to do a story on the AWACS, an aircraft with sophisticated command, control and communications equipment. Air Force officials were reluctant to allow journalists aboard the AWACS because "they were sure that we were going to reveal classified material," Rochelle told the Press Club forum. When officials finally relented and allowed journalists to write about the aircraft, "they loved the story . . . . They were happy that they let us do that. But they didn't learn any lessons from it," Rochelle said.[24]

The AWACS story was not the only instance in which pool reporters showed that they were sensitive to operational security concerns, the CNN reporter said. Shortly after arriving in the Gulf, journalists learned that there were not yet enough U.S. troops in the area to withstand an Iraqi attack if Saddam Hussein decided to move into Saudi Arabia. They did not report this information. Rochelle told the Press Club audience, "I think you've heard Gen. Schwarzkopf talk about how grateful he was that we didn't reveal how minimal the U.S. presence was in the early days.

That was part of the restrictions that we accepted as being able to cover what was going on in that area."[25]

The pool was disbanded on Aug. 26, 1990, after more than 300 U.S. and foreign journalists had arrived in Saudi Arabia.

Unilateral Coverage of Desert Shield

JIB personnel turned their attention to establishing procedures for independent, unilateral news coverage. Journalists arriving in Saudi Arabia submitted story requests to JIB public affairs officers (PAOs), who arranged trips and interviews. Journalists were taken to units in groups, because transportation and military personnel who could act as escorts were limited, but filed only for their own news organizations.

Journalists were told not to visit military units on their own, because field commanders did not want dozens of reporters and photographers driving unidentified vehicles in their areas, or taking the unit's time with unexpected visits. The military high command also did not want to have to commit resources to looking for news personnel who became lost in the desert.[26]

Reporting limitations were exacerbated by the fact that the JIB was overwhelmed by thousands of story requests submitted by hundreds of reporters, Capt. Sherman said. He added that repeated requests to Central Command for more vehicles and equipment elicited little response.[27]

These prohibitions and limitations resulted in numerous complaints from journalists, leading some reporters to refuse to sign the ground rules agreement, and to strike out on their own. Some of these reporters did not have much experience covering military affairs, and had little knowledge about what types of information would compromise security, according to JIB personnel. This, in turn, eroded commanders' confidence in the media, Capt. Sherman said.[28]

Journalists had their own complaints. James LeMoyne, a *New York Times* correspondent whose family includes military officers and who had covered previous conflicts, said in a *Times* article and an interview for this study that Pentagon officials closely monitored all news coverage of Desert Shield.[29] Press officers let reporters know that if they asked hard questions, they would be perceived as "anti-military" by Armed Forces personnel, he said.[30] Correspondents who wrote critical stories also jeopardized future requests for interviews with field commanders.[31] After LeMoyne wrote a story in October 1990 that quoted U.S. troops questioning President Bush's policies and reasons behind the U.S. presence in Saudi Arabia, many print reporters were denied access to Army units for more than a month, he said. An interview between LeMoyne and Gen. Schwarzkopf was canceled. Although the head of Central Command gave interviews to other reporters, it was six weeks until LeMoyne's interview was rescheduled. Gen. Schwarzkopf apologized during the interview, telling LeMoyne that the delay had been unavoidable. The reporter said such experiences "effectively dampened critical reporting" among the U.S. press corps.[32]

Journalists also complained that some escorts were intrusive, telling military personnel not to answer certain types of questions and stopping some television interviews "because they did not like what was being portrayed," LeMoyne said. These problems caused so much resentment that in October 1990, 18 print reporters wrote a letter of complaint to Gen. Schwarzkopf, Joint Chiefs of Staff Chairman Gen. Colin Powell and Defense Secretary Cheney. In an interview for this study, LeMoyne said the letter had little effect, and that he regretted that journalists had not taken a harder line with Defense Department officials:

> I have since re-read that letter and I'm astounded as to how polite we were. The letter is so diplomatic, and we bent over backwards so far to be nice. If I had it all to do over again, I'd be really forceful about it. . . . If every major media organization said, "We won't accept these rules" and [had] made a stink about it in November, I really don't think the Pentagon would have done what it did.[33]

Public affairs officers interviewed for this study did not think that some of LeMoyne's criticisms were valid. Central Command Public Affairs Officer Capt. Ron Wildermuth stated in an interview for this study that Gen. Schwarzkopf had not canceled his interview with LeMoyne because of critical stories. However, Capt. Wildermuth and other PAOs agreed that the lack of JIB resources and inexperienced escorts hurt journalists' efforts to cover the buildup.[34]

The Hometown Program

While journalists based in Dhahran were becoming more bitter about the military's assertions that personnel and transportation shortages were limiting access to the field, Pentagon officials were authorizing the Military Airlift Command (MAC) to fly journalists from small- and medium-sized print and broadcast operations to the Gulf, and providing them with short, supervised visits with their hometown units.

This effort, which began in August and was known as the Hometown Program, was based on a highly successful prototype used by the Defense Department during the Vietnam War. While the program was in effect during Operation Desert Shield, more than 150 journalists were flown free to Saudi Arabia on military aircraft for two-to-four-day trips to visit their local units.[35] Although Hometown participants were not supposed to cover other units or activities, the Office of the Assistant Secretary of Defense for Public Affairs directed command and base public affairs officers in Saudi Arabia to "arrange media events . . . such as visits to field hospitals, AWACS aircraft, etc. if deemed appropriate."[36]

After President Bush increased the U.S. military presence in Saudi Arabia in November 1990, the Office of the Assistant Secretary of Defense for Public Affairs issued another message, calling the Hometown Program "an increasingly crucial element in the DOD effort to keep the American public — and particularly the families and communities of our forces deployed in support of Operation Desert Shield — informed about the missions and accomplishments of our armed forces in this massive operation."[37]

Reporters for the networks and large publications were furious that local reporters who were concentrating on what reporters call "Hi, Mom" stories were getting better access to units than correspondents based in Dhahran. Some local reporters whose publications and broadcast outlets had sent them to the Gulf independently as correspondents also were angry, because military officials would not help them hook up with hometown units. Stephanie Glass, who spent weeks in Saudi Arabia for the *San Antonio Light*, said in an interview for this study that she had covered military-affairs stories for the paper, and had made informal arrangements to meet military personnel after arriving in Dhahran. She said the Joint Information Bureau provided no assistance, even after she called back to a unit in Texas and asked them to intervene. She finally found members of local units by going to a Dhahran supermarket and asking soldiers leaving the store whether they were from San Antonio.[38]

The program was phased out on Jan. 6, 1991, shortly before the war began, because the Pentagon needed the available public affairs personnel and resources to handle the influx of journalists arriving to cover the conflict.[39]

Special Access for Special Projects

Hometown media operations were not the only organizations to receive special treatment from the Defense Department. At least one private video production company also got special access to units in the field. A Minneapolis-based firm called Quantum Diversified received free air travel from the Defense Department and preferential access to units in Saudi Arabia because it was working on a video about the National Guard that Pentagon personnel believed would present a positive image of the U.S. military presence in the Gulf.

A message from the National Guard Bureau Public Affairs Office to U.S. Central Command in September 1990 said that Douglas Mattson, head of the Quantum production team, "needs to photograph as many units as he can in Saudi Arabia" and "has approval from the Secretary of Defense for Public Affairs and the National Guard Bureau to complete this work."[40] U.S. Central Command sent a message to military officers asking them to cooperate on the project, which they described as having "far reaching scope."[41] An Oct. 2, 1990 message from the Minnesota Air Reserve Center to U.S. Central Command states that the Quantum project "is for multiple uses: internal, Public Broadcast System, recruiting etc."[42]

The National Guard and Office of the Assistant Secretary of Defense for Public Affairs helped the Quantum crew — which was supported by private funding obtained from what one DOD official called "well-financed patriots"[43] — acquire Saudi visas and transportation to the Gulf. The Guard also provided a public affairs escort for the October 1990 trip, which included stops at bases in Germany and Spain as well as Saudi Arabia.[44]

Maj. Robert Dunlap, who works in the National Guard Bureau's Public Affairs Office in the Pentagon, said the Bureau and Pete Williams' office were willing to help Mattson because "he wasn't one of these guys that was going to slip over there and, you know, in a fly-by-night operation cover the war, and put out a bunch of bad news stories."[45]

Quantum Diversified also received assistance for their project from NFL Films, which produces videos of National Football League games, and from Northern

Lights Communications of Minneapolis, whose most-publicized previous project was an 800-number hotline that Indianapolis 500 fans could call to listen to the conversations between drivers and pit crews.

In an interview for this study, Maj. Dunlap said the Guard would work with organizations as long as their script "is going to not put us in an unfavorable light. I mean, it doesn't make any sense to give someone help when they're going to make you look like a bunch of buffoons."[46]

When Quantum Diversified wanted to go back to the Gulf last March to get additional footage of U.S. forces after the ground war had ended, they received additional help from the Broadcast Pictorial Branch of the Directorate for Defense Information, part of Williams' office. On March 1, 1991, Army Lt. Col. Steven M. Titunik, Chief of the Branch, wrote a letter to Mattson saying his office would provide U.S. Central Command with a recommendation that "they assist you in shooting the video material you seek for your production(s)."[47] The letter refers to the project as one or more videos that would be produced by Quantum Diversified, Northern Lights Communications and NFL Films "highlighting Operation Desert Storm for free distribution to all families who had an immediate family member serving in the Operation."[48]

The letter stated that the Defense Department would make a final review of the Quantum Diversified tape, which could be used for commercial purposes.[49]

Lt. Col. Titunik also sent a letter to the Public Affairs Office of the Military Airlift Command (MAC), asking their assistance in getting Mattson's crew to the Gulf.[50] Capt. David S. Wirwahn, the State Public Affairs Officer for the Minnesota Air Reserve National Guard, also wrote to MAC, requesting that they receive transportation to the Gulf. Capt. Wirwahn — who left the Guard and worked for Quantum Diversified for a time — said the video crew was "operating on a special OASD/PA command information mission and is not associated with conventional media."[51]

On March 21, 1991, U.S. Central Command sent a memorandum to the Office of the Assistant Secretary of Defense for Public Affairs, as well as to Army, Air Force, Marine Corps and Navy officials, granting theater clearance for Quantum Diversified personnel so they could "obtain video coverage of U.S. military units which participated in Desert Storm."[52]

In an interview for this study, Lt. Col. Titunik said Quantum Diversified had gotten "the exact same support" as other video production firms. "If you have a script and you want some material and you're factual and you're truthful and you have a rational point of view, we assist you."[53]

Lt. Col. Titunik said he first learned about the project in a Feb. 18 letter from the head of NFL Films, Steve Sabol, who said he wanted to work with Quantum Diversified and Northern Lights to produce a series of "energy-packed patriotic presentations" that would "uplift and inspire."[54] A later letter from Quantum Diversified spoke of the video as a "positive picture" that would be made "out of tribute" to the U.S. forces who served in the Gulf, Lt. Col. Titunik said.[55]

He stated that Quantum Diversified "went over to the Middle East just like anybody else would have done, you know. No one provided them anything, anything that anybody else didn't get."⁵⁶ Lt. Col. Titunik said several private companies received Pentagon technical assistance on Gulf War videos. He said the Pentagon helps any firm "as long as it's not some weirdo group like the KKK or the Nazi Party or the Aryan Nation or some oddball group, but once they tell us who they are and who they represent and what they want to do, if it's feasible and if it's in the best interest and if it also promotes the understanding, we don't have difficulty as long as it's not going to cost the government money."⁵⁷

In an interview for this study, Mattson stated that Quantum Diversified's entire interest in the project involved the production and distribution of a video that the firm would distribute free to U.S. military personnel who had served in Desert Storm. He declined to discuss who was funding the project. Richard Fons, Chief Executive Officer of Northern Lights Communications, which has been affiliated with Quantum Diversified, said the two organizations had severed their relationship with NFL Films, although that company still had some video footage from the project.⁵⁸ NFL Films Public Relations Director Kathy Davis said the company was looking for corporate financing to finish their video.⁵⁹

President Bush Lays the Groundwork for War

Throughout September and October 1990, the percentage of Americans who endorsed the President's decision to send troops to the Middle East declined, and his overall approval rating slipped more than 20 points.⁶⁰ By early November there also were signs that the U.S.-led multinational coalition that was pressuring Iraq to withdraw from Kuwait was beginning to fragment because of disagreements about what measures to take.

On Nov. 8, 1990, two days after the midterm elections, Bush announced that he was deploying additional troops to Saudi Arabia "to prepare for a possible offensive option" to ensure that "aggression against Kuwait will not stand" if international economic sanctions were not effective in pressuring Iraq to withdraw.⁶¹ It marked the President's first public departure from previous pronouncements that the U.S. military mission in Saudi Arabia was strictly defensive. He stated that he would prefer to act under the authorization of the United Nations, but that the United States was prepared to act unilaterally if necessary.⁶²

The President's remarks drew mixed reactions from Congress and the public. Opinion polls showed that a majority of respondents still backed the President's actions concerning Iraq, but protests against a military solution in the Gulf increased, and the President found himself faced with hecklers at public speeches.

To counteract eroding public support, the White House began a campaign to convince the public that a U.S. offensive might be necessary to preserve U.S. interests and stability in the Middle East, and to return the country to the Kuwaiti people. The Bush administration's efforts were reinforced by a public relations and lobbying campaign run by private U.S. firms hired by the Kuwaiti government.

Kuwaitis Spend Millions on Campaign to Encourage Intervention

Immediately after the invasion, the Kuwaiti government asked the United States to use military intervention to oust Iraqi troops. On Aug. 2, 1990, Kuwait's ambassador to the United States told reporters that his government had asked the Bush administration for military assistance, and that "we expect our friends to stand by us."[63] The Kuwaitis were encouraged when the President sent troops to Saudi Arabia, but they wanted to ensure that the United States kept an offensive option open in case the Iraqis did not withdraw.

On Aug. 20, 1990, a group of Kuwaiti government representatives hired Hill and Knowlton, one of the most influential public relations firms in the United States, to convince Congress and the public to support U.S. military involvement in the crisis. The Kuwaitis thought that Hill and Knowlton might be especially sympathetic to their cause when they read an Aug. 16 commentary in *USA Today* written Robert Dilenschneider, President and Chief Executive Officer of Hill and Knowlton/USA, which criticized the media for publishing widely diverse opinions about U.S. military options in the Gulf. Recalling the World War II slogan, "loose lips sink ships," Dilenschneider urged the media to stand behind the President. He wrote:

> Let's keep the public informed and even chart progress via the media. But President Bush and his strategists need all the help they can get. . . . Let's stop giving Saddam the benefit of our best thinking and give those we have entrusted with our defense all the help and tools they need to do the job.[64]

Another advantage the Kuwaitis had in hiring Hill and Knowlton was that many of its executives had served in the Reagan and Bush administrations. One was Craig Fuller, the company's new President and Chief Operating Officer of Public Affairs/Worldwide, who had been Vice President Bush's chief of staff.

From August until January, Hill and Knowlton ran an extensive public relations campaign for the Kuwaitis. In a foreign agents registration statement filed with the Justice Department, Hill and Knowlton officials said they had developed press kits that were sent to reporters, members of Congress and federal officials; coordinated print and broadcast interviews; and organized a group called Americans for a Free Kuwait.[65] The firm, which was paid more than $10 million for its efforts, also provided

> . . . general monitoring of congressional activities with regard to the Persian Gulf crisis, including coverage of congressional debate, committee action, and public statements of members. Registrant contacted congressional staff members, chiefly of leadership offices . . . to provide information relative to Kuwait.[66]

In an interview for this study, Hill and Knowlton executive Nathaniel Clevenger said that the firm also sent more than two dozen video news releases (VNRs) to more than 700 television stations around the world.[67] Clevenger said Hill and

Knowlton got footage from Kuwaiti government contacts in the Gulf and then made editorial decisions "as to what was to be seen and what was not to be seen. Or what needed to be seen."[68] Many U.S. stations ran the releases as straight news, without identifying the source of the footage or script information because of their "trust" in Hill and Knowlton's news judgment, Clevenger said.[69]

During the fall and winter, the Kuwaiti government also hired other firms to help with the lobbying and PR effort. By December 1990, as Congress was considering whether to authorize President Bush to use military force to push Iraqi troops out of Kuwait, a half-dozen firms were promoting the Kuwaiti agenda with Congress and the American people. For example, the Kuwaiti government paid Neill and Company $50,000 a month to provide:

> . . . advice and information on issues in the United States Congress relating to the development of U.S. policy in the Persian Gulf and. . . .legislative advisory services to the Embassy of Kuwait to promote and strengthen the relations between the government of Kuwait and the United States.[70]

Members of Congress from both parties were outraged by the situation. Rep. Jimmy Hayes (D-La.) stated that it should be illegal for foreign governments to run a "war lobby" and to "buy" U.S. public opinion. He and other lawmakers vowed to support tougher legislation to increase reporting requirements for U.S. firms working for these governments and their representatives.[71]

The Pentagon-Press Battle Heats Up as War Nears

Three weeks after President Bush announced he was doubling the size of the U.S. force in the Gulf to prepare for possible offensive action, the United Nations passed a resolution giving Iraq until Jan. 15, 1991 to comply with previous U.N. demands that Iraqi forces leave Kuwait. After that date, U.S. and coalition forces would be authorized to use "all necessary means" to force Iraq to withdraw.[72] In the wake of these events, editors and bureau chiefs in Washington began meeting with Williams to discuss pool arrangements and ground rules if combat occurred. They also wanted to ensure that the Pentagon would provide transportation to the Gulf for additional media personnel, because commercial flights probably would be canceled. The debate that these meetings engendered foreshadowed the problems that would face both the Pentagon and the press during Operation Desert Storm.

On Dec. 14, 1990, Williams sent Washington news executives who had Pentagon reporters on their staffs a memorandum that included a draft of proposed pool procedures and media ground rules that would go into effect if war broke out.[73] In his memo, Williams said that the Pentagon would fly 120 additional media personnel to Saudi Arabia in the event of hostilities, and enclosed a list of how many personnel each medium would be permitted.[74]

The pool procedures were to be implemented in three phases. Phase I, which would begin immediately, would involve two pools that would be formed by the Dhahran JIB from media personnel already in Saudi Arabia. These pools would go on trial deployments at least once every two weeks so journalists could "familiarize themselves with troops and equipment, cover activities in the areas to which the pools are sent, and exercise their ability to file news stories from the field," the plan said.[75]

Phase II would involve deploying the two pools when hostilities were imminent, so they would be in place to cover the first stages of combat. If it were not feasible to move the pools into the field, they would be taken to forward positions as quickly as conditions permitted. Additional pools would be deployed "as soon as possible" to expand coverage. The size of these new pools "will be determined by the availability of transportation and other operational factors," the contingency plan said.[76]

All pool material would undergo security review by military escorts in the field before being transmitted to Dhahran.[77]

The plan stated that Phase III would begin "when open coverage is possible and would provide for unilateral coverage of activities. The pools would be disbanded and all media would operate independently, although under U.S. Central Command escort."[78]

The proposed ground rules were 2-1/2 pages long. One provision said that all interviews with members of the Armed Services would be on the record, effectively prohibiting reporters from conducting background or off-the-record interviews with military personnel. Another stipulated that journalists "must remain with your military escort at all times, until released, and follow instructions regarding your activities."[79]

The proposed ground rules told reporters what types of information they could and could not release. The latter category included information regarding future operations, information on intelligence collection activities and ongoing operations against hostile targets, and information about postponed or canceled operations.[80]

News Executives Criticize Proposed Rules

Williams' memorandum unleashed a torrent of criticism from news editors and executives. *New York Times* Washington Editor Howell Raines wrote in a Dec. 21 letter to Williams that the proposals were "unacceptably restrictive" and that some provisions "seem to be in direct contradiction to our group discussions at the Pentagon."[81]

Many media executives objected strenuously to the ground rules. In a letter to Williams, Knight-Ridder Washington Bureau Chief Clark Hoyt stated:

> The proposed rules far overstep the common-sense bounds necessary to protect the security of U.S. military operations. The specific rules about what is "releasable" and "not releasable" are at once so broad and so vague that they are bound to lead to disagreement and misinterpretation even now, in advance of war. On the field, under combat conditions, the potential for misunderstanding and inconsistent interpretation is enormous.[82]

The proposal requiring media escorts even after unilateral coverage had gone into effect also provoked angry responses. *Washington Post* Assistant Managing Editor for Foreign News Michael Getler wrote in a Dec. 18 letter to Williams that this idea seemed to be "simply another means of controlling everything."[83]

The proposed security reviews also were criticized. Hearst Newspapers Washington Bureau Chief Charles J. Lewis wrote in a Dec. 20 letter to Williams that such reviews went beyond the spirit and provisions of the Sidle Report, which had been prepared by military and media personnel after the invasion of Grenada and was supposed to be the blueprint for the Pentagon's wartime media policies. Lewis wrote:

> I'm sorry to see on-site "security review" in your plans. As you know, when the national Pentagon pool was first launched in 1984 [as a result of the Sidle Report], no such reviews were contemplated. Correspondents were to comply with the "Vietnam-era rules," which didn't require prior review. . . . Those rules won a very high degree of compliance.
>
> Unfortunately, the practice of prior censorship has become embedded in the Pentagon pool concept in recent years, mainly because all parties quickly recognized that the pool was reliant on military communications.[84]

Bureau Chiefs Fight for Pentagon Privileges

Williams' memo also sparked another disagreement that revealed the divisiveness and competition among the press corps, factors that later would undermine efforts to present a united front against media restrictions during the war. A number of news executives believed their organizations had not been allocated enough seats on the plane that Williams said the Pentagon would provide to fly media personnel to Dhahran if war broke out.[85] An intense lobbying campaign ensued as media executives fought to secure space for their personnel. Clark Hoyt of Knight-Ridder protested that his organization, which represented 28 newspapers with a combined daily circulation of 3 million, had been allocated only two seats, while individual newspapers, such as *The New York Times* and *The Washington Post*, had received three seats each.[86] *Newsday* Washington Bureau Chief Gaylord Shaw was unhappy that his newspaper had been given only one seat, pointing out that *Newsday*'s commitment to Gulf coverage "has equalled or exceeded some newspapers on the list that were granted two or three seats on the flight."[87] KFWB News, a Group W radio station in Los Angeles that twice had sent reporters to cover the U.S. buildup in the Gulf, protested that it had not been allocated any seats.[88]

According to journalists and former military officials interviewed for this study, the bickering undermined the media's independence and ability to confront the Pentagon effectively.

"The fight over who would get how many seats on the plane showed Pentagon officials well before the war how dependent even the larger, well-financed media were going to be on DOD facilities," said one journalist who covers the Pentagon and asked not to be identified.[89] "It sent a signal that although bureau chiefs and reporters might make a great deal of noise about media restrictions, they would never take a united, hard line against whatever media restrictions the Pentagon finally decided to put in place, because they didn't want to lose whatever favors DOD might bestow — favors that could give a competing newspaper or network an advantage."[90]

The Military Revises the Proposed Rules

Military officials said in interviews for this study that they changed the pool procedures and ground rules in the wake of journalists' criticism. Col. Bill Mulvey, Director of the Dhahran JIB during the war, said in an interview for this study that PAOs in the Gulf realized after discussions with correspondents that many of the restrictions could not be justified on the grounds that they protected operational security. He and other JIB personnel "really sort of laughed at ourselves for even putting them in in the first place," he said.[91]

On Jan. 4, 1991, Williams again met with the news executives, and on Jan. 7, he issued a memorandum with revised ground rules and guidelines that incorporated some of their suggestions.[92] The rules had been reduced to one page and no longer told reporters what information they would be permitted to release. The security-review process was still in place, but included a specific proviso that pool reports and visuals would be reviewed only "to determine if they contain information that would jeoparidize an operation or the security of U.S. or coalition forces. Material will not be withheld just because it is embarrassing or contains criticism."[93]

The guidelines also provided details about the security-review appeals process. If a reporter disagreed with a military escort's decision to change or delete parts of a story, the material would be sent to the Dhahran JIB for a review by the Director. If the disagreement could not be resolved at that time, the material would be forwarded to Williams, who would review it with the appropriate bureau chief.[94]

In his memo, Williams told news executives that he agreed with many of the criticisms of the earlier versions of the ground rules and guidelines. He wrote:

> You will note that we eliminated many of the earlier proposed ground rules, especially those which would have failed the critical test for combat ground rules: whether that information would jeopardize the operation, endanger friendly forces, or be of use to the enemy. As many of you noted, while every military operation has unique characteristics, past experience shows that reporters understand their heavy responsibility in covering combat. In the end, it is that professionalism upon which we will depend.[95]

Williams also revised the allocation of seats on the military plane that would fly supplemental news personnel to the Gulf. In his memo he allocated an additional seat to Knight-Ridder and *Newsday*, and provided a total of four seats to media that had not been included on the first list. *USA Today* received two of those seats, and *Business Week* and Voice of America were allocated one each.[96]

Media Executives Criticize the New Pentagon Proposals

Williams' Jan. 7 memo set off a new round of protests. Many editors and media executives disagreed with Williams' assertion that the Pentagon planned to rely on journalists' sense of responsibility and professionalism. They noted that key provisions which they previously had objected to — such as the requirement that journalists stay with military escorts at all times and follow all the escorts' instructions — had not been changed. They also protested that the security-review process was overly restrictive, and amounted to de facto censorship. *New York Times* editor Raines wrote in a Jan. 8, 1991 letter that the ground rules and guidelines "remain fundamentally flawed," and that the idea of a constant escort "was never accepted by or even discussed with our group."[97] He wrote:

> [the ground rules] can only be interpreted as an effort to impose a rigid censorship in place of a common-sense understanding about specific disclosures that would endanger lives. *By combining these categories of reportable information with the requirement for a "security review," you have created a system of censorship* unlike anything in recent combat history. [Emphasis is Raines's.][98]

The American Society of Newspaper Editors also criticized the security-review proposal. ASNE President Burl Osborne and Larry Kramer, a representative of the ASNE Press, Bar and Public Affairs Committee, sent a letter to Williams on Jan. 8, 1991 to "strongly protest" the review system.[99] The letter stated:

> In a world where "spin control" of the news has become commonplace, this form of prior restraint is a tool to gain control over what the American public sees or hears from the battlefield. There was no such prior review in Vietnam, and there were few security breaches of any consequence.[100]

The Society of Professional Journalists sent a letter expressing similar views to Defense Secretary Cheney, stating that the security-review provision "turns military personnel into editors and producers and constitutes an unnecessary prior restraint on the news."[101]

The presidents of the three network news operations and CNN sent a joint letter to Defense Secretary Cheney stating that the proposed ground rules and guidelines went "far beyond what is required to protect troop safety and mission security."[102] They charged that the security review would "set up cumbersome barriers to timely and responsible reporting" and would compromise "the free flow of information with official intrusion and government oversight."[103]

In a Jan. 8 letter to Williams, *Washington Post* Assistant Managing Editor Getler prophesied what would happen if the review system were put in place:

> . . . it will cause a nightmare for us and, ultimately, for you and the American public. It will inevitably, from day one of hostilities, involve grim fights between reporters and PAO's. It will involve missed deadlines

on stories that had no right to be withheld or delayed. It will poison the atmosphere between the press and the Pentagon and erode credibility to the point where there will be widespread mistrust of that information that is put out in Washington or Riyadh by the Defense Department.[104]

Editors and executives also were concerned because the new ground rules and guidelines made no mention of unilateral coverage, leading some news executives to fear that pools would be used throughout hostilities.

They also were alarmed by a new provision that said reporters who tried to initiate unilateral coverage would "not be permitted into forward areas" and that commanders "will exclude from the area of operation all unauthorized individuals."[105]

At a Jan. 10, 1991 Pentagon press briefing, *Newsday* reporter Patrick J. Sloyan asked Williams whether this meant that reporters who tried to make contact with units on their own would be arrested.[106] "I don't know that I would call it arrest," Williams said, explaining that correspondents trying to work outside the pools would be "escorted back to a rear unit, and as soon as possible, back to Dhahran."[107]

The Pentagon Makes Final Adjustments

As a result of the criticism, Pentagon officials again revised the guidelines, but left the ground rules essentially unchanged. The final versions of both were released Jan. 15, 1991.

The escort provision was less restrictive, stating that an escort "may be required because of security, safety, and mission requirements as determined by the host commander" at U.S. tactical or field locations and encampments.[108]

The revised guidelines also provided more detail about what escorts would be looking for in security reviews. The new language said materials would be reviewed "to determine if they contain sensitive information about military plans, capabilities, operations, or vulnerabilities . . . that would jeopardize the outcome of an operation or the safety of U.S. or coalition forces."[109]

The appeals process was changed so that journalists retained final control over whether information would be printed. If there were a disagreement about a pool report in the field, it would be sent "immediately" to Dhahran (not just "expeditiously," as the previous version had stated), and would be reviewed not only by the JIB Director but also by "the appropriate news media representative." If no agreement were reached, the material would be forwarded "immediately" to Washington for review by Williams and the appropriate bureau chief. The revised guidelines stated that "the ultimate decision on publication will be made by the originating reporter's news organization."[110]

Williams Defends the Ground Rules and Guidelines

Williams vigorously defended the ground rules and guidelines in public appearances. In an appearance on ABC-TV's *Good Morning America*, he said they represented "an evolution" of the rules put into effect as a result of the Sidle Report. Combat pools in the Gulf were an "extension" of the DOD national media pool, and were necessary in part because of the "enormous number of reporters" who were in Dhahran waiting to see whether hostilities would occur.[111] An ABC commentator asked whether Williams could guarantee that if a major operation began, the press would be in a position to see it. The Assistant Secretary of Defense — who 10 months earlier had been severely criticized in the Hoffman Report for acquiescing to Cheney's plan to delay the DOD national media pool so it missed the initial fighting in Panama — replied:

> Absolutely. That is the whole goal of this operation. And what we have to do is, I think we've learned our lesson from Panama, where [we] took reporters down and treated them to a briefing on the history of the Panama Canal while some of the operation was still going on. And that is unacceptable. What we're doing is a very thorough planning of this. We learned our lesson from Panama. We're gonna sit down and make the media pool plan match the operational plan.[112]

Williams picked up support from former CBS newsman and anchor Walter Cronkite, who said, "I don't think these [restrictions] are so unreasonable. I think that they're workable."[113] Cronkite said he did consider the security reviews a form of censorship, "but censorship is required in a military operation of this kind and I don't think most of the press really objects to that."[114]

Cronkite added that he thought "vigilance . . . is absolutely essential" to ensure that the military lived up to its pledge that security reviews and appeals would be handled swiftly. He said the escort question was "very difficult," but that journalists would need help with transportation in a desert environment, and if the escorts allowed journalists to report freely, the system could work.[115]

In a teleconference with PAOs in Dhahran and Riyadh four days before the war began, Williams explained in detail how the guidelines and ground rules were supposed to work.

He explained that escorts were to act as facilitators, getting reporters where they needed to be, answering questions about units and performing security reviews. He reminded the PAOs that escorts should "keep their eye on the general picture" and not try to be with a reporter every second because "it's possible to escort someone to death."[116] On the other hand, journalists "can't just sort of say, 'Thank you for getting me here, I'll catch you later.' That's not permissible. They just can't be wandering off, vanishing for days a time. That won't cut it," Williams said.[117]

Later in the teleconference, Bob Taylor, Williams' principal deputy, appeared to suggest that escorts also should restrict photojournalists' access to certain types of situations. When Col. Mulvey pointed out that the guidelines were silent about whether photographers could take pictures of prisoners of war — which he believed would be a violation of the Geneva Convention — Taylor said:

> I think that the point is that the media is not a party to the Geneva Convention, so they may be able to take the pictures; the public affairs officers are just going to assure that the opportunity isn't given to them.[118]

Williams and Marine Lt. Col. Fred Peck, Deputy Director of Public Affairs at Marine Headquarters, stressed that the ground rules applied only to what was reported, not to what was asked. "There is no such thing as an impermissible question," Williams said. "There's nothing in these ground rules that says anything about the questions that reporters can ask. Reporters can ask any questions they like."[119] He told PAOs that "it's never a good idea in my opinion to stop an interview or raise your hand or wave your hands or anything like that."[120]

During security reviews, escorts were to ask journalists to omit "only things that would jeopardize an operation or put lives at risk," Williams said. Reviewers were not to "question anything or withhold anything just because it's embarrassing or it criticizes us," Williams said.[121]

Williams also explained why Pentagon officials had gone beyond the system of media restrictions used during the Vietnam War, when security reviews were not used. The conflict in Southeast Asia was a multi-year operation, and a daily story was one of many thousands, he explained. The Defense Department expected any war in the Gulf to last only a few months, "so every day's reporting becomes that much more important and that much bigger a percentage of what's said about the total operation," Williams said.[122] He told the PAOs that so far, "the very accurate picture that people in America are getting of this operation is a good one."[123]

Another factor in the decision to expand the scope of the media restrictions was that Vietnam involved primarily "a series of skirmishes," whereas a war in the Gulf would be "more of a set piece . . . a big, widely coordinated plan." A third factor was the advance of technology, which by 1990 allowed video to be transmitted live from the battlefield. The security review was instigated "because it's incumbent upon us to stick a little bit of breathing space in here, a little time for reflection on critical information," Williams said.[124]

These factors contributed to the need for pool coverage, he continued. Two 18-member pools had undergone trial deployments in Saudi Arabia, but "it may be that two 18-member pools isn't enough to cover the whole Army," so the Defense Department was still thinking about how many pools should be allowed in the field, Williams said.[125]

The guidelines and ground rules contained no provisions for unilateral coverage, and Williams and other Pentagon officials emphasized that public affairs officers should discourage journalists from trying to go out in the field on their own. Williams said reporters placed themselves and others in danger by driving unescorted vehicles in the desert, where they could easily be mistaken for the enemy. They also could put an unwanted burden on field commanders, who might feel obliged to provide the unexpected journalist with food, water and transportation needed for the troops. In addition, allowing reporters to make independent contact with units would be unfair to pool reporters who were playing by the rules, and would destroy the pool operation, Williams said. He told the PAOs:

> . . . the point is, we can't be flexible on this at the beginning or we've lost all control over the pools. The pools will be useless and pointless . . . the pool members who are out there trying to do their jobs will be

overwhelmed by all these adventurers and soldiers of fortune who are trying to get out there and join up with them on their own. And it'll weigh the pools down to the point where it will be an unwieldy beast.[126]

Williams said field commanders had been told that if a reporter appeared unannounced, they should "escort those reporters back to the rear and as soon as possible send them back to Dhahran." He added:

> . . . we will treat them like any other nonmilitary person who shows up at a unit and tries to join up. . . . Whatever those rules are, those rules will be followed. If that means they'll be detained, or some very large burly guys escort them back, that may happen.[127]

Williams added that the Pentagon would consider pulling press credentials of reporters who went unilateral. When Col. Mulvey reminded him that the Saudi government was responsible for accrediting correspondents, Williams said the Pentagon would work with the Saudis on that issue.[128]

Williams said "there may be a time" when pools would be disbanded and "we start to work a little more towards more sort of unilateral coverage."[129]

Col. Mulvey said during the teleconference that when some pool journalists in Dhahran had heard that unilateral coverage would not be allowed, they had cheered.[130]

The fact that journalists in Dhahran supported efforts by the Pentagon to stifle independent reporting shows how intensely rival media competed to wring every advantage from the pool system. Many of the details concerning how combat pools would function were worked out during the fall among Pentagon personnel, representatives of major media, public affairs officers in the Gulf and correspondents based at the Dhahran JIB. Many of the correspondents who participated in the discussions worked for the networks, wire services and largest newspapers, which were the only organizations able to maintain a constant presence in the Gulf. Mid-sized and smaller media could not afford to maintain reporters in Dhahran continuously, and sent over staffers for a few weeks at a time.

This meant that reporters for the major media had more input than other correspondents into the way the pools were organized. They also had more influence than other journalists because the Defense Department officials were most concerned about how the national media were going to cover the war.

As a result, when the combat pools were organized, representatives of the major media, in conjunction with military personnel, decided their organizations would have permanent pool slots.[131] Other media would divide up the remaining slots on a rotating basis. This caused enormous resentment, especially among the hundreds of print reporters trying to get into the pools. Frank Aukofer, Washington Bureau Chief of *The Milwaukee Journal* and a longtime participant in the DOD National Media Pool, pointed out that the system prevented highly qualified correspondents from smaller news organizations from having much of an opportunity to cover the war.

"There were no principles of 'open coverage' or 'press freedom' involved" in the major media's decision to ensure that they retained permanent pool slots, Aukofer wrote in *Nieman Reports*.[132] It was simply a tactic to reduce competition for access to the battlefield, he wrote.[133]

Hearst Newspapers' Lewis said the system led to a "constant brawl" among print reporters for pool slots. The continuing "ugly fracas" prevented correspondents in Dhahran from organizing effective opposition to the Pentagon's restrictions. "I was horribly frustrated about it, because I would tell people that we were spending too much time fighting among ourselves [when] we should be fighting with the military," he said.[134]

Some journalists and smaller media organizations did fight the Pentagon, by filing suit against White House and Defense Department officials in U.S. District Court in New York.[135] The plaintiffs — who included Pulitzer Prize-winning *Newsday* columnist Sydney Schanberg — stated that the Pentagon's pool regulations and other wartime media policies violated their First and Fifth Amendment rights. The suit challenged the preferential treatment that the Pentagon had provided to selected media, such as the provision of a military aircraft to fly a group of correspondents to Dhahran after the outbreak of hostilities, and the assurance of special access to military units for participants in the Hometown Program.[136]

No major media joined the suit. Some editors and executives feared that they might lose their access to the pools if the Pentagon decided to retaliate, and others believed a loss in court could set a poor precedent for future actions against the Pentagon. The Reporters Committee for Freedom of the Press, which had considered filing a lawsuit against the Reagan administration after the media were prevented from covering the invasion of Grenada in 1983, said the suit was "a long shot," because "judges are more willing to tolerate prior restraints on speech than at any time in the last 50 years."[137]

The War Begins

During the first two weeks of January, diplomats made frantic efforts to work out an agreement between Iraq and the United States and its coalition partners. On Jan. 9, 1991, Secretary of State James A. Baker III and Iraqi Foreign Minister Tariq Aziz met in Geneva, but failed to reach any agreement. The next day, the U.S. Congress began debating whether to authorize President Bush to use military force to drive Iraqi troops out of Kuwait. On Jan. 12, 1991, the House approved the measure, 250 to 183, and the Senate also voted in favor, 52 to 47. The same day, United Nations Secretary General Javier Pérez de Cuéllar traveled to Baghdad to meet with Saddam Hussein, but was unable to resolve the crisis. When the U.N.-mandated Jan. 15 deadline for Iraq's withdrawal passed, the world braced for war.

In Saudi Arabia, preparations for possible wartime media coverage were well under way. In early January, more than 60 journalists had been part of a trial deployment of seven combat correspondent pools. On Jan. 14, the Pentagon sent the final versions of the ground rules and guidelines to Dhahran. By the next day, more than 70 journalists in eight pools had been sent into the field. On Jan. 16, about 6:30 p.m. Washington time, U.S. and coalition aircraft began the initial air attacks against Iraqi forces. The operation would be known as Desert Storm. In Washington, President Bush told the nation, "The liberation of Kuwait has begun . . . . we will not fail."[138]

Some pool reporters who witnessed the first action of the war were very pleased with how the system for reviewing and moving copy functioned that night. A public affairs officer awakened Associated Press reporter Edith Lederer and *Chicago Tribune* correspondent David Evans, who were on an air base in Saudi Arabia, and drove them to the flight line where U.S. aircraft were taking off, according to a *Washington Journalism Review* article.[139] Later, as the reporters wrote a quick lead, the escort drove them to a construction shack that had a phone. They dictated their copy to an AP staffer in the Dhahran International Hotel, and the story was released as a pool report as U.S. and allied bombs began falling on Baghdad. The system "worked perfectly," Lederer said. "It showed that even in this restrictive system, we could actually break news for our media colleagues. Unfortunately, the problem is that this one case stood out like a beacon for everything that followed."[140]

Journalists Complain About Pool Limitations

Despite this auspicious beginning, the Pentagon ground rules and guidelines soon generated dozens of complaints. Within days, journalists and media executives were deluging the Joint Information Bureau at Dhahran and Williams' office at the Defense Department with complaints about the pools, the security reviews and the delays in transmitting copy.

Correspondents were especially angry about the lack of pools. In an interview for this study, Col. Mulvey estimated that there were 600 journalists and support staff in Dhahran on Jan. 17.[141] The next day, 120 additional media representatives arrived on the special flight arranged by Williams. JIB officials had thought most of the passengers would be support personnel, but the majority were reporters and photographers. Public affairs officers were able to add several additional pools during the first weeks of the war, but hundreds of journalists spent days sitting in the Dhahran International Hotel, waiting and hoping for a pool slot.

The problem was that many commanders did not want to take journalists, JIB personnel said in interviews for this study. Lt. Col. Larry Icenogle, Deputy Director for Combat Media Pool Operations for the Dhahran JIB, said that when he had arrived in Saudi Arabia in late December and had seen the plan to deploy seven combat pools, his reaction had been, "Wait a minute, we got one pool here to cover the whole Army? You've got to be kidding me."[142] He organized one more pool for the Army before the war began, which meant there were fewer than 30 journalists covering hundreds of thousands of Army troops once the war began. After the start of hostilities, "we started expanding the number of pools, but we certainly weren't able to do it fast," because many commanders would not agree to take journalists, Lt. Col. Icenogle said.[143] In some cases commanders used the fact that pools were already in the field as a rationale for not accepting correspondents into their units, Lt. Col. Icenogle said, adding that he "simply could not find enough commanders" to accommodate the number of additional pools that the JIB wanted to form. Col.

Mulvey said in an interview that some commanders were reluctant to take reporters because they were not convinced that journalists could maintain operational security.[144] Army commanders, for example, were concerned that journalists might give away the westward deployment of ground forces, which were being massed for a surprise move into Kuwait.[145]

Different branches of the service had different attitudes about journalists, which partly reflected the feelings of top-level officers. The Marines, led by Lt. Gen. Walter Boomer, the former Marine public affairs chief, called the JIB repeatedly asking that more journalists be sent to their units, and went to great lengths to provide transportation and communications facilities for correspondents. Shortly before the ground war began, two Marine divisions had a total of more than 30 journalists with them. By contrast, no Army division had a full seven-member combat pool, although just before the ground assault began, some commanders agreed to take a few journalists. At the start of the ground campaign, more than 190 journalists were deployed in pools.[146] At the time, the Pentagon estimated that between 800 and 1,600 journalists were in Saudi Arabia.[147]

Col. Mulvey said the number of journalists in Dhahran was "overwhelming," and created difficulties, especially in light of the fact the JIB had fewer staff than he had requested. The optimum number of journalists his operation could have handled was 200, he said.[148]

Many editors believed that the only reason the JIB could handle so few was that top-level military commanders and Pentagon officials did not want to provide the resources and personnel to enable the media to provide large-scale, independent coverage of the war. The pools provided a rationale for limiting the number of journalists in the theater and controlling the stories they could cover.

Hearst Newspapers Washington Bureau Chief Charles Lewis said in an interview for this study that even if the Pentagon's highest estimate were correct, the number of journalists in Saudi Arabia "was ridiculously low, in a country the size of the eastern United States, [with] 720,000 fighting personnel."[149]

Journalists also protested the fact that the pool system meant that JIB personnel had become the *de facto* assignment editors for the U.S. news media. Author David Halberstam — who as a *New York Times* reporter in South Vietnam won praise from the State Department for the fairness of his reporting and later a Pulitzer Prize for his coverage of the war — discussed the pool system on ABC's *Nightline* shortly after the Gulf conflict began. "I can't remember a story broken by a pool," he said. "I think a pool takes away the editing function and the assignment function from a newspaper and from a journalist and essentially grants it to the United States government, to the Army."[150]

The pools in the Gulf went to the places that the PAOs designated. Shortly after the war began, ABC correspondent Judd Rose, a member of Combat Correspondent Pool #10, reported that members of his pool had wanted to visit a Patriot battery because the air-defense system had been used against a Scud the night before. Instead, the pool was sent to a facility where military trucks, guns and equipment were being repaired.[151] Hearst Bureau Chief Lewis stated in a letter to Pete Williams after the war that this "power to define coverage amounts to censorship of far more dangerous proportions than any 'blue pencil' editing."[152]

Col. Mulvey denied that PAOs were dictating what journalists could cover. He said the Joint Information Bureau solicited journalists' requests and story ideas, but could only send reporters to units where the commanders were willing to accept them.[153] Journalists replied that this simply meant that military personnel had direct control over who and what reporters were able to see. *New York Times* reporter Malcolm W. Browne, who won a Pulitzer Prize for his reporting from Vietnam, wrote that the pool system had turned each journalist into "an unpaid employee of the Department of Defense."[154] News executives in the United States who had cooperated with the Pentagon to work out the pool system felt betrayed by what some called "censorship by access."

Editors and news executives also were concerned because the Pentagon's control of the visuals of the air war, combined with the daily televised briefings from Riyadh and the Pentagon, meant that the entire picture of the conflict that the American people were receiving was being controlled by the U.S. military. Some thought this control reflected the feelings of officers such as Gen. Schwarzkopf, who had served in Vietnam. Many of these officers were bitter about media coverage of that war and wanted to limit journalists' access to the field, according to former military personnel and journalists interviewed for this study.[155]

Some Pentagon officials readily acknowledged that they believed the Pentagon's control of information was a good idea. One of these was Lt. Gen. Thomas Kelly, Director of Operations for the Joint Staff, who conducted many of the Gulf War briefings in Washington. Lt. Gen. Kelly — who said in an interview for this study that he carries a copy of the Constitution in his briefcase — stated that the briefings were "the most significant part of the whole operation" because

> for the first time ever, the administration — the Department of Defense — was talking directly to the American people, using the vehicle of a press briefing, whereas in Vietnam, everything was filtered through the press. I think that was a major advantage for the government. The press, wittingly or unwittingly, between Riyadh and Washington, was giving us an hour-and-a-half a day to tell our story to the American people .... the American people were getting their information from the government — not from the press ....
>
> I think the lesson for the future is, that we should endeavor to do that more.[156]

Reporters Try to Go Unilateral

As the war entered its second week, increasing numbers of reporters in Saudi Arabia abandoned the pool system and began trying to cover the war unilaterally. A CBS television crew led by Bob Simon, an experienced Middle East correspondent, disappeared in late January after being turned away while trying to visit the 1st Cavalry Division.[157] Simon had been captured by Iraqi forces and was held until the end of the war. Military officers used Simon as an example of why reporters should not go unilateral, but many experienced journalists believed the pool system, with its tight control over access and information, pressured Simon into striking out on his own. "I cannot help feeling that part of the responsibility lies in a system that goads people into taking unnecessary — or necessary — risks," wrote *New York Times* reporter Browne.[158]

Although U.S. military personnel turned away some unilaterals, they detained others. Wesley Bocxe, a photographer working for *Time*, was blindfolded, searched and held for more than 30 hours by a National Guard unit.[159] By mid-February, more than two-dozen journalists had been detained or threatened with detention by U.S. forces before being sent back to Dhahran.[160] JIB officials insisted that journalists were not being singled out, and that all unescorted civilians were being detained by the military to protect operational security. But many journalists, including former military officers, rejected this explanation. Col. David Hackworth, the highly decorated U.S. Army officer who was covering the Gulf conflict for *Newsweek*, said in an interview for this study that he believed the pool system was being used not to control security, but to control public perceptions about the war. Journalists "were treated not unlike animals in the zoo, and the military was the zookeeper, throwing them bits and scraps of meat," he said.[161]

When Col. Hackworth realized that the pool system would never provide the access he wanted to the troops, he scrounged up a uniform and military credentials, painted his 4-wheel-drive vehicle desert colors and put Army markings on it, and set out to contact units on his own. He said he found soldiers and officers in the field anxious to share their story with journalists. When commanders who were not well-disposed to the media came by, the soldiers hid Hackworth so he wouldn't be sent back. "They were very angry about the freedom of the press, because many of them thought that's what they were fighting for — freedom," Col. Hackworth said.[162]

But military personnel were not the only people trying to stop the unilaterals. Many pool reporters were furious with journalists who didn't abide by the rules. On one hand, they feared that unilaterals might further alienate the Pentagon, resulting in the pools being even more restricted, and on the other they worried that unilaterals might have more access to military personnel and events, and therefore a competitive advantage. Several confrontations occurred between pool reporters and unilaterals. Robert Fisk, an experienced Middle East reporter working as a unilateral for the London *Independent*, wrote that during the battle of Khafji, an NBC-TV pool reporter with the Marines became infuriated when Fisk showed up on the scene. Fisk wrote that the reporter:

> responded with an obscenity and shouted: "You'll prevent us from working. You're not allowed here. Get out. Go back to Dhahran." He then called over a Marine public-affairs officer, who announced, "You're not allowed to talk to U.S. Marines, and they're not allowed to talk to you."

It was a disturbing moment. By traveling to Khafji, the *Independent* discovered that the Iraqis were still fighting in the town long after allied military spokesmen had claimed that it had been liberated. For the NBC reporter, however, the privileges of the pool and the military rules attached to it were more important than the right of journalists to do their job.[163]

The battle of Khafji in late January became a flashpoint for several controversies between the military and the media. Journalists in Dhahran complained bitterly that they had been kept from the fighting, and that the only pool reporters near the scene were kept miles away from the town itself. They were angry that unilateral reporters from The Associated Press and *The New York Times* had gotten much better stories than the pool reporters.

AP reporters Fred Bayles and John King said in interviews for this study that after hearing about the fighting in Khafji, they had driven up from Dhahran on their own and hooked up with a Marine unit. Bayles said:

> We spent the night and part of the next day with them, and took fire. We were with them when they were ambushed. . . . They basically said, "You're here, it's not safe, this is why. If you want to stay, you're responsible for yourselves," etc. I said, "Fine." Those were the ground rules. Part of the issue, too, was that at that time they had some reconnaissance units that were trapped behind enemy lines. They pulled us out and asked us not to mention anything about it, and we didn't. We were able to get back and forth and file our stories. We filed our stories without going through censors, and we respected the conditions that were put on us by the regimental commander. . . . Our copy moved quickly. It got on the wire while the fighting was still going on.[164]

Long after the AP reporters had begun covering the Khafji fighting, King saw a pool stopped at a roadblock, waiting to get near the scene.[165] Other eyewitness reports also were filed by Malcolm Browne, who had given up on the pools and had accompanied a Saudi unit that had become involved in the fighting.

Col. Mulvey strongly defended pool coverage of Khafji. He pointed out that the battle primarily involved Iraqi troops fighting Saudi and Qatari forces, and that the pools were designed only to provide coverage of U.S. forces. "Orders from Central Command were that this was a Saudi fight, and the Saudis would control it," Col. Mulvey said. "Saudi participation in the battle of Khafji was never intended to be covered by our pool system." U.S. Marines stayed back and provided artillery support, and the pools provided extensive coverage of the Marines' role, producing 57 pages of pool reports, he said. Col. Mulvey eventually made special arrangements with a Saudi commander to have a pool accompany Saudi forces into the area, although this took several days to arrange.[166] By that time, the riveting accounts provided by unilateral reporters had further undermined journalists' trust in the ability of the pool system to get journalists to the scene of the action.

Communications Problems Plague the Pools

Another situation that infuriated journalists and frustrated JIB personnel involved difficulties in getting copy from the field to Dhahran. Reporters' stories sometimes took days to reach the Joint Information Bureau, and some never arrived. In early February, *Wall Street Journal* reporter John Fialka wrote Col. Mulvey a letter about delays in releasing his pool reports. The letter stated:

> There were at least two cases last week where pool reports were delayed 40 hours or more in getting in from the field. At a time when ground combat hasn't started yet, this is simply unacceptable and a cruel fraud on reporters out in the field who are working on the assumption that they are disseminating news. As one benchmark for discussing this issue, you should consider that news of the Battle of the Wilderness in Virginia in the Civil War took only 24 hours to reach New York. . . .
>
> If these two cases are any indication of the condition of the courier/censorship system you have set up, then I would say it is close to brain dead on the eve of combat when the public (ours and yours) assumes it will get prompt news reports.[167]

JIB personnel agreed that communications problems were, to use Col. Mulvey's word, "horrible."[168] He and other JIB personnel said the major problem was that the Pentagon did not provide the public affairs operation with sufficient resources. For example, repeated requests to Central Command for tactical and commercial fax machines and tactical phone lines, which would have enabled print correspondents to file from the field, produced little response. As a result, print copy, along with videocassettes, audio tapes and rolls of film, had to be brought in from the field by courier. JIB personnel had hoped couriers could use air transportation, but their requests that helicopters and other aircraft be dedicated to the public affairs operation were not granted. Instead, pool products from land-based units were transported by a system that became known as the "Pony Express." A series of couriers drove pool material from forward units to a rendezvous point in the rear, where they handed off pool products to other drivers. These couriers would then drive to King Khalid Military City — which might be eight hours from the rendezvous point — in hopes of meeting a C-130, which was scheduled to leave for Dhahran at 6 p.m. each evening. If the plane were grounded because of bad weather or were needed for a military operation, couriers then had to drive hundreds of miles to Dhahran, a trip which could take an additional eight hours.[169]

"Inadequate communications hurt us, lack of dedicated airframes hurt us and the sheer magnitude of the travel distances hurt us," Lt. Col. Icenogle said in an interview for this study.[170]

JIB personnel had begun asking for communications and transportation assets months earlier, Lt. Col. Icenogle stated:

All those requests were documented last summer. We sent request after request for them — additional phones, radios, vehicles with radios so we could stay in touch with the guys out in the field, tactical fax machines, a tactical telephone line, another secure phone.[171]

At one point the Joint Information Bureau was so desperate for a tactical phone line, which cost $25,000, that Lt. Col. Icenogle suggested putting everyone on MREs [meals ready to eat] for the rest of the war and using the savings to get a phone line.

He said he believed that Central Command officials "in their heart of hearts really wanted to help us, but I never felt that our requests got the emphasis they deserved. For whatever reason, we didn't get the equipment that we needed, and we paid the price. We paid the price in credibility, in the interminable delays. . . . We were so close to making the whole thing work, it's just a damn shame that the lack of hardware kept us from doing it."[172]

In the after-action reports, JIB personnel suggested that the public affairs operation be given dedicated transportation and communications facilities. They also stated that the Pentagon should work out guidelines so journalists could bring their own communications equipment into the field without interfering with military communications or compromising operational security.

Escorts Create Controversy

The debate about communications difficulties paled in comparison to the controversies concerning escorts and security reviews. Pete Williams and Col. Mulvey stressed repeatedly that escorts were to act as facilitators, helping pool members get to the units they had been assigned to cover, setting up interviews, providing technical information when necessary. The escorts were not supposed to interfere with journalists' news-gathering efforts, Williams said.[173]

When escorts conducted security reviews, they were to look only for possible violations of the ground rules, and were to be concerned only with information that might endanger operational security or troop safety. Material was not to be marked for deletion because it contained information that criticized or embarrassed the military.[174]

Col. Mulvey emphasized that the reviews were not a form of censorship, but a process that was supposed to involve both the escort and the journalist, and over which the media were to have final control. He said:

> We felt that it was very important that it [the review] be done together with the reporter because the reporter was the only one that could make a change to the copy. We did not have authority to get out a blue pen or pencil and change a work or strike something out or cut something out as a censor would do back in World War II or whatever to remove something. So what the escort would do would be to appeal to the reporter, "I think this paragraph is a violation of the ground rules. . . . But the escort couldn't take it out.[175]

Despite the written guidelines and oral briefings provided by Williams and Col. Mulvey, a number of escorts did not follow the rules. Within days of the start of the war, journalists reported that escorts were interfering with their attempts to interview troops. Some were telling soldiers not to answer specific types of questions. Stephanie Glass, who covered the war for the *San Antonio Light*, said some PAOs spoke for personnel being interviewed, "like a ventriloquist act." When she asked one escort not to finish the sentences of the people she was talking with, she was told she would be put back on the press bus if she were "going to be a smart ass."[176]

Other PAOs carried written advisories that they read to the troops before allowing journalists to ask questions. AP correspondent Fred Bayles said reporters dubbed these advisories the "Miranda warning."[177] An escort working with ABC reporter Judd Rose said, "What I would ask you not to do is to portray anything that might be negative."[178] Glass said one serviceman told her that his commanding officer had said "if he did not have anything nice to say, he shouldn't say anything at all."[179]

Escorts chided journalists for talking with military personnel in restaurants and other public places if an escort were not present. *The Boston Globe*'s Walter Robinson had so little access to the troops before the war started that he began interviewing them at the Hardee's restaurant in Dhahran. When he mentioned this to a JIB officer he was told, "The rules are the rules and they're pretty clear and you can't interview any soldier anywhere without an escort."[180] The officer planned to send someone to the Hardee's to put a stop to such discussions, Robinson said in an interview for this study.[181]

Sometimes military personnel tried to restrict pool members' access if they or other officers did not approve of a reporter's stories. Phil Davison of the British paper *Independent on Sunday* said in an interview for this study that an officer tried to eject him from the pool because he didn't approve of a military-analysis piece that Davison had written.[182] UPI correspondent Anthony O. Miller protested, and the officer backed down. But Miller said the incident showed that "as late as one hour before we embarked on convoying up for the grand invasion through the minefield, they were about the task of trying to make certain the coverage went a certain way."[183]

Another incident involved *Los Angeles Times* reporter Douglas Jehl, a pool reporter covering the 1st Armored Division, who wrote a story during the first weeks of the war about a large number of U.S. military vehicles that had been stolen from an Army facility. In a Feb. 4, 1991 memorandum to Col. Mulvey, Jehl said he had been told that the story had raised concerns among Army commanders "because it was based on information supplied by anonymous sources and contained information regarded as contrary to the best interests of the Army."[184] Jehl's military escort had met with the Division's public affairs officer and then had told Jehl his access to the division would be "severely limited," and that a PAO had to be present during any conversation that the reporter had with an officer or soldier. Jehl also would not be permitted access to any meeting, office, tent or other facility in which he might hear or see sensitive information.

In his memorandum, Jehl pointed out that no one had questioned the accuracy of his story. The report had not violated any ground rules and had passed a security review. The reporter said that the proposed curbs on his access resulting from officers' reactions to the story "will greatly restrict my ability to cover the war as part of the Pentagon pool," and "will undermine arrangements for pool reporting developed over months of consultation."[185] *Los Angeles Times* editors backed up Jehl's protests, and the additional restrictions were not implemented.[186]

Escorts' interference with news-gathering activities was one of the major problems addressed in a letter sent to Defense Secretary Cheney by 17 top-level news executives and editors on June 24, 1991.[187] An attachment to the letter that detailed problems with Persian Gulf media restrictions praised the "handful" of PAOs who "went to extraordinary lengths to help reporters get the story — and to get the story transmitted rapidly back from the field."[188] But it said many other escorts "saw their duty not as facilitating but controlling." The letter stated:

> The interference had nothing to do with operational security. It had everything to do with sanitizing the nature of war and polishing the image of the military.
>
> These experiences — shared by every type of news medium, with every service and in every part of the war theater — make it clear that we cannot again be subjected to a system that requires all newsgathering to be performed under the control of military monitors.[189]

Security Reviews Add to Tensions Between Military and Media

The ways in which some escorts conducted security reviews caused additional arguments between journalists and public affairs personnel. Reporters said some escorts deleted words or passages that might have proved embarrassing to the U.S. military, or allowed military officers to do so. The most publicized incident involved *Detroit Free Press* reporter Frank Bruni, who had described U.S. pilots returning from missions early in the war as "giddy." The wing commander thought the word was inappropriate, and had it changed to "proud."[190]

Escorts who were unsure about technical details or operational security considerations in specific instances sometimes sent stories up the chain of command for review. A story by Malcolm Browne concerning Stealth bombing missions was sent all the way to Stealth headquarters at the Tonopah Test Range in Nevada for review because the escort was unfamiliar with the aircraft and did not know whether the story was technically correct or contained classified information. By the time the report arrived back in Saudi Arabia and was released, it was "hopelessly stale," Browne wrote.[191]

In other cases, Army officers were conducting their own independent reviews of stories. Hearst Newspapers' Lewis said a major in the Army's 7th Corps became "famous" among reporters for editing copy that had been dropped off for the JIB courier.[192] This was a violation of the news media guidelines, which said only escorts would review copy, and led to further delays in the transmission of pool reports.[193]

Col. Mulvey acknowledged that "there were some horror stories," and that sometimes "the system failed." But he added that these problems resulted from individual errors, not from the escort or security-review procedures themselves.[194]

Col. Mulvey said some of the difficulties journalists encountered in the field happened because many PAOs were inexperienced, and had not had sufficient training to handle wartime situations as effectively as the Pentagon had hoped. Another problem was that the JIB was understaffed. Col. Mulvey had asked for 57 people, and by the end of the war he had 52, many of whom had arrived weeks after the war had begun.[195]

Col. Mulvey believed that overall, the security-review process had worked well. He pointed out that of 1,351 print reports, only five had been appealed to the Pentagon, and four of those were quickly cleared for release by Williams. Only one report, a story by *Washington Times* reporter Michael Hedges on military intelligence-gathering techniques, went to the last stage of the appeals process, with Williams contacting the paper's editor to ask him to approve the deletion of information that military officers believed jeopardized operational security and troop safety. The documents surrounding this controversy are part of a public report by the Senate Governmental Affairs Committee regarding its February 1991 hearings concerning Pentagon rules on media access during the Gulf War. They illustrate some of the fundamental problems that faced the military and the media in trying to deal with operational security issues.[196]

A Disputed Pool Report Raises Major Questions

Hedges' story, written after he had been in the field for weeks, was based on an interview with intelligence-battalion commander Lt. Col. Bill Moore. It contained detail about the intelligence battalion's mission to "take vague and contradictory information and create an accurate picture of what the Iraqis are doing, while deceiving and confusing them."[197] The story said the troops' activities included sending long-range reconnaissance teams into enemy territory to report on Iraqi troop positions, intercepting and translating Iraqi radio transmissions, and trying to deceive the Iraqi military through such ruses as creating fake bunkers. The report also included a description of the Trailblazer system, which could scan Iraqi radio frequencies, allow interpreters to listen to enemy conversations, and enable U.S. forces to pinpoint Iraqi radio sites within 10 meters.[198]

The story was cleared by Hedges' public affairs escort, a major, and sent to Dhahran, where JIB personnel thought the story violated Ground Rule #5, which stated that "information on intelligence collection activities, including targets, methods, and results" should not be released.[199] Hedges and print pool coordinator Nicholas Horrock of the *Chicago Tribune* did not agree. In an interview for this study, Hedges said the story was "well-sourced" and that he "was not predisposed to self-censor it," especially since he had not been told that the information was classified.[200] "My feeling was that if the Iraqis had access to any standard manuals of electronic warfare, they would know this stuff," Hedges said.[201] He stated:

> I feel that it was a report that did not reveal any sensitive, critical military information . . . . the battalion commander in the field and the major in the field were both much closer to the actual situation than

anybody back in Dhahran. . . . . I think among ourselves out in the field we had a real clear understanding of what was sensitive and what I shouldn't write, and I just felt they were being overly sensitive back in the rear.[202]

JIB personnel wanted the five paragraphs about the Trailblazer deleted, as well as references to U.S. personnel operating in enemy territory. They also wanted to remove descriptions of deception techniques such as providing canvas and plywood vehicles with bogus radio and thermal signatures to fool Iraqi pilots, and replicating the radio signals of a U.S. tank battalion in one place while that battalion moved under cover of radio silence to a different attack location.[203]

When Col. Mulvey and pool coordinator Horrock could not agree on how to handle the story, the article and suggested changes were sent to Williams, who did not see it until Feb. 16, five days after it had been filed. Williams agreed with Col. Mulvey that the report violated Ground Rule #5. Williams asked *Washington Times* Editor-in-Chief Arnaud de Borchgrave in a Feb. 16 memorandum to review the report, emphasizing that "the final decision [on whether to change the report] rests with the news organization, not the Pentagon."[204] Williams said the Pentagon was asking that some of the information in the story not be released because "Our intelligence officers consider this information to be of the most sensitive nature. They believe its publication could put field intelligence officers at risk."[205] Williams also wrote:

> Michael may have accurately reported precisely what the intelligence officer in the field told him. However, while military officials must use discretion in talking to reporters, the entire approach of putting reporters into the field is based on the concept that reporters will not simply report all they see and hear but will, instead, use their discretion and comply with the ground rules on sensitive information. If military officers believe otherwise, they will be reluctant to share information that is essential to the understanding of an operation.
>
> We encourage military personnel to give reporters as complete a picture of their operations as possible. In doing that, they sometimes discuss sensitive information. But they trust reporters to abide by the ground rules to prevent publication of such sensitive details.[206]

De Borchgrave agreed that the material should be deleted. The report was retyped and released as a pool report in Dhahran.

In an interview for this study, Col. Mulvey said this incident showed that the security-review system worked, and that it was not censorship. The key point was that the editor, not the Pentagon, made the final decision, he stated.

However, the issues concerning how to define what types of information are a security risk — and how to handle such information — are still being debated.

Military officers interviewed on background for this study disagreed about whether information in the story jeopardized operational security. Some agreed with Hedges that the article did not contain any material that a well-informed intelligence officer would not have been aware of. Others said the information about communications intelligence was especially sensitive, and that some of that information might still be classified. They were surprised that documents about this controversy were available in a public report.

Some officers thought that the entire story should have been deleted, because it talked about intelligence-collection activities, which was forbidden by Ground Rule #5. Others said the deletions that had been made were arbitrary, and that phrases and sentences left in the story contained the same information as those that had been removed.

Journalists said the incident showed that military personnel did not always agree on what types of information compromised military security, and had unfairly blamed the press for not being able to make decisions that they could not make themselves.

News executives and editors pointed out that many journalists had gone to great lengths to protect operational security. *U.S. News & World Report* columnist David Gergen, who worked in the White House press office during the Reagan administration, wrote that the magazine's staff "learned nearly two weeks in advance where allied ground forces would strike and that amphibious operations were a fake, but it withheld disclosure. Several other news organizations made similar decisions."[207]

Public affairs officers agreed that military personnel did not always agree about where to draw the line concerning what types of data might compromise security. But they added that journalists in the Gulf had violated security guidelines in obvious ways dozens of times. Most of the violations were inadvertent, and were committed by inexperienced reporters, they said.[208] They cited instances in which television correspondents had discussed in detail where Scud missiles had landed, thus providing the Iraqis with targeting information, and stories by print reporters that identified the exact location of units they were covering.[209]

JIB personnel said such incidents increased military officers' distrust of reporters, and made it more difficult to convince commanders to allow journalists into their units. The PAOs agreed that the security-review process had created some problems, but they believed that like the pools and the escorts, the reviews had been necessary in the Gulf, and had not unduly hindered press coverage.[210]

The Media Try to Fight Back

Journalists had a very different view of the restrictions, and inundated Williams' office with dozens of protest letters throughout the war. Associated Press Executive Editor and Senior Vice President Al Rossiter Jr. at one point compared the U.S. press restrictions with those of the Iraqis:

> U.S. officials correctly pointed out that the movements and reports of Western journalists in Baghdad are tightly controlled by the Iraqi government. . . .

But I suggest the same thing is happening to Western journalists attempting to cover the war from Saudi Arabia. UPI reporters in Saudi Arabia are permitted to see only what you and public affairs officers of the various services and those of the alliance want us to see. We do not have free access to the various military units and current pool arrangements are highly restrictive.[211]

The Pentagon Bars the Media from Dover

The protests did not lead to any significant changes in the Pentagon's policies. Meanwhile, the Bush administration took additional steps to restrict media access to other types of information and images about the conflict. On Jan. 21, 1991, five days after the start of the war, Williams issued a memorandum barring the media from covering the arrival of casualties at Dover Air Force Base, the transshipment point for military personnel who die overseas.[212]

Williams insisted that this was not an effort to control news coverage. "There is an idea somehow that we're trying to sort of pretend like people don't get killed in a war, and that we do that by not allowing coverage at Dover, which, of course, is ludicrous," he told a National Press Club audience after the war.[213] "There really wasn't anything happening at Dover other than the caskets being unloaded and shipped on, and that wasn't the only place it happened."[214]

Journalists — pointing out that events at Dover had nothing to do with operational security and troop safety — believed there was another explanation. They remembered the angry White House reaction during the invasion of Panama when two networks and CNN had used a split screen to provide simultaneous live coverage of President Bush joking with reporters before a news conference while the bodies of servicemen killed in the invasion were arriving at Dover. Presidential spokesman Marlin Fitzwater said the images had been unfair. President Bush chided the media at a subsequent press briefing, saying he had received numerous letters from viewers who thought he had been insensitive.[215]

Williams' memorandum barring the media from covering the arrival of casualties also announced that the Pentagon had canceled ceremonies honoring the arriving war dead at Dover.[216] Williams said the cancellation was designed to protect survivors' privacy, and to avoid "hardships for family members and friends who may feel obligated to travel great distances" to attend the Dover ceremonies.[217]

Williams later told reporters that "families of those who were killed in action should decide where the services are. Now naturally they are going to want those as close to home as possible."[218]

But some organizations of veterans and military families disagreed. They regarded the cancellation of ceremonies as an insult to Armed Forces personnel who had given their lives for their country, and believed that the decision to bar the media from covering the arrival of casualties was an attempt to conceal the reality of war from the public. These groups, including the Vietnam Veterans of America Foundation, Veterans for Peace and the Military Families Support Network, joined with journalists and the American Civil Liberties Union to file a lawsuit in U.S.

District Court in Washington challenging the Pentagon's actions. The plaintiffs' court documents stated:

> The intent of barring the public and press from witnessing the return of America's war dead is to control and limit media coverage of the effects of the war: specifically, to limit the emotional impact and significance of the fact that Americans are being killed. . . .[219]

As of Jan. 1, 1992, a final court decision in the case had not been rendered.

The Administration Tries to Control Environmental News

Administration officials also tried to restrict information about the environmental effects of the Gulf War. On Jan. 25, 1991, the Department of Energy San Francisco Operations Office issued a memorandum entitled, "Media Policy on War Issues." The memo stated that the public affairs office at DOE headquarters "has requested that all DOE facilities and contractors *immediately* discontinue any further discussion of war related research and issues with the media until further notice." [Emphasis is DOE's.][220]

The memo, first discussed in a *Scientific American* article in May 1991, outlined "the extent of what we are authorized to say about environmental impacts of fires/oil spills in the Middle East."[221] According to the memo, appropriate comments included, "most independent studies and experts suggest that the catastrophic predictions in some recent news reports are exaggerated," and "predictions [about the environmental consequences of the war] remain speculative and do not warrant any further comment at this time."[222]

In the *Scientific American* article and an interview for this study, John Belluardo, the DOE public information officer who wrote the memorandum, said it was not designed to stifle debate about the possible effects of the war on the environment, but to prevent the Iraqis from obtaining information that might enable them to hamper U.S. military operations.[223] When asked why the policy remained in effect for months after the war had ended, Belluardo said it was because "we are still in a transition period."[224]

The Media Lose Ground on the Home Front

Media executives and editors fought the restrictions on information in Washington and the Gulf, but their efforts to obtain met with little sympathy from the U.S. public. A poll by the Times Mirror Center for the People & the Press in January 1991 found that 76 percent of Americans thought the U.S. military was censoring news reports from the Gulf, and 79 percent thought this was a good idea.[225] Seventy-eight percent thought the military was telling them as much as possible under the circumstances, and was not hiding bad news about the war. Fifty-seven percent of the public that the military should exert more control over war coverage.[226]

President Bush's approval ratings jumped sharply after the start of the war. The day after the war began, 86 percent of respondents in a *New York Times*/CBS News poll approved of the job the President was doing.[227] It was a jump of 20 percentage points over the previous week's figure, and was the highest rating for a U.S. President in 30 years.[228] In the ensuing weeks, the President's overall rating stayed above 70 percent.[229]

As the President's popularity soared, his backers began criticizing some journalists and their coverage of the conflict. The most visible target was CNN reporter Peter Arnett, the only reporter for a major Western news organization who had been allowed to stay in Iraq after the war began.

Arnett's Reporting Creates Controversy

Arnett, who had covered more than a dozen wars and had won a Pulitzer Prize for his reporting of the Vietnam conflict, operated under Iraqi government restrictions. He traveled with escorts and his reports were censored. CNN announcers told viewers about the restrictions, and a message superimposed on the screen told viewers that the reports had been cleared by Iraqi censors.

Arnett's work in Iraq infuriated administration supporters in Congress, who thought his reporting was irresponsible. Their anger increased after Arnett reported Iraqi statements that U.S. bombs had damaged a baby formula factory. Pentagon spokesmen had insisted that the facility was used to produce biological weapons.

On Feb. 4, 1991, 21 members of the House signed a letter to CNN President Tom Johnson, protesting that Arnett's "unsubstantiated claims of widespread devastation of civilian targets" was discouraging the American people and U.S. troops. The letter urged CNN to stop airing Arnett's reports:[230]

> In our judgment some of this reporting actually poses additional danger to the lives of U.S. servicemen and servicewomen. . .
>
> CNN's reporting of Peter Arnett's coverage of Saddam Hussein. . .gives the demented dictator a propaganda mouthpiece to over 100 nations. The risks this presents — inciting fanatics and endangering our service personnel — lends great urgency to suggestions that CNN review its current policies on airing the voice of Baghdad.[231]

CNN executives said they received numerous calls and letters protesting Arnett's coverage, but stood behind their reporter.[232]

The rhetoric about Arnett escalated in early February, when Sen. Alan Simpson (R-Wyo.) told reporters Arnett was a "sympathizer" and his reporting from Baghdad was "repulsive."[233] The senator said Arnett's Vietnam coverage had been biased, and his Vietnamese brother-in-law had worked with the Viet Cong.[234]

The reporter's colleagues were outraged. David Gergen, who worked in the White House press office under President Reagan, wrote in *U.S. News & World Report* that "a press that sends a reporter behind enemy lines serves less as a mouthpiece for the other side than as the eyes and ears for his own country."[235]

David Halberstam, who met Arnett when both men were based in Saigon, said Simpson's allegations were "just dead wrong" and were part of a campaign by the

Bush administration to create anti-press sentiment.[236] Arnett's son wrote an impassioned defense of his father in *The New York Times*, stating that Sen. Simpson's "guilt-by-association tactics" were "more in keeping with a dictatorship than a democracy," and that the allegations that family had ties with the Viet Cong were false and painful.[237]

Journalists also pointed out the irony that Sen. Simpson was criticizing Arnett for providing support for Saddam Hussein when the senator himself had met with the Iraqi dictator in April 1990 and allegedly had sympathized about Hussein's problems with the Western press. Sen. Simpson denied this, saying his remarks had been taken out of context.

However, Arnett had been in Jerusalem during Sen. Simpson's Middle East visit, and "was one of a handful of journalists . . . who were called to the U.S. consulate to be upbraided by Sen. Simpson and others . . . . and why were we upbraided? We were misrepresenting Saddam Hussein," Arnett said during a speech at the National Press Club on March 19, 1991. CNN never used the footage, "But we do still have the video, senator," Arnett said.[238]

On March 20, Sen. Simpson apologized to Arnett in a letter sent to *The New York Times*. He wrote that he should not have repeated rumors about Arnett's family, and should not have called the reporter a "sympathizer." The word "dupe" or "tool" would have been more in context, Simpson wrote.[239]

Arnett spent considerable time defending his reporting after returning to the United States. In a series of articles, speeches and interviews, he said he had tried to document not only the obvious effects of the war, such as civilian casualties, but also "the rapid deterioration of Iraqi society and the frustration of the average man on the street."[240] He got information about economic and political life past the censors by working it into the unscripted question-and-answer sessions with CNN announcers.[241] The negative reaction to his reporting occurred because "the American people weren't quite clear about what we were doing," Arnett said, adding that the U.S. media had to accept part of the blame for the fact that the U.S. public did not have a clear idea about the function of a free press in wartime.[242]

The Media Look for Support

Arnett's point was underscored by the results of a March 1991 poll by the Times Mirror Center for the People & the Press, which showed that the percentage of Americans who thought censorship was a good idea has increased to 83 percent.[243] With so much of the U.S. public solidly behind the Pentagon's press restrictions, journalists and media executives looked elsewhere for support in their efforts to increase access to the battlefield. Initially they hoped members of Congress, who had authorized President Bush to use force in the Gulf and stood to pay a high political price if the war did not go well, would pressure the Defense Department to ease the restrictions so lawmakers would have more access to objective information. In January, 16 House members wrote to Defense Secretary Cheney that the media restrictions "seriously undermine First Amendment rights and may well prevent the American public from receiving accurate and objective information on this international crisis."[244] Several lawmakers also introduced resolutions calling for the restrictions to be revised, and for pools to be expanded. Neither the letter nor the resolutions had much effect.

As problems with pools, escorts and security reviews continued, news executives stepped up behind-the-scenes pressure for congressional action, and in February 1991, the Senate Governmental Affairs Committee held a hearing on the Pentagon's wartime media restrictions.[245] Witnesses included Pete Williams; Walter Cronkite; war correspondents such as Pulitzer Prize winners Malcolm Browne and Sydney Schanberg; and former Pentagon personnel, including the authors of the Sidle and Hoffman reports.

The journalists who testified at the hearing stated that they believed the Gulf restrictions went beyond what was needed to protect operational security and troop safety. The former public affairs officers who appeared before the committee agreed.

Barry Zorthian, chief Pentagon public affairs spokesman during the Vietnam War, said he believed that the Pentagon's policies resulted from commanders' perceptions that the public had turned against the Vietnam War because of negative press coverage. These officers wanted to ensure that information about the Gulf conflict "will be controlled and based largely on official sources," Zorthian said.[246]

Fred S. Hoffman, who had analyzed Pentagon restrictions during the invasion of Panama, said pools and security reviews should be discontinued. Voluntary ground rules were sufficient to protect military secrecy, he said.[247]

Retired Maj. Gen. Winant Sidle, who had supervised an extensive study of the military-media relationship after the invasion of Grenada, also recommended that security reviews be discontinued.[248] But the former head of the Sidle Panel believed that the pool system was essential because of the large number of journalists who had shown up to cover the conflict.

He testified that although the panel's report called for pools to be disbanded "as quickly as possible," panel members had recognized that unilateral coverage might have to be limited in cases where security, logistics and the size of an operation created special problems. "This is certainly the case in Saudi Arabia today," he said.[249]

Maj. Gen. Sidle and other former officers who testified before the committee urged the military and the media to try to settle their differences and reestablish a relationship based on mutual respect and cooperation. The dispute over media restrictions was "not necessary and not one the nation needs in the face of all our other major concerns in the Gulf and elsewhere," Zorthian said.[250]

Three days after the Senate hearing, the ground war began, and the Pentagon tightened its control of news coverage.

The Ground War Begins

At 8 p.m. on Feb. 23, 1991, U.S. and coalition forces began a large-scale ground offensive against Iraqi forces in Kuwait. At 10:30 p.m., Defense Secretary Cheney announced that press briefings at the Pentagon and in Riyadh would be suspended "until further notice."[251] Cheney told reporters, "Up to now we've been as forthcoming as possible about military operations, from this point forward, we must limit what we say." The inadvertent release of any detail might compromise the operation, so "we will have nothing to say about it for many more hours," Cheney stated.[252] He expressed confidence that the public would support his decision:

> I want to assure all of you that we understand our solemn obligation to the American people to keep them informed of developments, but I am confident that they understand that this policy is necessary to save lives and to reduce American casualties, as well as those of coalition forces.[253]

The news blackout ended half a day later, after it had become apparent that the United States was going to win the ground war with minimal resistance from the Iraqis and very few U.S. casualties.

But journalists were outraged about the latest Pentagon effort to control news coverage. Some reporters in Dhahran, tired of watching the war on CNN as they waited for a pool assignment, climbed into rented vehicles and drove toward Kuwait City.

Reporters who were on the battlefield as unilaterals produced some important stories. The first live report from the field came minutes after Cheney's announcement about the blackout, when Bob McKeown used a satellite phone to call CBS from a location somewhere south of Kuwait. ABC's Forrest Sawyer, who was traveling with an Egyptian unit, transmitted the first pictures of the battlefield the same evening with a portable satellite set-up.

Meanwhile pool reporters, many of whom had been accepted by Army units only days or hours before the fighting began, found it impossible to get their stories and copy back to Dhahran. Many units had not worked out procedures for moving copy back from their forward positions, and were moving so quickly that JIB couriers had difficulty making contact. Military communications facilities were occupied with operational traffic, so journalists had no way to communicate with the Joint Information Bureau. Stories written by some pool correspondents did not arrive until days after the ground war had ended. Some copy never arrived at all. *Washington Post* Assistant Managing Editor Michael Getler told an Accuracy in Media forum after the war that *The Post* had received a total of one story during the ground war from its three correspondents on the front lines.[254]

Hearst Bureau Chief Charles Lewis, who was with the 2nd Armored Division during the 100-hour ground war, said in an interview for this study that he tried for days to get the division to send back his stories from the front. Lewis finally took the copy back himself, hitching a ride from Kuwait City to Dhahran and walking into the JIB at 7 p.m. on March 1, the day after the ground war ended. One of his stories was four days old.[255]

AP photographer John Gaps said his film took so long to get back to Dhahran that the pictures were "almost too late for textbooks."[256]

After the ground campaign ended, JIB personnel in Dhahran tried to help journalists get to Kuwait City, where public affairs officers had opened another Joint Information Bureau. PAOs at the JIB in the Kuwaiti capital provided information and assistance to unilaterals. There were no pools.

On Feb. 28, 1991, Iraq accepted U.S. terms for a ceasefire. As military action tapered off, efforts by journalists and policy analysts to evaluate the impact of the Pentagon's media restrictions intensified. Many editors and executives agreed with an assessment provided by Zorthian, who told a National Press Club forum that the war had ended and "the press lost."[257]

More Information About the War Comes to Light

During the spring, news executives and editors discussed the best strategy for confronting the Pentagon. At the same time, as more information became available about the extent to which the Defense Department and the White House had controlled images and information concerning the war, many journalists took a closer look at traditional reporting practices.

Some editors and reporters concluded that although journalists had spent considerable time and effort trying to overcome battlefield restrictions, they had not been equally concerned with more subtle White House and Pentagon techniques for managing the news. As a result, many journalists had cooperated — wittingly or unwittingly — with the Bush administration's efforts to present a sanitized view of the Gulf conflict. *New York Times* columnist Anthony Lewis wrote, "Self-examination is urgently needed in our business after our performance in the Persian Gulf War." He added:

> . . . the control and the censorship, outrageous as they were, cannot excuse the compliant, unquestioning attitude of the American press. We glorified war and accepted its political premise, forsaking the independence and skepticism that justify freedom of the press.[258]

Retired Rear Adm. Eugene J. Carroll Jr. of the Center for Defense Information, a graduate of the Army and Navy War Colleges who fought in Vietnam, agreed with this assessment. He said in an interview for this study that the news media had allowed themselves to become part of "a Madison Avenue-type public relations campaign" that had been carefully orchestrated to protect the President's high public-opinion ratings, which reached 91 percent at the end of the war.[259]

Some of the information-control techniques used by the White House and the Pentagon included:

- **Controlling the visuals of the war**

During the early days of the Gulf conflict, the Pentagon released videos showing laser-guided ordnance hitting targets with unerring accuracy. Viewers saw one bomb go down what looked like a smokestack or ventilator shaft (the image was reminiscent of Luke Skywalker's winning salvo in the film *Star Wars*) and watched as other precision-guided ordnance hit bridges, runways and buildings with unerring accuracy.

CNN reporter John Holliman issued a cautioning note in early February when he said on *Larry King Live*:

> If you look at the information that we get from the Pentagon, we've seen a lot of great pictures of the Nintendo-like surgical strikes. We have seen, to my knowledge, not one picture taken from a B-52 on a carpet bombing raid. Until we see pictures like that, we're not going to know, really, what is going on as far as the massive killing and destruction that the B-52s are the only things capable of providing.
>
> I'd like to see what the B-52s are doing, really. I'm sure a lot of people have been killed in this war so far. We haven't really seen many people killed. I don't necessarily want to see a long line of dead bodies, but the fact that we aren't seeing any really says to me that we're not getting the full picture.[260]

One reason the public wasn't getting the full picture was that the Pentagon restricted photographic access to the conflict. U.S. photographers' coverage of the air war consisted primarily of planes taking off, landing and being serviced. All requests by journalists to fly on B-52 missions were rejected. Photo editors in the United States protested that the pictures were "bland" and showed "no negative aspects" of the war. Photographers pressed for more access to bombing missions, to no avail.[261]

After the Gulf War ended, journalists learned how misleading the visuals had been. On March 15, 1991, Air Force Chief of Staff Gen. Merrill A. McPeak — who had admitted that the Air Force might have "the appearance" of an integrity problem after failing to disclose that two Stealth aircraft had missed their targets during the Panama invasion — gave a comprehensive briefing on the air campaign in the Gulf.[262] Rather than reiterating the glowing reports presented in earlier briefings, he stated that the weather had been so bad that U.S. and coalition pilots had not been able to see 40 percent of their primary targets during the first 10 days of the war.[263] Gen. McPeak also announced that less than 9 percent of the 84,200 tons of bombs dropped by U.S. forces during the war were precision-guided munitions — the type shown in the Pentagon videos. The rest of the ordnance — more than 75,000 tons — were "dumb" bombs, which had no precision-guidance capabilities.[264]

Rear Adm. Carroll criticized "the very unrealistic picture of a 'surgical' war" that had been presented by the Pentagon. He wrote in a letter to *The Washington Post* that videos used during one of Gen. Schwarzkopf's briefings showed how misleading the Pentagon's portrait of the war had been. Rear Adm. Carroll stated:

> In his Jan. 30 briefing at Riyadh, Gen. Norman Schwarzkopf stated that U.S. aircraft had flown 790 sorties against 33 bridges in Iraq. He then showed films of a series of direct hits on bridges to promote the image of perfect accuracy.
>
> But if every bomb hit a bridge, why was it necessary to make 790 attacks? This equates to 24 attacks against each bridge. Assuming that each bridge required two hits to put it out of use, and each aircraft dropped only one bomb, then 8 percent of the attacks were successful.

If each attack involved more than one bomb (highly likely), then hits were fewer than 8 percent. This is a far cry from the perfection shown on the TV screens of America.[265]

Another aspect of the war that viewers did not see much of, especially in the early weeks of the war, were U.S. or Iraqi casualties. Editors and media executives said one reason why was that some Pentagon personnel reportedly kept journalists away from areas where casualties had occurred, limiting the media's ability to show the effects of the war on the troops.[266] But another reason was that some U.S. editors practiced self-censorship, refusing to print graphic battlefield photographs. Photographer Ken Jarecke took a picture of the charred corpse of an Iraqi soldier who apparently had died while trying to climb out of his burning truck. When the photo arrived at the AP photo desk in New York, it was taken off the wire. AP photo editor Tom Stathis said in an interview for this study that the photograph was "too gruesome." The picture was published for the first time in the United States in the July-August 1991 issue of *American Photo* magazine, along with a commentary by Jarecke on journalistic self-censorship during the Gulf War. "I think people should see this," he wrote. "If we're big enough to fight a war, we should be big enough to look at it."[267]

- **Minimizing Iraqi military casualties**

Throughout the conflict, the U.S. military declined to release estimates of the enemy body count. When asked about Iraqi casualties during a Jan. 30, 1991 briefing, Gen. Schwarzkopf — who later told reporters he had felt compelled to lie about body counts during the Vietnam War — said, "I'm anti-body count. Body count means nothing, absolutely nothing, And all it is is a wild guess that tends to mislead people as to what's going on."[268] During Pentagon and White House briefings, spokesmen said repeatedly that the body count was impossible to estimate.

After the war, the National Resources Defense Council, a public interest group, filed a Freedom of Information Act request with the Pentagon concerning the Iraqi body count. The Defense Intelligence Agency responded that approximately 100,000 Iraqis had been killed and 300,000 wounded during the war.[269] Because "little information is available which would enable this Agency to make an accurate assessment," those figures had an "error factor of 50% or higher," the letter stated.[270]

According to military personnel interviewed for this study, many of the Iraqis died in the massive bombing carried out by B-52s. One military officer interviewed on background said the Iraqi troops were "bombed into jelly."[271]

Thousands of Iraqis were buried alive in the trenches during the U.S.-led ground assault. *Newsday* staffer Patrick J. Sloyan wrote an article in September 1991 that described how U.S. forces used combat earthmovers, and plows mounted on tanks, to move across 70 miles of trenches.[272] Two thousand Iraqis surrendered, but thousands more who were dead, injured or firing their weapons were buried under tons of sand, Sloyan wrote. The tactic was used by three brigades of the 1st Mechanized Infantry Division to minimize U.S. casualties, and not a single American soldier died during that phase of the ground assault.[273]

However, Sloyan wrote, the division pool reporters had not seen that part of the operation. The tactic had been "hidden from public view."[274] An Army spokesman objected to that phrase, saying that the tactic had been explained to pool reporters, who later had been shown the breach. The spokesman added that a May 18, 1991 story in the *Topeka Capital-Journal* quoted a division commander at a news conference stating that Iraqis who had chosen to fight had been buried.[275]

In a follow-up article, Sloyan wrote that pool members had not been permitted to witness the assault. He quoted Leon Daniel, a UPI correspondent and pool member, saying that when reporters moved through the breach after the attack had been completed on Feb. 25, "We were all wondering where the bodies were. We never saw any bodies."[276]

First Brigade commander Col. Lon Maggart told Sloyan, "I know burying people like that sounds pretty nasty, but it would be even nastier if we had to put our troops in the trenches and clean them out with bayonets."[277]

Some readers were dismayed by the stories. In a letter to the editor, Bill Stewart wrote that his initial reaction had been disbelief, because "I have always been told that America does not engage in terrorism and torture."[278]

The brigades' actions were neither. The tactic had been designed by officers trying to protect the lives of their troops. They believed that what they did was necessary and justifiable.

But as *Newsday* columnist Sydney Schanberg wrote:

> If this is indeed the moral judgment you make, then what's wrong with Sloyan's reporting what happened? Since the American people were asked to consent to the war, why shouldn't they be treated as adults and told war's bloody truths?[279]

- **Minimizing Iraqi civilian casualties**

Shortly after the start of the U.S. military buildup in Kuwait in August 1990, President Bush stated, "We have no argument with the people of Iraq."[280]

Throughout the war, Pentagon officials and administration spokespersons emphasized that U.S. forces were focusing on military targets. On Jan. 18, 1991, Gen. Schwarzkopf told reporters in Riyadh:

> We're doing absolutely everything we possibly can in this campaign to avoid injury or hurting or destroying innocent people. We have said all along that this is not a war against the Iraqi people.[281]

After the war, President Bush said in a speech that U.S. air strikes had been "the most effective yet humane in the history of warfare."[282]

But United Nations, U.S. and international public health teams painted a different picture. In the months after the war, they reported on the bombing raids' devastating impact on civilians.

Members of a United Nations Security Council mission that visited Iraq in March 1991 wrote that "nothing that we had seen or read had quite prepared us for the particular form of devastation" that they found in Iraq.[283]

A Harvard study team said in May that the situation was a "public health catastrophe," and predicted that at least 170,000 children under the age of 5 would die within one year.[284]

A later study by an international team of scientists, health workers and human rights advocates found that the war — in conjunction with economic sanctions and the civil unrest that followed the conflict — had left more than 100,000 children "either moderately or severely malnourished and therefore at increased risk of dying."[285]

None of these studies addressed the plight of the Shiites and Kurds, who tried to follow President Bush's suggestion that "the Iraqi people take matters into their own hands and force Saddam Hussein the dictator to step aside."[286] Thousands died in revolts against the Iraqi leader after the ceasefire. The U.S. news media, unfettered by pools or press restrictions, presented graphic stories and visuals outlining the plight of the rebels. This coverage, which included photographs of dead Kurdish children, spurred the U.S. public to demand that the White House react to the situation. The result was Operation Provide Comfort, during which U.S. troops helped set up a relief program for Kurdish refugees.

- **Exaggerating U.S. successes in the air war**

Some statements about U.S. triumphs on the battlefield during the early days of the war were misleading. One example involved statements made by Lt. Gen. Thomas Kelly regarding the success rate of U.S. Air Force missions.

At a Jan. 18, 1991 briefing, he confirmed for reporters that aircraft going into the area of operations had performed with "80 percent effectiveness."[287] Many news media used that figure. Three days later, Lt. Gen. Kelly said, "the aircraft are launching; 80 percent of them are successful in delivering their ordnance."[288] However, some reporters had heard about bad weather in the Gulf and wanted the briefer to explain how military officials could assess the success of these missions when visibility was so poor. After Lt. Gen. Kelly said the cloudy weather was, in fact, "limiting our ability to measure completely the effect of what we've done," a reporter pressed for clarification.

"For several days you've been saying that you've had an 80 percent success rate. Can you tell us how you quantify that if you can't assess the damage?" the journalist asked.[289] Lt. Gen. Kelly replied:

> Well, we can't completely assess the damage . . . . but we can make some assessment of the damage. What I mean with the 80 percent is, the sorties are launched, they go to their targets, they successfully drop their ordnance, and that's what we're saying the success rate of the sortie is.[290]

In an interview for this study, Lt. Gen. Kelly denied that he had misled reporters, saying there had been a policy change about how to define success rate during the early days of the war.[291]

The Bush administration also made exaggerated claims about how much damage U.S. bombing raids had done to Iraq's nuclear facilities. In a speech to the Reserve Officers Association on Jan. 23, 1991, the President stated, "Our pinpoint attacks have put Saddam out of the nuclear bomb-building business for a long time to come."[292] On Feb. 22, Defense Secretary Cheney said, "We've destroyed his capacity to produce weapons of mass destruction, nuclear and biological weapons."[293] These assessments were incorrect. After the Gulf War, United Nations inspectors found evidence of a widespread nuclear research program, which included facilities that U.S. intelligence and military personnel had been unaware of during the war. In September 1991, Iraqi military personnel temporarily detained U.N. inspectors who had taken possession of documents concerning the program, which focused on processes for producing atomic bombs, hydrogen bombs and missiles capable of carrying nuclear weapons.[294]

- **Exaggerating the success of U.S. weapons**

U.S. officials also made misleading statements concerning the success of U.S. weapons in the Gulf. On Jan. 25, 1991, Lt. Gen. Kelly said that more than 200 Tomahawks "have been fired to date very successfully."[295] The publication *Navy News & Undersea Technology* said the Tomahawk had "a readiness rate of better than 98%."[296] The Defense Department's Interim Report to Congress on the Gulf Conflict stated that of the 288 Tomahawks reportedly fired during the war, "282 are assessed to have successfully transitioned to a cruise profile for a 98 percent launch success rate."[297]

The Tomahawk's performance was mentioned in numerous news stories, including an article in *Fortune* that said the missile could "deliver a 1,000-pound warhead to a target the size of a mailbox with almost as much accuracy as the postal service."[298] However, reporters didn't ask Pentagon briefers to clarify their statements about the weapon's success. They learned in April 1991 what the descriptions meant when an article in the *Bulletin of Atomic Scientists* entitled "Awestruck press does Tomahawk PR" appeared. The author, Eric H. Arnett, a program associate in the Science and International Security Program at the American Association for the Advancement of Science, explained that terms such as "launch success rate" had nothing to do with the Tomahawk's accuracy or ability to hit targets. It meant simply that the missile had gotten out of its launcher without getting stuck.[299]

Arnett — who recently completed a book on cruise missiles and U.S. security — wrote that there was "little firm evidence that the Tomahawks' performance was even adequate," and that one Navy source involved with the launchings had said, "We don't know how many have actually hit their targets."[300]

In an interview for this study, Arnett was critical of reporters who did not question Pentagon statistics, saying the Defense Department used the numbers to control public opinion and justify asking Congress for a larger budget.[301] He said:

> It's well known in the field that the military uses all kinds of strange definitions for effectiveness, so for me the thing I wanted to ask . . .

was, well, what's your definition of effectiveness or success? But these reporters very seldom asked that until . . . weeks into the war, when the impression that it was all sort of a high-tech wonder had already set in. And that impression couldn't be knocked down.[302]

U.S. officials also exaggerated the success of the Patriot. Night after night U.S. viewers saw Patriots hitting Iraqi Scuds. President Bush told workers during a visit to the Raytheon corporation's Patriot plant that the weapon had intercepted 41 of 42 Iraqi missiles.[303] What the public did not see or hear about during the war was the fact that although the Patriot hit the Scud, it did not always destroy the warhead, which then hit the ground with full explosive force. Meanwhile, debris from the rest of the Scud and the Patriot scattered over a wide area, causing further damage. Gen. Powell spoke of the Patriot's drawbacks at a House defense appropriations subcommittee hearing in February, but his remarks received little coverage. He told lawmakers, "There have been cases where both missiles did not explode entirely in the air as a result of the interception" by the Patriot.[304] In such cases, the Scud sometimes "breaks into different pieces, and so you have had cases where the warhead has landed and gone off," he said.[305]

Additional questions about the air-defense system were raised when a battery of Patriots failed to detect an incoming Scud that subsequently struck a U.S. barracks just outside Dhahran, killing 28 military personnel and wounding more than 90. Months later Pentagon investigators revealed that software problems had been the principal cause of the defense system's failure to pick up the incoming missile.[306]

MIT Professor Theodore A. Postol, an engineer and physicist who has worked with the Defense Department, stated in testimony before the House Armed Services Committee in April 1991 that preliminary data concerning damage and casualties resulting from Patriot interceptions raised "serious questions about the measure of effectiveness that has been used to portray the success of [the] Patriot."[307]

Postol said in an interview for this study that he was concerned that the Defense Department's restrictions on the press, coupled with the fact that most reporters are "pretty impressively ignorant" about technology, meant that the government was both "the disseminator and assessor of the effectiveness of the various weapons systems" used in the Gulf.[308] Although future decisions about whether to continue funding such systems would have an impact on major defense issues, including Star Wars, and would involve billions of dollars from U.S. taxpayers, the public was not getting enough objective, independent information about these concerns, Postol said. "When the media don't really try to get to the bottom of statements or statistics, it takes the American people out of the debate to a certain extent," he said.[309]

Former Defense Department official Pierre Sprey provided a similar assessment in his testimony before the House Armed Services Committee. He told lawmakers, "The country has been poorly served by the shamelessly doctored statistics and the hand-selected video clips of isolated successes that were pumped out to the media during the war in order to influence post-war budget decisions."[310]

New York Times columnist Tom Wicker said revelations about the ways in which the Pentagon manipulated statistics was "a damning commentary on the controlled information policy exercised by the Pentagon during the war."[311] He wrote:

> The real, and dangerous, point is that the Bush administration and the military were so successful in controlling information about the war that they were able to tell the public just about what they wanted the public to know.
>
> Perhaps worse, press and public largely acquiesced in this disclosure of only selected information.[312]

As journalists learned more about the ways in which the Pentagon and the White House had controlled perceptions about the war, one effort to ensure that the press would have more access to information and the battlefield in future conflicts failed. On April 16, 1991, U.S. District Court Judge Leonard B. Sand dismissed the lawsuit brought against the Pentagon by a number of smaller media and individual writers.[313] The judge said that although the suit raised "profound and novel questions" about the wartime role of the press in a democracy, "The Court should not now be evaluating a set of regulations that are currently being reviewed for probable revision, to determine their reasonableness in the context of a conflict that does not exist and the precise contours of which are unknown and unknowable."[314]

Journalists Confront the Pentagon

As editors and media executives prepared to confront the Pentagon about the restrictions, Defense Department officials began damage control. Pete Williams, who had written several articles stating that during the Gulf conflict "the press gave the American people the best war coverage they ever had,"[315] said in a speech before the National Press Club on Freedom of Information Day that it was a "myth" that the media restrictions prevented reporters from doing their jobs properly.[316] However, Williams conceded that the Defense Department "could have done a better job" helping reporters get into the field, training escort officers and transmitting copy.[317] He said he had sent a letter to every reporter who had been in the Gulf, asking for criticisms and suggestions.[318]

On April 15, 1991, more than a dozen editors and bureau chiefs met to work out a unified strategy for dealing with the Pentagon. The group included representatives from major newspapers, wire services, the networks and CNN, and newsmagazines. On April 29, the group sent a letter to Defense Secretary Cheney "as the first step in a process that we hope will lead to improved combat coverage and improved understanding between the military and the media over our respective functions in a democracy."[319]

The letter said the editors and executives "strongly disagree" with Williams' statements that the war coverage had been the best ever, and believed that "the flow of information to the public was blocked, impeded or diminished by the policies and practices of the Department of Defense," which had abridged "our right and role to produce timely independent reporting of Americans at war."[320] The letter stated that journalists wanted to prevent the Gulf restrictions from becoming "a model for the future."[321]

The letter struck journalists who had suffered under the pool system as poetic justice. *Milwaukee Journal* Washington Bureau Chief Frank Aukofer, who had encountered numerous difficulties while trying to obtain a pool slot, wrote:

> I read the newspaper story about their protest with bitter amusement. It was, for the most part, the same closed little group of collaborators who had helped the Defense Department set up the pools, and had done it to protect their own asses — er, access — while freezing out news organizations not deemed worthy to join their elitist clique. As it turned out, they became pawns of the Pentagon.[322]

Cheney did not agree that the restrictions had had a negative impact on news coverage, and said that the public supported his position. He told *USA Today*, "As I get out around the country, I do not find any sense of unhappiness or outrage on the part of the American people that somehow the press was mistreated. I just don't think it's there."[323] He and other Defense Department officials pointed out that polls showed the U.S. public had approved of the coverage, and believed they had received enough information about the war.[324]

In late June, 17 additional top-level news executives and editors sent a follow-up letter to Cheney that included a report documenting the problems with the pools, escorts and security reviews, and containing a Statement of Principles that they wanted as the foundation for future ground rules and guidelines.[325] The 10 principles included provisions that:

- Independent reporting would be the principal means of coverage;
- Pools should be limited to the first 24 to 36 hours of a deployment and should be disbanded rapidly in favor of independent coverage; some special-purpose pools would be appropriate for special events or in places where open coverage was impossible, but would not cancel the principle of independent coverage;
- Journalists should be given access to all major military units;
- Journalists should be allowed to ride on military vehicles whenever feasible;
- The military would supply PAOs with "timely, secure, compatible transmission materials" for pool material and would make these facilities available when possible for journalists engaging in independent coverage;
- PAOs would not interfere with the reporting process.
- Security reviews would be eliminated.[326]

The letter requested that Cheney schedule a meeting with a representative group of editors and executives "at your earliest opportunity."[327]

In September 1991, Cheney met with six representatives of the group, and again defended the restrictions and the coverage of the Gulf conflict. "Cheney described it as the best-covered war ever. We described it as the worst coverage ever," said Burl Osborne, publisher of the *Dallas Morning News* and former President of the

American Society of Newspaper Editors.[328] However, Cheney agreed that bureau chiefs and editors should meet with Williams to continue trying to resolve disagreements.

By January 1, 1992, the five-member steering committee for the group had reached agreement on all major points contained in the Statement of Principles except the elimination of the security review, committee member Clark Hoyt said in an interview for this study.

But many executives and editors were skeptical, pointing to the fact that with each succeeding conflict after the Vietnam War, the press policies enacted by the Pentagon had become more restrictive. "No one has any sense that there's going to be any significant improvement" in the media restrictions as a result of the current negotiations, *Los Angeles Times* Foreign Policy Editor Tom McCarthy said in an interview for this study.[329] "They make no attempt to abide by the rules once they set them," McCarthy said. "The fact is, when you get with a unit, the unit commanders — and the Pentagon essentially allows this to occur — can change the rules . . . anytime they want to. So you can sit down with Pete Williams-type people and even with Dick Cheney and negotiate agreements, but then when you're placed with a unit, all bets are off."[330]

Milwaukee Journal Washington Bureau Chief Aukofer also is skeptical. He wrote:

> We should not expect anything different in the future. When the crunch comes, military people become soldiers first and public affairs specialists somewhere behind that. Everything is subverted to the military objectives. All the good-faith planning in the world will not change that.[331]

Proposals Don't Address Some Issues

Other journalists and military personnel pointed out that the proposed rules do not address basic problems that wartime coverage creates between the Pentagon and the press.

For example, many journalists believe that the media should provide their own communication and transportation resources whenever possible.

Former Rear Adm. Carroll of the Center for Defense Information said such a step is crucial to ensure independent coverage. "As long as they are tied to the military communications system, and they must file their reports for transmission . . . there is a measure of either explicit or implicit control of the news," he said.[332]

Public affairs officers who worked in the Gulf and were unable to get sufficient resources for media operations said that journalists should be willing to invest in vehicles and equipment, and work with the Pentagon on procedures to protect operational security.[333]

Television's capacity for delivering battlefield information in real time is another crucial problem that has not been addressed, despite a specific recommendation in the 1984 Sidle Report that military and media personnel make that issue a priority.[334] In a March speech to the National Newspaper Association, Gen. Powell said that during the conflict the other briefers and I always had to remember that every word we said was being heard by the enemy at the same moment we said it. We went to too great an expense to eliminate the enemy's ability to follow our actions on the battlefield to then give it away for free on TV.

Even so, I had more than one tantrum in my office over the past few weeks as sensitive information was doled out to fit 30-second slots. The worst time was the evening a TV reporter described to the world the new secret technique the Air Force was using to locate and destroy Iraqi tanks — a technique that could be countered if known by the Iraqis.[335]

Another issue that created problems in the Gulf involved the number of journalists who showed up to cover the war. Although there was controversy about how many journalists actually were working in Saudi Arabia — reporters and some PAOs believed the Pentagon's generally accepted estimate of 1,400 to 1,500 was much too high — public affairs officers said there were too many journalists for the military to handle, regardless of whether there had been pool or unilateral coverage. "You could not have 200 or 300 guys following the 24th Infantry Division in rented jeeps — it simply would not be possible," Pete Williams said.[336]

Many editors and news executives agreed that the numbers were a problem, but were unsure how to limit them in the future. Most preliminary suggestions involved giving priority to the large media with national audiences. This was unacceptable to journalists working for mid-sized and alternative media, who pointed out that some of the most original and incisive stories about the Gulf had come from reporters who were not part of the media establishment that usually covers the Pentagon and the White House.

The Media Assess Their Own Failures

While executives and editors were reevaluating what to do about Pentagon restrictions, some journalists were analyzing what to do about the profession's traditional newsgathering practices. They believed that although a handful of reporters had done an excellent job trying to cover the U.S. buildup in the Gulf and to put subsequent events in perspective, many media had been too complacent about accepting the Pentagon's restrictions and presenting the official view of the war.

Some commentators said that problems with coverage began long before the war started. They pointed out that there had been a dearth of analytical reporting about the Persian Gulf situation and the U.S. role there in the months and years before the United States decided to send troops to the region. Few media discussed the fact that the U.S. government and American corporations had played an important part in the strengthening of the Iraqi military, and that in the months before Saddam Hussein decided to invade Kuwait, the United States had sent the Iraqi dictator a number of conciliatory signals. After Iraq invaded Kuwait, coverage focused on the military buildup, and few stories put the U.S. role in events preceding the crisis into context.

"Nearly every one of America's major news outlets seemed to be carried away with enthusiasm for the buildup in the Gulf. Journalists were not asking the hard questions while there was still time for debate," said PBS correspondent Bill Moyers, a former press secretary for President Johnson during the Vietnam War.[337]

Mike Moore, former editor of *Quill*, published by the Society of Professional Journalists, agreed. Moore, who tracked pre-war newspaper coverage in the Gulf for months, said although some media examined the implications of U.S. actions in the Persian Gulf, many became cheerleaders for the war.[338] The press did not provide enough analysis of the Bush administration's decisions during the fall, and did not press Congress hard enough about the issue. As a result, when President Bush went to lawmakers for formal authorization to use force if necessary to get Saddam Hussein out of Kuwait, "many senators and representatives said that they did not necessarily want to do what they were about to do, but that it was too late in the game to debate it," Moore said.[339]

"Reporters, editors like to portray themselves as watchdogs. Watchdogs of the government on behalf of the American people. If you're going to portray yourself as a watchdog, you've got to bark once in a while," he continued. "You've got to bark before we've got 4 or 500,000 troops in the Mideast."[340]

Former war correspondent and CBS anchorman Walter Cronkite provided a similar assessment in a National Press Club forum after the Gulf War.

"We've been greatly concerned about freedom of the press and how we assure it in wartime circumstances," he said. "But it occurs to me that if the news media were as interested in covering the peace, and the things that lead up to war — to commit just some small part of the appropriation that they had to dig into their pockets to find to cover the war — we might not have these wars . . . . it's just possible that this country would have been alerted . . . because of the news coverage, and very possibly Hussein would not have moved into Kuwait in the first place."[341] □

CONCLUSIONS AND RECOMMENDATIONS

The sole purpose of such [military public affairs] activity is to expedite the flow of information to the public: propaganda has no place in Department of Defense public affairs programs.

Principles of Information
Defense Secretary Richard Cheney

The most eloquent arguments against politically based information policies during wartime are made by military officers. They have seen firsthand that information-control efforts that go beyond operational security and troop safety can endanger U.S. troops and undermine the entire war effort, as they did during the Vietnam conflict.[1]

The Pentagon's Principles of Information, reissued by Defense Secretary Cheney in 1990, commit the Defense Department to information policies free of political influence. But as the previous chapters have shown, White House and Pentagon leaders repeatedly have violated both the letter and the spirit of these Principles in an effort to shape the American people's perceptions about military operations. Col. Summers has pointed out in his book *On Strategy* and in other writings that military involvement in political efforts to maintain public support for a war is counterproductive for several reasons. It alters the relationships among the trinity comprising the public, the Armed Forces and the government, and undercuts the democratic ideal that in the United States, the military is the army of the people, not the President.

This chapter summarizes the responsibilities of the military, Congress and the media regarding coverage of U.S. military operations abroad, and the ways in which each institution could contribute to a reevaluation of government information policies to ensure that they are consistent with democratic principles.[2]

The Responsibilities of the Military

In a democracy, continued support for the military, especially in a protracted war, depends upon public acceptance of the political objectives of the conflict and the cost of those objectives.[3] That acceptance is based partly on the people's faith that their government officials are telling them the truth. Because the objectives and the cost of U.S. involvement in World War II were clear, the American people supported the war despite the enormous casualties, Summers has stated. Because the nation's leaders could not convince the public of the importance of the political objectives in either Korea or Vietnam, support for those wars declined as casualties increased, according to Summers and other analysts.[4]

When the public loses faith in the objectives of a war, it also loses faith in the Armed Forces, as military officers and analysts have pointed out.[5]

- **Military officers should be straightforward about what happens on the battlefield**

Years after the Vietnam War had ended, Gen. Schwarzkopf acknowledged that one reason the people lost faith in the Armed Forces was that they believed their military officers had not told them the truth about what had occurred during the conflict.[6] In his interview with *Life* magazine after the Gulf War, Schwarzkopf acknowledged that actions he had participated in during Vietnam, such as fabricating enemy body counts, had contributed to this:

> There was a loss of confidence on the part of the American people in their military leadership. We probably deserved a lot of it — not all of it — for not having the intestinal fortitude to stand up and say, "All right, we won't take this shit anymore, and career be damned."[7]

Some officers, such as Col. Hackworth, did just that.[8] Others, including Schwarzkopf, stayed in the services and tried to effect changes from within.[9] Two years after the United States withdrew its troops from South Vietnam, Gen. Fred Weyand, the last U.S. commander in that country, wrote an article outlining what the military must do differently during the next war. Gen. Weyand argued that the military should never again go along with civilian leaders' attempts to make a war look as if it were a policy alternative with little cost. In the article, Weyand wrote about the responsibilities of the leaders of the Armed Forces:

> As military professionals we must speak out, we must counsel our political leaders and alert the American public that there is no such thing as a "splendid little war." There is no such thing as a war fought on the cheap. War is death and destruction. The American way of war is particularly violent, deadly and dreadful. . . .we should have made the realities of the war obvious to the American people. . . .The Army must make the price of involvement clear *before* we get involved, so that America can weigh the probable costs of involvement against the dangers of uninvolvement. [Emphasis is Gen. Weyand's.][10]

Other military officers agreed. Summers said the Armed Forces should never mislead the public by using inflated statistics or by presenting information in a manner designed to hide the costs and mistakes made on the battlefield:

> . . . as Vietnam illustrated, this divergence between what we were doing and what we said we were doing led to such serious problems as the "credibility gap" and the loss of public support. . . . In the future we must take care to avoid jeopardizing American public support for their military with misstatements — either intentional or unintentional — of what we are about.[11]

● **The military should avoid involvement in political efforts to build support for wars**

When military officials agree to participate in politically based policies designed to control the flow and content of information, they may be endangering their own troops. Vietnam provides several examples. Col. Hackworth pointed out in his book, *About Face*, that the White House insistence on using enemy body counts to convince the American public that the war was going well put so much pressure on field commanders that they sometimes exposed soldiers to enemy fire in order to provide them.[12] At other times field commanders lied about body counts, contributing to false estimates of enemy troop strength.[13] Some Armed Forces and intelligence officials also contended that U.S. military officers deliberately lowered estimates of the North Vietnamese and Viet Cong order of battle because the White House and Pentagon feared that Congress and the American people would not support the war if they knew the extent of the enemy's strength. High-ranking military officers such as Gen. Westmoreland vigorously denied these charges. The debate about the accuracy of enemy troop-strength estimates continues today. The implications are extremely important, because lowered order of battle figures could have resulted in unrealistic battle plans and increased U.S. casualties.

Media restrictions based on political factors also are counterproductive for the Armed Forces because they prevent Defense Department officials from obtaining and evaluating objective, independent accounts of how military personnel and equipment have performed in the field.[14] As previous chapters in this study have shown, ample evidence exists that numerous decisions about information control during the limited wars of the '80s and '90s were politically motivated, going far beyond what was needed to protect military operations or troops. During the Grenada operation, the military concealed the fact that U.S. troops went to war armed with faulty intelligence reports, inadequate maps and poor operational plans. This was concealed from the American people as President Reagan and Defense Secretary Weinberger talked of the operation as a "brilliant campaign" that had been "extremely skillfully handled."[15]

In Panama, military officers anxious to maintain congressional support for the Stealth program were not truthful about the aircraft's first test in combat, leading Defense Secretary Cheney to say that the aircraft performed flawlessly when in fact it had missed both its targets.[16]

The Gulf conflict marked the most extensive use of politically based information-control strategies since the Vietnam War. The public was given optimistic statistics about the success rates of weapons systems and aircraft, without being told how the Pentagon was defining the terms.

● **The military should avoid trying to sanitize war with heavily edited visuals and euphemisms**

Joint Chiefs of Staff Chairman Gen. Colin Powell provided one rationale for the Pentagon's concern with the visual images of war when he told the National Newspaper Association after the Gulf conflict that military philosopher Carl von Clausewitz had warned military leaders to beware of the power of "transient images."[17] But Clausewitz also believed that people should see the reality of war. He wrote:

> Kind-hearted people might of course think there was some ingenious way to disarm or defeat an enemy without too much bloodshed, and might imagine this is the true goal of the art of war. Pleasant as it sounds, it is a fallacy that must be exposed. . . . It would be futile — even wrong — to try and shut one's eyes to what war really is from sheer distress at its brutality.[18]

The Pentagon, however, repeatedly has tried to hide the true face of war by controlling the images of the conflict, frequently with the cooperation of the media. During the early years of the Vietnam War, television journalists reached an agreement with military officials not to show gruesome pictures of casualties or graphic battlefield scenes.[19] The Defense Department also prepared plans to send its own camera teams to South Vietnam, and shipped their antiseptic footage to local stations that could not afford to send crews to Saigon.[20]

The trend continued in Grenada — when the networks ran the Pentagon's footage of the first two days of the war after their own camera crews had been barred from the island — and in Panama, where the television crew in the DOD pool was prevented from filming the early hours of the battle. The manipulation of visual images reached its apex in the Gulf, where night after night television screens were filled with images of U.S. and coalition precision-guided bombs striking their targets with incredible accuracy. After the war, journalists learned that only 8.8 percent of the bombs dropped by the United States had precision-guidance systems.[21]

Former officers such as Col. Hackworth have been disturbed by this trend. He has stated repeatedly in his articles and in interviews that he fears that the sterile images of war presented during the conflicts in Grenada, Panama and the Persian Gulf might lead the American people to believe that "limited" wars are not very violent, and are an acceptable alternative to diplomacy. "My young son is 14," Hackworth said. "It looked to him like the [Gulf] War was Star Wars fun, and bloodless, and war is good. We have to understand that war is horrible."[22]

As it emphasized coverage of high-tech weapons, the Defense Department de-emphasized coverage of U.S. and enemy casualties. In the conflicts of the '80s and '90s, TV journalists and still photographers were discouraged from taking pictures of the dead and wounded. They were barred for several days from a U.S. military hospital treating U.S. soldiers during the Panama invasion, and were prevented from covering the arrival of the bodies of troops killed in the Gulf War at Dover Air Force Base in Delaware.[23]

Throughout the operations in Grenada, Panama and the Persian Gulf, Pentagon briefers encouraged reporters to tell the public how many enemy tanks, aircraft and other equipment had been "killed" by U.S. and allied forces. Weapons counts replaced the enemy body counts of the Vietnam era. At a Jan. 23, 1991 briefing, Gen. Powell even referred specifically to the "body count" of aircraft destroyed by the coalition.[24] However, when reporters asked Gen. Schwarzkopf about the body count of enemy soldiers at a Jan. 30, 1991 briefing, Schwarzkopf chided them and said, "Body count means nothing, absolutely nothing."[25]

Another facet of this technique of controlling public perceptions by altering language involves creating euphemisms for battlefield events. Former U.S. officers, such as Col. Summers, have criticized this practice. Summers wrote that euphemisms actually eroded public support for the Vietnam War:

> In order to smooth our relations with the American people we began to use euphemisms to hide the horrors of war. We became the Department of the Army (not the *War* Department) and our own terminology avoided mention of the battlefield. [Emphasis is Summers'.] We did not kill the enemy, we "inflicted casualties"; we did not destroy things, we "neutralized targets." These evasions allowed the notion to grow that we could apply military force in a sanitary and surgical manner. In so doing we unwittingly prepared the way for the reaction that was to follow [when high casualties in Vietnam showed Americans what war was really like].[26]

By hiding battlefield realities from the American people, the Pentagon has given them an unrealistic idea of what war is like. Military and civilian officials may regret this decision if a future conflict is not as brief as those in Grenada, Panama or the Persian Gulf, and U.S. casualties are not as low as they were in those operations.

● **The military should support information policies that uphold Constitutional principles**

One reason why the history of the relationship between the Pentagon and the press is replete with officers who have worked to ensure that journalists have access to the battlefield, and that media restrictions are limited to matters of military — not political — security, is that preserving the media's right to information is part of the Armed Forces' fundamental mission of protecting the Constitution and its principles.

When Defense Department officials go along with White House efforts to try to sustain public support for a conflict by manipulating the statistics, language and images of war, they are preventing the American people from receiving independent information that will enable them to make objective judgments about the nation's leaders and their policies. The military then becomes, to use Gen. Weyand's terms, an "arm on the Executive Branch" rather than "an arm of the American people."[27]

Such political censorship also interferes with Congress' Constitutional responsibility to act as a check on the power of the President. When members of Congress deliberate about whether to commit U.S. troops abroad, they should be able to base their decisions on well-researched and objective information. When that information includes misleading statistics and visuals, lawmakers' abilities to make a reasoned, well-founded decision about whether the nation should go to war are impaired.

● **The Pentagon should establish a system for documenting operational security violations and discussing them with journalists**

Disagreements and misunderstandings about the types of information that must be restricted to protect operational security and troop safety are at the heart of the tension between the Pentagon and the press. The Pentagon might alleviate this problem by instituting a system for documenting operational security violations involving the media, and the real or potential effects of these violations.

Documentation procedures should be written into the public affairs plan for each operation. The results should become part of the Armed Forces' after-action reports and should be disseminated to public affairs officers, field commanders and journalists. Discussing these cases would help military and media personnel reduce future violations. The press could learn more about the military's views about the kinds of information that could compromise operational security if it were broadcast or published, and Armed Forces personnel could learn more about distinguishing operational from political considerations by hearing editors' and reporters' views about information-control procedures that seem to be driven by political rather than military factors.

The Defense Department could use these discussions to assist public affairs officers and field commanders who will be dealing with the media, and executives and editors could use them to train reporters and photographers who will be sent to the battlefield during future conflicts.

No system for tracking security violations was in place during the operations in Grenada and Panama. Public affairs personnel currently are reviewing pool reports and stories that appeared in the Pentagon's Early Bird news digest during the Gulf War for possible violations.[28] Capt. Ron Wildermuth, Public Affairs Officer for the U.S. Central Command, said in an interview for this study that military personnel would bear partial responsibility for some of these violations, either because they revealed sensitive information to reporters, or failed to recognize such information in news reports they were reviewing.

In one example, Capt. Wildermuth described a Navy pilot who flew over an island off the Kuwaiti coast and saw a message spelled out with rocks that said, "We surrender." He passed on the information to officials aboard his ship, who in turn talked to journalists about it. Subsequent stories were cleared by security reviewers before U.S. military officials could mount an operation to visit the island and learn whether the message had been left, as they suspected, by Iraqi troops.

By the time U.S. forces arrived, no Iraqi soldiers could be found. Wildermuth said that U.S. military officers believed that Iraqi officials may have learned about the situation from news reports, traveled to the island, and executed the soldiers.[29]

Neither journalists nor field commanders routinely see public affairs after-action reports, which means that military discussions about how journalists did or did not observe operational security and troop safety never reach the officers in the field or the editors and reporters responsible for covering military affairs.[30]

The Responsibilities of Congress

During the past 30 years, politically based media restrictions, which sanitize battlefield images and are designed to promote support for U.S. military intervention, have profoundly affected the way in which Congress has exercised its power to send the Armed Forces into battle. Nevertheless, Congress traditionally has not become involved in conflicts between the military and the media, opting instead to stay on the sidelines while the two institutions have aired their differences in the press and, during the Persian Gulf conflict, in the courts. Because media restrictions have increased — and have affected the amount and content of information upon which Congress bases its decisions — lawmakers must become more involved in the debate about U.S. information policies.

- **Congress must assist the effort to reevaluate information policies that restrict in-depth, objective war reporting**

Congress is the only branch of government that is Constitutionally empowered to declare war. Lawmakers must take every step to ensure that they have the maximum amount of independent information on which to base such decisions. Like the American people, members of Congress receive much of their information from the press. During the past three decades, however, journalists have been prevented from gathering some of the in-depth, objective information that lawmakers need to evaluate whether U.S. troops should be sent abroad.

The Vietnam War provides an example of what can happen when such information is not available. The optimistic representations about how well the war was going and the falsified body counts gave Congress a distorted picture of that conflict.[31] If the House and Senate had known the reality of what was going on in the field, they might have taken additional steps to limit U.S. involvement.

Distorted information led Congress to relinquish to the President some of its authority over the deployment of U.S. military forces to South Vietnam. In 1964, lawmakers passed the Gulf of Tonkin Resolution, which granted the President power to act unilaterally in terms of U.S. military involvement in South Vietnam.[32] Congress approved the measure after the Johnson administration announced that U.S. ships twice had been attacked by North Vietnam without provocation.

Later, discrepancies arose concerning the early official reports of those incidents, and evidence emerged that the second incident probably had never occurred.[33] If Congress had known the truth about the Gulf of Tonkin incidents, it might not have granted President Johnson such broad powers.

The Resolution also put the military in a nearly untenable position. To ensure civilian control over the Armed Forces, the Constitution gave only Congress the power to declare war. A formal declaration of war affirms that the Armed Forces are being sent abroad by the representatives of the people, not by a single person in the White House. Troops sent to Southeast Asia were fighting without this declaration, and as the war became unpopular the public began turning not only against the White House, but also against the military. As Col. Summers stated, when the American people criticize their Armed Forces for carrying out the orders of civilian authorities, it puts the military and the country in "a dangerous position."[34]

- **Congress should help define where the line should be drawn between information policies based on military security and those based on political considerations**

In order for journalists and military personnel to carry out their Constitutional responsibilities, there must be clearer guidance about where the line should be drawn between media restrictions that are necessary to protect operations and troops, and restrictions that are put in place to protect political agendas and public opinion ratings.

To help the Pentagon and the press delineate that line, Congress should hold hearings to examine wartime information policies. Such hearings cannot be patterned on the quick, half-day affair sponsored in February 1991 by the Senate Governmental Affairs Committee. Instead, full-scale hearings should be held to examine the historical, political, and military background of White House and Pentagon efforts to control information during military conflicts overseas. If lawmakers assist in the effort to reexamine and redraw the parameters of media restrictions, they will take an important step toward ensuring that they and their successors will have the most complete information possible upon which to base future decisions about whether the nation should go to war.

- **Congress should question nominees for Defense Secretary about their commitment to open information policies**

Confirmation hearings provide lawmakers with opportunities to examine and influence the attitudes of persons nominated to head the Defense Department. Nominees should be questioned closely about their attitudes toward news coverage of military activities, to ascertain the extent of their commitment to information policies based on military, not political, considerations.

- **Congress must monitor and restrict efforts by foreign governments to influence U.S. public opinion**

Representatives of the Kuwaiti government spent millions of dollars to hire the public relations firm Hill and Knowlton to produce video news clips and press kits supporting U.S. military involvement in the Middle East crisis.[35] Such actions have serious implications, especially in light of the firm's statements that the news stories were seen by millions of U.S. viewers, often with no disclaimers identifying Kuwaiti government representatives as the sponsors of the clips.[36] Hill and Knowlton's worldwide public relations operation is headed by the man who was George Bush's Chief of Staff when Bush was Vice President. Other officers of the company served in the Reagan and Bush administrations. Part of Hill and Knowlton's job was to monitor congressional hearings and to provide information to members of key committees that were considering different aspects of the Middle East situation and the role that the United States should play in resolving it.[37] Hill and Knowlton also "arranged appointments with congressional members and staff . . . [and] provided information to Administration officials."[38] These facts raise serious questions about the ability of foreign special interests to shape U.S. public opinion, and the extent to which this may have been done with the support or tacit approval of the White House.

Congress should implement measures immediately to limit the extent to which the information it uses to decide whether U.S. troops should be committed abroad can be manipulated by foreign governments. The House and Senate should support Democratic and Republican lawmakers' efforts to pass legislation strengthening the Foreign Agents Registration Act (FARA), which requires that companies and individuals working on behalf of foreign governments and organizations register with the Justice Department. Congress then must ensure that the Justice Department enforces the provisions of such legislation vigorously.[39]

Congress also should follow the General Accounting Office recommendation that the Federal Regulation of Lobbying Act be strengthened.[40] Vague language in the act — which requires disclosure of persons and organizations that finance lobbyists' efforts to influence federal legislation — prevents effective enforcement, according to the GAO.[41]

The Responsibilities of the Media

During the past 30 years, the press has not been aggressive enough in pursuing its role of informing the public and Congress about military affairs. As this study indicates, journalists too often have been poorly informed about military affairs, especially operational matters. Too often as well, they have failed to oppose politically based restrictions on wartime coverage effectively, and have published without verification information from Pentagon and White House sources that has been carefully edited to conform with a political agenda. In doing so, the media have fulfilled the wishes of Arthur Sylvester, Assistant Secretary of Defense for Public Affairs during the Vietnam era, who said that in wartime, the media should become the "handmaiden" of government.[42]

To prevent the Executive Branch and the military from coopting the press, journalists and media executives should consider concentrating on two major objectives: clarifying the principles that they believe future wartime information policies should be based upon, and initiating steps to improve journalists' knowledge of the military and coverage of U.S. military operations.

- **The media should formulate a more unified response to restrictive information policies**

One reason that the White House and the Defense Department have been able to promulgate media restrictions that go beyond the needs of operational security and troop safety is that the media never have presented united opposition to such rules. During the Grenada operation, television news executives and journalists were enraged about being barred from the conflict for two days. They filed angry protests with the White House and Pentagon, but nevertheless used the footage that the Reagan administration provided during the news blackout.

The Sidle Panel hearings, held after the Grenada operation, highlighted the media's inability to formulate a unified response to the press restrictions. Some journalists boycotted the proceedings, others provided testimony. Major media organizations said it would be inappropriate for their representatives to be members of a panel convened by the government, but agreed to abide by the provisions of the panel's report.

When the spirit of those provisions was violated during the Gulf War, the media again remained divided on an appropriate course of action. Maj. Gen. Sidle himself told a Senate committee in February 1991 that some of the restrictions during the conflict were unnecessarily stringent.[43] But when some journalists in Dhahran tried to organize protests, their calls went unheeded by reporters who had received good pool assignments, and others who were afraid they would lose all access to the battlefield if they pulled out of the pool system.[44] When more than a dozen nonestablishment news organizations and writers filed suit against George Bush and Defense Department officials on the grounds that the restrictions were unconstitutional, the suit got little support from other members of the media. The suit was dismissed as moot after the war ended, but not before the federal judge hearing the case said it had raised important Constitutional issues that needed to be examined.[45]

Media restrictions will not change a great deal until the press has substantive alternatives to the current system and is willing to pursue them. A major step in this direction was taken in June 1991, when executives of 17 major media sent a letter to Defense Secretary Cheney that protested the Gulf restrictions and included a Statement of Principles concerning future war coverage.[46] These principles could provide a foundation for action if executives and editors could agree on how to implement them. For example, one principle stated that during the next conflict, the primary form of coverage would be independent. Does this mean these media will boycott future combat pools if the Pentagon insists that such pools are the only feasible means of covering a war? How will these executives respond if the military says it will detain reporters working outside the pool system who try to contact military units on their own? How will the media deal with genuine concerns about operational security, such as those involving real-time television coverage of the battlefield, and inadvertent violations by inexperienced reporters?

If the media are going to make a serious effort to change the government's information policies, there should be more discussion about how to implement new principles, and how to respond to possible Pentagon objections and concerns about operational security and troop safety.

- **The media should provide more of their own transportation and communications facilities during military operations**

Journalists should reduce their reliance on the military to get them to the battlefield and to transmit copy and visuals to their editors. Retired Navy Rear Adm. Eugene Carroll, now with the Center for Defense Information, pointed out in an interview for this study that the more the media depend on the military for such facilities, the more control they cede to the Pentagon over media operations.[47] This becomes a crucial factor in wartime coverage when Defense Department officials can not or will not dedicate aircraft, vehicles and communications equipment for journalists' use.

Although both the Hoffman and Sidle reports call for the Pentagon to dedicate increased facilities for the media, public affairs officers during the Gulf War were unable to get all the equipment they needed. Despite their best efforts, copy from the field was delayed as the aircraft and vehicles they had available were held up by bad weather, and communications facilities were occupied with military transmissions or were operating at less than peak efficiency because of technical difficulties.[48] The media could alleviate such problems by purchasing vehicles needed to move journalists into the field, and communications equipment to send stories and video back to the United States.

This does not mean that journalists should never avail themselves of military facilities. Sometimes only military transportation might be capable of moving journalists to the battlefield. Smaller media may have experienced reporters ready to cover a war, but may lack the resources to provide complete transportation and communications packages. In such cases, joint efforts may be the only way that journalists will be able to collect information, or transmit copy and visuals.

- **Journalists should take a more critical stance toward information provided by the government**

The media should not continually report official information without verification. Journalists should ask how the information was gathered, who the original source was, and how terms were defined — just as they would for information from any other source. Unfortunately, this has not been part of many war correspondents' daily routines.

A similar situation occurred with the coverage of Grenada. As Mark Hertsgaard pointed out in his book *On Bended Knee — The Press and the Reagan Presidency*:

> In retrospect, it is remarkable how credulous leading American journalists were of information given them by a government which had both lied to them about whether an invasion was planned and then censored them by preventing them from covering it. But it was a trust built into the way most journalists approached the task of reporting on their government.
>
> "Most of the inaccurate stuff came out of the press conferences [held in Washington by Defense Secretary Weinberger and other military officials]. But we took it hook, line and sinker," conceded ABC's John McWethy.[49]

As Mike Moore, former editor of *Quill*, the magazine of the Society of Professional Journalists, said, "We too often take government handouts. We too often accept government analogies and metaphors. . . . We've got to be more critical. That's part of our job."[50]

- **Editors should send only experienced reporters to cover wars**

As Korean War veteran and former *Washington Post* staffer Peter Braestrup pointed out in an interview for this study, editors wouldn't think of sending someone who knew nothing about sports to cover a football game.[51] Experienced military affairs reporters would have an excellent background for scrutinizing the official story, and for reducing the distrust and resentment that military officers feel when they must deal with reporters who know little about the Armed Forces.

Some of the best reporting has come from military veterans such as David Evans, the former Marine who covered the Gulf conflict for the *Chicago Tribune*. With the end of the draft, chances of finding reporters who have been in the Armed Forces are diminishing, but military service is not an absolute prerequisite for good war reporting. For example, reporters who have covered a Pentagon or local military-affairs beat also can take considerable experience into a wartime situation.

- **Journalists should stop accepting Pentagon tours of the battlefield**

These tours, many of which lasted only a couple of days, were used effectively during the Vietnam conflict,[52] and were reinstated during the military buildup in the Gulf in the fall of 1990. They involved taking reporters and photographers, mostly from small- and medium-sized media, on escorted visits to specific military units. During Operation Desert Shield, the Defense Department flew more than 150 journalists to Saudi Arabia to interview hometown troops.[53] Such junkets do not provide the time, resources or freedom to do independent reporting. Some editors and military officers have argued that these tours were the only way that media from smaller cities and towns could get stories about what local units were doing during the Gulf War. But when journalists completely relinquish control of their itinerary to the Pentagon or any government agency, questions arise about whether they have crossed the line between reporting and public relations.

- **The media must stop using handouts and video news releases prepared by public relations firms working for foreign governments**

Using this type of material without verification or independent, supplemental reporting distorts the debate about whether to send U.S. troops to war by providing Congress and the American people with information packaged as objective news but designed to shape public opinion. It also undercuts the media's credibility in arguing that Pentagon press restrictions can be dangerous because they preclude access to independently gathered information.

- **The media should stop censoring graphic images of war**

Self-censorship of battlefield images has been used in every conflict since World War II, and contributes to the impression that war can be antiseptic and bloodless — an impression that chills military officers who have seen combat. Adm. Carroll, a veteran of Korea and Vietnam, said "putting a nice face" on war is wrong, and that the American people need to know what war is really like in order to assess whether it is an acceptable policy option.[55]

Using sanitized images of war also has contributed to government public relations efforts to maintain support for military operations abroad. White House adviser Michael Deaver said the reason Americans supported the Grenada invasion so wholeheartedly was that "they didn't have to watch American guys getting shot and killed. They can't stand that every night."[56]

Editors should not cause unnecessary grief for the family and friends of wartime casualties by using visuals in which individuals can by identified. Otherwise they should not hesitate to print or broadcast pictures in which dead or wounded soldiers appear, if the images are a legitimate part of the story.

- **The media should do more in-depth reporting on the issues leading to the involvement of U.S. troops abroad**

The media must make an effort to provide more in-depth foreign coverage that places U.S. policy in a historical, economic and political context. The press also must pursue follow-up stories examining the long-term impact of the U.S. involvement in conflicts abroad on the United States and other nations. After the Gulf War, the media ran numerous high-profile stories on victory parades and joyous reunions between military personnel and their families. But several major policy stories that shed new light on the decision to go to war went almost unheeded. Many media overlooked the fact that it was July 1991 before Congress finally obtained State Department cables concerning the meeting between former U.S. Ambassador to Iraq April Glaspie and Iraqi leader Saddam Hussein shortly before he invaded Kuwait. Several senators said the cables showed Glaspie had misled Congress when she testified in April 1991 that she had given Hussein strong indications the United States would not stand by if Iraq followed its expansionist tendencies.[57]

Many media also have neglected to do follow-up stories regarding the long-term impact of U.S. conflicts on the other countries involved. Such information might affect future congressional deliberations about whether committing U.S. troops overseas is preferable to pursuing other options. For example, long-term objectives for the invasion of Panama included the promotion of democracy and a reduction of drug trafficking. But nearly two years later, top government officials have been implicated in corruption, narcotics-related activities continue and political parties allied with supporters of Gen. Manuel Noriega are gaining strength. A CNN report in September 1991 about Noriega's trial on drug-related charges showed one Panamanian lamenting that the problem with the U.S. invasion was that the Pentagon had taken away Ali Baba, but had left the 40 thieves.[58]

Improving the Military-Media Relationship

The different Constitutional roles and cultural values of the military and the media will always create conflict between the two institutions. Many military officers believe this is good for democracy. Gen. Powell said in a speech after the war that only a "challenging, untrusting" press can get the in-depth, factual information that the public needs to hold government officials accountable.[59] The issue, then, is not whether there should be friction between the Pentagon and the press, but at what point does such friction become counterproductive to their ability to function in a democratic society. Gen. Dugan summarized the situation in his *New York Times* article in May 1991:

> I believe Americans appreciate tension between the media and officialdom as an appropriate background in which government institutions work, indeed, work better. The issue is: How much tension? And how can it be better managed?[60]

Dugan and other officers, such as Maj. Gen. Sidle and Col. Summers, called for a renewed dialogue between Pentagon and press personnel. Dugan wrote:

> . . . there are no simple answers for improving relations. Nevertheless, it would be advantageous for both institutions to find a continuing, independent forum for discussion and for researching ways to better serve the public interest. Both the military and the media view themselves as professions. It would be a useful start if each viewed the other in the same light — and acted accordingly.[61]

To make such a start, the military and the media need to take several steps.

- **The Pentagon and the press should explore setting up a top-level joint working group to discuss information policies**

Such a group would be most effective if it included top-level Pentagon personnel; media executives and editors; military-affairs reporters; and representatives of major media associations. The group would meet on a regular basis to discuss fundamental information-policy issues.

Bureau chiefs and Defense Department public affairs officers have had meetings to discuss specific media restrictions, and these sessions have provided an opportunity for airing day-to-day issues involving journalists and public affair officers working in the field. But personnel at these levels cannot set policy for their institutions. During the controversy about the press restrictions during the Gulf War, bureau chiefs met with Pentagon officials to complain bitterly about the DOD rules. One Pentagon official interviewed on background for this study referred to these sessions as "yawners," because they involved problems that personnel at the middle-management level could not resolve.[62]

- **The military should continue providing public affairs officers with additional training**

For years the Pentagon has sent public affairs officers to study for master's degrees at journalism schools and departments. This practice not only enables PAOs to learn about the press as an institution, but also gives them an opportunity to meet future reporters and see how they are trained. Journalism students also learn about military life and values from these PAOs on an informal basis.

- **Journalism schools and departments should offer classes in military-affairs reporting**

Press organizations and executives could support the efforts of journalism schools and departments to offer classes in this area. Many schools offer classes in sports reporting; a course in a field that is much more important to the national interest could be added to many curricula. Such courses, however, should not be exercises in how to produce public-relations copy about military units and operations, but serious efforts to provide students with enough background about the history, role and structure of the U.S. military to evaluate information provided by the government about military affairs, and to write stories that are factually correct and in an accurate context.

- **More media should establish military-affairs beats**

Large newspapers, magazines and broadcast operations already do this, but small- and medium-sized organizations in cities and towns with a significant military presence would do well to commit resources to this beat. Journalists working this beat could learn the intricacies of the military bureaucracy while producing stories about the impact of military events and issues on their readers, much the way a city hall reporter learns about local government bureaucracy in the course of covering that beat.

- **The Pentagon should continue "Army 101" for inexperienced reporters**

During the Gulf conflict, the Pentagon began a series of classes for reporters dubbed "Army 101." The courses covered the basics of the military command structure, strategy and weapons systems. The Defense Department should continue such classes and should make them available to reporters outside Washington who want to learn to cover the military.

- **The Defense Department should revive** *Military Media Review*

This journal was devoted to exploring the Pentagon-press relationship, and enabled media and military personnel to exchange information and opinions. The *Review* was discontinued in 1989 because of funding and personnel shortages.

In the end, the effectiveness of efforts to improve the military-media relationship will depend upon the individuals involved. All the recommendations in Pentagon after-action reports and military-media conferences, and those made in this study, will yield few results unless Pentagon and press personnel become convinced of the value of improving their relationship, and commit the necessary time, effort and resources to resolving the problem. As Maj. Gen. Sidle said:

> In the final analysis, no statement of principles, policies or procedures, no matter how carefully crafted, can guarantee the desired results, because they have to be carried out by people — the people in the military and the people in the media. So it is the goodwill of the people involved, their spirit, their genuine efforts to do the job for the benefit of the United States, on which a civil and fruitful relationship hinges.[63]

□

NOTES

Chapter I
Executive Summary

1. Sprey, P. M., *Statement*, testimony before the House Armed Services Committee, April 22, 1991, p. 1. Sprey is a former Special Assistant to the Assistant Secretary of Defense for Systems Analysis.

2. Postol, Theodore A., *Lessons for SDI from the Gulf War PATRIOT Experience: A Technical Perspective*, testimony before the House Armed Services Committee, April 16, 1991, pp. 1-6; *Appendix to Testimony*, p. 1; interview with the author, May 1, 1991. Postol has worked for the Congressional Office of Technology Assessment and as a scientific adviser to the Chief of Naval Operations in the Pentagon. He currently is Professor of Science, Technology, and National Security Policy in the Program in Science, Technology, and Society at the Massachusetts Institute of Technology.

3. *Total Tonnage Expended — US-Only*, updated version of graphic used for Defense Department briefing by Gen. Merrill A. McPeak, March 15, 1991. Original graphic was updated March 21, 1991 to reflect revised figures, which showed that precision-guided bombs comprised a slightly higher percentage of total tonnage than the original figures showed.

4. See Defense Department briefings, Federal News Service transcripts, January 17-24, 1991.

5. Ibid. See especially Federal News Service transcripts, Defense Department briefings on Jan. 21, 1991, pp. 4, 21 and 25; Jan. 22, 1991, pp. 1-5, 13-17; Jan. 23, 1991, pp. 2-3.

6. "Worst Weather in 14 Years," a section of *Audibles*, graphic accompanying Gen. McPeak's press briefing on March 15, 1991.

7. Kelly, Lt. Gen. Thomas, interview with the author, Aug. 16, 1991.

8. See, among others, message from National Guard Bureau, Washington, D.C. (PA) to U.S. Commander-in-Chief, Central Command (CCPA), on Sept. 27, 1990, 2102 Zulu, Subject: Request for Media Travel, Operation Desert Shield; message from U.S. Commander-in-Chief, Central Command (CCPA) to U.S. Central Command, Air Force, Forward Headquarters Element, on Oct. 1, 1990, 1025 Zulu, Subject: Media Travel, Operation Desert Shield; message from Minnesota Air Reserve Center Headquarters (MNAG-PAO) to U.S. Commander-in-Chief, Central Command (CCPA) on Oct. 2, 1990, 2100 Zulu, Subject: Documentary Film Crew, Operation Desert Shield. Also, interview with Doug Mattson of Quantum Diversified, by the author, June 14, 1991.

9. Dunlap, Maj. Robert, National Guard Bureau, Office of Public Affairs, interview with the author, July 15, 1991.

10. *Harvard Study Team Report: Public Health in Iraq After the Gulf War*, May 1991, pp. 1, 5-13.

11. Ahtisaari, Martti, United Nations Under-Secretary General for Administration and Management, *Report to the Secretary-General on humanitarian needs in Kuwait and Iraq in the immediate post-crisis environment*, March 20, 1991, pp. 5, 7-13.

12. "Media Policy on War Issues," memo from John Belluardo, Public Information Officer, Department of Energy, San Francisco Operations Office, Jan. 25, 1991. First cited in a May 1991 *Scientific American* article by John Horgan entitled "U.S. gags discussion of war's environmental effects."

13. Dilenschneider, Robert, speech to Georgetown University business students, shown on the Cable-Satellite Public Affairs Network (C-SPAN) April 3, 1991, transcript, p. 1. Dilenschneider left Hill and Knowlton on Sept. 26, 1991.

14. Ibid.

15. Hill and Knowlton executive Nathaniel Clevenger, in an interview with research associate Elizabeth Baker, June 2, 1991.

16. White House press conference, Jan. 5, 1990, Federal News Service transcript, p. 8.

17. Humphries, Naval Lt. Cmdr. Arthur A., "Two routes to the wrong destination: Public affairs in the South Atlantic war," *Naval War College Review*, June 1983. Discussed in Braestrup, Peter, *Battle Lines — Report of the Twentieth Century Fund Task Force on the Military and the Media* (New York: Priority Press Publications, 1985), Chapter 5.

18. Hoffman, Fred S., *Review of Panama Pool Deployment — December 1989*, written for the Department of Defense, March 9, 1990, p. 6.

19. See Cheney's statements during a Defense Department briefing on Jan. 11, 1990, Federal News Service transcript, p. 20, and Gordon, Michael, "Report says general knew of Stealth fighter's failure," *The New York Times*, July 2, 1990, p. A13.

Chapter II
The Military-Media Relationship

1. The Principles of Information were formulated by Defense Secretary Caspar Weinberger in the wake of criticism that the media had been excluded from covering the U.S. invasion of Grenada in 1983, according to Greg Martin, a civilian assistant to Assistant Secretary of Defense for Public Affairs Pete Williams. Martin was interviewed by research associate Donine Henshaw on May 16, 1991. A full discussion of the Principles of Information appears later in this chapter.

2. Hackworth, David H., interview with the author, June 3, 1991.

3. "Newsweek's troops in the Persian Gulf," *Newsweek*, March 11, 1991, p. 4; interview with the author, June 3, 1991.

4. Ibid., "Newsweek's troops in the Persian Gulf."

5. Powell, Gen. Colin, speech to the National Newspaper Association, March 15, 1991, transcript, p. 10.

6. Evans, David, interview with research associate Elizabeth Baker, May 1991, p. 2.

7. Interview with Col. Hackworth by the author, June 3, 1991.

8. Von Clausewitz, Carl, *On War*, Indexed Edition, edited and translated by Michael Howard and Peter Paret (Princeton, N.J.: Princeton University Press, 1984), Book VIII, Chapter 6, page 610.

9. Ibid., p. 605.

10. Ibid., pp. 606-10.

11. Ibid., Book I, Chapter 1, p. 89.

12. Summers, Col. Harry G. Jr., *On Strategy — A Critical Analysis of the Vietnam War* (New York: Del! Publishing, 1984).

13. Ibid., p. 37.
14. Summers, Col. Harry G. Jr., "Western media and recent wars," *Military Review*, May 1986, p. 10.
15. Wildermuth, Capt. Ron, Public Affairs Officer for the U.S. Central Command, interview with the author, July 8, 1991.
16. Weyand, Gen. Fred C., quoted in *On Strategy*, p. 33. These comments originally appeared in an article by Gen. Weyand entitled, "Vietnam myths and American realities," *CDRS CALL*, July/Aug. 1976.
17. See Summers, "Western media and recent wars," pp. 10-15.
18. Braestrup, Peter, *Battle Lines — Report of the Twentieth Century Fund Task Force on the Military and the Media — Background Paper* (New York: Priority Press Publications, 1985), p. 13. The Twentieth Century Fund is an independent research foundation that undertakes policy studies of economic, political, and social institutions and issues. The Task Force on the Military and the Media comprised representatives of the Pentagon and the press, plus persons with experience in government and politics.
19. Clifford, Clark, with Holbrooke, Richard, "Annals of Government (The Vietnam Years — Part I)," *The New Yorker*, May 6, 1991, p. 76. Based on Clifford and Holbrooke's book, *Counsel to the President* (New York: Random House, 1991).
20. See Summers, *On Strategy*, pp. 79, 45-58.
21. Clifford, with Holbrooke, "Annals of Government, Part I," p. 76.
22. Ibid., pp. 76-80; Clifford, with Holbrooke, "Annals of Government (The Vietnam Years — Part II), *The New Yorker*, May 13, 1991, pp. 50-60. Also see Hammond, William M. "The Army and public affairs: Enduring principles," *Parameters — U.S. Army War College Quarterly*, June 1989, pp. 70-71.
23. See Summers, *On Strategy*, p. 68; Mueller, John E., *War, Presidents and Public Opinion* (Lanham, Md.: University Press of America, 1985), pp. 62-65; Hammond, William M., *U.S. Army in Vietnam — Public Affairs: The Military and the Media, 1962-1968* (Washington, D.C.: Center of Military History — United States Army, 1988), p. 387.
24. Summers, *On Strategy*, p. 54.
25. Ibid., pp. 54-55.
26. See, for example, Braestrup, *Battle Lines*, pp. 61, 74-75; Dugan, Gen. Michael J., "Generals vs. journalists, cont.," *The New York Times*, May 24, 1991, p. A19; Todd, Greg, "Of slants and censorship," *Military Media Review*, July 1987, p. 13; Howell, Maj. Cass D., "War, television and public opinion," *Military Review*, Feb. 1987, pp. 71-74.
27. See Summers, *On Strategy*, p. 68; Mueller, *War, Presidents and Public Opinion*, p. 65; Hammond, *The Military and the Media*, p. 387.
28. Dugan, "Generals vs. journalists, cont." Dugan was removed as Air Force Chief of Staff in September 1990 by Defense Secretary Cheney after he spoke with reporters about U.S. military options in the Persian Gulf. Cheney said Gen. Dugan had violated Pentagon rules by discussing with reporters possible military targets inside Iraq and information about U.S. troop strength in the Gulf. Some media speculated that Gen. Dugan's openness with reporters bothered Cheney and President Bush. The *Los Angeles Times*, in a Sept. 19, 1990 editorial entitled, "The silencing of a general," said Dugan's conduct "on one level is not much more heinous than the crime of excessive candor."

29. Braestrup, *Battle Lines*, p. 135.
30. Ibid.
31. Ibid.
32. Ibid., pp. 133-35.
33. Ibid, pp. 136-40.
34. Dugan, "Generals vs. journalists, cont."
35. Todd, "Of slants and censorship," *Military Media Review*, July 1987, p. 13.
36. Sharpe, Col. Gerald W., "A look at the media-military relationship," *Military Media Review*, April 1987, pp. 8-9.
37. Braestrup, *Battle Lines*, p. 134.
38. Interview by the author with retired Army Maj. Gen. Winant Sidle, April 13, 1991; see also, testimony of Fred Hoffman, former Principal Deputy Assistant Secretary of Defense for Public Affairs before the Senate Governmental Affairs Committee, Feb. 20, 1991, transcript, p. 4.
39. Hammond, "The Army and public affairs: Enduring principles," p. 58.
40. Ibid., p. 60.
41. Quoted in Halloran, Richard, "Soldiers and scribblers: A common mission," *Parameters — U.S. Army War College Quarterly*, Spring 1987, p. 10.
42. Hammond, "The Army and public affairs: Enduring principles," p. 65.
43. Ibid., pp. 65-68; Braestrup, *Battle Lines*, pp. 27-36.
44. Braestrup, *Battle Lines*, pp. 47, 60.
45. See, for example, Hammond, *The Military and the Media*, pp. 11-22, and Braestrup, *Battle Lines*, pp. 61-63.
46. Hammond, *The Military and the Media*, p. 195.
47. Black, Justice Hugo, *New York Times Co. v. United States*, 403 U.S. 713 (1971), p. 717.
48. See, for example, Humphries, "Two routes to the wrong destination: Public affairs in the South Atlantic war, " pp. 70-71; Braestrup, *Battle Lines*, pp. 81-82.
49. A wealth of material on this subject is available in *1984: Civil Liberties and the National Security State*, hearings before the House Judiciary Subcommittee on Courts, Civil Liberties, and the Administration of Justice, 98th Cong., 1st and 2nd Sess., Serial No. 103, 1984. Floyd Abrams wrote a comprehensive piece on the subject entitled, "The new effort to control information, " which appeared in the Sept. 25, 1983 edition of *The New York Times Magazine*. See also, for example, "Who keeps tabs on the spies?" *The Christian Science Monitor*, editorial, Sept. 29, 1981, p. A24; Reston, James, "Washington — Reagan and the press, " *The New York Times*, Nov. 2, 1983, p. A31; Sheinfeld, Lois P. "Washington vs. the right to know; four more years of secrecy," *The Nation*, April 13, 1985, p. 426.
50. See U.S. Senate Select Committee on Secret Military Assistance to Iran and the Nicaraguan Opposition, and U. S. House of Representatives Select Committee to Investigate Covert Arms Transactions with Iran, *Report of the Congressional Committees Investigating the Iran-Contra Affair — With Supplemental, Minority, and Additional Views*,

November 1987, especially pp. 85-103 and related documents; also see, for example, letter from U.S. Comptroller General to Rep. Jack Brooks, Chairman of the House Committee on Government Operations, regarding the General Accounting Office report on unauthorized actions of the State Department Office of Public Diplomacy for Latin America and the Caribbean, Sept. 30, 1987; staff, House of Representatives Committee on Foreign Affairs, *Staff Report — State Department and Intelligence Community Involvement in Domestic Activities Related to the Iran/Contra Affair,* Sept. 7, 1988.

51. Gailey, Phil, "U.S. bars coverage of Grenada action; news groups protest," *The New York Times,* Oct. 27, 1983, p. A1; The Associated Press, "Admiral says it was his decision to tether the press," *The New York Times,* Oct. 31, 1983, p. A12.

52. Cannon, Lou and Hoffman, David, "Invasion secrecy creating a furor — Speakes complained in memo," *The Washington Post,* Oct. 27, 1983, p. A1; Cannon, Lou, "White House press aide resigns in row over Grenada policy," *The Washington Post,* Nov. 1, 1983, p. A22.

53. See "Transcript of address by President on Lebanon and Grenada," *The New York Times,* Oct. 28, 1983, p. A10.

54. See Roberts, Steven V., "Younger voters tending to give Reagan support," *The New York Times,* Oct. 16, 1984, p. A1; Dickenson, James R., "Bombing, invasion in eerie focus — anniversaries of Beirut and Grenada affect both presidential candidates," *The Washington Post,* Oct. 24, 1984, p. A10; Clines, Francis X., "Reagan finds refreshment in a fountain of youthful support," *The New York Times,* Oct. 28, 1984, p. D1.

55. See House Judiciary Subcommittee on Courts, Civil Liberties, and the Administration of Justice, *1984: Civil Liberties and the National Security State,* pp. 3-14, 425-515.

56. Chairman of the Joint Chiefs of Staff Media-Military Relations Panel (Sidle Panel) Report, released by the Pentagon on Aug. 23, 1984.

57. Greg Martin interview with research associate Donine Henshaw, May 16, 1991.

58. Sidle Panel Report, Introduction, p. 1.

59. Dorfman, Ron, "Bringing the war back home," *The Quill,* January 1984, p. 15.

60. Sidle Panel Report, p. 3.

61. Ibid., pp. 16, 3.

62. Ibid., p. 16.

63. Ibid., p. 4. The report notes in the "Comments" section on page 8 that media representatives unanimously opposed pools in general, but would cooperate in pool arrangements "if that were necessary for them to obtain early access to an operation."

64. Ibid., p. 8.

65. Ibid.

66. Ibid., pp. 8-12.

67. Ibid., p. 12.

68. Ibid.

69. Letter from Gen. Sidle to Gen. Vessey that accompanied the Sidle Panel Report, p. 2.

70. Ibid., p. 1.

71. Defense Department, *Summary Sheet, DOD National Media Pool Deployments,* p. 2.

72. Willey, Maj. Barry E., "Military-media relations come of age," *Parameters — U.S. Army War College Quarterly,* March 1989, pp. 76-84.

73. Thompson, Mark, "With the press pool in the Persian Gulf," *Columbia Journalism Review,* Nov./Dec. 1987, pp. 43-45.

74. Ibid., p. 43.

75. Hoffman, Fred S., *Review of Panama Pool Deployment — December 1989,* March 9, 1990.

76. Ibid., p. 6.

77. Ibid., pp. 1, 7-8.

78. Ibid., p. 7.

79. Ibid., pp. 6-8.

80. Ibid., p. 1.

81. Ibid., p. 7.

82. Ibid., p. 2.

83. Ibid., p. 7.

84. Ibid., pp. 1, 3-4, 8.

85. Ibid., p. 8.

86. Ibid.

87. Greg Martin interview with research associate Donine Henshaw, May 16, 1991. Cheney made one substantive change in the Principles, changing the sentence "Requests for information from organizations and private citizens will be answered responsively and as rapidly as possible," to "Requests for information from organizations and private citizens will be answered in a timely manner."

88. See, for example, CNN reporter Carl Rochelle's discussion of the pool at a March 19, 1991 forum at the National Press Club entitled, "The war and the media: A retrospective," transcript, pp. 6-7.

89. Interviews by the author with Col. Bill Mulvey, May 27, 1991; Lt. Col. Larry Icenogle, June 28, 1991; and Capt. Mike Sherman, June 19 and June 20, 1991.

90. LeMoyne, James, "A correspondent's tale — Pentagon's strategy for the press: good news or no news," *The New York Times,* Feb. 17, 1991, p. E3; LeMoyne interview with research associate Sue Mullin, Aug. 15, 1991.

91. Interviews by the author with Col. Mulvey, Lt. Col. Icenogle and Capt. Sherman.

92. Ibid.

93. Apple, R. W. Jr., "Correspondents protest pool system," *The New York Times,* Feb. 12, 1991, p. A14. Also see an exchange between Pete Williams and *Newsday* reporter Patrick Sloyan during the Jan. 8, 1991 Pentagon press briefing, Federal News Service transcript, p. 5.

94. Interview with Col. Mulvey by the author, May 24, 1991.

95. Sidle, Maj. Gen. Winant, *Statement before the U.S. Senate Committee on Governmental Affairs,* Feb. 20, 1991, pp. 2-3.

96. Ibid., p. 3.

97. Summers, Col. Harry G. Jr., *Pentagon Rules Governing Press Access to the Persian Gulf War*, testimony before the Senate Governmental Affairs Committee, Feb. 20, 1991, p. 3.

98. Hoffman, Fred S., *Statement*, testimony before the Senate Governmental Affairs Committee, Feb. 20, 1991, pp. 1, 4.

99. Interviews by the author with Col. Mulvey and Lt. Col. Icenogle.

100. Letter to Defense Secretary Cheney, June 24, 1991, signed by Roone Arledge, President, ABC News; James K. Batten, Chairman of the Board and Chief Executive Officer, Knight-Ridder Inc.; Louis D. Boccardi, President and Chief Executive Officer, The Associated Press; Max Frankel, Executive Editor, *The New York Times*; Peter S. Prichard, Editor, *USA Today*; Michael G. Gartner, President, NBC News; Katharine Graham, Chairman of the Board, The Washington Post Co.; Tom Johnson, President, CNN; Peter Kann, Publisher and President, *The Wall Street Journal*; David Laventhol, Publisher, *Los Angeles Times*; Jason McManus, Editor-in-Chief, Time Warner Inc.; Donald Newhouse, President, *Star-Ledger*; Eric Ober, President, CBS News; Burl Osborne, Publisher and Editor, *The Dallas Morning News*; Arnold Rosenfeld, Editor-in-Chief, Cox Newspapers; Al Rossiter Jr., Senior Vice President/Executive Editor, United Press International; Richard M. Smith, Editor-in-Chief and President, Newsweek Inc.

101. *Statement of Principles*, attachment to June 24, 1991 letter to Defense Secretary Cheney sent by 17 publishers and news executives.

102. Ibid.

103. Interviews, on background, with the author.

104. Williams, Pete, "View from the Pentagon — Let's face it, this was the best war coverage we've ever had," *The Washington Post*, March 17, 1991, p. D1.

105. *The Nation, et al. v. United States Department of Defense, et al.*, United States District Court, Southern District of New York, Jan. 10, 1991. Plaintiffs were *The Nation, Harper's, In These Times*, Pacific News Service, *The Guardian, The Progressive, Mother Jones, The L.A. Weekly, The Village Voice, The Texas Observer*, Pacifica Radio News, Sydney Schanberg, E.L. Doctorow, William Styron, Michael Klare and Scott Armstrong. Agence France-Press and Michael Sargent later filed a separate suit that was consolidated with *The Nation et al.*. Defendants were the Defense Department, Richard Cheney, Pete Williams, Gen. Colin Powell and President Bush.

106. Decision by The Honorable Leonard B. Sand, *The Nation, et al. v. United States Department of Defense, et al.*, April 16, 1991.

Chapter III
Pentagon Information-Management Techniques

1. *House of Commons Defence Committee First Report: The Handling of the Press and Public Information During the Falklands Conflict* (subsequently referred to as the HCDC Report), 1982-83 Sess., HMSO Dec. 1982, Vol. I (HC 17-1), pp. xiv-xvii.

2. Ibid.

3. Gillmor, Donald M., Barron, Jerome A., Simon, Todd F., and Terry, Herbert A., *Mass Communication Law — Cases and Comment* (St. Paul, Minn.: West Publishing Co., 1990) 5th Ed., pp. 2-3; Dorsen, Norman, Bender, Paul, and Neuborne, Burt, *Political and Civil Rights in the United States* (Boston: Little, Brown and Co., 1976), 4th Ed., Vol. I, pp. 16-18.

4. Ibid.

5. Gillmor, et al., *Mass Communication Law*, p. 3; Dorsen, et al., *Political and Civil Rights*, p. 17. See also, Emery, Edwin, and Emery, Michael, *The Press and America — An Interpretive History of the Mass Media* (Englewood Cliffs, N.J.: Prentice-Hall, Inc., 1984), 5th Ed., pp. 55-58.

6. See Britain's *Officials Secrets Act, 1911*, Sections 2-6. Information also was provided by Maurice Frankel, Director of the Campaign for Freedom of Information, an organization in Great Britain that is working for passage of a Freedom of Information Act and liberalization of the *Official Secrets Act*, during a telephone interview with the author from his office in London, May 31, 1991.

7. Knightley, Phillip, "The Falklands: How Britannia ruled the news," *Columbia Journalism Review*, Sept./Oct. 1982, p. 51.

8. Hoffman, "Pool Deployment," pp. 1, 7.

9. See exchange between Pete Williams and *Newsday* reporter Patrick Sloyan during the Jan. 8, 1991 press briefing, Federal News Service transcript, p. 5.

10. Hoffman, "Pool Deployment," p. 12; Maraniss, David, "Wounded put off-limits to reporters; interview on Panama 'Not in good taste,' Army general says," *The Washington Post*, Dec. 24, 1989, p. A14.

11. LeMoyne, James, "A correspondent's tale — Pentagon's strategy for the press: good news or no news," *The New York Times*, Feb. 17, 1991, p. E3.

12. SouthCom after-action report, p. iii.

13. Bray, former Capt. Linda, interview with research associate Donine Henshaw, July 15, 1991.

14. SouthCom after-action report, p. iii.

15. LeMoyne, "A correspondent's tale"; interview with research associate Sue Mullin, Aug. 15, 1991.

16. SouthCom after-action report, pp. 15, 19-20.

17. Apple, R.W. Jr., "The press: correspondents protest pool system," *The New York Times*, Feb. 12, 1991, p. A14.

18. Ibid.; also, interview with research associate Kathy Scotta, April 26, 1991.

19. Apple, "Correspondents protest."

20. SouthCom after-action report, pp. 51-53.

21. Interview with *Boston Globe* correspondent Walter Robinson by research associate K. J. Scotta, May 8, 1991.

22. LeMoyne, "A correspondent's tale"; Henry, William A. III, and Cloud, Stanley W., "Looking over their shoulders," *Time*, Jan. 21, 1991, p. 41.

23. Copeland, Peter, interviewed on C-SPAN, transcript, p. 4.

24. LeMoyne, "A correspondent's tale"; interview with research associate Sue Mullin, Aug. 15, 1991.

25. Browne, Malcolm W., "The military vs. the press," *The New York Times Magazine*, March 3, 1991, p. 45.

26. Ibid., pp. 44-46.

27. LeMoyne, "A correspondent's tale."

28. Ayres, B. Drummond Jr., "U.S. concedes bombing hospital in Grenada, killing at least 12," *The New York Times*, Nov. 1, 1983, p. Al.

29. See Federal News Service transcripts of Defense Department briefings of Dec. 22, 1989 and Jan. 25, 1990.

30. See comments by Schwarzkopf during "Operation Urgent Fury," a *Frontline* program originally shown on PBS on Feb. 2, 1988, transcript, pp. 17-21.

31. Defense Department briefing, Dec. 20, 1989, Federal News Service transcript, pp. 6-7; interview with Lt. Gen. Kelly by the author, Aug. 16, 1991.

32. "Our planes on alert until cease-fire firm," question-and-answer interview with McPeak by the editorial board and news staff of *USA Today*, March 20, 1991, p. A13. This article was part of a package of background information about McPeak sent to the author by the Air Force Office of Public Affairs.

33. Weinberger, Caspar, "Operation Urgent Fury," *Frontline*, transcript, p. 24.

34. Schwarzkopf, "Operation Urgent Fury", pp. 20-21.

35. See, for example, Defense Department briefing, Dec . 26, 1989, Federal News Service transcript, p. 5.

36. Gordon, Michael, "Stealth's Panama mission reported marred by error, " *The New York Times*, April 4, 1990, p. B5.

37. See McPeak, Defense Department briefing, March 15, 1991, and two graphics accompanying the briefing, entitled *Total Tonnage Expended — US Only* and *Audibles*. See also the question-and-answer interview with McPeak in *USA Today*, March 20, 1991, in which he does not answer directly a question concerning whether 70 percent of the bombs that lacked precision guidance missed their targets, stating instead that bombs that miss by 10 meters can still inflict considerable damage on the target.

38. The Associated Press, "Ammo explosion in Kuwait kills 3 GIs," printed in *The Arizona Daily Star*, July 24, 1991, p. A6.

39. The discussion about body counts unfolded over a period of months. See, for example, United Press International, "U.S. lowers estimate of civilian casualties to 202, plans to release 100 POWs," *Los Angeles Times*, Jan. 13, 1990, p. A7; Omang, Joanne and Dana Priest, "Accounting for Panama's dead: Uncertainty and confusion," *The Washington Post*, Jan. 7, 1990, p. A23; Rohter, Larry, "Panama and U.S. strive to settle on death toll," *The New York Times*, April 1, 1990, sec. 1, pt. 1, p. 12; Hockstader, Lee, "In Panama, civilian deaths remain an issue," *The Washington Post*, Oct. 6, 1990, p. A23; Cousins, Norman, "What's the truth on Panama casualties?" *The Christian Science Monitor*, Oct. 16, 1990, p. 18; Freed, Kenneth, "Panama tries to bury rumors of mass graves — allegations persist that up to 4,000 civilians were killed in the U.S. Invasion," *Los Angeles Times*, Oct. 27, 1990, p. A3; Panvini, Col. Joseph S., "Estimates of Panamanian casualties not a secret," letter to the editor, *The Christian Science Monitor*, Nov. 16, 1990, p. 20; United States Southern Command, Fact Sheet, "Operation Just Cause: One Year Later (Panamanian Fatalities and Common Graves)," Dec. 14, 1990, revised Jan. 3, 1991.

40. SouthCom, Fact Sheet, pp. 1-2.

41. "Bush outlines gulf lessons for Air Force Academy grads," *Air Force Times*, June 10, 1991, p. 23.

42. See, among others, *Harvard Study Team Report* and the United Nations *Report to the Secretary-General on humanitarian needs*; The Associated Press, "Bombing left Baghdad

'a high-tech trap,' doctor finds," printed in *The Arizona Daily Star*, April 10, 1991, A7; Tyler, Patrick E., "Health crisis said to grip Iraq in wake of war's destruction," *The New York Times*, May 22, 1991, p. A4; The Associated Press, "Gulf dead: 150,000-plus," printed in the *Tucson Citizen*, May 29, 1991, p. A1; Cowell, Alan, "Malnutrition ravages children of an Iraqi city," *The New York Times*, June 1, 1991, p. A4; Tyler, Patrick E., "Postwar Iraq on brink of disaster, U.S. finds," *The New York Times*, June 3, 1991, p. A1.

43. See transcript of ABC-News *20/20*, March 15, 1991, p. 6; also see Ryan, Michael, "Here's to the winners," *Life*, March 18, 1991, p. 34.

44. Schwarzkopf, Defense Department briefing in Riyadh, Jan. 30, 1991, Federal News Service transcript, p. 17.

45. See Pete Williams' discussion of the issue at the Defense Department briefing of March 12, 1991, Federal News Service transcript, p. 12.

46. Hardzog, Robert C., Chief, Freedom of Information and Privacy Act Staff, Defense Intelligence Agency, letter to Robert S. Norris, Senior Staff Analyst for the National Resources Defense Council, May 22, 1991. Letter was in response to the Council's March 14, 1991 FOIA request.

47. Interview, on background, with the author, Feb. 17, 1991.

48. See, for example, Gen. Schwarzkopf's briefing of Jan. 30, 1991 and Gen. McPeak's briefing of March 15, 1991.

49. Hackworth, Col. David H., *The Real Story*, CNBC, July 10, 1991, transcript, p. 5.

50. See Defense Department briefings, Federal News Service transcripts, Jan. 17, 1991–Jan 23, 1991.

51. Williams, Pete, speech to the National Press Club, March 14, 1991, Federal News Service transcript, p. 3.

52. Cheney, Richard, Defense Department briefing, Jan. 23, 1991, Federal News Service transcript, pp. 1-2.

53. Powell, Gen. Colin, testimony before the Senate Armed Services Committee, Feb. 21, 1991.

54. Schwarzkopf, Gen. H. Norman, "Talking with David Frost," broadcast on PBS March 27, 1991, transcript, p. 4.

55. See the Times Mirror Center for the People & the Press, *The People, the Press and the War in the Gulf: Part II — A Special Times Mirror News Interest Index*, released March 25, 1991, p. 2.

56. Ibid., pp. 2-3.

Chapter IV
Issues Raised by Media Restrictions

1. Carroll, Rear Adm. Eugene J. Jr., interview with the author, June 19, 1991.

2. Ibid.

3. Hackworth, Col. David H., *The Real Story*, transcript, p. 1.

4. See, for example, Hertzgaard, Michael, *On Bended Knee — The Press and the Reagan Presidency* (New York: Farrar Straus Giroux, 1988), p. 211.

5. See, for example, Shribman, David, "Poll shows support for presence of U.S. troops in Lebanon and Grenada," *The New York Times*, Oct. 29, 1983, p. A9; Hilts, Philip L., "565,000 jam ABC's phone lines — call-in poll endorses invasion of Grenada 8 to 1," *The Washington Post*, Oct. 30, 1983, p. A18; Sussman, Barry, "Reagan talk gains support for policies," *The Washington Post*, Oct. 30, 1983, p. A1; Nagy, David, "Reagan turns Grenada, Lebanon to political advantage," *Reuters*, Nov. 5, 1983; and Dickenson, James R., "Bombing, invasion in eerie focus — anniversaries of Beirut and Grenada affect both presidential candidates," *The Washington Post*, Oct. 24, 1984, p. A10.

6. See Chapter VIII for further discussion of this point. Other information about these issues can be found in the testimony of former Senior Deputy Assistant Secretary of State for Intelligence and Research Francis McNeil before the Senate Foreign Relations Subcommittee on Terrorism, Narcotics, and International Operations, April 4, 1988; testimony of Drug Enforcement Administration officials before the House Judiciary Subcommittee on Crime, Oversight Hearings on Enforcement of Narcotics, Firearms, and Money Laundering Laws, July 28, 1988; testimony of DEA Administrator John Lawn and former Chief Assistant U.S. Attorney in the Southern District of Florida Richard Gregorie before the same subcommittee on July 12, 1988; testimony of former Special Assistant to President Reagan for National Security Affairs Norman Bailey before the House Select Committee on Narcotics Abuse and Control, hearing on U.S. Foreign Policy and International Narcotics Control, March 29, 1988; letter from Nancy Kingsbury, Associate Director of the General Accounting Office, National Security and International Affairs Division, to Rep. Bill Alexander (D-Ark.), Aug. 3, 1988, and letter from Nicholas Rostow, Special Assistant to the President and Legal Adviser, to Ms. Kingsbury, July 13, 1988; Mullen, Francis, *NNBIS—Major Changes Needed*, memorandum from former DEA Administrator written in January 1984 and quoted in hearings by the House Government Operations Subcommittee on Legislation and National Security Information concerning Continued Review of the Administration's Drug Interdiction Efforts, March-September 1984, p. 421. Also see U.S. Senate Select Committee on Secret Military Assistance to Iran and the Nicaraguan Opposition, and U.S. House of Representatives Select Committee to Investigate Covert Arms Transactions with Iran, *Report of the Congressional Committees Investigating the Iran-Contra Affair, with Supplemental, Minority, and Additional Views*, November 1987, p. 110. Information from these hearings is summarized in Sharkey, Jacqueline, "The Contra-Drug Tradeoff," *Common Cause Magazine*, Sept./Oct. 1988, pp. 23-33.

7. See, for example, Sandler, Norman D., "Approval of military actions may be transitory," *United Press International*, Oct. 30, 1983.

8. Roberts, Steven V. "Younger voters tending to give Reagan support," *The New York Times*, Oct. 16, 1984, p. A1; Clines, Francis X., "Reagan finds refreshment in a fountain of youthful support," *The New York Times*, Oct. 28, 1984, p. D1.

9. See, for example, Bernstein, Richard, "Latins in U.N. council assail the U.S. on invasion," *The New York Times*, Oct 26, 1983, p. A18; Taylor, Stuart Jr., "Legality of Grenada attack disputed," *The New York Times*, Oct. 26, 1983, p. A19; Taylor, Stuart Jr., "Legal basis for invasion — U.S. suggests exception to U.N. Charter; others see version of 'Brezhnev Doctrine,'" *The New York Times*, Oct. 27, 1983, p. A22; Bernstein, Richard, "U.S. vetoes U.N. resolution 'deploring' Grenada invasion," *The New York Times*, Oct. 29, 1983, p. Al (the U.N. Security Council approved a resolution on Oct. 28, 1983 "deeply deploring" the invasion as a "flagrant violation of international law." The United States immediately vetoed the resolution). Also see "Mr. Reagan's illegal invasion of Grenada," remarks by Rep. Richard L. Ottinger, *Congressional Record — Extensions of Remarks*, Oct. 27, 1983, p. E 5166; Feder, Barnaby J., "U.S. was warned

by Mrs. Thatcher — she urged caution on Reagan — London played no role," *The New York Times*, Oct. 26, 1983, p. A1; Gwertzman, Bernard, "Allies' criticism of U.S. raises wider questions," *The New York Times*, Oct. 27, 1983, p. A21; "Britain's Grenada shut-out," *The Economist*, March 10, 1984, p. 21 (U.S. Edition, p. 31).

10. See, for example, Adkin, Mark, *Urgent Fury: The Battle for Grenada*, (Lexington, Mass.: Lexington Books, 1989); Major Adkin was the Barbados Defence Force Caribbean Operations staff officer who helped plan the deployment and use of the Caribbean Peacekeeping Force during the operation. Also see a review of the book by Ronald H. Cole, an historian in the Office of the Joint Chiefs of Staff, which appeared in *The Friday Review of Defense Literature*, published by the American Forces Information Service in the Pentagon, Sept. 15, 1989, p. 2. Also see remarks of Gen. Schwarzkopf in PBS *Frontline* program, "Operation Urgent Fury," Feb. 2, 1988, Journal Graphics Inc. transcript, pp. 17-24; Perry, James M. and Fialka, John J., "As Panama outcome is praised, details emerge of bungling during the 1983 Grenada invasion," *The Wall Street Journal*, Jan. 15, 1990, p. A12.

11. Braestrup, *Battle Lines*, p. 9.

12. See discussions of the origins of the First Amendment in Gillmor et al., *Mass Communication Law*, pp. 2-5; Dorsen et al., *Political and Civil Rights*, pp. 15-17; Emery, *The Press and America*, pp. 54-58.

13. Emery, *The Press and America*, pp. 54-59.

14. Abrams, Floyd, testimony before the House Judiciary Subcommittee on Courts, Civil Liberties, and the Administration of Justice, Nov. 2, 1983. See House, 98th Cong., 1st and 2nd Sess., House of Representatives, Judiciary Subcommittee on Courts, Civil Liberties, and the Administration of Justice, *1984: Civil Liberties and the National Security State*, Serial No. 103, 1984, p. 7.

15. Summers, "Western Media and Recent Wars," pp. 10-11.

16. Hammond, *The Military and the Media*, pp. 284-87.

17. Hackworth, Col. David H., *About Face — The Odyssey of An American Warrior* (New York: Simon & Schuster, 1989), pp. 601-02.

18. Hammond, *The Military and the Media*, pp. 286-87.

19. O'Rourke, Lawrence, journalists' roundtable discussion shown on C-SPAN, March 29, 1991, transcript, p. 23.

20. Dilenschneider, Georgetown speech, transcript, p. 1.

21. Massey, Donald F., Senior Vice President, Hill and Knowlton/Washington, *Short Form Registration Statement* under the Foreign Agents Registration Act of 1938, as amended, Attachment III, received by the Justice Department Criminal Division on June 3, 1991.

22. See *Exhibit A to Registration Statement* under the Foreign Agents Registration Act of 1938, as amended, filed by Pintak/Brown International, received by the Justice Department Criminal Division on Oct. 16, 1990; *Exhibit A to Registration Statement*, filed by Neill and Company, received by the Justice Department Criminal Division, Jan. 22, 1991. Full discussions of firms who have represented Kuwait and registered under the U.S. Foreign Agents Registration Act (FARA) can be found in *O'Dwyer's FARA Report*, published monthly by J.R. O'Dwyer Co., New York, N.Y.

23. Ibid., Neill and Company.

24. Lee, Gary, "Kuwaitis pay $5.6 million to publicity firm," *The Washington Post*, Dec. 19, 1990, p. A21.

25. Levine, Peter, Counsel for the Senate Governmental Affairs Subcommittee on Oversight of Government Management, *Statement*, testimony before the subcommittee hearing on Enforcement and Administration of the Foreign Agents Registration Act, June 20, 1991, p. 1. See also, *A History and Guide to the Foreign Agents Registration Act for PR Firms*, J.R. O'Dwyer Co., New York, N.Y., pp. 3-7.

26. Ibid., *A History and Guide to the Foreign Agents Registration Act.*

27. Richard, Mark, Deputy Assistant Attorney General, Criminal Division, Justice Department, *Statement Before the Subcommittee on Oversight of Government Management, Committee on Governmental Affairs, United States Senate, Concerning the Disclosure of Foreign Lobbying Under the Foreign Agents Registration Act of 1938, as Amended*, June 20, 1991, pp. 6, 12.

28. Ibid., p. 3.

29. See Levine, *Statement*, pp. 2-9; GAO, National Security and International Affairs Division, *Foreign Agent Registration — Justice Needs to Improve Program Administration* (GAO/NSIAD-90-250), July 30, 1990; Glickman, Rep. Dan (D-Kan.), *Statement*, testimony before the Senate Governmental Affairs Subcommittee on Oversight of Government Management About the Foreign Interests Representation Act of 1991, June 20, 1991, pp. 1-3. The late Sen. John Heinz (R-Pa.) was working on legislation to strengthen FARA at the time of his death last spring.

30. Rep. Dan Glickman (D-Kan.) introduced legislation to broaden and strengthen the Foreign Agents Registration Act in April 1991, and the Justice Department also has recommended changes in the law, according to testimony by Mark Richard, Deputy Assistant Attorney General, Criminal Division, Justice Department, before the Senate Governmental Affairs Subcommittee on Oversight of Government Management on June 20, 1991. The June 20 hearing was one of a series that the subcommittee is holding during 1991 regarding lobbying issues.

31. GAO, July 30, 1990, FARA report, p. 7.

32. Mendelowitz, Allan I., Director, Trade, Energy, and Finance Issues, National Security and International Affairs Division, GAO, *Foreign Agent Registration and Former High-Level Federal Officials Representing Foreign Interests*, testimony before the Senate Committee on Commerce, Science, and Transportation, Sept. 27, 1990, p. 5.

33. Cronkite, Walter, testimony before the Senate Governmental Affairs Committee, Feb. 20, 1991, transcript p. 39.

34. Powell, Gen. Colin, speech to the National Newspaper Association, March 15, 1991, p. 9.

35. Fromkin, David, *A Peace to End All Peace — The Fall of the Ottoman Empire and the Creation of the Modern Middle East* (New York: Avon Books, 1989).

36. Ibid., p. 15.

37. See Perkins, Bradford, "[Report from the] Delegate to the Advisory Committee on Historical Diplomatic Documentation," *Organization of American Historians Newsletter*, August 1990, p. II-7.

38. Ibid.

39. Ibid. In August 1953, supporters of Mosadeq — who had incurred the enmity of

Western nations by nationalizing a British-owned oil company in Iran — forced Shah Mohammed Reza Pahlavi to leave the country. Mosadeq was soon overthrown by a CIA-supported coup which returned the shah to the throne and solidified his power. Popular opposition to the Shah led to his overthrow in 1979. In the resulting power vacuum, Ayatollah Ruhollah Khomeini took control.

40. Interview with the author, July 17, 1991.

Chapter V
The Vietnam War

1. See "Bush: 'What we are doing right,'" *The Washington Post*, Nov. 16, 1990, p. A24; the article comprises excerpts from a CNN interview with President Bush on Nov. 15, 1990. In 1971, the Senate Foreign Relations Committee and its Chairman, J. William Fulbright, asked the Library of Congress to measure the quantitative costs of the war. The result was a study entitled, "Impact of the Vietnam War," published later that year and reproduced in part in *America in Vietnam — A Documentary History* (New York: W. W. Norton & Co., 1989), edited with commentaries by William Appleman Williams, Thomas McCormick, Lloyd Gardner and Walter LaFeber. Sen. Fulbright's introduction states that as of 1971, there were 827,000 South Vietnamese, U.S. and allied military casualties and 1 million civilian casualties in the South. More than 714,000 North Vietnamese and Viet Cong had been killed in action. U.S. troops did not withdraw from South Vietnam until 1973. Stanley Karnow, in his book, *Vietnam — A History* (New York: The Viking Press, 1983), said the final casualty figure for North and South Vietnamese was 4 million (see p. 11).

2. Bryan, C.D.B., *Friendly Fire* (New York: G. P. Putnam's Sons, 1976), p. 362. The author states in his book that his interviews with Gen. Schwarzkopf were tape-recorded.

3. Ryan, Michael, "Here's to the Winners," *Life*, March 18, 1991, p. 34.

4. "The Bear — Gen. H. Norman Schwarzkopf knows soldiers and loves them, knows war and hates it," *U.S. News & World Report*, Feb. 11, 1991, p. 39.

5. See Summers, *On Strategy*, especially pp. 21-70; and his article, "Western media and recent wars," in the May 1986 issue of *Military Review*, pp. 4-17.

6. See Hammond, *The Military and the Media*, p. 22. There are numerous examples of turning to the press in Col. Hackworth's *About Face*. On page 786, for example, he talks of leaking information about problems with Vietnamization in the Delta to Ward Just of *The Washington Post*. Also see Neil Sheehan's book, *A Bright Shining Lie — John Paul Vann and America in Vietnam* (New York: Random House, 1988), pp. 5-6. Vann, who went to South Vietnam as an Army lieutenant colonel in 1962 and eventually became one of the most important Americans in the country, also began talking freely with the media. Like Col. Hackworth, Vann also left the military after his experiences in Southeast Asia. Vann returned to South Vietnam as a civilian, where he continued working with U.S. and South Vietnamese forces as an adviser and de facto field commander until he was killed in a helicopter crash in 1972.

    People such as Hackworth and Vann chose the journalists they spoke with carefully. These officers, like others, had little use for inexperienced reporters who spent their time in the Saigon hotels and wrote stories based solely on the MACV briefings.

7. Hammond, *The Military and the Media*, pp. 16-17, 29-30, 44-45, 72, 93, 160, 366-67. Note, for example, that in 1963, Defense Secretary Robert McNamara, furious that U.S. Army advisers were making critical comments to reporters about the South Vietnamese government and Armed Forces, and about the progress of the war, ordered the Joint Chiefs of Staff Chairman to limit these statements. The Continental Army

Command then told newly assigned personnel to confine their remarks to "areas of personal responsibility and knowledge," and to leave general statements about the conflict to higher-ranking officers.

8. The term "Cong" is an abbreviation of "Cong-san," meaning "Communist," according to Edwin Diamond, former senior editor of *Newsweek* and former senior fellow in political science at Massachusetts Institute of Technology. In an article entitled, "Who is the 'enemy'?" in the Winter 1970-71 issue of *Columbia Journalism Review*, Diamond examined the various terms that U.S. media used when referring to the "enemy" in Vietnam. He pointed out that in the mid-1950s, "there were south of the 17th parallel in Vietnam thousands of Northerners, Southerners, Communists, Resistance fighters, socialists, religious factionalists, nationalists, and other dissidents who opposed the French — and American — supported government in Saigon." These various dissident groups surfaced in 1960 as the National Liberation Front of South Vietnam and resented the term Viet Cong, which had been coined by Saigon newspapers in 1956. The Front called the term a "contemptuous appellation which lumps together Communists and others," according to Diamond.

9. Hammond, *The Military and the Media*, p. 13.

10. Hammond, *The Military and the Media*, p. 15. The quote is from Cable 1006, a directive from the U.S. Information Agency, the State Department and the Defense Department dated Feb. 21, 1962.

11. Ibid.

12. Ibid.

13. Ibid.

14. Ibid., pp. 11-13, 29, 93.

15. Ibid., pp. 12, 29. See also Sheehan, *A Bright Shining Lie*, pp. 88-91, 94-95, 99, 270-292.

16. Ibid.

17. See, for example, Hammond, *The Military and the Media*, pp. 16-17, 134, 145, 240-42.

18. Hammond, *The Military and the Media*, pp. 16-17.

19. Bigart, Homer, "Saigon's regime rejects pressures for reforms," *The New York Times*, June 3, 1962, quoted in Hammond, *The Military and the Media*, p. 15.

20. Ibid.

21. Halberstam, David, "Curbs in Vietnam irk U.S. officers: Americans under orders to withhold news," *The New York Times*, Nov. 22, 1962, quoted in Hammond, *The Military and the Media*, p. 15.

22. Hammond, *The Military and the Media*, pp. 15-16.

23. Ibid.; see pp. 29-38 concerning the January 1963 battle of Ap Bac, and pp. 52-53 concerning Gen. Harkins' rejection of assessments by Col. Daniel B. Porter, Senior Adviser in South Vietnam's IV Corps Tactical Zone in February 1963, and Australian counterinsurgency adviser Col. F. P. Serong, who was attached to Gen. Harkins' staff, in March 1963. Also see Sheehan, *A Bright Shining Lie*, pp. 66-351. These pages include a lengthy discussion of conditions before and after the Ap Bac battle, and Gen. Harkins' refusal to accept Lt. Col. Vann's criticisms of the situation.

24. Hammond, *The Military and the Media*, p. 22.

25. Ibid.

26. Hackworth, *About Face*, p. 778.
27. Ibid. Also see p. 572.
28. Ibid., pp. 667, 778-79. See also Sheehan, *A Bright Shining Lie*, p. 125, in which Sheehan discusses Army Lt. Col. John Paul Vann's acceptance of exaggerated body counts from Vietnamese commanders. Dr. Hammond discusses this issue in *The Military and the Media* on pp. 182, 284 and 317-19.
29. Hackworth, *About Face*, 571-72.
30. Ryan, "Here's to the winners," p. 34. Also see Gen. Schwarzkopf's reference to falsified body counts during his interview with Barbara Walters on ABC-TV's *20/20*, March 15, 1991, transcript, p. 5.
31. Hammond, *The Military and the Media*, especially pp. 318-19. Dr. Hammond pointed out that State Department analysts had reached similar conclusions. Fred Green of the Bureau of Intelligence and Research wrote in September 1967 that MACV statistics were "highly questionable or incomplete." Dr. Hammond cited several sources for his discussion of these events, including a document entitled, "Military Results and Initiative in Vietnam," Office of the Assistant Secretary of Defense for Systems Analysis, Oct. 17, 1967; Mission Council Action Memo 233, Oct. 6, 1967; and Green's memo to William Bundy, Sept. 22, 1967. Also see Hackworth, *About Face*, especially pp. 572-73; interesting information also can be found on pp. 668, 772-74.
32. Ibid.
33. Sheehan, *A Bright Shining Lie*, pp. 273-83.
34. Ibid., p. 283; Hammond, *The Military and the Media*, p. 33-34; Braestrup, Peter, *Big Story* (New Haven, Ct.: Yale University Press, 1983), p. 4. Braestrup's book originally was published in 1977 in two volumes by Westview Press in cooperation with Freedom House.
35. Hammond, *The Military and the Media*, p. 37.
36. Ibid., pp. 29-34; Sheehan, *A Bright Shining Lie*, pp. 203-83.
37. Clifford, Clark with Richard Holbrooke, "Annals of Government (The Vietnam Years — Part I), *The New Yorker*, May 6, 1991, p. 46.
38. U.S. Congress, House, Government Operations Subcommittee on Foreign Operations and Government Information, *Government Information Plans and Policies (Part 4 — Vietnam News Coverage)*, 88th Cong., 1st Sess., May 24, 1963, pp. 387-420. Also see U.S. Congress, House, Committee on Government Operations, *United States Information Problems in Vietnam*, 88th Cong., 1st Sess., Oct. 1, 1963.
39. Hilsman, Roger, testimony before the House Government Operations Subcommittee on Foreign Operations and Government Information, May 24, 1963, p. 389.
40. Ibid., pp. 388, 390.
41. Hammond, *The Military and the Media*, p. 76.
42. Ibid.
43. Ibid., pp. 76-78.
44. Ibid., p. 77. Dr. Hammond is quoting from U.S. Congress, Senate, *Congressional Record*, 88th Cong., 2d Sess., April 27, 1964, p. 8889.
45. Summers, *On Strategy*, p. 48; Karnow, *Vietnam*, pp. 373-76.

46. Karnow, *Vietnam*, p. 375.

47. Ibid., pp. 375-76.

48. To this day, there is disagreement about several aspects of the U.S. operations in the Gulf. See Karnow, *Vietnam*, pp. 364-76; Hammond, *The Military and the Media*, pp. 99-101, 370; Stillman, Don, "Tonkin: what should have been asked," *Columbia Journalism Review*, Winter 1970-71, pp. 21-22; and two books by Lt. Gen. Phillip B. Davidson, *Secrets of the Vietnam War* (Novato, Ca.: Presidio Press, 1990), pp. 129-32, and *Vietnam at War — The History — 1946-75* (Novato, Ca.: Presidio Press, 1988), pp. 317-22. The second incident occurred during bad weather. U.S. forces engaged in considerable shooting. However, the enemy was seen only as radar and sonar blips, and after-action debriefing of the *Maddox* crew raised doubts as to whether the enemy had been present at all. The sonar had been malfunctioning and manned by an overeager operator, and the radar images may have been caused by unusual weather effects. In addition, many crew members were not combat veterans, and Lt. Gen. Davidson wrote that under zero visibility conditions, their reports of torpedo noises and sightings, radar contacts and sinkings could have been combat hysteria. Information concerning doubts about whether there had been a second attack was promptly relayed to Washington, but failed to alter President Johnson's portrayal of the incident as a second North Vietnamese attack.

49. Friendly, Fred W., "TV at the turning point," *Columbia Journalism Review*, Winter 1970-71, p. 14.

50. Stillman, "Tonkin: what should have been asked," pp. 21-25.

51. Hammond, *The Military and the Media*, pp. 78-79. Dr. Hammond is quoting from Rowan's memo to Secretary of State Dean Rusk, June 4, 1964, on the improvement of the U.S. informational/psychological program in South Vietnam.

52. Ibid., pp. 80-82. Dr. Hammond is quoting from State Department Message 59 to the U.S. mission in Saigon, July 7, 1964. This message superseded all previous messages about public affairs except the one concerning Zorthian's appointment.

53. Ibid., pp. 80-83; the need for journalists to travel in small groups is discussed on pp. 366-67. One example of the use of the pool system that Dr. Hammond discussed involved Gen. Westmoreland's decision in February 1968 to limit the number of correspondents who could visit bases in the northern sectors of South Vietnam. For example, only 15 journalists at a time could visit the base at Khe Sanh. According to Dr. Hammond, one reason for limiting access only to small groups of journalists was that more than 600 correspondents had been accredited in Saigon. Gen. Westmoreland said in a Feb. 27, 1968 cable to Adm. Ulysses S. Grant Sharp that limiting press access was necessary to "ease press transportation and housekeeping requirements for our field commanders." Gen. Westmoreland also was concerned that many reporters newly assigned to South Vietnam were inexperienced and might inadvertently reveal information about activities at the northern bases that would be valuable to the North Vietnamese and Viet Cong.

54. Sylvester, Arthur, testimony, U.S. Congress, Senate, Foreign Relations Committee, *News Policies in Vietnam*, 89th Cong., 2d Sess., Aug. 17 and 31, 1966, p. 68.

55. Hammond, *The Military and the Media*, p. 82.

56. Ibid., pp. 81-83; also see Sheehan, *A Bright Shining Lie*, p. 94. Sheehan discussed the fact that members of Congress and Pentagon officials sometimes went along on these trips. He wrote that one of MACV's favorite destinations was the South Vietnamese unit advised by Army Lt. Col. John Paul Vann, because of the unit's high body count

(often falsified) and Vann's skill as a briefer. After Lt. Col. Vann had presented his upbeat, positive briefings with charts, graphs and slides, he sometimes quietly took the Pentagon representatives aside for private, more realistic briefings that neither lawmakers nor reporters were invited to attend.

57. Ibid., pp. 82, 93, 102-03. Assistant Secretary of Defense for Public Affairs Arthur Sylvester told the Senate Foreign Relations Committee in August 1966 that in one 13-month period, the Pentagon had provided more than 80 journalists with short tours of South Vietnam. See his testimony, Aug. 17 and 31, 1966, p. 68.

58. Ibid., p. 68.

59. Clark, Sen. Joseph S., statement, Senate Foreign Relations Committee hearings, Aug. 17 and 31, 1966, p. 108.

60. Hammond, *The Military and the Media*, p. 102-03.

61. Ibid., pp. 94-95.

62. Ibid., p. 184. Dr. Hammond bases his account of this incident on an interview with U.S. mission spokesman Barry Zorthian, and on CBS reporter Morley Safer's article, "Television covers the war"; both are part of *News Policies in Vietnam*, Aug. 17 and 31, 1966, pp. 90-92. Sylvester denied the account during his testimony to the Senate Foreign Relations Committee; see p. 71. Sylvester rephrased his sentiments, saying on page 67 of his testimony that "American newsmen in Vietnam need help from their government if they are to report accurately and objectively to the American public." But Dr. Hammond wrote that Zorthian confirmed the original account during a 1984 interview. Sylvester died in 1979.

63. Ibid., p. 135.

64. Hammond, *The Military and the Media*, pp. 192-93. Dr. Hammond is quoting from a cable that Gen. Westmoreland sent to Lt. Gen. John L. Throckmorton on Aug. 6, 1965.

65. Ibid.; see, for example, pp. 44-45, 72, 93, 160.

66. Ibid., p. 136.

67. Ibid., p. 160.

68. Ibid., p. 241. Dr. Hammond is discussing a message from Adm. Sharp to MACV dated Aug. 9, 1966.

69. Hackworth, *About Face*, p. 569-71.

70. Clifford, with Holbrooke, "Annals of Government (The Vietnam Years — Part I)," p. 64.

71. Shockley, Col. Henry A., testimony before the House Select Committee on Intelligence, hearings, "The 1968 Tet Offensive in South Vietnam: II," Dec. 3, 1975, p. 1657-60.

72. Hackworth, *About Face*, p. 713.

73. Ibid., pp. 744-45.

74. Ibid., p. 713.

75. Col. Hackworth alludes to this situation throughout *About Face*. Especially interesting are incidents mentioned on pages 587-646. For example, in 1968, during the time he was assigned to the Pentagon, Col. Hackworth was one of 16 Army officers asked to express their views in writing on problems facing the Army for Gen. Westmoreland, who had gone from being Commander of the U.S. forces in Vietnam to being Army Chief of Staff. Col. Hackworth's report, which summarized years of other reports he had prepared in South Vietnam and during his time in Washington, stated, "The U.S.

Army has badly botched the war. I have concluded, after exhaustive study, that we have lost." The report, excerpts of which appear on pages 613-15, discussed the corruption and indifference of the South Vietnamese Armed Forces, the failure of the U.S. Army to understand the nature of guerrilla warfare, and the unwillingness of the U.S. military to listen to assessments that did not agree with their preconceived ideas concerning how the war was going. The excerpts concluded with the statement, "To succeed in today's Army one must be quick on his feet and dazzle all with shifty footwork. To be a winner you cannot rock the boat and you must be willing to change your positions to accommodate the views of your 'superiors.' I found my head starting to nod in agreement though I knew down deep inside that I was in complete disagreement! My growing Pavlovian tendencies scared me to my roots!"

76. Ibid., pp. 791-95. Hackworth put in for retirement shortly after filming the "Issues and Answers" program. Pentagon officials began a formal investigation of his career and threatened to court martial him on a series of charges, including violations of currency regulations and gambling. Hackworth retained Washington, D.C. lawyer Joseph Califano and eventually was allowed to retire without incident.

Col. Hackworth's television appearance is an example of one of the most important ways in which the press can help Armed Forces officers in wartime. As Col. Summers wrote in a May 1986 *Military Review* article, "Western media and recent wars," one of the functions of the media is to serve as "unofficial links" between field commanders and government officials in Congress, the White House and the Pentagon itself. The media enable officers to bypass formal communications channels that have been "deliberately blocked in order to conceal military incompetence or inadvertently clogged by bureaucratic arteriosclerosis," Summers wrote.

77. Hammond, *The Military and the Media*, p. 139. Dr. Hammond is quoting from a message from Defense Secretary McNamara to Gen. Westmoreland, March 2, 1965.

78. Ibid., p. 139. Dr. Hammond is quoting from a message from Gen. Westmoreland to Defense Secretary McNamara, March 3, 1965.

79. Ibid., pp. 138-40, 144, 160-61, 193-95.

80. Summers, *On Strategy*, p. 255.

81. Hammond, *The Military and the Media*, p. 195.

82. Ibid., pp. 237-38.

83. Hammond, "The press in Vietnam as agent of defeat: A critical examination," *Reviews in American History*, June 1989, pp. 315-16.

84. Hammond, *The Military and the Media*, p. 322.

85. Ibid. Also based on Dr. Hammond's interview with the author, June 13, 1991. The role of escorts varied during the Vietnam War. Peter Braestrup said in an interview for this study that when he was in South Vietnam for *The Washington Post*, escorts did not always accompany reporters, but when they did, they acted as guides, arranging transportation and communications, and facilitating access with units in the field.

At times, however, journalists were required to have escorts in the hopes that the presence of these military personnel would have a chilling effect on troops who talked with the press. On pages 140-43 of his book, Dr. Hammond wrote that Ambassador Maxwell D. Taylor became so concerned about stories that discussed U.S. bombing missions in Laos that in March 1965 he considered closing the Da Nang and Bien Hoa Air Bases, where U.S. pilots lived and worked, to any journalist without an escort. Dr. Hammond wrote that the ambassador believed this would "reduce the access of the Saigon correspondents to South Vietnamese and American airmen and limit the amount of specific information they could acquire."

South Vietnamese officials followed up on this idea, closing the Da Nang base to unescorted correspondents. Local U.S. commanders then said journalists could not enter American service clubs or canteens at the base. Associated Press Managing Editor Wes Gallagher said preventing free access to the base and requiring escorts for reporters was "clearly aimed not at security matters but at controlling what American fighting men might say."

86. Ibid., pp. 236-37, 321. Also see Sylvester's testimony before the Senate Foreign Relations Committee, Aug. 17 and 31, 1966, pp. 67-69, 97-98, 108-09.

87. Sylvester, testimony before the Senate Foreign Relations Committee, Aug. 17 and 31, 1966, p. 68.

88. Hammond, *The Military and the Media*, p. 333.

89. Ibid., pp. 289-90, 333-35.

90. Ibid., p. 334. Dr. Hammond is quoting from Gen. Westmoreland's speech at the National Press Club, Nov. 21, 1967.

91. Ibid., pp. 333-82; Summers, *On Strategy*, pp. 33-44.

92. See, for example, Lt. Gen. Phillip B. Davidson, who excoriates the press in *Vietnam at War*, pp. 483-92; William A. Hamilton, who served two years in Vietnam and is now a syndicated columnist, and who delivered a speech entitled, "A Vietnam soldier's view of the media: the transition to reality," at the Accuracy in Media "War and the media" conference in Washington, D.C. on April 25-26, 1991.

93. See, for example, Braestrup, *Big Story*, pp. xi-xiii, 467-68, 511-12. Braestrup stated that media coverage of the offensive, which presented Tet as a disaster for the U.S. and South Vietnamese war effort, was a "distortion of reality." This distortion resulted from numerous factors, Braestrup wrote. The attacks on Saigon and the U.S. Embassy were personally threatening to journalists based in the capital, which contributed to reporters' impressions that the offensive was a catastrophe. The shock of these attacks after months of U.S. statements about how well the war was going resulted in stories that reflected not only journalists' subjective reactions to Tet, but also their resentment about "prior manipulation by the Administration." Many reporters, accustomed to basing their stories on easily understood themes, were unprepared to cope with "the unusual ambiguities and uncertainties" surrounding Tet. This situation was exacerbated by President Johnson's inability to take the initiative and provide journalists with a news agenda based on definite U.S. plans. The president's indecisiveness fueled additional stories focusing on Tet as a disaster for U.S. interests, Braestrup wrote. For another explanation of the coverage, see Mohr, Charles, "Once again — Did the press lose Vietnam?" *Columbia Journalism Review*, Nov.-Dec. 1983, pp. 51-56.

94. See Hammond, *The Military and the Media*, p. 372; Braestrup, *Big Story*, pp. xiii, 505-06; Mueller, *War, Presidents and Public Opinion*, pp. 57, 106.

95. Hammond, *The Military and the Media*, p. 372.

96. Clifford, with Holbrooke, "Annals of Government (The Vietnam Years — Part II)," *The New Yorker*, May 13, 1991, p. 52.

97. Braestrup, *Big Story*, pp. xi-xiii; 466-68; 505-06.

98. Hammond, *The Military and the Media*, p. 372, citing polling data from Roper in *Big Story*, Westview Press edition, Vol. I, p. 687. Support for President Johnson decreased even as support for the war and for U.S. policy increased after the start of Tet, according to statistics cited by Dr. Hammond. The percentage of the public who disapproved of his handling of the war had risen from 47 percent to 63 percent by the end of February 1968.

99. Adams, Samuel A., "Vietnam cover-up: Playing war with numbers," *Harpers*, May 1975, pp. 41-73.

100. Adams, testimony, U.S. Congress, House, Select Committee on Intelligence, hearings, *U.S. Intelligence Agencies and Activities: The Performance of the Intelligence Community*, Part 2, 94th Cong., 1st Sess., Sept. 18, 1975, p. 683.

101. Adams, "Vietnam cover-up," pp. 43-44.

102. Ibid. Six years after his article appeared, Adams' allegations about the U.S. military's alterations of the enemy order of battle became the starting point for a CBS-TV documentary that resulted in a libel suit by Gen. Westmoreland. Adams was a paid consultant for the program and also was interviewed on camera. However, the documentary, "CBS Reports — The Uncounted Enemy: A Vietnam Deception" went beyond Adams' assertions in the *Harper's* article and testimony before the House Select Committee on Intelligence. The program stated that Gen. Westmoreland headed a conspiracy to alter the figures that resulted in deceiving the President as well as Congress and the American people about the enemy order of battle.

The documentary quickly became controversial. CBS was criticized for not showing more interviews that supported Gen. Westmoreland's position, for not interviewing a key member of his staff who had a great deal of responsibility for the order of battle, for not identifying Adams as a paid consultant in his televised interview, for interviewing one person twice and allowing him to see other interviews critical of Gen. Westmoreland. More serious, in a legal sense, were several errors of fact and context. For example, one military officer critical of changes made to enemy troop estimates was misidentified as a member of Westmoreland's staff, and was presented as having received orders to change the estimates from Gen. Westmoreland himself; another officer's answer to a hypothetical question about altering order of battle figures was presented as a response to something Gen. Westmoreland actually had done; one officer's characterization of the estimates as "crap" was linked to figures prepared by the U.S. military when actually it referred to figures prepared by the South Vietnamese and used by the U.S. military.

In September 1982, Gen. Westmoreland filed a $120 million libel suit against CBS and some of its employees, including consultant Adams. The case went to trial more than two years later, in October 1984. It resulted in thousands of pages of previously classified U.S. documents about the Vietnam War being declassified, providing a riveting look at how the government had made decisions about the conflict.

The trial lasted more than three months. Both sides presented military officers who supported their position. The case was settled just before it went to the jury. There was no monetary settlement, and no retraction by CBS. Instead, CBS and Gen. Westmoreland signed a joint statement. The statement said that CBS "respects General Westmoreland's long and faithful service to his country and never intended to assert, and does not believe, that General Westmoreland was unpatriotic or disloyal in performing his duties as he saw them." The general and his attorney said the statement amounted to an apology by the network, cleared his name and restored his honor. Gen. Westmoreland said in the statement that he "respects the long and distinguished journalistic tradition of CBS and the rights of journalists to examine the complex issues of Vietnam and to present perspectives contrary to his own."

103. See, for example, Davidson, *Secrets of the Vietnam War*, pp. 29-92. During the war, Davidson spent two years as chief intelligence officer for Gen. Westmoreland and Gen. Abrams.

104. Graham, James C., letter to the editor, *Harper's*, July 1975, Appendix V, House Select Committee on Intelligence hearings, "The 1968 Tet Offensive in South Vietnam: II," Dec. 3, 1975, pp. 2003-04.

105. Adams, testimony before the House Select Committee on Intelligence, Sept. 18, 1975, pp. 684-85.

106. Graham, Lt. Gen. Daniel, testimony before the House Select Committee on Intelligence, "The 1968 Tet Offensive in South Vietnam: II," Dec. 3, 1975, p. 1653.

107. Ibid.

108. Ibid.

109. McArthur, Richard G., testimony before the House Select Committee on Intelligence, "The 1968 Tet Offensive in South Vietnam: II," Dec. 3, 1975, p. 1656.

110. McClory, Rep. Robert, statement during House Select Committee on Intelligence hearings, "The 1968 Tet Offensive in South Vietnam: II," Dec. 3, 1975, p. 1662-63.

111. Westmoreland, Gen. William, letter to Rep. Dale Milford, December 1975, p. 1. The exchange of correspondence between Rep. Milford and Gen. Westmoreland comprises Appendix VI, House Select Committee on Intelligence, "The 1968 Tet Offensive in South Vietnam: II," Dec. 3, 1975.

112. Ibid.

113. Ibid., pp. 1-2.

114. Ibid., p. 2.

115. Testimony about this was presented during the Westmoreland-CBS trial by two military officers, Army recon specialist Daniel Friedman and Howard Embree, a West Point graduate who went through Ranger and Airborne training and became an adviser to the South Vietnamese Army in Quang Tri province. The two men, witnesses for CBS, built booby traps on the witness stand in a matter of minutes. Friedman stated that to make such a device, "All you have to do is to be able to tie a knot." Their testimony is recounted in *Vietnam on Trial — Westmoreland vs. CBS*, by Bob Brewin and Sydney Shaw (New York: Atheneum, 1987), pp. 295-99. This book, considered the most authoritative on the controversy, was written by two reporters who were given access to documents by both sides in the case, interviewed the principals before and after the trial, and submitted a draft of the book to each of the principals for comments on factual and contextual accuracy, and fairness.

116. Hackworth, *About Face*, p. 627.

117. Ibid., p. 694.

118. Latham, Aaron, "Introduction to the Pike Papers," *The Village Voice*, Feb. 16, 1976, p. 70.

119. U.S. Congress, House, Select Committee on Intelligence, Final Report, January 1976, printed in *The Village Voice*, Feb. 16, 1976, p. 92. The quotes here are taken from Section II of the report, "The Select Committee's Investigative Record," and appeared on pages 76-77 of the *Voice*.

120. Ibid. The debate about the effects of enemy troop estimates continues today, as can be seen in Lt. Gen. Davidson's *Secrets of the Vietnam War*, which devotes two chapters to refuting Adams' statistics and arguments. Adams cannot reply; he died of a heart attack in 1988.

121. See, for example, the discussion of this issue in Hammond, *The Military and the Media*, pp. 385-88; Hammond, "The press in Vietnam," pp. 312-23; Mueller, *War, Presidents and Public Opinion*, which discusses public opinion during the wars in Korea and Vietnam, with pages 58-65 and 155-67 being especially useful; Michael D. Sherer's article, "Vietnam war photos and public opinion," in the Summer 1989 issue of *Journalism Quarterly*, pp. 391-95 and page 530.

122. Summers, Col. Harry G., testimony, Senate Governmental Affairs Committee, Feb. 20, 1991, pp. 1-2.

123. Hammond, *The Military and the Media*, p. 387. Dr. Hammond is citing Mueller, *War, Presidents and Public Opinion*, pp. 60, 154-56.

124. Summers, *On Strategy*, p. 68.

125. Sidle, interview with the author, April 13, 1991.

126. Hammond, "The press in Vietnam," p. 318; also see Hammond, *The Military and the Media*, p. 35.

127. Sheehan, *A Bright Shining Lie*, p. 271.

128. Ibid. Sheehan returned from his last year of covering the war in 1966, and in 1971 obtained the Pentagon Papers for *The New York Times*.

129. Howell, Maj. Cass D., "War, television and public opinion," *Military Review*, February 1987, p. 72.

130. Hammond, "The press in Vietnam," p. 315. Hammond is citing statistics from a study done by Northwestern University researcher Lawrence Lichty, which the researcher detailed in an article entitled, "Comments on the influence of television on public opinion," in *Vietnam as History: Ten Years After the Paris Peace Accords* (Washington, D.C.: Woodrow Wilson International Center for Scholars, 1984), a book edited by Peter Braestrup. Also see Dr. Hammond's discussion of this issue in *The Military and the Media*, pp. 237-38.

131. Mueller, *War, Presidents and Public Opinion*, p. 167. In a footnote, the author pointed out that a 1967 Harris poll once reported, "For most Americans television helps simplify the enormous complexities of the war and the net effect is that when they switch off their sets, 83 percent feel more hawkish than they did before they turned them on." However, this statement was based on responses to the question, "Has the television coverage of the war made you feel more like you ought to back up the boys fighting in Vietnam or not?"

132. Ibid., p. 164.

133. Zorthian, Barry, *Statement Before Senate Government Affairs Committee on Pentagon Press Rules in the Persian Gulf War*, Feb. 15, 1991, delivered during hearings of Feb. 20, 1991, transcript, p. 2.

134. Sidle, testimony before the Senate Governmental Affairs Committee, Feb. 20, 1991, transcript, p. 77.

135. Sidle, interview with the author, April 13, 1991. Also see Braestrup, Peter, *Battle Lines*, pp. 61-75, which addresses security concerns and details additional violations.

136. Hammond, *The Military and the Media*, pp. 374-75.

137. Sidle, interview with the author, April 13, 1991.

138. Zorthian, Barry, statement during "The war and the media: A retrospective," National Press Club, March 19, 1991.

139. Zorthian, *Statement*, Senate Governmental Affairs Committee, delivered Feb. 20, 1991, transcript, p. 3.

140. Hackworth, *About Face*, pp. 668, 778.

141. Ibid., p. 844.

142. Hammond, *The Military and the Media*, pp. 284-86. For a complete analysis of the M-16 controversy, see Fallows, James, *National Defense* (New York: Vintage Books, 1981), pp. 76-95.

143. Howell, "War, television and public opinion," p. 77.

Chapter VI
The Falklands/Malvinas War

1. In addition to British books written about Falklands news coverage, excellent background information on how Vietnam influenced British officials responsible for controlling the coverage can be found in Peter Braestrup's *Battle Lines*, which devotes a chapter to the Falklands War, and Michael J. Arlen's article, "The Air — The Falklands, Vietnam, and our collective memory," *The New Yorker*, Aug. 16, 1982, p. 70.

2. Harris, Robert, *GOTCHA! The Media, the Government and the Falklands Crisis* (London: Faber and Faber Inc., 1983), p. 62. The word "Gotcha!" is the enormous front-page headline that ran in early editions of Rupert Murdoch's London-based newspaper, the *Sun*, on May 4, 1982. It accompanied a picture of the Argentine ship *General Belgrano*, which had been torpedoed the day before by a British submarine. More than 350 Argentine troops died in the incident. Harris said later editions carried a more subdued headline: "DID 1200 ARGIES DROWN?"

3. Ibid. Also see Feron, James, "British reporters tell new side of Falkland story," *The New York Times*, July 3, 1982, p. A2. The *Times* story quotes ITN reporter Michael Nicholson as saying, "it was a question of, 'Look what you people did in Vietnam, turning a nation against the war.'"

4. Ibid. See also, Morrison, David E., and Tumber, Howard, *Journalists at War — The Dynamics of News Reporting During the Falklands Conflict* (London: Sage Publications Ltd., 1988), pp. 168-69.

5. Ibid., p. 65.

6. Ibid.

7. See Adams, Valerie, *The Media and the Falklands Campaign* (London: MacMillan, 1986), p. vii.

8. See HCDC Report, pp. xii-xv; Feron, "British reporters tell new side of Falkland story"; Karl, Patricia A., "Media Diplomacy, " *Proceedings of the Academy of Political Science*, Vol. 34, No. 4, 1982, p. 146.

9. HCDC Report, p. xii.

10. Ibid, p. xvii.

11. Ibid., p. vii. See also, Willis, David K., "Falklands fallout: A tale of British reporters chafing," *The Christian Science Monitor*, June 23, 1982, p. A1.

12. Knightley, "The Falklands: How Britannia ruled the news, " p. 53.

13. HCDC Report, pp. xv-xvi; Adams, *The Media and the Falklands Campaign*, pp. 6-7; Morrison and Tumbler, *Journalists at War*, pp. 167-70 (timetable for delays for major stories is on page 169).

14. HCDC Report, p. xix; Adams, *The Media and the Falklands Campaign*, p. 6.

15. Harris, *GOTCHA!*, p. 68. See also Clarke, Gerald, "Covering an Uncoverable War," *Time*, May 17, 1982, p. 53.

16. Ibid., p. 68.

17. Ibid., pp. 68-69.

18. See Harris, *GOTCHA!*, p. 70; Morrison and Tumber, *Journalists at War*, p. 169.

19. Ibid.

20. Harris, *GOTCHA!*, pp. 60-61.

21. Ibid., p. 61.

22. Ibid., p. 121.

23. HCDC Report, p. viii; Morrison and Tumber, *Journalists at War*, pp. 227-40; Harris, *GOTCHA!*, pp. 71-92; Lewis, Flora, "Foreign Affairs — Double Standards," *The New York Times*, June 3, 1982, p. A23; Panter-Downes, Mollie, "Letter from London," *The New Yorker*, May 31, 1982, p. 91-93.

24. Morrison and Tumber, *Journalists at War*, p. 228.

25. HCDC Report, p. viii; Lewis, Flora, "Double Standards."

26. "Dare call it treason," editorial, *Sun*, May 7, 1982.

27. Harris, *GOTCHA!*, p. 75.

28. Ibid., p. 94.

29. Ibid., p. 93.

30. HCDC Report, p. xliii.

31. Ibid., p. xiii.

32. Harris, *GOTCHA!*, pp. 99-100; Smith, Mark S., The Associated Press, "British blunders made Falklands 'a close thing,'" *Los Angeles Times*, Nov. 7, 1982, p. A1.

33. Harris, *GOTCHA!*, pp. 99-100.

34. Adams, *The Media and the Falklands Campaign*, p. 207.

35. Harris, *GOTCHA!*, p. 100.

36. Ibid., p. 99.

37. See, for example, the discussion of the *General Belgrano* incident in *War and Peace News*, produced by the Glasgow University Media Group (Milton Keynes, Great Britain: Open University Press, 1985), beginning on page 29. Also see Apple, R. W. Jr., "Secrets case won, Briton quits post," *The New York Times*, Feb. 18, 1985, p. A3; The Associated Press, "British official denies deception on '82 sinking of Argentine ship," *The New York Times*, Feb. 19, 1985, p. A6; "Defence aide renews Falklands cover-up charge," *Reuters*, March 13, 1985.

38. See *Official Secrets Act, 1911*, Section 2.

39. Braestrup, *Battle Lines*, p. 82.

40. Humphries, "Two routes to the wrong destination," pp. 70-71.

41. Joyce, Edward M., CBS News President, *Statement* to the House Judiciary Subcommittee on Courts, Civil Liberties, and the Administration of Justice, Hearings on Civil Liberties and the National Security State, Nov. 2, 1983.

Chapter VII
The Invasion of Grenada

1. See, for example, Crossette, Barbara, "Grenada looks to Cuban ways and U.S. tourists," *The New York Times*, Feb. 7, 1982, p. Al; Massing, Michael, "Grenada before and after," *The Atlantic*, February 1984, p. 76.

2. "Serpent in Caribbean island paradises," *U.S. News & World Report*, May 19, 1980, p. 25.

3. See Tyler, Patrick E., "The making of an invasion: Chronology of the planning," *The Washington Post*, Oct. 30, 1983, p. A1. Also see Dam, Kenneth W., Deputy Secretary of State, "The larger importance of Grenada," *Current Policy No. 526*, U.S. Department of State, Nov. 4, 1983; Motley, Langhorne A., Assistant Secretary of State for Inter-American Affairs, "The decision to assist Grenada," *Current Policy No. 541*, submitted as testimony before the House Armed Services Committee, Jan. 24, 1984.

4. In his nationally televised speech two days after the invasion, President Reagan talked about Bishop's attempt to establish better relations with the United States, stating, "Whether or not he was serious, we'll never know." See "Transcript of address by President on Lebanon and Grenada," *The New York Times*, Oct. 28, 1983, p. A10.

5. Statements by medical school Chancellor Charles Modica and Vice Chancellor Geoffrey Bourne on "Operation Urgent Fury," *Frontline*, Feb. 2, 1988, Journal Graphics Inc. transcript, p. 13.

6. Tyler, "The making of an invasion."

7. Cody, Edward, "Cuba condemns Grenada coup, will review tie," *The Washington Post*, Oct. 22, 1983, p. A1.

8. Tyler, "The making of an invasion." Also see Motley, State Department *Current Policy No. 541*; Dam, State Department *Current Policy No. 526*; and the Department of State and Department of Defense, *Grenada — A Preliminary Report*, Dec. 16, 1983.

9. Motley, State Department *Current Policy No. 541*, p. 2.

10. See, for example, St. Lucia Prime Minister John Compton's remarks on *The MacNeil/Lehrer News Hour*, PBS, Oct. 27, 1983. Also see Motley, State Department *Current Policy No. 541*, pp. 2-3.

11. See Tyler, "The making of an invasion."

12. Statements by Modica, Geoffrey Bourne and former Carter White House official Peter Bourne on "Operation Urgent Fury," Journal Graphics Inc. transcript, pp. 14-16.

13. Tyler, "The making of an invasion."

14. Ibid.

15. Ibid.; also see a report from *United Press International*, Oct. 23, 1983, distributed as regional news in the New York area.

16. Ayres, B. Drummond Jr., "U.S. Marines diverted to Grenada in event Americans face danger," *The New York Times*, Oct. 22, 1983, p. A1.

17. Hiatt, Fred, "U.S. says situation still unclear as naval force nears Grenada," *The Washington Post*, Oct. 23, 1983, p. A24.

18. Ibid.

19. Madigan, Nick, *United Press International* report, Oct. 22, 1983, filed from Bridgetown, Barbados, for international distribution.

20. Prial, Frank J., "American envoys going to Grenada," *The New York Times*, Oct. 23, 1983, p. A1.

21. Ibid.

22. See Motley, State Department *Current Policy No. 541*, which has a chronological accounting of U.S. actions leading up to the invasion. Also see Tyler, "The making of an invasion."

23. Tyler, "The making of an invasion."

24. Ibid.; Cannon, Lou and Hoffman, David, "Speakes complained in memo; invasion secrecy creating a furor," *The Washington Post*, Oct. 27, 1983, p. A1; Cannon, Lou, "White House press aide resigns in row over Grenada policy," *The Washington Post*, Nov. 1, 1983, p. A22.

25. Gailey, Phil, "U.S. bars coverage of Grenada action; news groups protest," *The New York Times*, Oct. 27, 1983, p. A1.

26. Maraniss, David, "Information blackout revives old issues," *The Washington Post*, Nov. 15, 1983, p. A2.

27. Braestrup, *Battle Lines*, p. 3.

28. Tyler, "The making of an invasion"; also see Motley, State Department *Current Policy No. 541*; "D-Day in Grenada — the U.S. and friends take over a troubled Caribbean isle," *Time*, Nov. 7, 1983, p. 28.

29. Braestrup, *Battle Lines*, p. 89; Hertsgaard, *On Bended Knee—The Press and the Reagan Presidency* (New York: Farrar Straus Giroux, 1988), pp. 213-14. Also see Taylor, Stuart Jr., "In wake of invasion, much official misinformation by U.S. comes to light," *The New York Times*, Nov. 6, 1983, p. A20; Cannon and Hoffman, "Speakes complained in memo"; Cannon, "White House press aide resigns"; Castro, Janice, "Keeping the press from the action — for the first time, a major U.S. military operation is blacked out," *Time*, Nov. 7, 1983, p. 65.

30. Hertsgaard, *On Bended Knee*, p. 214.

31. Ibid.

32. Letter from President Reagan to Sen. Strom Thurmond, Oct. 25, 1983.

33. Kaufman, Michael T., "1,900 U.S. troops, with Caribbean allies, invade Grenada and fight leftist units; Moscow protests; British are critical," *The New York Times*, Oct. 26, 1983, p. A1.

34. "Text of Reagan's announcement of invasion," *The New York Times*, Oct. 26, 1983. A different rationale was presented by the Joint Task Force Commander for the Grenada operation, Vice Adm. Joseph Metcalf III, during a Columbia University seminar on the military and the media held on Feb. 24, 1991. At that time, Adm. Metcalf said, "We were told to go, you know, install a friendly government." The remarks are on page 30 of the transcript.

35. Ibid.

36. McQuiston, John T., "School's chancellor says invasion was not necessary to save lives," *The New York Times*, Oct. 26, 1983, p. A20; Omang, Joanne, "Americans in Grenada, calling home, say they were safe before invasion," *The Washington Post*, Oct. 26, 1983, p. A11; Logeman, Henry G., *United Press International* report, Oct. 25, 1983.

37. Friendly, Jonathan, "Reporting the news in a communique war," *The New York Times*, Oct. 26, 1983, p. A23.

38. *United Press International* report, Oct. 27, 1983, for regional distribution.

39. Gailey, "U.S. bars coverage of Grenada."

40. Ibid; Cannon and Hoffman, "Speakes complained in memo."

41. Hertsgaard, *On Bended Knee*, p. 215; Cannon and Hoffman, "Speakes complained in memo"; Cannon, "White House press aide resigns."

42. Cannon and Hoffman, "Speakes complained in memo."

43. Ibid.; Friedrich, Otto, "Anybody want to go to Grenada? Angry reporters finally get to a story after it is all but over," *Time*, Nov. 14, 1983, p. 70.

44. See Gailey, "U.S. bars coverage of Grenada"; Castro, "Keeping the press from the action."

45. Hunter, Marjorie, "U.S. eases restrictions on coverage," *The New York Times*, Oct. 31, 1983, p. A12.

46. "Grenada — and Mount Suribachi," *The New York Times*, Oct. 28, 1983, p. A26.

47. Gailey, "U.S. bars coverage of Grenada."

48. Ibid.; *The New York Times*, "Grenada — and Mount Suribachi"; Cannon and Hoffman, "Speakes complained in memo"; Weinraub, Bernard, "U.S. press curbs: the unanswered questions," *The New York Times*, Oct. 29, 1983, Section 1, page 1.

49. Farrell, William E., "U.S. allows 15 reporters to go to Grenada for day," *The New York Times*, Oct. 28, 1983, p. A13; "White House admits Pentagon censorship," *Baltimore Sun*, Oct. 28, 1983. Also see Friendly, Jonathan, "Weinberger tied to curb on press," *The New York Times*, Nov. 13, 1983, Section 1, p. 19; Kaiser, Charles, "An off-the-record war," *Newsweek*, Nov. 7, 1983, p. 83; Castro, "Keeping the press from the action."

50. Cronkite, Walter, statements made on *CBS Newswatch*, transcript reprinted in *Congressional Record*, Senate, Oct. 29, 1983, p. S14964.

51. Ibid.

52. Gailey, "U.S. bars coverage of Grenada"; Castro, "Keeping the press from the action." Also see Friendly, "Reporting the news in a communique war"; testimony of Fred C. Ikle, Under Secretary of Defense for Policy, before the House Armed Services Committee, Jan. 24, 1984, *Full Committee Hearing on the Lessons Learned as a Result of the U.S. Military Operations in Grenada*, House Armed Services Committee, 98th Cong., 2d. Sess., Jan. 24, 1984, pp. 2-3.

53. The *Newsweek* magazine printed the Sunday before the invasion had substantial information about a possible U.S. invasion. In addition to articles mentioned earlier in this chapter, other pre-invasion stories included UPI reporter Nick Madigan's story on Oct. 24, 1983, which talked about three helicopters and a U.S. Navy jet carrying Marines landing in Barbados; Michael Kaufman's *New York Times* story, "50 Marines land at Barbados field," which ran the morning of the invasion, and Edward Cody's story, "Grenada puts military on alert, warns of U.S. threat to invade," which ran in *The Washington Post* on Oct. 24, 1983, the day before the invasion, on page A4.

54. Maraniss, "Information blackout revives old issues"; Gailey, "U.S. bars coverage of Grenada."

55. Kaiser, "An off-the-record war."
56. See Ikle's testimony before the House Armed Services Committee, and remarks made by Adm. Metcalf during the Columbia University seminar on the military and the media, transcript, pp. 28-29. Background interviews with the author regarding this subject were done during the spring of 1991.
57. Friedrich, "Anybody want to go to Grenada?" Adm. Metcalf repeated this rationale at the Columbia University seminar, transcript, p. 29.
58. *The Associated Press*, "Admiral says it was his decision to tether the press," *The New York Times*, Oct. 31, 1983, p. A12; Friendly, "Weinberger tied to curb on press"; Kaiser, "An off-the-record war."
59. Friedrich, "Anybody want to go to Grenada?"
60. Ibid.; interview with Tim Ross, by the author, Sept. 7, 1991.
61. Castro, "Keeping the press from the action."
62. Cody, Edward, "The day war roared into St. George's picture-book harbor," *The Washington Post*, Oct. 28, 1983, p. A1, and "The invasion of Grenada — U.S. forces thwart journalists' reports," *The Washington Post*, Oct. 28, 1983, p. A16; Diederich, Bernard, "Images from an unlikely war — a report from the battle," *Time*, Nov. 7, 1983, p. 30, and "War news: under new management," *Worldview*, July 1984, p. 7.
63. Cody, "The day war roared into St. George's"; Diederich, "Images from an unlikely war" and "War news: under new management."
64. Cody, "The day war roared into St. George's."
65. Ibid.; Diederich, "Images from an unlikely war."
66. Diederich, "War news: under new management."
67. Cody, "The day war roared into St. George's."
68. Ibid.
69. Ibid.
70. Castro, "Keeping the press from the action."
71. Editor's note at the end of Cody's "The invasion of Grenada," Oct. 28, 1983.
72. Cody, "The invasion of Grenada."
73. Ibid.
74. Editor's note at the end of a story by Associated Press correspondent Kernan Turner, "Admiral fights 2 battles: with Grenada and press," *The Washington Post*, Oct. 31, 1983.
75. Ibid.
76. Diederich, "Images from an unlikely war."
77. Ibid.
78. Ibid.
79. Ibid.
80. Ibid.
81. Ibid.

82. Janka, Les, "Grenada, the media, and national security," *Armed Forces Journal International*, December 1983, p. 9.
83. Ibid.
84. Ibid.
85. Ibid.
86. Hertsgaard, *On Bended Knee*, p. 214; Friendly, "Weinberger tied to curb on press"; Middleton, Drew, "Barring the press from the battlefield," *The New York Times Magazine*, Feb. 5, 1984, pp. 69, 92. Cannon, "White House press aide resigns."
87. Hertsgaard, *On Bended Knee*, p. 214.
88. Castro, "Keeping the press from the action."
89. Friedheim, Jerry W., *Statement* of the position of the American Newspaper Publishers Association, printed in the *Congressional Record*, Senate, Oct. 29, 1983, p. S14961.
90. Gailey, "U.S. bars coverage of Grenada."
91. Joyce, Edward M., letter to Defense Secretary Weinberger, Oct. 25, 1983.
92. This phrase became almost a motto after President Reagan used it in his Oct. 27, 1983 speech. See "Transcript of address by President on Lebanon and Grenada," *The New York Times*, Oct. 28, 1983, p. A10.
93. Weicker, Sen. Lowell, remarks in *Congressional Record*, Senate, Oct. 28, 1983, p. S14884.
94. Ibid.
95. There were exceptions, including such journalists as Cody, Diederich and Bohning.
96. See Castro, "Keeping the press from the action."
97. Metcalf, Vice Adm. Joseph, comments during Columbia University seminar, transcript, p. 30.
98. See "Transcript of address by President on Lebanon and Grenada."
99. Interview with Capt. Ron Wildermuth, by the author, July 8, 1991.
100. Friedrich, "Anybody want to go to Grenada?"
101. Shales, Tom, "Grenada: A question of news control; limited to military footage, networks cry foul," *The Washington Post*, Oct. 28, 1983, p. B1.
102. Ibid.
103. Ibid.
104. Ibid.
105. Castro, "Keeping the press from the action."
106. Shales, "Grenada: A question of news control."
107. Joyce, Fay S. "First evacuees arrive in U.S. from Grenada," *The New York Times*, Oct. 27, 1983, p. A1; Sinclair, Ward, "Student evacuees return, praise U.S. military," *The Washington Post*, Oct. 27, 1983, p. A1.
108. Sinclair, "Student evacuees return."
109. Joyce, "First evacuees arrive."

110. McFadden, Robert D., "From rescued students, gratitude and praise," *The New York Times*, Oct. 28, 1983, p. A1.

111. Ibid.

112. Ibid.

113. *The New York Times* story, "First evacuees arrive in U.S. from Grenada," says in paragraph 4 that the students "seemed divided, however, on whether the invasion was necessary to save their lives," but never elaborates on that observation or quotes a single student expressing that point of view. *The Washington Post* story, "Student evacuees return, praise U.S. military," makes no mention of other viewpoints. The last two paragraphs of the story quote student Jean Joel of Albany, N.Y., saying that the night before the intervention, a Grenadian officer came to the school to warn students and "to reassure us of our safety." The officer told students the island's problems were internal and the students were not involved in them. *The Washington Post* story, "Americans in Grenada, calling home, say they were safe before invasion," was by Joanne Omang.

114. McFadden, "From rescued students, gratitude and praise."

115. McFadden's Oct. 28, 1983 story stated in paragraph 2 that many students said "they had not been directly threatened or endangered by the turmoil and fighting and some said they believed their safety had been used as an excuse by the United States to invade Grenada." Follow-up quotations were presented later in the text.

116. Clines, Francis X., "The view from a capital colored by Grenada," *The New York Times*, Nov. 4, 1983, p. B6.

117. Smith, Hedrick, "Capitol Hill outcry softens as public's support swells," *The New York Times*, Nov. 4, 1983, p. A18.

118. Balz, Dan, and Edsall, Thomas B., "The invasion of Grenada — GOP rallies around Reagan; Democrats divided on Grenada," Oct. 26, 1983, p. A8.

119. Sussman, Barry, "Grenada move earns Reagan broad political gains, poll shows," *The Washington Post*, Nov. 9, 1983, p. A3.

120. Hilts, Philip J., "565,000 jam ABC's phone lines; call-in poll endorses invasion of Grenada, 8-1," *The Washington Post*, Oct. 30, 1983, p. A18; Sussman, Barry, "Reagan's talk gains support for policies," *The Washington Post*, Oct. 30, 1983, p. A1.

121. Hilts, "565,000 jam ABC's phone lines."

122. Sussman, "Grenada move earns Reagan broad political gains."

123. Ibid.

124. "Reagan rating slips after a sharp rise, Harris poll shows," *The New York Times*, Dec. 16, 1983, p. A26.

125. See, for example, Nagy, David, "Reagan turns Grenada, Lebanon to political advantage," *Reuters*, Nov. 5, 1983; Dickenson, James R., "Bombing, invasion in eerie focus — anniversaries of Beirut and Grenada affect both presidential candidates," *The Washington Post*, Oct. 24, 1984, p. A10; Roberts, Steven V., "Younger voters tending to give Reagan support," *The New York Times*, Oct. 16, 1984, p. A1; Clines, Francis X., "Reagan finds refreshment in a fountain of youthful support," *The New York Times*, Oct. 28, 1984, p. D1.

126. Hoffman, David, "Reagan entertains students, hails rescue from Grenada," *The Washington Post*, Nov. 8, 1983, p. A1.

127. See, for example, Sussman, "Grenada move earns Reagan broad political gains," in which a *Washington Post*-ABC News poll shows that 57 percent of Americans thought that the way President Reagan handled foreign policy was increasing the chances for war. A *New York Times* article by William Schneider entitled, "Despite foreign policy popularity boost, doubts about Reagan persist," indicated that more than 60 percent of women held that view, and a majority of men. A Gallup poll taken during Oct. 26-27, 1983 showed that 47 percent of respondents thought the President was "too quick to employ U.S. military forces," as opposed to the 43 percent who thought he used the Armed Forces wisely to resolve foreign policy issues.

128. See "Transcript of the President's news conference on Rumsfeld and Grenada," *The New York Times*, Nov. 4, 1983, p. A16; Hoffman, David and Oberdorfer, Don, "He calls it a 'rescue mission' — Grenada no invasion to Reagan," *The Washington Post*, Nov. 4, 1983, p. A1.

129. Cannon, Lou, "Reagan's upbeat mood returns after week that rocked nation," *The Washington Post*, Oct. 30, 1983, p. A2.

130. Ibid.

131. Ibid.

132. Ibid.

133. Hoffman, "Reagan entertains students"; Sandler, Norman D., "Approval of military actions may be transitory," *United Press International*, Oct. 30, 1984.

134. Clines, Francis X., "Medical students cheer Reagan at a White House ceremony," *The New York Times*, Nov. 8, 1983, p. A10; Hoffman, David, "Reagan entertains students."

135. Ibid.

136. Interview, on background, with the author.

137. Wildermuth, interview with the author, July 8, 1991.

138. Interview, on background, with the author.

139. Wildermuth, interview with the author, July 8, 1991.

140. Ibid. *Washington Post* reporter Phil McCombs says in an Oct. 28, 1983 article entitled, "Barbados, a restless press; 150 miles from the war, the bad news is no news," that public affairs officer Capt. Dean Chamberlain told him there were 325 reporters on Grenada on Oct. 27.

141. Wildermuth, interview with the author, July 8, 1991.

142. Wildermuth, interview with the author, July 10, 1991. U.S. journalists were from The Associated Press, United Press International, Reuters, U.S. News & World Report, the networks, including CNN, and two Caribbean news operations.

143. Ibid.

144. See Pentagon document entitled, *News Media Processed From Barbados to Grenada*, which gives the number of journalists who went in each pool from Oct. 27, 1983 until Oct. 31, 1983, when open coverage was instituted.

145. Kaiser, "An off-the-record war"; Friedrich, "Anybody want to go to Grenada?"

146. Friedrich, "Anybody want to go to Grenada?"

147. Braestrup, *Battle Lines*, pp. 99-100; based on personal correspondence from Ricks.

148. McCombs, "Barbados, a restless press."

149. Ibid.
150. Wildermuth, interview with the author, July 8, 1991; Braestrup, *Battle Lines*, p. 101.
151. The Associated Press, "Admiral says it was his decision to tether the press"; Turner, "Admiral fights 2 battles."
152. Wildermuth, interview with the author, July 8, 1991.
153. See "Text of Reagan's announcement of invasion."
154. Cody, Edward, "Medical school director says he backs invasion," *The Washington Post*, Oct. 31, 1983, p. A23.
155. Ibid.
156. Ibid.
157. Panicali, Joseph, "Operation Urgent Fury," Journal Graphics Inc. transcript, p. 23.
158. Painter, Lucy, "Operation Urgent Fury," Journal Graphics Inc. transcript, p. 23.
159. Nunn, Sen. Sam, "Operation Urgent Fury," Journal Graphics Inc. transcript, p. 22.
160. Weinberger, Defense Secretary Caspar, "Operation Urgent Fury," Journal Graphics Inc. transcript, p. 24.
161. Schwarzkopf, Gen. H. Norman, "Operation Urgent Fury," Journal Graphics Inc. transcript, p. 18.
162. Ibid., p. 21.
163. Ibid., p. 24.
164. Ibid.
165. See comments by student Lucy Painter, "Operation Urgent Fury," Journal Graphics Inc. transcript, p. 27.
166. See "Transcript of address by President on Lebanon and Grenada."
167. Cody, "The day war roared into St. George's."
168. Custer, Scott, "Operation Urgent Fury," Journal Graphics Inc. transcript, p. 19.
169. Ibid., p. 25.
170. Ibid., p. 20.
171. Schemmer, Ben, publisher of *The Armed Forces Journal*, quoting from the Commander-in-Chief, Atlantic, after-action report on "Operation Urgent Fury," Journal Graphics Inc. transcript, p. 20.
172. Ibid.
173. Atkinson, Rick, "Estimates of casualties in Grenada are raised," *The Washington Post*, Nov. 9, 1983, p. A1.
174. Custer, "Operation Urgent Fury," Journal Graphics Inc. transcript, p. 19.
175. Ayres, B. Drummond Jr., "U.S. says Grenada invasion is succeeding; 600 Cubans seized after heavy resistance," *The New York Times*, Oct. 27, 1983, p. A1.
176. Ayres, B. Drummond Jr., "U.S. concedes bombing hospital in Grenada, killing at least 12," *The New York Times*, Nov. 1, 1983, p. A1.

177. Ayres, "U.S. concedes bombing hospital in Grenada"; Cody, Edward, "U.S. bomb strike mistakenly hit hospital; 20 dead; asylum was near Grenadan Army post," *The Washington Post*, Nov. 1, 1983, p. A1; "U.S. admits mistaken attack on Grenadian hospital," *The Christian Science Monitor*, Nov. 2, 1983, p. A2. Rear Adm. Carroll's statement was made during an interview with the author, June 19, 1991.

178. See "Pentagon account of attack," transcript of Pentagon statement on the bombing of the hospital, *The New York Times*, Oct. 31, 1983, p. A16.

179. Atkinson, Rick and Hiatt, Fred, "Weeks after Grenada invasion, questions rise over casualty accounting," *The Washington Post*, Nov. 12, 1983, p. A21.

180. Ibid.

181. Atkinson and Hiatt, "Weeks after Grenada invasion"; UPI report, Nov. 8, 1983, for regional distribution.

182. Ibid.

183. See Atkinson, "Estimates of casualties in Grenada are raised"; UPI report, Nov. 8, 1983.

184. Atkinson, "Estimates of casualties in Grenada are raised."

185. Atkinson and Hiatt, "Weeks after Grenada invasion."

186. Sussman, "Reagan's talk gains support for policies."

187. Johnson, Haynes, "Echoes — President could emulate 'surefire' cornhuskers, Redskins," *The Washington Post*, Jan. 29, 1984, p. A2.

188. Henry, William A. III, "Journalism under fire: A growing perception of arrogance threatens the American press," *Time*, Dec. 12, 1983, p. 76.

189. Clurman, Richard M., "The media learn a lesson," *The New York Times*, Dec. 2, 1983, p. A27.

190. Henry, "Journalism under fire."

191. Shales, "A question of news control."

192. Maraniss, "Information blackout revives old issues."

193. Henry, "Journalism under fire."

194. Ibid.

195. Ibid.; Hilts, "565,000 jam ABC's phone lines."

196. Ibid.

197. Ibid.

198. Ibid.

199. Maraniss, "Information blackout revives old issues."

200. Ibid.

201. Hunter, "U.S. eases restrictions on coverage."

202. See House Judiciary Subcommittee on Courts, Civil Liberties, and the Administration of Justice, *1984: Civil Liberties and the National Security State*, hearings during 98th Cong., 1st and 2d. Sess., Serial No. 103, 1984, pp. 393-515.

203. Joyce, Edward M., *Statement* before the House Judiciary Subcommittee on Courts, Civil Liberties, and the Administration of Justice, Nov. 2, 1983, transcript in *1984: Civil Liberties and the National Security State*, p. 11.

204. See the Sidle Panel Report, released Aug. 23, 1984.

205. Braestrup, *Battle Lines*, p. 8.

206. Ibid., p. 6.

207. Whitney, Craig R., quoted in *Battle Lines*, p. 8.

208. Wildermuth, interview with the author, July 8, 1991.

Chapter VIII
The Invasion of Panama

1. *Section 5 — Classified Information Procedures Act Submission* by Frank A. Rubino, Esq. and Jon A. May, Esq., attorneys for the defense, in *United States v. Manuel Antonio Noriega, et al.*, United States District Court, Southern District of Florida, March 18, 1991, p. 27.

2. See testimony of Norman Bailey, former Director of Planning for the National Security Council staff and former Special Assistant to President Reagan for National Security Affairs, before the House Select Committee on Narcotics Abuse and Control, March 29, 1988, pp. 79-80. Also see testimony of Francis McNeil, former Senior Deputy Assistant Secretary of State for Intelligence and Research, before the Senate Foreign Relations Subcommittee on Terrorism, Narcotics, and International Operations, April 4, 1988, p. 9.

3. *Section 5 CIPA Submission*, p. 36; *Transcript of Hearing Proceedings, United States v. Manuel Antonio Noriega, et al.*, United States District Court, Southern District of Florida, May 5, 1991, pp. 89-91.

4. Bailey, testimony, pp. 79-80.

5. Ibid., p. 79.

6. Ibid.

7. McNeil, testimony, p. 12.

8. Rosenthal, Andrew, "U.S. considered aid to Panama rebels — But Baker and other officials say the time wasn't ripe," *The New York Times*, Oct. 5, 1989, p. A1.

9. Hoffman, "Pool Deployment," p. 5.

10. Ibid., p. 7.

11. Sconyers, Air Force Col. Ronald T., *United States Southern Command Public Affairs After Action Report — "Operation Just Cause" — Dec. 20, 1989-Jan. 31, 1990*, Jan. 31, 1990, pp. i-ii; 1.

12. Hoffman, "Pool Deployment," p. 7.

13. Ibid., p. 2.

14. Staffers of *Time* magazine's Washington bureau did violate operational security, the Hoffman Report stated. The violation occurred after a *Time* representative was notified about the pool callout during a Christmas party, and there was a discussion of who should go for the magazine. This assignment "should have been established by the bureau chief in advance," the Hoffman Report said. The Report and Pentagon officials stated that the *Time* violation did not compromise Just Cause. The Report said the situation could have been avoided "if the *Time* bureau chief had been notified at his office during daytime business hours — something made impossible because of the high level Pentagon decision to delay the callout until after the evening news broadcasts on TV."

15. Hoffman, "Pool Deployment," pp. 7-8.

16. Ibid., p. 1.

17. Ibid., p. 1.

18. "Panama — One Year Later," journalists' roundtable discussion, C-SPAN, Dec. 20, 1990, transcript, p. 1.

19. Hoffman, "Pool Deployment," p. 3.
20. Ibid.
21. SouthCom after-action report, p. 6.
22. Hoffman, "Pool Deployment," p. 13.
23. Ibid., p. 14.
24. Ibid.
25. Ibid.
26. SouthCom after-action report, p. 57.
27. Ibid., p. 15.
28. Ibid., pp. 15, 19-20.
29. Ibid., p. 15.
30. Eisner, Peter, "So, what did happen?" *Hemisphere — A Magazine of Latin American and Caribbean Affairs*, Fall 1990, p. 21.
31. See Specter, Michael, "Second-Hand News Coverage Blamed on Military," *The Washington Post*, Dec. 22, 1989, p. A29, and later statements by Pete Williams at Dec. 22, 1989 Defense Department briefing, Federal News Service transcript, p. 8.
32. Hoffman, "Pool Deployment," p. 11.
33. Defense Department briefing, Dec. 20, 1989, 4:35 p.m., Federal News Service transcript, p. 5; interview with Lt. Gen. Kelly by the author, Aug. 16, 1991. Kelly said in the interview, "As of that time, there had been no reports of friendly fire casualties."
34. White House press briefing, Dec. 21, 1989, Federal News Service transcript, p. 3.
35. Defense Secretary Richard Cheney, briefing at a U.S. military installation in Panama, Dec. 25, 1989, Federal News Service transcript, p. 1.
36. Defense Department briefings, Federal News Service transcripts, June 19, 1990, pp. 1-2; June 20, 1990, pp. 8-9.
37. Defense Department briefing, June 19, 1990, Federal News Service transcript, p. 3.
38. Defense Department briefing, June 19, 1990, p. 2.
39. Defense Department briefing, Dec. 26, 1989, Federal News Service transcript, p. 5.
40. Defense Department briefing, Dec. 26, 1989, p. 11.
41. Jehl, Douglas, "Ranger force bore brunt of Panama toll," *Los Angeles Times*, Jan. 7, 1990, p. A1.
42. Sloyan, Patrick, "Candor Panama's first casualty; U.S. press restrictions guarded military's image," *Newsday*, Jan. 14, 1990, p. A3.
43. Defense Department briefing, Dec. 20, 1989, 4:35 p.m., Federal News Service transcript, pp. 6-7.
44. Ibid., p. 10.
45. Defense Department briefing, Dec. 21, 1989, Federal News Service transcript, p. 7; interview with Lt. Gen. Kelly by the author, Aug. 16, 1991.

46. See Jehl, Jan. 7, 1990; Sloyan, Patrick, Jan. 14, 1990 and "The war you won't see: Why the Bush administration plans to restrict coverage of gulf combat," *Newsday*, Jan. 13, 1991, p. C2.

47. Sloyan, Jan. 14, 1990.

48. Maraniss, David, "Wounded put off-limits to reporters; Interviews on Panama 'Not in good taste,' Army general says," *The Washington Post*, Dec. 24, 1989, p. 14.

49. "Stiner: Aircraft losses in Panama not surprising, given conditions," *Aerospace Daily*, March 1, 1990, p. 376.

50. Interview, on background, with the author.

51. Defense Department briefing, April 10, 1990, Federal News Service transcript, p. 5.

52. Ibid.

53. Defense Department briefing, Dec. 26, 1989, p. 5.

54. Defense Department briefing, April 10, 1990, p. 6.

55. Defense Department briefing, Jan. 11, 1990, Federal News Service transcript, p. 20.

56. Gordon, Michael, "Stealth's Panama mission."

57. Defense Department briefing, April 10, 1990, pp. 2 and 4.

58. Ibid., p.3.

59. Gordon, Michael, "Report says general knew of Stealth fighter's failure," *The New York Times*, July 2, 1990, p. A13.

60. Ibid.

61. Ibid.

62. McPeak, Gen. Merrill, "Three Themes for the Future," speech presented at the Air Force Association's National Symposium, Los Angeles, Calif., Oct. 26, 1990, pp. 2-3.

63. "Public Affairs Policies and Procedures," AF Regulation 190-1, Department of the Air Force, 1-4e., Chapter 1, p. 18.

64. SouthCom after-action report, pp. 49-50.

65. See, for example, United Press International, "U.S. lowers estimate of civilian casualties to 202, plans to release 100 POWs," *Los Angeles Times*, Jan. 13, 1990, p. A7; Omang, Joanne and Dana Priest, "Accounting for Panama's dead: Uncertainty and confusion," *The Washington Post*, Jan. 7, 1990, p. A23; Rohter, Larry, "Panama and U.S. strive to settle on death toll," *The New York Times*, April 1, 1990, sec. 1, pt. 1, p. 12; Healy, Eric, "War victims' bodies pulled from mass graves," *The Arizona Daily Star*, Sept. 16, 1990, p. A4; Hockstader, Lee, "In Panama, civilian deaths remain an issue," *The Washington Post*, Oct. 6, 1990, p. A23; Cousins, Norman, "What's the truth on Panama casualties?" *The Christian Science Monitor*, Oct. 16, 1990, p. 18; Freed, Kenneth, "Panama tries to bury rumors of mass graves — Allegations persist that up to 4,000 civilians were killed in the U.S. invasion," *Los Angeles Times*, Oct. 27, 1990, p. A3; Panvini, Col. Joseph S., "Estimates of Panamanian casualties not a secret," letter to the editor, *The Christian Science Monitor*, Nov. 16, 1990, p. 20; United States Southern Command, Fact Sheet, "Operation Just Cause: One Year Later (Panamanian Fatalities and Common Graves)," Dec. 14, 1990, revised Jan. 3, 1991.

66. SouthCom, Fact Sheet, pp. 1-2.

67. Ibid., p. 3.

68. Ibid., pp. 1, 4-5.
69. Rangel, Rep. Charles, "The Pentagon Pictures," *The New York Times*, Dec. 20, 1990, p. A31. Rangel's staff discussed the video footage in an interview with Center researcher Christine Stavem, March 14, 1991.
70. Defense Department briefing, Dec. 22, 1989.
71. MacKay, Robert, "Noriega 'cocaine' was witchcraft naming Bush," United Press International, Jan. 24, 1990; Meddis, Sam, "Noriega cache story may be so much corn," *USA Today*, Jan. 24, 1990, p. A4.
72. Defense Department briefing, Jan. 25, 1990, Federal News Service transcript, p. 5.
73. Defense Department briefing, Jan. 23, 1990, Federal News Service transcript, p. 5.
74. Defense Department briefing, Jan. 25, 1990, pp. 5-6.
75. Oppenheimer, Andres, speech during the Journalists and Editors Workshop on Latin America and the Caribbean, April 20, 1990, Miami, Fla. Workshop was sponsored by the *Miami Herald* and Florida International University.
76. Ibid.
77. Warren, James, "Instant reporters born for TV," *Chicago Tribune*, Dec. 21, 1989, p. A16; interview with CNN Public Relations Director Steve Haworth by research associate Elizabeth Baker, June 19, 1991.
78. Ibid.
79. Richmond, Ray, "CNN brings Panamanians live action," *The Orange County Register*, Dec. 21, 1989, p. A12.
80. Hanson, Christopher, writing under the pen name William Boot, "Wading around in the Panama pool," *Columbia Journalism Review*, March/April 1990, p. 18.
81. "Panama — One Year Later," C-SPAN.
82. SouthCom after-action report, p. 11.
83. Ibid.
84. Ibid., pp. 20-21.
85. Ibid., p. 54; Hoffman, "Pool Deployment," p. 14.
86. "A Conversation with Sam Donaldson," conducted by Marvin Kalb, sponsored by the Joan Shorenstein Barone Center on the Press, Politics and Public Policy, John F. Kennedy School of Government, Harvard University, March 12, 1990, pp. 5-8.
87. Ibid.
88. Hoffman, "Pool Deployment," p. 14.
89. Kaye, Jeff, "Fitzwater Assails Networks on Coverage," *Los Angeles Times*, Dec. 22, 1989.
90. Ibid.
91. Gerard, Jeremy, "The Noriega Case: Television — President complains about TV's use of split images," *The New York Times*, Jan. 6, 1990, p. A11.
92. White House press conference, Jan. 5, 1990, Federal News Service transcript, p. 8.

93. Gerard, "President complains."
94. Ibid.; see also Page, Susan, "Networks' split TV irks Bush," *Newsday*, Jan. 6, 1990, p. 5.
95. Copeland, Peter, "Army women went into Panama with weapons — and used them," *The Washington Times*, Jan. 2, 1990, p. A1.
96. SouthCom after-action report, p. 51.
97. Ibid.
98. Ibid.
99. Interview with research associate Donine Henshaw, April 11, 1991.
100. Interview with research associate Donine Henshaw, July 15, 1991.
101. Ibid.
102. SouthCom after-action report, p. 53.
103. "Public Affairs Policies and Procedures," AF Regulation 190-1, Department of the Air Force, 1-3d., Chapter 1, p. 18.
104. Hoffman, "Pool Deployment," p. 1.
105. Ibid.
106. SouthCom after-action report, p. 17.
107. Ibid., p. 12.

Chapter IX
The War in the Gulf

1. For the sake of clarity, the times of military actions in the Gulf are given in Eastern Standard or Eastern Daylight Savings Time. The invasion began on Aug. 2, 1990 at approximately 4 a.m. Kuwaiti time, which is Aug. 1, 1990 at approximately 9 p.m. EDT. For initial reports concerning the invasion, see Gordon, Michael R., "Iraq Army invades capital of Kuwait in fierce fighting," *The New York Times*, Aug. 2, 1990, p. A1; The Associated Press, "Iraqi invasion, step by step," *The New York Times*, Aug. 3, 1990, p. A9. A number of current books provide a historical look at the foundation of tensions between Iraq and Kuwait; one of the most well-researched is David Fromkin's, *A Peace to End All Peace* (New York: Avon Books, 1989), which explores the decisions made by European powers after World War I that set the stage for many of the region's current problems.
2. Bush, President George, speech at the Aspen Institute, Aspen, Colo., Aug. 2, 1990, Federal News Service transcript, p. 1; White House briefing, Aug. 2, 1990, Federal News Service transcript, p. 1.
3. President Bush, White House briefing, Aug. 2, 1990, pp. 1-2.
4. President Bush, address to the nation, Aug. 8, 1990, Federal News Service transcript pp. 1-2.
5. Ibid., p. 2; White House press conference, Aug. 8, 1990, Federal News Service transcript, p. 6. During his address, President Bush said that four principles guided U.S. policy: the immediate, complete and unconditional withdrawal of all Iraqi forces from Kuwait; the restoration of the Kuwaiti government; the security and stability of the Persian Gulf; and the protection of American citizens abroad.

6. Oreskes, Michael, "Poll on troop move shows support (and anxiety)," *The New York Times*, Aug. 12, 1990, Sec. 1, p. 13. Also see Oreskes' "Washington talk — Iraq puts election truisms to test," *The New York Times*, Aug. 10, 1990, p. A15. Reuters reported on Aug. 11, 1990 that a *Newsweek* poll showed that President Bush's approval rating had risen 10 percent since July, with 75 percent of respondents giving the President high marks. A CNN/Time poll gave the President an 83 percent approval rating for his performance regarding the invasion of Iraq, according to Reuters.

7. Oreskes, "Poll on troop move."

8. Ibid.

9. Wines, Michael, "Press left out of Gulf airlift," *The New York Times*, Aug. 9, 1990, p. A14.

10. President Bush, White House press briefing, Aug. 8, 1990, Federal News Service transcript, p. 2.

11. Ibid.

12. Defense Department press conference, Aug. 8, 1990, Federal News Service transcript, p. 7.

13. Defense Department briefing, Aug. 9, 1990, Federal News Service transcript, p. 10.

14. Ibid.

15. Defense Department press conference, Aug. 8, 1990, Federal News Service transcript, p. 7; Defense Department briefing, Aug. 9, 1990, Federal News Service transcript, p. 10.

16. Farhi, Paul and Mills, David, "Media shut out at the front lines," *The Washington Post*, Aug. 9, 1990, p. D4.

17. Hoffman, Fred S., *Statement*, Senate Governmental Affairs Committee, Feb. 20, 1991, transcript, p. 2.

18. Williams, Defense Department briefing, Aug. 9, 1990, Federal News Service transcript, p. 10.

19. Jones, Alex S., "News organizations angry at the lack of a press pool," *The New York Times*, Aug. 10, 1990, p. A10.

20. Sherman, Capt. Mike, interview with the author, June 19, 1991.

21. Capt. Sherman, interviews with the author, June 19, 20 and 24, 1991.

22. Rochelle, Carl, "The War and the Media: A Retrospective," National Press Club forum, March 19, 1991, transcript, p. 6.

23. Ibid., pp. 6-7.

24. Ibid., pp. 6-7.

25. Ibid., p. 7.

26. Capt. Sherman, interviews with the author, June 19 and 20, 1991.

27. Ibid.

28. Capt. Sherman, interview with the author, June 19, 1991.

29. LeMoyne, James, "A correspondent's tale"; interview with research associate Sue Mullin, Aug. 15, 1991.

30. Ibid.
31. Ibid.
32. Ibid.
33. LeMoyne, interview with research associate Sue Mullin, Aug. 15, 1991.
34. Wildermuth, Capt. Ron, interview with the author, July 8, 1991; Capt. Sherman, interviews with the author, June 19 and 20, 1991; Lt. Col. Larry Icenogle, interview with the author, June 28, 1991.
35. Message from U.S. Commander-in-Chief, Central Command (CCPA) to the Office of the Assistant Secretary of Defense for Public Affairs, and others, Jan. 6, 1991, 1400 Zulu, Subject: Hometown News Media Travel Temporarily Suspended.
36. See Message from the Office of the Assistant Secretary of Defense for Public Affairs to U.S. Commander-in-Chief, Central Command (CCPA), and others, Oct. 19, 1990, 1359 Zulu, Subject: Public Affairs Guidance — Media Travel for Hometown Coverage (Operation Desert Shield), p. 2.
37. Message from the Office of the Assistant Secretary of Defense for Public Affairs to U.S. Commander-in-Chief, Central Command (CCPA), and others, Dec. 22, 1990, 0919 Zulu, Subject: Hometown Media Travel — Amplifying Instructions.
38. Glass, Stephanie, interviews with research associate Maggy Zanger, Dec. 26 and Dec. 31, 1991.
39. Message from U.S. Commander-in-Chief, Central Command (CCPA) to the Office of the Assistant Secretary of Defense for Public Affairs, and others, Jan. 6, 1991, 1400 Zulu, Subject: Hometown News Media Travel Temporarily Suspended.
40. Message from National Guard Bureau, Washington, D.C. (PA) to U.S. Commander-in-Chief, Central Command (CCPA), Sept. 27, 1990, 2102 Zulu, Subject: Request for Media Travel, Operation Desert Shield.
41. Message from U.S. Commander-in-Chief, Central Command (CCPA) to U.S. Central Command, Air Force, Forward Headquarters Element, and others, Oct. 1, 1990, 1025 Zulu, Subject: Media Travel, Operation Desert Shield.
42. Message from Minnesota Air Reserve Center Headquarters (MNAGPAO) to U.S. Commander-in-Chief, Central Command (CCPA), and others, Oct. 2, 1990, 2100 Zulu, Subject: Documentary Film Crew, Operation Desert Shield.
43. Titunik, Lt. Col. Steven M., Chief, Broadcast Pictorial Branch, Directorate for Defense Information, Office of the Assistant Secretary of Defense for Public Affairs, interview with research associate Donine Henshaw, Nov. 8, 1991.
44. Ibid.; also an interview by the author with Maj. Robert Dunlap, National Guard Bureau Office of Public Affairs, Media Relations Branch, July 15, 1991.
45. Maj. Dunlap, interview with the author, July 15, 1991.
46. Ibid.
47. Lt. Col. Titunik, Army Lt. Col. Steven, letter to Doug Mattson, March 1, 1991.
48. Ibid.
49. Ibid.
50. Lt. Col. Titunik, memorandum to MAC Public Affairs Office, attention Master Sgt. Jones, Scott Air Force Base, March 21, 1991.

51. Wirwahn, Capt. David S., memorandum to Master Sgt. Jones, MAC Headquarters, Scott Air Force Base, March 22, 1991. The Minnesota Guard office said Capt. Wirwahn had left to go to work for Quantum Diversified. Mattson said Capt. Wirwahn had worked for the firm for a time, but no longer was employed there.

52. Message from U.S. Commander-in-Chief, Central Command, to the Office of the Assistant Secretary of Defense for Public Affairs, and others, March 21, 1991, 1900 Zulu.

53. Lt. Col. Titunik, interview with research associate Donine Henshaw, Nov. 8, 1991.

54. Ibid.

55. Ibid.

56. Ibid.

57. Ibid.

58. Fons, Richard, interview with research associate Donine Henshaw, Nov. 8, 1991.

59. Davis, Kathy, interview with research associate James Callard, Nov. 8, 1991.

60. See, for example, Morin, Richard, "How much war will Americans support?" *The Washington Post*, Sept. 2, 1990, p. B1; Gugliotta, Guy, "Gulf policy fosters anxious support; approval in poll solid despite concerns over cost, length of action," *The Washington Post*, Sept. 11, 1990, p. A1; Oreskes, Michael, "Poll finds strong support for Bush's goals, but reluctance to start a war," *The New York Times*, Oct. 1, 1990, p. A9; Oreskes, Michael, "Economy and Mideast standoff bring a drop in Bush's standing," *The New York Times*, Oct. 14, 1990, Sec. 1, Pt. 1, p. 1; Ladd, Everett Carll, "Is Bush's popularity in a nosedive? What the polls are really showing," *The Christian Science Monitor*, Oct. 19, 1990, p. 18; Morin, Richard, "Poll shows plunge in public confidence; Bush's rating plummets; overall national mood at two-decade low," *The Washington Post*, Oct. 16, 1990, p. A1; Devroy, Ann, "Bush shifts theme — again; GOP fortunes ignite White House feuding," *The Washington Post*, Nov. 5, 1990, p. A1; Apple, R. W. Jr., "The 1990 campaign; war clouds, no thunder; as guns are silent, so are the candidates," *The New York Times*, Nov. 6, 1990, p. A1.

61. "Bush: 'State of Kuwait must be restored or no nation will be safe,'" transcript of the President's remarks at the White House and excerpts from his news conference, *The Washington Post*, Nov. 9, 1990, p. A33.

62. Ibid.; also see Oreskes, Michael, "Mideast tensions; a debate unfolds over going to war against the Iraqis," *The New York Times*, Nov. 12, 1990, p. A1.

63. Al-Sabah, Shaikh Saud Nasir, Kuwaiti Ambassador to the United States, press conference, Aug. 2, 1990, Federal News Service transcript, p. 2.

64. Dilenschneider, Robert L., "Talking strategy in public bad idea," *USA Today*, Aug. 16, 1990, p. 10.

65. Massey, Donald F., Senior Vice President, Hill and Knowlton/Washington, *Short Form Registration Statement* under the Foreign Agents Registration Act of 1938, as amended, Attachment III, received by the Justice Department Criminal Dvision on June 3, 1991.

66. Ibid.

67. Clevenger, Nathaniel, interview with research associate Elizabeth Baker, May 28, 1991.

68. Ibid.

69. Ibid.

70. See *Exhibit B to Registration Statement* and *Retainer Agreement* filed by Neill and Company, received by the Justice Department Criminal Division, Jan. 22, 1991.

71. "H&K's Kuwait drive sparks Hayes plea for FARA reform," *O'Dwyer's FARA Report*, February 1991, p. 1; interview with Hayes' staff by research associate Donine Henshaw, Nov. 8, 1991.

72. See United Nations Security Council Resolution 678, which passed by a 12-to-2 vote. China abstained, and Cuba and Yemen opposed the Resolution.

73. Williams, Pete, letter to Washington bureau chiefs of the Pentagon press corps concerning plans for pools and a flight for auxiliary news staff in the event of hostilities in the Persian Gulf, Dec. 14, 1990. The term "bureau chief" was generic, referring to any news executive who supervised a member of the Pentagon press corps. This document and many others relating to the controversy about the Defense Department's media restrictions during the Gulf War can be found in U.S. Congress, Senate, Committee on Governmental Affairs, hearing, *Pentagon Rules on Media Access to the Persian Gulf War*, 102nd Cong., 1st Sess., Feb. 20, 1991.

74. Ibid.

75. "Department of Defense Contingency Plan for Media Coverage of Hostilities — Operation Desert Shield," Dec. 13, 1990, attachment to Dec. 14, 1990 memorandum from Pete Williams to Washington bureau chiefs.

76. Ibid.

77. Ibid.

78. Ibid.

79. "Operation Desert Shield news media ground rules," attached to Williams' memorandum to Washington bureau chiefs, Dec. 14, 1990, p. 1.

80. Ibid., pp. 1-3.

81. Raines, Howell, letter to Pete Williams, Dec. 21, 1990.

82. Hoyt, Clark, letter to Pete Williams, Dec. 18, 1990.

83. Getler, Michael, letter to Pete Williams, Dec. 18, 1990.

84. Lewis, Charles J., letter to Pete Williams, Dec. 20, 1990, p. 1.

85. See "Proposed news media listing for DOD contingency airlift," attachment to Williams' Dec. 14, 1990 memorandum to Washington bureau chiefs, Dec. 14, 1990. The plane could hold 120 people. Williams had allotted 10 seats each to the three networks and CNN; six to the networks' local affiliates; five each to the Associated Press, United Press International and Reuters; three each to *Time, Newsweek, U.S. News & World Report*; three each to five large newspapers, including *The New York Times, The Washington Post* and *The Wall Street Journal*; two each to five major radio news operations and one each to UPI Radio and Unistar Radio; two each to five other news organizations, including Knight-Ridder, the *Boston Globe*, Hearst Newspapers and Gannett News Service; and one each to 13 other media organizations, including Scripps-Howard, *The Christian Science Monitor*, the *Baltimore Sun, Newsday* and *The Milwaukee Journal*.

86. Hoyt, Clark, letter to Pete Williams, Dec. 17, 1990.

87. Shaw, Gaylord, letter to Pete Williams, Dec. 18, 1990.

88. Yaeger, Bill, KFWB News Executive Editor, letter to Pete Williams, Jan. 4, 1991.

89. Interview, on background, with the author.
90. Ibid.
91. Mulvey, Col. Bill, interview with the author, May 24, 1991.
92. Williams, Pete, memorandum to Washington bureau chiefs of the Pentagon press corps about ground rules and a flight for auxiliary staff in the event of hostilities in the Persian Gulf, Jan. 7, 1991.
93. See "Guidelines for news media," attached to Williams' Jan. 7, 1991 memorandum to Washington bureau chiefs, Jan. 7, 1991.
94. Ibid.
95. Williams, letter to Washington bureau chiefs, Jan. 7, 1991.
96. See "Proposed news media listing for DOD contingency airlift," attached to Pete Williams' Jan. 7, 1991 memorandum, dated Jan. 4, 1991.
97. Raines, Howell, letter to Pete Williams, Jan. 8, 1991.
98. Ibid.
99. Osborne, Burl and Kramer, Larry, letter to Pete Williams, Jan. 8, 1991, pp. 1-2.
100. Ibid., p. 1.
101. McMasters, Paul, National Freedom of Information Chairman, Society of Professional Journalists, letter to Defense Secretary Cheney, Jan. 10, 1991.
102. Arledge, Roone; Ober, Eric; Johnson, Tom; and Gartner, Michael G., letter to Defense Secretary Richard Cheney, Jan. 9, 1991.
103. Ibid.
104. Getler, Michael, letter to Pete Williams, Jan. 8, 1991.
105. "Guidelines for news media," dated Jan. 14, 1991, attached to Pete Williams' memorandum for Washington bureau chiefs of the Pentagon press corps about ground rules and guidelines for correspondents in the event of hostilities in the Persian Gulf, Jan. 15, 1991.
106. Sloyan, Patrick J., Defense Department briefing, Jan. 10, 1991, Federal News Service transcript, p. 5.
107. Ibid.
108. "Guidelines for news media," dated Jan. 14, 1991.
109. Ibid.
110. Ibid.
111. Williams, Pete, remarks on ABC-TV, *Good Morning America*, Jan. 11, 1991. A partial transcript of the program has been reprinted as part of the transcript of the teleconference briefing to public affairs officers in Saudi Arabia regarding the news media ground rules and guidelines, Jan. 12, 1991, *Pentagon Rules on Media Access to the Persian Gulf War*, pp. 380-84.
112. Ibid., p. 384.
113. Ibid., p. 383.

114. Ibid.
115. Ibid.
116. Ibid., pp. 387-88.
117. Ibid., p. 393.
118. Ibid., p. 397.
119. Ibid., p. 387.
120. Ibid., p. 394.
121. Ibid., pp. 390-91, 394.
122. Ibid., pp. 390-91.
123. Ibid., pp. 377-417.
124. Ibid., pp. 390-91.
125. Ibid., p. 407.
126. Ibid., p. 409.
127. Ibid., p. 409.
128. Ibid., pp. 409, 413.
129. Ibid., p. 408.
130. Ibid., p. 409.
131. Representatives from the major media believed this system was justified. For example, in an interview with research associate Elizabeth Baker on June 20, 1991, *Wall Street Journal* reporter John Fialka, who was the print pool coordinator for a short time, said, "Pete Williams and the bureau chiefs in Washington worked out a policy so that the pool would have representation from the major media in the United States, so in any given emergency you'd have somebody out there that could give broad coverage. You wouldn't want the *Phoenix Gazette* to have to report to the whole country. . . . You'd want *The New York Times* or other major papers to have kind of permanent representation, partly because they have a breadth of readership, and also partly because they are always going to be there. They are the organization that spent the money to have permanent people in Dhahran from the very beginning. The military knew that they could always find them, so the idea was to construct a pool system around them."
132. Aukofer, Frank A., "The press collaborators," Nieman Reports, Summer 1991, pp. 24-26.
133. Ibid.
134. Lewis, Charles, interview with the author, May 1991.
135. *The Nation, et al. v. United States Department of Defense, et al.*, United States District Court, Southern District of New York, Jan. 10, 1991. Plaintiffs were *The Nation, Harper's, In These Times,* Pacific News Service, *The Guardian, The Progressive, Mother Jones, The L.A. Weekly, The Village Voice, The Texas Observer,* Pacifica Radio News, Sydney Schanberg, E.L. Doctorow, William Styron, Michael Klare and Scott Armstrong. Agence France-Presse and Michael Sargent later filed a separate suit concerning denial of access to the pools for AFP. This suit was consolidated with *The Nation, et al..* Defendants were the Defense Department, Richard Cheney, Pete Williams, Gen. Colin Powell and George Bush.

136. See *The Nation, et al.*, First Amended Complaint, Jan. 24, 1991.

137. "Editorial — Military's efforts to control coverage as well as battle could cause backlash," *The News Media & the Law*, published by the Reporters Committee for Freedom of the Press, Winter 1991, back of front cover. A discussion of why the possibility of filing a lawsuit was considered and rejected after the Grenada invasion can be found in Peter Braestrup's *Battle Lines — Report of the Twentieth Century Fund Task Force on the Military and the Media — Background Paper* (New York: Priority Press Publications, 1985), pp. 120-28.

138. Bush, President George, address to the nation, Jan. 16, 1991, excerpted in "Tracking the Storm — Chronology," *Military Review*, September 1991, p. 72.

139. See Lamb, David, "Pentagon hardball," *Washington Journalism Review*, April 1991, p. 33.

140. Ibid.

141. Col. Mulvey, interview with the author, May 24, 1991.

142. Lt. Col. Icenogle, interview with the author, June 28, 1991.

143. Ibid.

144. Col. Mulvey, interview with the author, May 24, 1991.

145. Ibid.

146. This information was provided by Col. Mulvey in interviews with the author on May 24 and May 27, 1991, and by Lt. Col. Icenogle in an interview with the author on June 28, 1991.

147. The figure of 800 media personnel is from Lt. Col. Icenogle. The figure of 1,500 is the one that has been used most frequently by Pentagon personnel in the months since the war ended. This figure has been disputed by some correspondents who were in Dhahran, most notably Hearst Newspapers' Washington Bureau Chief Charles J. Lewis. He has pointed out that the figure does not account for the fact that many journalists signed up at both the Dhahran and Riyadh JIBs and may have been counted twice, or that the Pentagon's figure includes numerous support personnel who never went into the field or put any burden on JIB officials or resources. The 1,600 figure is used occasionally by Defense Department personnel, and was the figure cited by retired Maj. Gen. Winant Sidle in "The Gulf War reheats military-media controversy," *Military Review*, September 1991, pp. 52-63. Maj. Gen. Sidle, the leader of the Sidle Panel that prepared the 1984 report that led to the establishment of the DOD national media pool, wrote that 1,600 journalists were "too many." Such great numbers of correspondents "could never be allowed to roam the battlefield at will," and could mean that "pools may have to continue for the duration, as in Desert Storm," he wrote.

148. Col. Mulvey, interviews with the author on May 24 and May 27, 1991.

149. Lewis, Charles J., interview with the author, May 1, 1991.

150. Halberstam, David, *Nightline*, ABC-TV, Journal Graphics transcript #2523, Jan. 23, 1991, p. 9. The information about the State Department letter praising Halberstam's reporting is from an article by Dr. William M. Hammond, historian with the U.S. Army Center of Military History, "The press in Vietnam as agent of defeat: A critical examination," *Reviews in American History*, June 1989, p. 314 and Footnote 5. Dr. Hammond obtained the information from a State Department message to the U.S. Embassy in Saigon, Nov. 30, 1962.

151. Rose, Judd, *PrimeTime Live*, ABC-TV, Jan. 24, 1991, Journal Graphics transcript #177, p. 7.

152. Lewis, Charles J., letter to Pete Williams, March 13, 1991, p. 2.

153. Col. Mulvey, interview with the author, May 24, 1991.

154. Browne, Malcolm W., "The military vs. the press," *The New York Times Magazine*, March 3, 1991, p. 29.

155. For example, retired Army Col. David Hackworth, a Vietnam veteran who covered the Gulf conflict for *Newsweek*, stated in an interview with the author on June 3, 1991 that the media restrictions represented "the ghost of Vietnam."

156. Kelly, Lt. Gen. Thomas, interview with the author, Aug. 16, 1991.

157. Message from U.S. Central Command (CCPA) to Army and Marine officials, among others, Jan. 23, 1991, 0600 Zulu, Subject: Missing CBS News Team.

158. Browne, "The military vs. the press," p. 46.

159. Ibid.; interview with Wesley Bocxe by research associate K. J. Scotta, April 16, 1991.

160. Apple, R. W. Jr., "The press — correspondents protest pool system," *The New York Times*, Feb. 12, 1991.

161. Col. Hackworth, interview with the author, June 3, 1991.

162. Ibid.

163. Fisk, Robert, "Out of the pool," *Mother Jones*, May-June 1991, p. 58. This article comprised excerpts of dispatches that Fisk had filed for the *Independent*.

164. Bayles, Fred, interview with research associate Maggy Zanger, Dec. 26, 1991.

165. Ibid.

166. Col. Mulvey, interview with the author, May 27, 1991.

167. Fialka, John, memo to Col. Mulvey concerning "unconscionable delays in getting print pool reports in from the field," Feb. 9, 1991. Reprinted in *Pentagon Rules on Media Access to the Persian Gulf War*, p. 701.

168. Col. Mulvey, interview with the author, May 24, 1991.

169. Col. Mulvey, interviews with the author, May 24 and 27, 1991; Lt. Col. Icenogle, interview with the author, June 28, 1991.

170. Ibid.

171. Ibid.

172. Ibid.

173. Williams, teleconference briefing with public affairs officers in Saudi Arabia, *Pentagon Rules on Media Access to the Persian Gulf War*, pp. 387-417. Other information came from interviews by the author with Col. Mulvey, May 24 and 27, 1991.

174. Ibid.

175. Col. Mulvey, interview with the author, May 24, 1991.

176. Glass, Stephanie, interview with research associate Maggy Zanger, Dec. 26, 1991. Also see her remarks on page 4 of "Military Escorts: The Big Chill," one section of

"Covering the Persian Gulf War," an attachment to a letter sent by 17 news executives to Defense Secretary Cheney, June 24, 1991.

177. "Military Escorts: The Big Chill," p. 5; interview with Bayles by research associate Maggy Zanger, Dec. 26, 1991.

178. Rose, *PrimeTime Live*, Jan. 24, 1991, Journal Graphics transcript #177, p. 7.

179. Glass, "Military Escorts: The Big Chill," p. 5.

180. Robinson, Walter, interview with research associate K. J. Scotta, May 8, 1991.

181. Ibid.

182. Davison, Phil, interviews with research associate Elizabeth Baker, May 1991.

183. Miller, Anthony O., interview with research associate Elizabeth Baker, May 7, 1991.

184. Jehl, Douglas, memorandum to Col. William Mulvey concerning restrictions on pool coverage, Feb. 4, 1991.

185. Ibid.

186. McCarthy, Tom, *Los Angeles Times* Foreign Policy Editor, interview with research associate Maggy Zanger, Jan. 2, 1991.

187. Letter to Defense Secretary Cheney, June 24, 1991, signed by Roone Arledge, President, ABC News; James K. Batten, Chairman of the Board and Chief Executive Officer, Knight-Ridder Inc.; Louis D. Boccardi, President and Chief Executive Officer, The Associated Press; Max Frankel, Executive Editor, *The New York Times*; Peter S. Prichard, Editor, *USA Today*; Michael G. Gartner, President, NBC News; Katharine Graham, Chairman of the Board, The Washington Post Co.; Tom Johnson, President, CNN; Peter Kann, Publisher and President, *The Wall Street Journal*; David Laventhol, Publisher, *Los Angeles Times*; Jason McManus, Editor-in-Chief, Time Warner Inc.; Donald Newhouse, President, Star-Ledger; Eric Ober, President, CBS News; Burl Osborne, Publisher and Editor, *The Dallas Morning News*; Arnold Rosenfeld, Editor-in-Chief, Cox Newspapers; Al Rossiter Jr., Senior Vice President/Executive Editor, United Press International; Richard M. Smith, Editor-in-Chief and President, Newsweek Inc.

188. "Military Escorts: The Big Chill," p. 4.

189. Ibid.

190. Browne, "The military vs. the press," p. 45.

191. Ibid., pp. 44-46; interview with Col. Mulvey by the author, May 24, 1991.

192. Lewis, interview with the author, May 1, 1991.

193. Ibid.; also, Hedges, Michael, interview with research associate Maggy Zanger, Dec. 26, 1991.

194. Col. Mulvey, interview with the author, May 24, 1991.

195. Ibid.

196. See *Pentagon Rules on Media Access to the Persian Gulf War*, pp. 714-24.

197. See Hedges, Michael, report from Combat Correspondents Pool #1, Feb. 11, 1991. Reprinted in *Pentagon Rules on Media Access to the Persian Gulf War*, pp. 716-18.

198. Ibid.

199. See "Operation Desert Shield Ground Rules," Jan. 14, 1991.
200. Hedges, Michael, interview with research associate Maggy Zanger, Dec. 30, 1991.
201. Ibid.
202. Ibid.
203. Hedges, Feb. 11, 1991 pool report.
204. Williams, Pete, memorandum to *Washington Times* Editor-in-Chief Arnaud de Borchgrave about the appeal of a story by Michael Hedges regarding military intelligence, Feb. 16, 1991. Reprinted in *Pentagon Rules on Media Access to the Persian Gulf War*, pp. 714-15.
205. Ibid.
206. Ibid.
207. Gergen, "Why America hates the press."
208. Interviews by the author with Col. Mulvey, May 24 and 27, 1991; Lt. Col. Icenogle, June 28, 1991; Capt. Sherman, June 19 and 20, 1991; and Central Command Public Affairs Officer Capt. Ron Wildermuth, July 8, 1991.
209. Ibid.
210. Ibid.
211. Rossiter, Al Jr., letter to Pete Williams, Feb. 14, 1991.
212. Message from the Office of the Assistant Secretary of Defense for Public Affairs to the Commander-in-Chief, U.S. Central Command (CCPA), among others, Jan. 21, 1991, 1824 Zulu, Subject: Public Affairs Guidance — Operation Desert Story Casualty and Mortuary Affairs, pp. 1-2.
213. Williams, Pete, speech at the National Press Club, March 14, 1991, transcript, p. 19.
214. Ibid. After the war, Gen. H. Norman Schwarzkopf told the Senate Armed Services Committee that Pentagon planners thought 10,000 to 20,000 U.S. servicemen and women might be killed or wounded during the Gulf conflict. See the Federal News Service transcript of the committee's hearing regarding the conduct of the Persian Gulf War, June 12, 1991, p. 31.
215. A fuller discussion of this incident appears in Chapter VIII, "The Invasion of Panama." Also see, among others, Kaye, Jeff, "Fitzwater assails networks on coverage," *Los Angeles Times*, Dec. 22, 1989; Gerard, Jeremy, "The Noriega case: Television — President complains about TV's use of split images," *The New York Times*, Jan. 6, 1990, p. A11; Page, Susan, "Networks' split TV irks Bush," *Newsday*, Jan. 6, 1990, p. 5; and White House press conference, Jan. 5, 1990, Federal News Service transcript, p. 8.
216. Message from the Office of the Assistant Secretary of Defense for Public Affairs to Commander-in-Chief, U.S. Central Command (CCPA), among others, Jan. 21, 1991, 1824 Zulu, pp. 1-3.
217. Ibid., p. 1; Message from the Office of the Assistant Secretary of Defense for Public Affairs to the Commander-in-Chief, U.S. Central Command (CCPA), among others, Feb. 2, 1991, 0333 Zulu, Subject: Public Affairs Guidance — Operation Desert Storm Casualty and Mortuary Affairs, p. 1.
218. Williams, National Press Club speech, transcript, p. 19.

219. See *JB Pictures, Inc. et al. v. Department of Defense, et al.*, United States District Court, District of Columbia, Civil Action No. 91-0397, Feb. 22, 1991, p. 3. Plaintiffs were JB Pictures Inc., Military Families Support Network, Center for Investigative Reporting Inc., Veterans for Peace, Vietnam Veterans of America Foundation, Marc Asnin, Nat Hentoff, Vicki Kemper, Viveca Novak, Mark Peterson, Eli Reed, Steve Rubin and Alex Webb. Defendants were the Department of Defense and Secretary of the Air Force Donald B. Rice.

220. Belluardo, John, Public Information Officer, DOE San Francisco Operations Office, "Media Policy on War Issues," Jan. 25, 1991.

221. Ibid.; also see Horgan, John, "U.S. gags discussion of war's environmental effects," *Scientific American*, May 1991, p. 24.

222. Belluardo, "Media Policy on War Issues."

223. Horgan, "U.S. gags discussion of war's environmental effects"; interview with John Belluardo by research associate Kenny Langone, May 1991.

224. Ibid.

225. Times Mirror Center for the People & the Press, *The People, the Press and the War in the Gulf — A Special Times Mirror News Interest Index*, Jan. 31, 1991, pp. 1, 11.

226. Ibid., pp. 12, 16.

227. Kagay, Michael R., "War in the Gulf — Public opinion — Approval of Bush soars," *The New York Times*, Jan. 19, 1991, Sec. 1, p. 9.

228. Ibid.

229. See, for example, Clymer, Adam, "War in the Gulf — Public Opinion — Poll finds deep backing while optimism fades," *The New York Times*, Jan. 22, 1991, p. A12; Kagay, Michael R., "War in the Gulf — Public opinion — Slight decline is found in U.S. backing for war," *The New York Times*, Jan. 30, 1991, p. A11; Dowd, Maureen, "War in the Gulf — Public opinion — Americans back continued air strikes," *The New York Times*, Feb. 15, 1991, p. A15; Kagay, Michael R., "War in the Gulf — Poll — Public shows support for land war," Feb. 26, 1991, p. A17.

230. Letter from 21 House members to Tom Johnson, Feb. 4, 1991. The signers were Lawrence Coughlin, G.V. (Sonny) Montgomery, Charles Wilson, Charles Stenholm, Norman Dicks, Solomon Ortiz, John Murtha, Paul Kanjorski, Ben Erdreich, Sonny Callahan, Claude Harris, Beverly Byron, Bob Carr, Howard Coble, Don Sundquist, Bill Archer, Bill Emerson, Mel Hancock, Ben Gilman, Frederick S. Upton and Nancy L. Johnson.

231. Ibid.

232. Rosenstiel, Thomas B., "The media take a pounding — Pentagon rules and instant communication have changed the way war is reported — reporters come off as clumsy villains in the Gulf drama," *Los Angeles Times*, Feb. 20, 1991, p. A1. During a speech at the National Press Club on March 19, 1991, Arnett said that CNN eventually began receiving more positive than negative responses from viewers about this work. See the Federal News Service transcript of his speech, p. 10.

233. Kurtz, Howard, "Sen. Simpson calls Arnett 'sympathizer'; CNN reporter blasted for Iraq coverage," *The Washington Post*, Feb. 8, 1991, p. B1.

234. Ibid.

235. Gergen, David, "Why America hates the press," *U.S. News & World Report*, March 11, 1991, p. 57.

236. Toner, Robin, "Senator, press and crossed swords," *The New York Times*, Feb. 2, 1991, p. A14.

237. Arnett, Andrew, "The truth about my family," *The New York Times*, March 13, 1991, p. A25.

238. Arnett, National Press Club speech, Federal News Service transcript, p. 14.

239. Simpson, Sen. Alan, "'The word 'sympathizer' was not a good one,'" *The New York Times*, March 20, 1991, p. A28.

240. Arnett, National Press Club speech, Federal News Service transcript, p. 6.

241. Ibid., pp. 5-6.

242. Ibid., p. 10.

243. See the Times Mirror Center for the People & the Press, *The People the Press and the War in the Gulf: Part II — A Special Times Mirror News Interest Index*, released March 25, 1991.

244. Letter from 16 House members to Defense Secretary Cheney, January 1991. The letter was signed by Bruce F. Vento, Dante B. Fascell, Louis Stokes, Don Edwards, Edward J. Markey, Fortney Pete Stark, Lane Evans, Peter A. DeFazio, George Miller, Mary Rose Oakar, Peter H. Kostmayer, Les AuCoin, John Bryant, Jim Bacchus, Nancy Pelosi and James L. Oberstar.

245. See *Pentagon Rules on Media Access to the Persian Gulf War* for a transcript of the hearing and relevant appendices.

246. Zorthian, Barry, *Statement Before Senate Government Affairs Committee on Pentagon Press Rules in the Persian Gulf War*, Feb. 15, 1991, delivered Feb. 20, 1991, p. 3.

247. Ibid., p. 4.

248. Sidle, Maj. Gen. Winant, *Statement* before the Senate Governmental Affairs Committee, Feb. 20, 1991, p. 3.

249. Ibid., p. 2.

250. Zorthian, *Statement*, p. 5.

251. Cheney, Defense Secretary Richard, statement during Defense Department Special Briefing, Feb. 23, 1991, 10:30 p.m., DOD transcript, p. 1.

252. Ibid.

253. Ibid.

254. Getler, Michael, comments during a conference on media coverage of the Persian Gulf War, April 26, 1991, transcript, p. 3.

255. Lewis, letter to Williams, March 13, 1991, p. 4.

256. Gaps, John, interview with research associate Maggy Zanger, Dec. 26, 1991.

257. Zorthian, Barry, comments during "The War and the Media: A Retrospective," National Press Club Forum, March 19, 1991, transcript, p. 1.

258. Lewis, Anthony, "To see oursels. . .," *The New York Times*, May 6, 1991, p. A15.

259. Carroll, Rear Adm. Eugene, interview with the author, June 19, 1991; also see "The President's popularity," *The New York Times*, March 5, 1991, p. A20.

260. Holliman, John, *Larry King Live*, CNN, Feb. 9, 1991, Journal Graphics, transcript #234, pp. 2-3.

261. "Editors criticize curbs on photos," *The New York Times*, Feb. 21, 1991.

262. Gen. McPeak's statements about the failure to disclose the problems with the Stealth's performance were made during a speech, "Three Themes for the Future," presented at the Air Force Association's National Symposium in Los Angeles on Oct. 26, 1990. The briefing after the Gulf War was held March 15, 1991.

263. "Worst Weather in 14 years," a section of *Audibles*, graphic accompanying Gen. McPeak's press briefing on March 15, 1991.

264. *Total Tonnage Expended — US-Only*, updated version of graphic used for Gen. McPeak's briefing on March 15, 1991. Original graphic was updated on March 21, 1991 to reflect revised figures. The new statistics showed that the percentage of precision-guided bombs used by U.S. forces was slightly higher than the original figures had indicated.

265. Carroll Jr., Rear Adm. Eugene J., "Damage by allied bombs," letter to the editor, *The Washington Post*, March 2, 1991, NEED PAGE

266. Letter from 17 media executives and editors to Defense Secretary Cheney, attachment entitled "Covering the Persian Gulf War — Access: Limited, Restricted, Delayed," June 24, 1991, p. 7.

267. Jarecke, Ken, as told to Carol Squiers, "I, witness — The image of war," *American Photo*, July-August 1991, p. 120.

268. Schwarzkopf, Gen Norman, Defense Department Special Central Command Briefing, Jan. 30, 1991, Federal News Service transcript, p. 17. Gen. Schwarzkopf discussed his experiences with body counts during the Vietnam conflict with Barbara Walters on ABC-TV's *20/20* on March 15, 1991 (see transcript, p. 6), and with reporter Michael Ryan, who included the comments in an article for *Life* entitled, "Here's to the winners," March 18, 1991, p. 34.

269. Hardzog, Robert C., Chief, Freedom of Information and Privacy Act Staff, Defense Intelligence Agency, letter to Robert S. Norris, May 22, 1991.

270. Ibid.

271. Interview, on background, with the author.

272. Sloyan, Patrick J. "Buried alive — U. 5. tanks used plows to kill thousands in Gulf War trenches," *Newsday*, Sept. 12, 1991, p. 5.

273. Ibid.

274. Ibid.

275. Sloyan, Patrick, "Tough job completed by Army's big armor," *Newsday*, Sept. 13, 1991, p. 6.

276. Ibid.

277. Maggart, Col. Lon, "Buried alive."

278. Stewart, Bill, "Unearthing truth in Iraq," letter to the editor, *Newsday*, Sept. 19, 1991, p. 105.

279. Schanberg, Sydney, "The other POWs: A cringing press," *Newsday*, Sept. 24, 1991, p. 94.

280. President Bush, "Confrontation in the Gulf — Excerpts from President's news conference on Gulf crisis," *The New York Times*, Aug. 31, 1990, p. A11.

281. Schwarzkopf, Gen. Norman, Defense Department Special Briefing, Riyadh, Saudi Arabia, Jan. 18, 1991, Federal News Service transcript, p. 2.

282. "Bush outlines gulf lessons for Air Force Academy grads," *Air Force Times*, June 10, 1991, p. 23.

283. Ahtisaari, Martti, United Nations Under-Secretary General for Administration and Management, *Report to the Secretary-General on humanitarian needs in Kuwait and Iraq in the immediate post-crisis environment*, March 20, 1991, p. 5.

284. *Harvard Study Team Report: Public Health in Iraq After the Gulf War*, May 1991, pp. 3, 1.

285. International Study Team, *Health and Welfare in Iraq After the Gulf Crisis — An In-Depth Assessment*, October, 1991, p. 7. The team's work was financed by UNICEF, the MacArthur Foundation, the John Merck Fund and Oxfam-UK. The team included physicians, public health workers, law students, engineers and economists from the United States, Europe and the Middle East.

286. President Bush, shown on "The War We Left Behind," Journal Graphics transcript, p. 6.

287. Kelly, Lt. Gen. Thomas, Defense Department briefing, Jan. 18, 1991, Federal News Service transcript, p. 6.

288. Kelly, Defense Department briefing, Jan. 21, 1991, Federal News Service transcript, p. 4.

289. Ibid., pp. 5, 8.

290. Ibid., p. 8.

291. Kelly, interview with the author, Aug. 16, 1991.

292. Bush, President George, speech to the Reserve Officers Association, Jan. 23, 1991, Federal News Service transcript, p. 2.

293. Cheney, film clip from Feb. 22, 1991 press briefing, shown on *Nightline*, ABC-TV, June 12, 1991, transcript #2623, p. 1.

294. See, for example, Rosenthal, Andrew, "U.S. warns Iraqis it will use force to inspect arms," *The New York Times*, Sept. 19, 1991, A1; Lewis, Paul, "Iraqis said to stall on U.N. inspections," *The New York Times*, Sept. 23, 1991, p. A3, and "Baghdad detains 40 U.N. inspectors for twelve hours," *The New York Times*, Sept. 24, 1991, p. A1; Spielmann, Peter James, The Associated Press, "Iraqis detain U.N. officials, seize papers — Security Council likely to OK military escorts," *The Arizona Daily Star*, Sept. 24, 1991, p. A1; Lewis, Paul, "U.N. accepts Iraq proposal to free detained inspectors," *The New York Times*, Sept. 27, 1991, p. A6; Wines, Michael, "U.S. is building up a picture of vast Iraqi atomic program," *The New York Times*, Sept. 27, 1991, p. A6; Lewis, Paul, "Telltale clues found by the U.N. inspectors in Iraq," *The New York Times*, Sept. 29, 1991, p. A10; "Iraq tested missile to carry A-bomb, a U.N. report says," *The New York Times*, Oct. 5, 1991, p. A2; Broad, William J., "U.N. says Iraq was building H-bomb and bigger A-bomb," *The New York Times*, Oct. 15, 1991, p. A1; Schmitt, Eric, "U.S. says it missed 2 A-plants in Iraq," *The New York Times*, Oct. 10, 1991, p. A7; Sciolino, Elaine, "Iraq's nuclear program shows holes in U.S. intelligence," *The New York Times*, Oct. 20, 1991, A5.

295. Kelly, Defense Department briefing, Jan. 25, 1991, Federal News Service transcript, p. 6.

296. "Tomahawk cruise missiles score big," p. 1.

297. Defense Department, "Cruise Missile Operations," *Conduct of the Persian Gulf Conflict — An Interim Report to Congress*, July 1991, p. 6-8.

298. Saporito, Bill, "America's arsenal — This war doesn't mean a windfall — General Dynamics," *Fortune*, Feb. 25, 1991, p. 42. Cited in Arnett, Eric H., "Awestruck press does Tomahawk PR," *The Bulletin of Atomic Scientists*, April, 1991, p. 7.

299. Arnett, "Awestruck press does Tomahawk PR," pp. 7-8.

300. Ibid. Arnett is the author of *Sea-Launched Cruise Missiles and U.S. Security* (New York: Praeger Publishers, 1991). Also see discussion of the Tomahawk and other weapons and air-defense systems in Adam, John A., "Warfare in the information age," in a Special Report from *IEEE Spectrum*, the magazine of the Institute of Electrical and Electronics Engineers Inc., September 1991, pp. 2633.

301. Arnett, interview with the author and research associate William H. Wing, Aug. 16, 1991.

302. Ibid.

303. See "The next Scudbusters," *The Wall Street Journal*, Feb. 20, 1991, p. 14; Morgan, Dan and Lardner Jr., George, "Damage from intercepted Scuds suggests Patriot needs refinement," *The Washington Post*, Feb. 21, 1991, p. 23; Safire, William, "The great scud-Patriot mystery," *The New York Times*, March 7, 1991, p. 25.

304. Powell, remarks during a hearing before a House Appropriations subcommittee, Feb. 19, 1991, Federal News Service transcript, p. 31.

305. Ibid.

306. Schmitt, Eric, "Flaw in Patriot missile gave earlier warning," *The New York Times*, June 6, 1991, p. A7; Burns, Robert, The Associated Press, "Army knew Patriot's fault before fatal Scud hit," printed in *The Arizona Daily Star*, June 6, 1991, p. A5.

307. Postol, Theodore A., "Lessons for SDI from the Gulf War Patriot Experience: A Technical Perspective," testimony before the House Armed Services Committee, April 16, 1991, p. 5. Postol is a Professor of Science, Technology, and National Security Policy at the Massachusetts Institute of Technology. Also see the discussion of the Patriot in Riezenman, Michael, "Revising the script after Patriot," Special Report, *IEEE Spectrum*, September 1991, pp. 49-52, and Watson, George F., "The challenge of post-Gulf conflicts," pp. 53-57.

308. Postol, interview with the author and research associate William Wing, May 1, 1991.

309. Ibid. Also see the discussion of the media ' s coverage of weapons performance in Condry, John, "TV: live from the battlefield," Special Report, *IEEE Spectrum*, September 1991, pp. 47-48.

310. Sprey, *Statement*, p. 1.

311. Wicker, Tom, "An unknown casualty," *The New York Times*, March 20, 1991, p. A29.

312. Ibid.

313. Decision by The Honorable Leonard B. Sand, *The Nation. et al. v. United States Department of Defense et al.*, April 16, 1991.

314. Ibid., pp. 37-38.
315. See, for example, Williams, Pete, "The Persian Gulf, the Pentagon, the press," *Defense*, May-June 1991, p. 10.
316. Williams, Pete, speech to the National Press Club, March 14, 1991, Federal News Service transcript, pp. 1-2.
317. Ibid., p. 8.
318. Ibid., p. 9.
319. Letter from 15 news executives and editors to Defense Secretary Cheney, April 29, 1991. Persons signing the letter included Stan Cloud of Time, Nicholas Horrock of the *Chicago Tribune*, Howell Raines of *The New York Times*, Barbara Cohen of CBS News, Albert R. Hunt of *The Wall Street Journal*, Timothy J. Russert of NBC News, Michael Getler, the *Washington Post*; Clark Hoyt, Knight-Ridder Inc.; Evan Thomas, *Newsweek*; Andrew Glass, Cox Newspapers; Charles Lewis, Hearst Newspapers, George Watson, ABC News, William Headline, CNN, Jack Nelson, *The Los Angeles Times*; and Jonathan Wolman, Associated Press.
320. Ibid.
321. Ibid.
322. Aukofer, "The press collaborators," p. 24.
323. Cheney, Defense Secretary Richard, "Trimming the military," *USA Today*, June 27, 1991, p. 11a.
324. At his National Press Club speech on March 15, 1991, for example, Williams said, "What public in what other conflict can possibly have been given as much information as the American people in this war? And people responded to that coverage. A *Newsweek* poll found that 59 percent of Americans think better of the news media now than they did before the war. The ABC News-*Washington Post* poll out last weekend shows that by a 2-to-1 margin, those surveyed thought that the press gained respect. and partly because of the thorough job that the press did, the military gained respect. Thanks to reporters, the American people could see what our troops, our commanders and our weapons were doing." These remarks are on page 3 of the transcript provided by the Pentagon.
325. Letter from 17 news executives and editors to Defense secretary Cheney, June 24, 1991.
326. Ibid.
327. Ibid.
328. The Associated press, "Cheney defends U.S. Gulf War press rules," *The Washington Post*, Sept. 13, 1991, p. A20.
329. McCarthy, Tom, interview with research associate Maggy Zanger, Jan. 2, 1991.
330. Ibid.
331. Aukofer, "The pool collaborators," p. 26.
332. Rear Adm. Carroll, interview with the author, June 19, 1991.
333. This suggestions was made during numerous interviews for this study, including interviews by the author with Lt. Col. Icenogle, June 28, 1991, Col. Mulvey, May 24, 1991 and Mort Rosenblum, April 16, 1991.

334. See *Report by the Chief of the Joints Chiefs of Staff Media- Military Relations Panel (Sidle Panel)*, Recommendation 8d, page 6, August 1984.

335. Gen. Powell, speech to the National Newspaper Association, March 15, 1991, transcript, p. 5.

336. Williams, speech at the National Press Club, March 15, 1991, transcript, p. 17.

337. Moyers, Bill, "Project Censored," PBS-TV, Feb. 23, 1991, transcript, p. 2.

338. Moore, Mike, "Project Censored," PBS-TV, Feb. 23, 1991, transcript, p. 2.

339. Ibid., p. 4.

340. Ibid., p. 5.

341. Cronkite, Walter, comments during "The War and the Media: A Retrospective," National Press Club, March 19, 1991, transcript, pp. 35-36.

Chapter X
Conclusions and Recommendations

1. During the Vietnam War, White House insistence on presenting an optimistic picture of the conflict led the U.S. Armed Forces to falsify body counts and estimates of enemy troop strength. See, for example, Gen. Schwarzkopf's remarks in Michael Ryan's article, "Here's to the winners," *Life*, March 18, 1991, pp. 34-35; Sam Adams' May 1975 *Harper's* article, "Vietnam cover-up: Playing war with numbers"; and Col. Hackworth's statements in *About Face*, especially on p. 778.

2. See Summers, *On Strategy*, pp. 26-27, 33-59; "Western media and recent wars," pp. 6-13.

3. Summers, *On Strategy*, pp. 27, 31-55; "Western media and recent wars," p. 12; testimony before the Senate Governmental Affairs Committee, Feb. 20, 1991, transcript of written statement, p. 1.

4. Summers, "Western media and recent wars," p. 12; testimony before Senate Governmental Affairs Committee, p. 79. Also see Hammond, *The Military and the Media*, p. 387; Mueller, *Wars, Presidents and Public Opinion*, pp. 60-65.

5. See, for example, Summers, *On Strategy*, pp. 34-35, 54-55; Gen. Schwarzkopf's comments to author C.D.B. Bryan in *Friendly Fire*, pp. 346-47; Braestrup, *Battle Lines*, p. 9.

6. Ryan, "Here's to the winners," pp. 34-35.

7. Ibid., p. 35.

8. Hackworth, *About Face*, pp. 756-94.

9. Gen. Schwarzkopf describes his agonizing about whether to stay in the military after the Vietnam War in *Friendly Fire*, pp. 340-48; 362-63.

10. Gen. Weyand's article for *CDRS CALL*, July-Aug. 1976, is quoted in Summers' *On Strategy*, pp. 58-59.

11. Summers, *On Strategy*, p. 244.

12. Hackworth, *About Face*, p. 778.

13. See, for example, Ryan, "Here's to the winners," p. 34; Hackworth, *About Face*, pp. 571-72, 778-79; Hammond, *The Military and the Media*, pp. 318-19.

14. See, for example, Summers, "Western media and recent wars," pp. 10-11; Hammond, *The Military and the Media*, pp. 284-87; and Hackworth, *About Face*, pp. 822-34.

15. See "Transcript of address by President on Lebanon and Grenada," Oct. 28, 1983; "Operation Urgent Fury," Journal Graphics Inc. transcript, p. 24.

16. See *New York Times* reporter Michael Gordon's stories, "Stealth's Panama mission" and "Report says general knew of Stealth fighter's failure," as well as the Defense Department briefing of April 10, 1990, Federal News Service transcript, pp. 2-6.

17. Powell, Gen. Colin, speech to the National Newspaper Association, March 15, 1991, transcript, p. 7.

18. Clausewitz, *On War*, pp. 75-76.

19. Hammond, *The Military and the Media*, pp. 237-38.

20. Ibid., pp. 81-82.

21. See *Total Tonnage Expended — US Only*, updated version of graphic used for Defense Department briefing by Gen. Merrill A. McPeak, March 15, 1991.

22. Hackworth, interview with the author, June 3, 1991; interview on *The Real Story*, transcript, p. 5.

23. Maraniss, "Wounded put off-limits to reporters"; *JB Pictures, Inc. et al. v. Department of Defense, et al.*, United States District Court, District of Columbia, *Complaint for Declaratory and Injunctive Relief*, Feb. 22, 1991.

24. Powell, Gen. Colin, Defense Department special briefing, Jan. 23, 1991, Federal News Service transcript, p. 17.

25. Schwarzkopf, Gen. H. Norman, special Central Command briefing, Jan. 30, 1991, Federal News Service transcript, p. 17.

26. Summers, *On Strategy*, p. 63.

27. Gen. Weyand, quoted in *On Strategy*, p. 33.

28. The Early Bird is a compilation of newspaper and wire service reports about defense issues, and is prepared by the American Forces Information Service, Office of the Assistant Secretary of Defense for Public Affairs (AFIS/OASD-PA).

29. Wildermuth, interview with the author, Aug. 6, 1991.

30. When two *Wall Street Journal* reporters tried to get the lessons-learned reports on the Grenada operation in 1989 — six years after Operation Urgent Fury — they had to file Freedom of Information requests and then received heavily censored documents, one of which was a monograph written by historians at the Center of Military History. Such heavy security classification so long after the fact seems counterproductive. The reporters' story, "As Panama outcome is praised, details emerge of bungling during the 1983 Grenada invasion," appeared in the *Journal* on Jan. 15, 1990, p. A12.

31. Excellent discussions of this issue are included in Clark Clifford and Richard Holbrooke's book, *Counsel to the President*; Col. Hackworth's *About Face*, pp. 739-834; Sam Adams' *Harper's* article, "Vietnam cover-up"; and Peter Braestrup's *Battle Lines*, pp. 61-75.

32. Summers, *On Strategy*, p. 48; Karnow, *Vietnam*, pp. 373-76.

33. Karnow, *Vietnam*, pp. 364-76; Hammond, *The Military and the Media*, pp. 99-101; 370.

34. Summers, *On Strategy*, p. 54.

35. See Dilenschneider, speech at Georgetown University; Clevenger, interview with research associate Elizabeth Baker on May 28, 1991; Hill and Knowlton's Foreign Agents Registration Act filings with the Justice Department during 1990-91.

36. Clevenger, interview with research associate Elizabeth Baker, May 28, 1991.

37. See *Foreign Agents Registration Act Supplemental Statement, Attachment III, No. 12*, filed by Hill and Knowlton, dated Nov. 10, 1990, received by the Justice Department Criminal Division on Dec. 10, 1990.

38. Ibid.

39. The Justice Department has not always vigorously enforced FARA in the past, according to a July 1990 GAO report, *Foreign Agent Registration — Justice Needs to Improve Program Administration* (GAO/NSIAD-90-250), and testimony before the Senate Committee on Commerce, Science, and Transportation by Allan I. Mendelowitz, Director, Trade, Energy, and Finance Issues, National Security and International Affairs Division, GAO, on Sept. 27, 1990.

40. Socolar, Milton J., Special Assistant to the Comptroller General, *Testimony — Federal Lobbying — Federal Regulation of Lobbying Act of 1946 Is Ineffective*, provided for the Senate Governmental Affairs Subcommittee on Oversight of Government Management, July 16, 1991.

41. Ibid.

42. Hammond, *The Military and the Media*, p. 184.

43. Sidle, *Statement*, Senate Governmental Affairs Committee, Feb. 20, 1991, p. 2.

44. Interview with Hearst Newspapers' Washington Bureau Chief Charles J. Lewis by the author, May 1, 1991.

45. See decision by The Honorable Leonard B. Sand, *The Nation et al. v. United States Department of Defense et al.*, April 16, 1991.

46. Letter to Defense Secretary Cheney, June 24, 1991. The names of the media executives who signed the letter are listed in footnote 100 for Chapter II.

47. Carroll, interview with the author, June 19, 1991.

48. Interviews by the author with Lt. Col. Icenogle, June 28, 1991, and Col. Mulvey, May 24, 1991.

49. Hertsgaard, *On Bended Knee*, p. 233.

50. Moore, Mike, "Project Censored," broadcast on PBS, Feb. 23, 1991, transcript, p. 5.

51. Braestrup, interview with the author, May 20, 1991.

52. Hammond, *The Military and the Media*, p. 102.

53. Interview with Lt. Col. Michael Cox by research associate Donine Henshaw, March 14, 1991.

54. Carroll, interview with the author, June 19, 1991.

55. Hertsgaard, *On Bended Knee*, p. 212.

56. See, for example, Hoffman, David, "U.S. envoy conciliatory to Saddam; secret cables dispute Glaspie's account of meeting before war," *The Washington Post*, July 12, 1991, p. A1; Sciolino, Elaine, "Envoy's testimony on Iraq is assailed," *The New York Times*, July 13, 1991, p. A1.
57. CNN report, Sept. 7, 1991.
58. Powell, speech to the National Newspaper Association.
59. Dugan, "Generals vs. journalists, cont."
60. Ibid.
61. Interview, on background, with the author.
62. Sidle Panel Report, pp. 16-17.

APPENDIX A

Department of Defense Principles of Information

PRINCIPLES OF INFORMATION

It is the policy of the Department of Defense to make available timely and accurate information so that the public, Congress, and members representing the press, radio and television may assess and understand the facts about national security and defense strategy. Requests for information from organizations and private citizens will be answered responsively and as rapidly as possible. In carrying out this policy, the following Principles of Information will apply:

- Information will be made fully and readily available, consistent with statutory requirements, unless its release is precluded by current and valid security classification. The provisions of the Freedom of Information Act will be supported in both letter and spirit.

- A free flow of general and military information will be made available, without censorship or propaganda, to the men and women of the Armed Forces and their dependents.

- Information will not be classified or otherwise withheld to protect the government from criticism or embarrassment.

- Information will only be withheld when disclosure would adversely affect national security or threaten the safety or privacy of the men and women of the Armed Forces.

- The Department's obligation to provide the public with information on its major programs may require detailed public affairs planning and coordination within the Department and with other government agencies. The sole purpose of such activity is to expedite the flow of information to the public: propaganda has no place in Department of Defense public affairs programs.

The Assistant Secretary of Defense (Public Affairs) has the primary responsibility for carrying out this commitment.

Caspar W. Weinberger
Secretary of Defense

PRINCIPLES
OF INFORMATION

It is the policy of the Department of Defense to make available timely and accurate information so that the public, Congress, and the news media may assess and understand the facts about national security and defense strategy.

Requests for information from organizations and private citizens will be answered in a timely manner. In carrying out this policy, the following principles of information will apply:

- *Information will be made fully and readily available, consistent with statutory requirements, unless its release is precluded by current and valid security classification. The provisions of the Freedom of Information Act will be supported in both letter and spirit.*

- *A free flow of general and military information will be made available, without censorship or propaganda, to the men and women of the Armed Forces and their dependents.*

- *Information will not be classified or otherwise withheld to protect the government from criticism or embarrassment.*

- *Information will be withheld only when disclosure would adversely affect national security or threaten the safety or privacy of the men and women of the Armed Forces.*

- *The Department's obligation to provide the public with information on its major programs may require detailed public affairs planning and coordination within the Department and with other government agencies. The sole purpose of such activity is to expedite the flow of information to the public: propaganda has no place in Department of Defense public affairs programs.*

The Assistant Secretary of Defense for Public Affairs has the primary responsibility for carrying out this commitment.

Dick Cheney
Secretary of Defense

APPENDIX B

The Sidle Panel Report

INTRODUCTION

The Chairman of the Joint Chiefs of Staff (CJCS) Media - Military Relations Panel (known as the Sidle Panel) was created at the request of the Chairman, General John W. Vessey, Jr., who asked that I convene a panel of experts to make recommendations to him on, "How do we conduct military operations in a manner that safeguards the lives of our military and protects the security of the operation while keeping the American public informed through the media?"

Major General Winant Sidle, USA, Retired, was selected as chairman of this project and asked to assemble a panel composed of media representatives, public affairs elements of the four Military Services, the Office of the Assistant Secretary of Defense (Public Affairs) (OASD(PA)), and operations spokesmen from the Organization of the Joint Chiefs of Staff (OJCS).

The initial plan, concurred in by CJCS and ASD(PA), was to invite major umbrella media organizations and the Department of Defense organizations to provide members of this panel. The umbrella organizations, such as the American Newspaper Publishers Association (ANPA), the American Society of Newspaper Editors (ASNE), the National Association of Broadcasters (NAB), and the Radio Television News Directors Association (RTNDA), and their individual member news organizations decided that they would cooperate fully with the panel but would not provide members. The general reason given was that it was inappropriate for media members to serve on a government panel.

This decision, unanimous among the major news media organizations, resulted in a revised plan calling for the non-military membership of the panel to be composed of experienced retired media personnel and representatives of schools of journalism who were experts in military-media relations. The Department of Defense organizations involved agreed to provide members from the outset. Final panel membership is at Enclosure 1.

To provide initial input to the panel for use as a basis for discussion when the panel met, a questionnaire was devised with the concurrence of CJCS and ASD(PA) and mailed to all participants. It was also sent to a number of additional organizations and individuals who had expressed interest and to some who had not but were considered to be experts in the matter. As the result of these mailings, the panel had available 24 written inputs to study prior to meeting. Of these, 16 were from major news organizations or umbrella groups. All inputs are at Enclosure 2. The panel regretted that all who indicated interest could not appear before it, but time did not permit.

Although the news organizations involved did not agree to provide panel members, they all agreed to provide qualified personnel to make oral presentations to the panel. The only exception was an individual news organization which felt that its umbrella group should represent it.

The panel met from 6 February through 10 February 1984 at the National Defense University, Fort McNair, Washington, D.C. The meetings included three days for media and military presentations in open session and two days for panel study and deliberation in closed session. The presentations included those by 25 senior media representatives speaking for 19 news organizations, including umbrella organizations. The chiefs/directors of Public Affairs for the Army, Navy, and Air Force also made major presentations during the open sessions with the USMC, OJCS, and ASD(PA) panel members making informal comments during the closed sessions. The open sessions were covered by about 70 reporters representing nearly 30 news organizations. The schedule of presentations is at Enclosure 3.

The attached panel report is composed of two sections.

1. The Recommendations section, concurred and signed by all panel members.

2. The Comment section, explaining the recommendations and including comments, when appropriate, made by all concerned, to include both written and oral inputs to the committee and by the panel itself. This section is signed by the chairman but was approved unless otherwise indicated by the members of the panel. It is made available to explain the recommendations and to assist, via suggestions, in their implementation.

The panel recommends approval and implementation both in fact and in spirit of the recommendations made in Section I of this report.

Winant Sidle
Major General, USA, Retired
Chairman

Enclosure
Report

Second, Grenada. We realize that Grenada had shown the need to review media-military relations in connection with military operations, but you did not request our assessment of media handling at Grenada and we will not provide it. However, we do feel that had our recommendations been "in place" and fully considered at the time of Grenada, there might have been no need to create our panel.

Finally, the matter of responsibility of the media. Although this is touched on in the report, and there is no doubt that the news organization representatives who appeared before us fully recognized their responsibilities, we feel we should state emphatically that reporters and editors alike must exercise responsibility in covering military operations. As one of the senior editors who appeared before us said, "The media must cover military operations comprehensively, intelligently, and objectively." The American people deserve news coverage of this quality and nothing less. It goes without saying, of course, that the military also has a concurrent responsibility, that of making it possible for the media to provide such coverage.

The members of the panel have also asked me to express their appreciation for being asked to participate in this important study and their hope that our work will be of value to the military, the media, and to the American people.

Finally, the panel considers this covering letter an integral part of our report.

                                            Sincerely,

                                            Winant Sidle
                                            Major General, USA, Retired
                                            Chairman

Enclosure
Report

General John W. Vessey, Jr.
Chairman, Joint Chiefs of Staff
The Pentagon, Room 2E872
Washington, D.C. 20301

Dear General Vessey:

As you requested, enclosed are the final report and recommendations of the Sidle Panel, together with pertinent enclosures. The panel is unanimous in its strong belief that implementation of the recommendations, both in fact and in spirit, by the appropriate military authorities will set the stage for arriving at workable solutions for media-military relations in future military operations. We also believe that these solutions will be satisfactory to reasonable members of both the media and the military.

The report has three sections: an introduction, a recommendations section, and a comment section. We adopted this format because, while we were unanimous on the recommendations, there were some differences of opinion on some points in the comments. However, we all agreed that the comments were necessary to help explain the recommendations and that even the points on which we were not unanimous were worthy of consideration as suggestions and background for those who will implement the recommendations, should they be implemented. In any case, the entire panel has formally endorsed the recommendations, while I signed the comments. I should add that, where appropriate, I have mentioned the panel's degree of support in the comments.

The panel asked that I put three points in this letter that were not exactly germane to the report but required some comment on our part.

First, the matter of so-called First Amendment rights. This is an extremely gray area and the panel felt that it was a matter for the legal profession and the courts and that we were not qualified to provide a judgment. We felt justified in setting aside the issue, as we unanimously agreed at the outset that the U.S. media should cover U.S. military operations to the maximum degree possible consistent with mission security and the safety of U.S. forces.

REPORT

by

CJCS MEDIA-MILITARY RELATIONS PANEL (SIDLE PANEL)

SECTION I: Recommendations

Statement of Principle

The American people must be informed about United States military operations and this information can best be provided through both the news media and the Government. Therefore, the panel believes it is essential that the U.S. news media cover U.S. military operations to the maximum degree possible consistent with mission security and the safety of U.S. forces.

This principle extends the major "Principle of Information" promulgated by the Secretary of Defense on 1 December 1983, which said:

> "It is the policy of the Department of Defense to make available timely and accurate information so that the public, Congress, and members representing the press, radio and television may assess and understand the facts about national security and defense strategy. Requests for information from organizations and private citizens will be answered responsively and as rapidly as possible. . ." (Copy at Enclosure 4)

It should be noted that the above statement is in consonance with similar policies publicly stated by most former secretaries of defense.

The panel's statement of principle is also generally consistent with the first two paragraphs contained in "A Statement of Principle on Press Access to Military Operations" issued on 10 January 1984 by 10 major news organizations (copy at Enclosure 5). These were:

> "First, the highest civilian and military officers of the government should reaffirm the historic principle that American journalists, print and broadcast, with their professional equipment, should be present at U.S. military operations. And the news media should reaffirm their recognition of the importance of U.S. military mission security and troop safety. When essential, both groups can agree on coverage conditions which satisfy safety and security imperatives while, in keeping with the spirit of the First Amendment, permitting independent reporting to the citizens of our free and open society to whom our government is ultimately accountable.

"Second, the highest civilian and military officers of the U.S. government should reaffirm that military plans should include planning for press access, in keeping with past traditions. The expertise of government public affairs officers during the planning of recent Grenada military operations could have met the interests of both the military and the press, to everyone's benefit."

Application of the panel's principle should be adopted both in substance and in spirit. This will make it possible better to meet the needs of both the military and the media during future military operations. The following recommendations by the panel are designed to help make this happen. They are primarily general in nature in view of the almost endless number of variations in military operations that could occur. However, the panel believes that they provide the necessary flexibility and broad guidance to cover almost all situations.

RECOMMENDATION 1:

That public affairs planning for military operations be conducted concurrently with operational planning. This can be assured in the great majority of cases by implementing the following:

    a. Review all joint planning documents to assure that JCS guidance in public affairs matters is adequate.

    b. When sending implementing orders to Commanders in Chief in the field, direct CINC planners to include consideration of public information aspects.

    c. Inform the Assistant Secretary of Defense (Public Affairs) of an impending military operation at the earliest possible time. This information should appropriately come from the Secretary of Defense.

    d. Complete the plan, currently being studied, to include a public affairs planning cell in OJCS to help ensure adequate public affairs review of CINC plans.

    e. Insofar as possible and appropriate, institutionalize these steps in written guidance or policy.

RECOMMENDATION 2:

When it becomes apparent during military operational planning that news media pooling provides the only feasible means of furnishing the media with early access to an operation, planning should provide for the largest possible press pool that is practical and minimize the length of time the pool will be necessary before "full coverage" is feasible.

RECOMMENDATION 3:

That, in connection with the use of pools, the Joint Chiefs of Staff recommend to the Secretary of Defense that he study the matter of whether to use a pre-established and constantly updated accreditation or notification list of correspondents in case of a military operation for which a pool is required or the establishment of a news agency list for use in the same circumstances.

RECOMMENDATION 4:

That a basic tenet governing media access to military operations should be voluntary compliance by the media with security guidelines or ground rules established and issued by the military. These rules should be as few as possible and should be worked out during the planning process for each operation. Violations would mean exclusion of the correspondent(s) concerned from further coverage of the operation.

RECOMMENDATION 5:

Public Affairs planning for military operations should include sufficient equipment and qualified military personnel whose function is to assist correspondents in covering the operation adequately.

RECOMMENDATION 6:

Planners should carefully consider media communications requirements to assure the earliest feasible availability. However, these communications must not interfere with combat and combat support operations. If necessary and feasible, plans should include communications facilities dedicated to the news media.

RECOMMENDATION 7:

Planning factors should include provision for intra- and inter-theatre transportation support of the media.

RECOMMENDATION 8:

To improve media-military understanding and cooperation:

a. CJCS should recommend to the Secretary of Defense that a program be undertaken by ASD(PA) for top military public affairs representatives to meet with news organization leadership, to include meetings with individual news organizations, on a reasonably regular basis to discuss mutual problems, including relationships with the media during military operations and exercises. This program should begin as soon as possible.

b. Enlarge programs already underway to improve military understanding of the media via public affairs instruction in service schools, to include media participation when possible.

c. Seek improved media understanding of the military through more visits by commanders and line officers to news organizations.

d. CJCS should recommend that the Secretary of Defense host at an early date a working meeting with representatives of the broadcast news media to explore the special problems of ensuring military security when and if there is real-time or near real-time news media audiovisual coverage of a battlefield and, if special problems exist, how they can best be dealt with consistent with the basic principle set forth at the beginning of this section of the report.

The Panel members fully support the statement of principle and the supporting recommendations listed above and so indicate by their signatures below:

Winant Sidle, Major General, USA, Retired
Chairman

Brent Baker, Captain, USN

Fred C. Lash, Major, USMC

Keyes Beech

James Major, Captain, USN

Scott M. Cutlip

Wendell S. Merick

John T. Halbert

Robert O'Brien, Colonel, USAF
Deputy Assistant Secretary of Defense (Public Affairs)

Billy Hunt

Richard S. Salant

George Kirschenbauer, Colonel, USA

Barry Zorthian

A. J. Langguth

SECTION II:

RECOMMENDATION 1:

That public affairs planning for military operations be conducted concurrently with operational planning. This can be assured in the great majority of cases by implementing the following:

        a. Review all joint planning documents to assure that JCS guidance in public affairs matters is adequate.

        b. When sending implementing orders to Commanders in Chief in the field, direct that the CINC planners include consideration of public information aspects.

        c. Inform the Assistant Secretary of Defense (Public Affairs) of an impending military operation at the earliest possible time. This information should appropriately come from the Secretary of Defense.

        d. Complete the plan, currently being studied, to include a public affairs planning cell in OJCS to help ensure adequate public affairs review of CINC plans.

        e. Insofar as possible and appropriate, institutionalize these steps in written guidance or policy.

Comments

1. Under the current system of planning for military operations, provisions exist to include public affairs planning but it is neither mandatory nor certain that current joint planning documents are adequate from a public affairs standpoint. The basic purpose of this recommendation is to help assure that public affairs aspects are considered as soon as possible in the planning cycle for any appropriate military operation and that the public affairs planning guidance is adequate.

2. The panel was unanimous in feeling that every step should be taken to ensure public affairs participation in planning and/or review at every appropriate level. Recommendations 1a, b, and d are designed to assist in implementing this consideration.

3. Panel discussions indicated that it is difficult to determine in advance in all cases when public affairs planning should be included. The panel felt that the best procedure would be to include such planning if there were even a remote chance it would be needed. For example, a strictly covert operation, such as the Son Tay raid in North Vietnam, still requires addressing public affairs considerations if only to be sure that after action coverage adequately fulfills the obligation to inform the American people. Very small, routine operations might be exceptions.

4. Recommendation 1c is self-explanatory. The ASD(PA), as the principal public affairs advisor to both the Secretary of Defense and the Chairman, JCS, must be brought into the planning process as soon as possible. In view of the DOD organization, the panel felt that this should be the responsibility of the Secretary of Defense.

5. We received indications that some commanders take the position that telling something to his public affairs officer is tantamount to telling it to the media. All members of the panel, including its public affairs officers decried this tendency and pointed out that a public affairs specialist is the least likely to release material prematurely to the media. Although the panel did not consider the matter officially there is no doubt that public affairs officers are just as dedicated to maintaining military security as are operations officers and must know what is going on in a command if they are to do their job!

RECOMMENDATION 2:

When it becomes apparent during military operational planning that news media pooling provides the only feasible means of furnishing the media with early access to an operation, planning should support the largest possible press pool that is practical and minimize the length of time the pool will be necessary.

Comments

1. Media representatives appearing before the panel were unanimous in being opposed to pools in general. However, they all also agreed that they would cooperate in pooling agreements if that were necessary for them to obtain early access to an operation.

2. The media representatives generally felt that DOD should select the organizations to participate in pools, and the organizations should select the individual reporters. (See Recommendation 3.)

3. The media were unanimous in requesting that pools be terminated as soon as possible and "full coverage" allowed. "Full coverage" appeared to be a relative term, and some agreed that even this might be limited in cases where security, logistics, and the size of the operation created limitations that would not permit any and all bona fide reporters to cover an event. The panel felt that any limitations would have to be decided on a case-by-case basis but agreed that maximum possible coverage should be permitted.

4. The media agreed that prior notification of a pooling organization should be as close to H-Hour as possible to minimize the possibility of a story breaking too soon, especially if speculative stories about the operation should appear in media not in the pool or be initiated by one of their reporters not privy to the pool. This would require a pool media decision as to whether to break the story early, despite the embargo on such a break that is inherent in early notification for pooling purposes. The media representatives were not in agreement on this matter but did agree generally that they should not release aspects of the story that they had been made aware of during DOD early notification and which did not appear in the stories already out or in preparation; nor should this privy information be used to confirm speculation concerning an operation.

5. In this connection, the media generally did not agree with a view voiced by some members of the panel that, absolutely to guarantee security, pool notification would not be made until the first military personnel had hit the beach or airhead even though advance military preparation could speed the poolers to the site in the least time possible. The panel did not take a position on this, but some felt that carefully planned pool transportation could meet the media's objections in many, possibly most, cases. For example, in remote areas the pool could be assembled in a location close to the operation using overseas correspondent who would not have to travel from the United States. This is a subject worthy of detailed discussion in the military-media meetings proposed in Recommendation 8a.

6. In this connection, the panel recognized that in many areas of the world an established press presence would be encountered by U.S. forces irrespective of a decision as to whether or not a pool would be used. This consideration would have to be included in initial public affairs planning.

7. There was no unanimity among the media representatives as to whether correspondents, pooled or otherwise, should be in the "first wave" or any other precise point in the operation. All did agree that media presence should be as soon as possible and feasible. The panel believes that such timing has to be decided on a case-by-case basis.

8. Neither the media nor the panel agreed on use in a pool of full-time media employees who are not U.S. citizens. The media tended to agree that, if the parent organization considered such employees reliable, they should be allowed to be pool members. Based on public affairs experience in Vietnam, there were many cases where such employees proved entirely reliable; however, some did not. The panel suggests that this has to be another case-by-case situation.

9. There was also a divergence of opinion among the media as to what news organizations should make up a pool, although all agreed that the most important criterion was probably which organizations cover the widest American audience. Several media representatives suggested specific media pools, but, unfortunately, they varied widely. The panel was not in full agreement on this subject either, but did agree that the following types of news organizations should have top priority. The panel further agreed that DoD should take the factors discussed in this paragraph into account when designating news organizations to participate in a pool.

    a. Wire services. AP and UPI to have priority. A reporter from each and a photographer from either one should be adequate. In a crash situation where inadequate planning time has been available, a reporter from one wire service and a photographer from the other could provide a two-person pool.

    b. Television. A two-person TV pool (one correspondent, one film/sound man) can do the job for a brief time although perhaps minimally. All TV representatives agreed that a three-person team is better and can do more. A panel suggestion that a six-person team (one cameraman, one sound man, and one reporter each from ABC, CBS, NBC, and CNN) seemed agreeable to the four networks although the load on the two technicians would be difficult to handle. The panel has no suggestion on this except that TV pool representatives must have high priority with two representatives as the minimum and augmentation to depend on space available. This should be a matter of discussion at the meetings suggested in recommendation 8a. The question of radio participation in pools must also be resolved.

    c. News Magazines. One reporter and one color photographer.

    d. Daily newspapers. At least one reporter. The panel agreed with newspaper representatives that, although newspapers do use wire service copy and photos, at least one newspaper pooler is needed for the special aspects of newspaper coverage not provided by the wire services. Criteria suggested for use when deciding which newspaper(s) to include in a pool included: Circulation, whether the newspaper has a news service, does the newspaper specialize in military and foreign affairs, and does it cover the Pentagon regularly. There was some agreement among the media representatives that there are probably not more than 8-10 newspapers which should be considered for pooling under these criteria.

10. In addition to the type of embargo necessary when a pooling news agency is notified in advance about a military operation (i.e., nothing to be said about it until it begins) there is another type applicable to some military operations. This second type was used with great success in Vietnam and restricts media accompanying the forces from filing or releasing any information about the progress of the operation until the on-scene commander determines that such release will not impair his security by informing the opposing commander about his objectives. Normally, this is not a problem as general objectives quickly become apparent. In the case of a special objective, there might be some delay in authorizing stories until either the objective is attained or it is obvious the enemy commander knows what it is. In any case, this type of embargo is an option to planners that the media would almost certainly accept as opposed to not having correspondents with the forces from the outset or close to it. The panel did not have a consensus on this matter.

11. Media representatives emphasized the readiness of correspondents to accept, as in the past, the physical dangers inherent in military operations and agreed that the personal security of correspondents should not be a factor in planning media participation in military operations.

RECOMMENDATION 3:

In connection with the use of pools, the Joint Chiefs of Staff recommend to the Secretary of Defense that he study the matter of whether to use a pre-established and constantly updated accreditation or notification list of correspondents in case of a military operation for which a pool is required or just the establishment of a news agency list for use in the same circumstances.

Comments

1. The panel envisions that in either case the agency would select the individual(s) to be its representatives in the pool. In the case of the accreditation/notification list, there would presumably be several names from each news agency/organization to provide the necessary flexibility. The agency would have provided the names in advance to DoD. In the case of the news agency/organization list, DoD would decide which agencies would be in the pool and the agencies would pick the person(s) desired without reference to a list. There was no agreement as to whether DoD should have approval authority of the individuals named to be pool members. The media representatives were unanimously against such approval as were some members of the panel. However, other panel members believed that in the case of an extremely sensitive operation, DoD should have such authority.

2. There was no agreement among either those who appeared before the panel or among the panel itself on this matter. More in both groups seemed to favor simply establishing a news agency list including wire services, television, news magazines and newspapers from which to pick when DOD establishes a pool.

3. This particular problem is one that should be resolved in advance of a military operation and should be a subject of discussion in connection with the military-media meetings suggested in Recommendation 8a.

4. This recommendation does not concern the accreditation that would have to be given each correspondent covering an operation, either at first or later, by the senior on-site commander. Traditionally, this accreditation is limited to establishing that the individual is a bona fide reporter (represents an actual media organization).

RECOMMENDATION 4:

That a basic tenet governing media access to military operations should be voluntary compliance by the media with security guidelines or ground rules established and issued by the military. These rules should be as few as possible and should be worked out during the planning process for each operation. Violations would mean exclusion of the correspondent(s) concerned from further coverage of the operation.

Comments

1. The media were in support of this concept as opposed to formal censorship of any type, and all media representatives agreed that their organizations would abide by these ground rules. This arrangement would place a heavy responsibility on the news media to exercise care so as not to inadvertently jeopardize mission security or troop safety.

2. The guidelines/ground rules are envisioned to be similar to those used in Vietnam (a copy at Enclosure 6). Recognizing that each situation will be different, public affairs planners could use the Vietnam rules as a starting point, as they were worked out empirically during Vietnam by public affairs and security personnel and, for the most part, in cooperation with news media on the scene. All media representatives who addressed the issue agreed that the ground rules worked out satisfactorily in Vietnam.

RECOMMENDATION 5:

Public affairs planning for military operations should include sufficient equipment and qualified military personnel whose function is to assist correspondents in covering the operation adequately.

Comments

1. The military personnel referred to in this recommendation are normally called escorts; however, this term has developed some unfortunate connotations as far as the media are concerned. In any case, the panel's recommendation is designed to provide personnel who, acting as agents of the on-scene commander, will perform such functions as keep the correspondents abreast of the situation; arrange for interviews and briefings; arrange for their transportation to appropriate locations; ensure they are fed and housed, if necessary; and be as helpful as possible consistent with security and troop safety.

2. Almost all of the media representatives agreed that such escorts are desirable, especially at the beginning of an operation, to assist in media coverage. As the operation progresses and the reporters become familiar with what is going on, the media representatives were generally less enthusiastic about this type of assistance.

3. All the media were against escorts if their goal was to try to direct, censor, or slant coverage. However, most agreed that pointing out possible ground rule violations and security problems would be part of the escort's responsibility.

4. The point was made to the panel and the media representatives that escorts were often required in Vietnam, especially after about mid-1968, without many problems arising. One of the major advantages of escorts was making sure the reporters had a full and accurate understanding of the operation being covered.

5. The senior on-scene commander will decide how long escorting should continue after an operation begins.

RECOMMENDATION 6:

Planners should carefully consider media communications requirements to assure the earliest feasible availability. However, these communications must not interfere with combat and combat support operations. If necessary and feasible, plans should include communicative facilities dedicated to the news media.

Comments

1. Media representatives were unanimous in preferring provision for use of their own communications or using local civilian communications when possible. They were also unanimous, however, in the need for access to military communications if nothing else were available, especially in the opening stages of an operation.

2. Permitting media coverage without providing some sort of filing capability does not make sense unless an embargo is in force.

3. Although not discussed in depth during the panel meetings, communications availability is an obvious factor in determining press pool size. Planners should consider the varying deadlines of the different types of media. For example, newsmagazine reporters usually have more time to file thus permitting courier service as a possible satisfactory solution from their standpoint.

4. There was considerable discussion of the possibility of media-provided satellite uplinks being a future threat to security if technology permits real-time or near real-time copy and film/tape processing. The media representatives felt that such a possibility was not imminent; however, the discussions resulted in Recommendation 8d being included in the report. One panel member made the point that such real-time or near real-time capability has long existed for radio news including the Murrow reporting during World War II.

RECOMMENDATION 7:

Planning factors should include provision for intra- and inter-theater transportation support of the media. There was no Panel comment on this matter.

RECOMMENDATION 8:

To improve media-military understanding and cooperation:

a. CJCS should recommend to the Secretary of Defense that a program be undertaken by ASD(PA) for top military public affairs representatives to meet with news organization leadership, to include meetings with individual news organizations, on a reasonably regular basis to discuss mutual problems, including relationships with the media during military operations and exercises. This program should begin as soon as possible.

b. Enlarge programs already underway to improve military understanding of the media via public affairs instruction in service schools and colleges, to include media participation when possible.

c. Seek improved media understanding of the military through more visits by commanders and line officers to news organizations.

d. CJCS should recommend that the Secretary of Defense host at an early date a working meeting with representatives of the broadcast news media to explore the special problems of ensuring military security when and if there is real-time news media audiovisual coverage of a battlefield and, if special problems exist, how they can best be dealt with consistent with the basic principle set forth at the beginning of this section of the report.

Comments

1. The panel became convinced during its meetings with both media and military representatives that any current actual or perceived lack of mutual understanding and cooperation could be largely eliminated through the time-tested vehicle of having reasonable people sit down with reasonable people and discuss their problems. Although some of this has occurred from time to time through the years, there has not been enough, especially in recent years. The panel envisages that these meetings would be between ASD(PA) and/or his representatives and the senior leadership of both media umbrella organizations and individual major news organizations. A number of media representatives appearing before the panel said that they thought the media would be happy to participate in such a program. The program should include use of the Chiefs/Directors of Public Affairs of the Services, some of whom are already doing this.

2. Such meetings would provide an excellent opportunity to discuss problems or potential problems involving future military operations/exercises such as pooling, security and troop safety, accreditation, logistic support, and, most importantly, improving mutual respect, trust, understanding, and cooperation in general.

3. The panel does not exclude any news organizations in this recommendation, but practicality will lead to emphasis on meetings with major organizations. It would be equally useful for commanders in the field and their public affairs officers to conduct similar meetings with local and regional media in their areas, some of which are also underway at this time.

4. Both the panel and the media representatives lauded the efforts underway today to reinsert meaningful public affairs instruction in service schools and colleges. Many officers are sheltered from becoming involved with the news media until they are promoted to certain assignments where they suddenly come face-to-face with the media. If they have not been adequately informed in advance of the mutual

with each other, they sometimes tend to make inadequate decisions concerning media matters. In this connection, several media representatives told the panel they would be, and in some cases have already been, delighted to cooperate in this process by talking to classes and seminars.

5. Several media representatives also were enthusiastic about undertaking an effort to inform their employees about the military, primarily through visits of commanders and other appropriate personnel to their headquarters or elsewhere in their organizations. It was also apparent that some media are concerned with this problem to the point that they are taking an introspective look at their relations not only with the military but other institutions.

General Comments:

1. The panel agreed that public affairs planning for military operations involving allied forces should also consider making plans flexible enough to cover allied media participation, even in pools in some cases.

2. It was pointed out to the panel and should be noted that planners may also have to consider the desires of U.S. Ambassadors and their country teams when operations take place in friendly foreign countries. Some of these problems can, of course, be handled by the commanders and senior public affairs personnel on the scene, but they should be alerted to them in advance.

3. The media representatives all agreed that U.S. media should have first priority in covering U.S. military operations. The panel generally agreed that this must be handled on a case-by-case basis, especially when allied forces are involved.

Final Comment:

An adversarial -- perhaps politely critical would be a better term -- relationship between the media and the government, including the military, is healthy and helps guarantee that both institutions do a good job. However, this relationship must not become antagonistic -- an "us versus them" relationship. The appropriate media role in relation to the government has been summarized aptly as being neither that of a lap dog nor an attack dog but, rather, a watch dog. Mutual antagonism and distrust are not in the best interests of the media, the military, or the American people.

In the final analysis, no statement of principles, policies, or procedures, no matter how carefully crafted, can guarantee the desired results because they have to be carried out by people -- the people in the military and the people in the media. So, it is the good will of the people involved, their spirit, their genuine efforts to do the job for the benefit of the United States, on which a civil and fruitful relationship hinges.

The panel believes that, if its recommendations are adopted, and the people involved are infused with the proper spirit, the twin imperatives of genuine mission security/troop safety on the one hand and a free flow of information to the American public on the other will be achieved.

In other words, the optimum solution to ensure proper media coverage of military operations will be to have the military -- represented by competent, professional public affairs personnel and commanders who understand media problems -- working with the media -- represented by competent, professional reporters and editors who understand military problems -- in a nonantagonistic atmosphere. The panel urges both institutions to adopt this philosophy and make it work.

Winant Sidle
Major General, USA, Retired
Chairman

APPENDIX C

Review of Panama Pool Deployment—December 1989
The Hoffman Report

REVIEW OF PANAMA POOL DEPLOYMENT
DECEMBER 1989

Prepared by:
Fred S. Hoffman
March 9, 1990

Excessive concern for secrecy prevented the Defense Department's media pool from reporting the critical opening battles of the U.S. invasion of Panama.

Because of a secrecy-driven decision by Defense Secretary Dick Cheney, the pool was called out too late and arrived too late to cover the decisive U.S. assaults in that brief war. Military leaders played NO part in shaping that decision.

Cheney said his first priority was safeguarding the security of the operation and that "I was aware of the conflict" between that imperative and the goal of getting the pool to Panama in time.

As Cheney's public affairs advisor, Assistant Defense Secretary Pete Williams should have foreseen the consequences of a late pool deployment. He should have tried to convince Cheney that the pool had to be launched early enough to reach Panama before the operation kicked off.

Over the five-year history of Pentagon-sponsored pools, including a year-long series in the Persian Gulf, hundreds of newsmen and newswomen demonstrated they could be trusted to respect essential ground rules, including operational security.

Unless the Defense Department's leaders are prepared to extend that trust in hot war situations, the pool probably will be of little value.

Excessive secrecy concern also prevented timely detailed planning for the pool's coverage of Operation Just Cause.

A lack of helicopters--which could have been avoided with proper planning--prevented the pool from reporting much of what was left of the action by the time the pool reached Panama.

Some U.S. military concern in Panama for the safety of the pool members impeded coverage. This concern, while understandable, should not have been allowed to limit the pool's reporting opportunities. Newsmen and women cover wars at their own risk.

The result of all this was that the 16-member pool produced stories and pictures of essentially secondary value.

Southern Command Public Affairs Officers (PAOs) had little success in getting the pool to any remaining newsworthy action in the mop-up of the already-defeated Panama Defense Force (PDF) and ragtag Dignity Battalion holdouts.

PAOs tried to find "story ideas," as one of them put it, but too many of these turned out to be disappointments or dry holes.

Overall, there were important instances of less than effective leadership and performance in the Office of the Assistant Secretary of Defense Public Affairs and among some of the senior PAOs in Panama; lapses in staff work, flawed procedures and problems in organization.

Southern Command PAOs failed to provide regular operational briefings for the pool to keep it informed of developments all through Panama. There was only one such briefing, more than 24 hours into the pool's four-day deployment.

Malfunctioning fax equipment and understaffing at the Pentagon, plus communications problems at the Southern Command Media Center in Panama, caused serious delays in getting out print pool reports and still photos.

The decision to send a news pool from Washington was highly questionable. The story could have--and, in my opinion, should have--been covered by a pool formed from U.S. news personnel already in Panama.

Such a pool could have been put in place before American forces attacked. It could have had a front-row view of the assault on Noriega's main headquarters, the Commandancia, a short distance down the hill from Southern Command headquarters on Quarry Heights. Some locally-based U.S. news personnel could have been pre-positioned to cover attacks on other key objectives as well.

Colonel Ron Sconyers, then the Southern Command's Public Affairs Officer, suggested to Williams that the story could be covered by a pool drawn from American news personnel already in Panama--personnel with whom he had worked. Sconyers had mustered such a pool many times before on smaller operations without any security breach.

It should be noted here that the Pentagon pool was established to enable U.S. news personnel to report the earliest possible action in a U.S. military operation <u>in a remote area where there was no other American press presence.</u> Panama did not fit that description.

But Williams, following discussions with Cheney, sent the national pool from Washington.

It appears that a key reason for this decision was what Cheney later described in an interview as a "desire to avoid being criticized for not using it" in the Panama situation.

As it turned out, the Pentagon pool landed in Panama about four hours after U.S. troops launched their attacks on key targets.

Even then, whatever helicopter lift Southern Command PAOs could round up was swiftly snatched away for higher priority operational purposes. Ground transportation was deemed too risky because of sniping. Also, the Bridge of the Americas which spans the Panama Canal was closed for hours on the first day of the operation.

The helicopter situation eased after about 36 hours, but the story was rapidly winding down by that time.

From the outset, the newsmen and women in the pool met one frustration after another.

PAOs in Panama unwittingly fed the pool's justified irritation by hauling its members to some "events" that had nothing to do with the fighting they so badly wanted to see and report.

As a result, there were suggestions that the pool was being manipulated to serve the Bush Administration's political and diplomatic interests.

So far as I could determine, there was no effort to manipulate the pool in Panama. Rather, it was a matter of maladroitness, sometimes good intentions gone awry, and unanticipated obstacles.

Some examples:

Late that exhausting first day, the pool was taken to meet the arriving U.S. ambassador for a news conference. One pooler described this happening as "worthless." Asked why this was done, an escort officer explained that there was nothing else going on at the time and that it was a matter of poolers "either doing that or hanging around the press center."

This was especially irksome to the pool because its members had been exposed, shortly after landing in Panama, to a briefing by John Bushnell, U.S. Embassy Charge d'Affaires. A reporter who was there described it as a lecture on the history of Panama.

What the pool apparently didn't know was that Bushnell was a last-minute stand-in. The SouthCom PAOs had expected the star of the event to be the newly-sworn-in Panamanian President Endara making his first appearance before the press. But Endara refused to do this at an American base. So the intended "exclusive" bombed, and Bushnell was drafted in Endara's place.

Sometimes the pool was diverted from a promising objective because escort officers discovered, belatedly, the presence of Special Operations soldiers. Such troops are under standing orders to shun the press.

More than once, the pool encountered unit commanders who had no idea what it was all about and felt they had to check up the chain of command. Obviously, word about the pool and its mission had not reached down through the military echelons, as should have been assured by senior PAOs of the Southern Command and the 18th Airborne Corps, which did the fighting.

I could find no evidence--except for standing orders governing Special Operation troops, including the Rangers--that any senior civilian official or military commander had issued written or verbal instructions to refuse interviews or other contact with news personnel. The restrictions on the Rangers were eased on the second day of the operation.

One senior PAO did advise Major General James Johnson, commander of the 82nd Airborne Division, not to talk with newsmen. Johnson accepted this advice from Lieutenant Colonel Ned Longsworth, who said he had received guidance to that effect.

But, when asked about this, Longsworth said he could not recall who gave him such guidance. This remains a mystery.

In my discussions with the top generals involved in Operation Just Cause I heard only expressions of support for the pool concept and regret that it didn't work as it should have in Panama. Skeptics may regard these expressions as tinged with after-the-fact wisdom, but I believe they can be viewed as hopeful indicators for the future.

General Max Thurman, who heads the Southern Command, said, "I think we made a mistake by not having some of the press pool in with the 18th Airborne Corps so they could move with the troops."

Army Lieutenant General Carl W. Stiner, who commanded all the combat troops in the invasion, said he could have received a smaller pool at Ft. Bragg, NC, and taken it with him to Panama ahead of the paratroop deployment. It could have been briefed, sequestered and positioned to witness the opening of the attack, said Stiner, who flew to Panama on Monday, Dec. 18. The assaults began early Dec. 20.

Stiner's scenario would have required a much earlier callout of the pool. It actually was mustered the evening of Tuesday, Dec. 19.

In fact, the pool question still was being discussed in the White House Oval Office as late as Tuesday afternoon and a "go" order wasn't given by Williams to his staff and the Southern Command PAO until about 5 pm that day for a 7:30 pm callout start--only 5 1/2 hours before H-hour.

· Major General Will Roosma suggested that, in the future, the Pentagon media pool members should exercise several times a year with airborne troops in conjunction with periodic Emergency Deployment Readiness Exercises. In that way "they become part of the team" and gain experience, said Roosma, who is Stiner's deputy in command of the 18th Airborne Corps.

More frequent pool exercises--the pool was called out only once last year prior to the Panama deployment--might well serve to implant necessary ground rules and prescribed procedures more deeply in the minds of pool members and their bureau chiefs, particularly those new to pool duty.

Periodic pool exercises with various elements of the armed forces, especially those with quick reaction missions, would help accustom line outfits to contact with news people.

There was a breach of OPSEC rules by staff members of Time magazine's Washington bureau reached at a Christmas party during the Panama pool callout on the evening of Dec. 19, only a few hours before the pool was due to take off from Andrews Air Force Base, MD.

This breach resulted from an open discussion at the party about who would go for Time-- an assignment that should have been established by the bureau chief in advance. As Time bureau chief Stanley Cloud acknowledged: "More people knew than should have known."

But that secrecy rule violation likely could have been avoided if the Time bureau chief had been notified at his office during daytime business hours--something made impossible because of the high level Pentagon decision to delay the callout until after the evening news broadcasts on TV.

So far as I could determine, the Time violation did not compromise the operation.

-0-

Some of the key problems that eventually burdened the pool had their genesis in overstress on secrecy and subsequent fumbles at the Pentagon and the Southern Command in November.

As a consequence, about a month of possible planning time was lost and, when Operation Just Cause was mounted, there was no public affairs plan.

On Nov. 13, the Joint Staff sent a Top Secret warning order to the Southern Command and other commands, signalling readiness for possible operations against Panama. In that message, the Joint Staff asked the Southern Command to submit a public affairs plan and directed Southern Command to "be prepared to accept a media pool."

On Nov. 22, the Southern Command Public Affairs Office sent a Top Secret fax to the Pentagon public affairs Plans unit. That fax was far short of a fully-fleshed plan. It provided bare-boned public affairs guidance.

Lieutenant Commander Gregory Hartung, a Plans officer, took the fax message to his boss, Colonel Peter Alexandrakos. Alexandrakos prepared a Top Secret memorandum and began the process of coordinating the proposed guidance among relevant offices. As is customary, Alexandrakos invited comments.

That same day, Nov. 22, Hartung was summoned to the Pentagon's Inter American Affairs Office.

Hartung said he was informed by a staff officer there that then Deputy Assistant Secretary of Defense Richard C. Brown "had discussed this document at an inter agency meeting...and that they decided, because this scenario was so inflammatory, that it should be held 'close hold' at OASD(PA) until such time that it became necessary to have such guidance and then staffed at that time."

According to Hartung's recollection, he was told to "stick it in the safe and forget about it."

In an interview, Brown said the proposed guidance document "was dynamite."

"It really told about the mission," Brown said. "Given that it could be leaked, there was concern about possible compromise."

One of Brown's top aides said the security concern centered on the way the document was being circulated for coordination. This aide said that the Inter American Affairs Office "never told Public Affairs to stop what they were doing." Adding:

"They were advised, however, to do it in the proper channels."

Although there are differing versions of what advice Hartung was given, the result was that the message was put into a safe and effectively buried there.

While the document failed to meet the requirement for a complete PA plan, it should have served to alert staff officers that follow-through action was imperative.

Four Public Affairs staff officers, three of them at the Pentagon and one at the Southern Command, failed to follow through--to question why nothing was being done to fulfill the Joint Staff's requirement for a public affairs plan for what turned out to be Operation Just Cause.

The Inter American Affairs objections were never brought to the attention of Williams, as should have happened. This demonstrates a weakness in the planning system. It needs closer oversight in the OASD(PA) front office.

If the normal planning process had been carried out, it is quite likely that some of the problems which cropped up for the pool during Operation Just Cause would've been anticipated. A careful plan would have provided for earmarking helicopters to move the pool, for dedicating aircraft to carry photographic and other pool products to the United States, and for adequate communications facilities to accommodate not only the pool, but the hundreds of other reporters and photographers who flooded into the country.

The Southern Command did have a contingency plan for accommodating the pool, but its provisions were very general. What was needed was a specific plan tailored to the upcoming operation.

As Major General Roosma of the 18th Airborne Corps said, "a public affairs annex to an operational plan must be written in great detail."

"The time to prepare such a plan is not during great crisis, but before hand," Roosma said.

-0-

The first discussion of a possible pool to cover the Just Cause Operation came on Sunday, December 17, in a meeting at which President Bush presided in his study. That was the meeting that produced the decision to send American troops into Panama.

Cheney said the Department of Defense pool would be activated to go in with the initial forces, according to White House spokesman Marlin Fitzwater, who was present. Bush asked whether the pool would come from Washington or would be organized in Panama. The President was told it would come from Washington, Fitzwater said. Bush indicated concern as to whether this could be done while still protecting operational security.

The issue came up again at the White House on Tuesday afternoon, 10 hours or so before the operation was due to start. Vice President Quayle asked if the pool couldn't be organized in Panama rather than being dispatched from Washington, Fitzwater said, adding:

"No one had a good answer as to why it had to come from Washington."

According to this account, Bush and Quayle remained skeptical that the pool would be able to maintain secrecy.

In the last analysis, Fitzwater said, "the President left it up to him (Cheney)."

Meanwhile on Monday morning, Williams said he was called to Cheney's office and told that the President had decided to proceed with an operation against Noriega and that a pool would be used to cover it.

"You can't mention this to anybody," Williams quoted Cheney as telling him.

Williams said he had several conversations with Cheney on Monday and Tuesday.

"There was never any doubt in anyone's mind that there was going to be a pool," Williams said.

However, the issue of whether it would be a pool drawn from news people already in Panama or the national media pool in Washington appears to have been a live one until late Tuesday afternoon.

"The Secretary and I talked about whether to use a national or regional pool," Williams recalled. In the end, he said, "We decided to use the national pool because we were confident OPSEC could be preserved, we were accustomed to it and we had used a pool" the previous May (in connection with a troop reinforcement to Panama).

Another reason for this decision, Williams said, was a belief that the Washington-based pool members "knew the ground rules."

Cheney mentioned somewhat different reasons for opting to send the pool from Washington--a decision that the Defense Secretary said was in accord with Williams' recommendation.

"The pool was created for this kind of situation," said Cheney.

On this, Cheney was misinformed. As mentioned earlier, the pool was organized as a vehicle to provide U.S. news personnel early access to fighting by American forces in remote areas--not a Panama with a resident U.S. press corps and an existing American base structure.

This illustrates how the perception of the pool's purpose has become skewed since it was established in the wake of the Pentagon's ill-advised denial of news reporting access to battles on the Caribbean island of Grenada in 1983.

Cheney also said he had a "sense of special loyalty to people who cover the Pentagon" and that "it was important that there be that kind of coverage."

Actually, the news pool that flew to Panama included only one Pentagon "regular," NBC's Fred Francis.

As for the timing of the pool callout--the most critical factor in the outcome of its deployment--Cheney said his decision was conditioned by an overriding need to maintain the "maximum security possible to avoid compromising the operation and to preserve the element of surprise."

Despite the attempt to keep a secrecy lid firmly in place, reports were appearing on TV and on the news wires Tuesday depicting unusual military activity at bases in the United States and Panama.

Alluding to these reports, Cheney said "we were very concerned about the situation--that the PDF (Panama Defense Force) might be waiting for us."

So, Cheney said, "we basically decided to notify the pool after the evening news Tuesday to minimize the possibility of leaks."

The 7:30 pm callout guaranteed that the pool would reach Panama hours after the operation began just before 1 am Wednesday.

Cheney said "I did it with full knowledge" of what his decision would mean for the pool.

The Pentagon chief made it clear it was basically his decision, but Williams obviously was in full agreement.

"We decided 7:30 pm was a good time to call it out," Williams said.

"I never suggested an earlier callout," he said when asked about this.

General Colin Powell, Chairman of the Joint Chiefs of Staff, recalled the White House discussion about the pool on Tuesday and said "the final judgement was made in the Oval Office and that was that we ought to have a pool."

Did Powell make any recommendations to Cheney or Williams on how and when the pool should be called out? The four-star general said he was "left out of the pattern" in this regard, that he discussed the pool with Cheney "in only the most general terms" and that "I left it up to Pete Williams."

Lieutenant General Tom Kelly, the Joint Staff Director of Operations, said "we didn't play any role" in the framing of the civilian decisions on the pool callout.

Williams said he didn't hear from senior military leaders on the question of the timing of the pool deployment.

Bound by a secrecy rule laid down by Cheney, Williams informed only two members of his staff on Monday, December 18, of the upcoming operation and the likelihood of a news pool being formed to cover it. These two were Deputy Assistant Secretary Bob Taylor and Major John Smith, Williams' Military Assistant.

It wasn't until the next morning that Williams brought his own planning staff into the process and several hours after that on Tuesday that Williams began discussions with Southern Command PAO Sconyers about a probable pool.

Therefore, more than 24 hours of immediate planning time was lost.

Taylor was set to work gathering information to refresh Williams' knowledge of pool callup procedures and similar matters. Smith, who had served in the Southern Command, provided information on the public affairs setup down there.

There was some "brainstorming," as Smith described it, but apparently no detailed planning on that Monday.

The only conversation outside the small circle of knowledge in Williams' office came about midday on Monday. It was initiated by mid-level officers from the Joint Staff who wanted to discuss possible airlift arrangements for a media pool deployment. These discussions were inconclusive because options offered from the Joint Staff would have landed the pool in Panama about 12 hours after the attacks opened.

Even after Williams brought in his planning staff to start detailed preparations on Tuesday, debate over whether to use a Panama-based pool or send one from Washington lingered into the afternoon.

The discussion became moot after the White House meeting, and Williams called Sconyers at SouthCom at about 5 pm to inform him that the national media pool would be heading his way that night.

To have made the pool deployment a success, a firm decision on sending it should have been made, if not on Monday, by Tuesday morning.

The pool could have been called out about midday Tuesday and flown to Panama to arrive by early evening—in plenty of time to be sequestered, briefed and prepositioned near possibly several objectives to witness the major attacks.

In Panama, chief PAO Sconyers received some indications on Monday, December 18, that there might be a military operation against Noriega, but this was not confirmed for him until Tuesday morning when an operations officer gave him a detailed briefing including specific objectives.

Colonel Sconyers said he was told he could not share that information with anybody. These security restraints, he said, barred him from starting preparations.

At that time, he said, he was thinking in terms of using a locally based pool and this conditioned some of his moves.

As of Tuesday morning, he said he considered asking for specific assignment of helicopters to support the pool, but he didn't feel at that time that he would need them for the Panama-based pool. He intended to place that pool to observe the fighting below Quarry Heights and possibly at Ft. Amador.

After he was notified officially at 5 pm Tuesday that the national media pool would be coming from Washington, Sconyers said he asked for helicopter support. By this time, virtually all the helicopters were assigned to carry combat troops.

Looking back, General Thurman said he might have been able to reach out and place possibly two helicopters at the disposal of the pool if he had known on Monday that it was coming from Washington. Sconyers did manage to get a small UH-1 helicopter for the pool. But a Huey holds only eight. So he asked for a larger one, and a CH-47 was eventually provided, only to be taken away Wednesday morning after ferrying the newsmen and newswomen from Howard AFB to Ft. Clayton, where the pool got to watch TV broadcasts of President Bush's speech and a Pentagon news conference by Cheney and General Powell.

Although Sconyers did not have definite word on Monday that an operation against Noriega was in the offing, he was reading signs and probably should have anticipated the need for helicopters to move a pool, even if that pool was organized in Panama.

In his long term planning, Sconyers and his staff had arranged for filing facilities at a media center on Quarry Heights, but these were designed to serve a limited pool, not the horde of newsmen and women who flooded in starting the day after the pool reached Panama.

In any event, those media center filing facilities, particularly telephone lines, proved to be inadequate even for the pool and were overwhelmed when the larger number of reporters converged on that center. Sconyers also underestimated a need for more people to handle the big influx of newsmen and women. He was offered additional help early on, but declined at the time.

The upshot was that he found himself spending much of his time and energies in arranging billeting, food and other necessary services for hundreds of news people. To that extent, he was diverted from serving the pool.

Back in Washington, Colonel Alexandrakos, head of OASD(PA)'s Plans division, and some of his staff began the callout as ordered at about 7:30 pm Tuesday. Pool members were supposed to report to Andrews AFB by 9:30 pm for a planned departure at 11 pm.

Immediately, the Plans officers manning the phones ran into difficulties in getting the word to some of the news people on the pool roster.

Some of this difficulty could be attributed to the fact that the callout came during the week before Christmas when there were news staff parties and there were news people on vacation.

The situation wasn't helped by apparent confusion in the callout process at the Pentagon.

Alexandrakos said he was ordered by Deputy Assistant Secretary Taylor in mid-callout to expand the pool by going back to all the wire services and inviting each to send a reporter and a photographer.

Taylor said in an interview Alexandrakos apparently had not understood that there were supposed to be slots on the pool for two representatives of each of the three wire services. That decision was made earlier on Tuesday, Taylor said.

The pool already had been expanded in an unprecedented way when Williams offered NBC the opportunity to bring along on the flight to Panama a satellite uplink dish which, together with its associated equipment, weighed more than a ton.

NBC arranged for that satellite dish and two technicians with an outside company which provides such services.

In effect, this add-on widened the radius of knowledge outside the normal pool. It created the potential for an OPSEC breach by technicians who never had been involved in pool activities and never had been subjected to the discipline of OPSEC ground rules. The satellite uplink, however, did help the NBC correspondent, Fred Francis, in beaming his broadcasts from Panama. There is no evidence that the addition of the technicians led to any security compromise.

As another byproduct of the confusion which surrounded the callout, the primary pooler for one newspaper and his alternate both showed up at Andrews. The alternate, who did not make the trip, then called home. Normally this would be a violation of a ground rule, but an escorting officer gave permission for the call.

Apart from the incident at the Time magazine Christmas party, there was another report of a security breach allegedly involving the pool.

This report reached President Bush when he spoke to House Speaker Tom Foley about 7 hours before the attacks opened. It did not check out.

A top aide to the Speaker said he is convinced a newsman's probing call to Foley was prompted by reports on TV and news wires of military movements around bases in the United States and Panama, not by any leak from the pool. This view is supported by the fact that the President told associates he spoke with Foley at about 6 pm Tuesday, which was 1 1/2 hours before the callout began.

Most of the poolers arrived at Andrews properly equipped. One lacked a passport. One lacked a shot record. Alexandrakos decided neither document was needed because the pool was going to be operating on and from U.S. bases in Panama.

Dick Thompson, Time magazine correspondent, had to rush from the Christmas party, so he didn't have a chance to change clothes or to pick up his writing tools. He went to tropical Panama in a winter suit.

The pool left Andrews at 11:26 pm and was informed, when airborne, where they were going and why. Most already suspected their destination was Panama.

-0-

Shortly after the pool landed at Howard AFB at 5 am Wednesday it became clear that it wasn't going to spring into action. A CH-47 helicopter arrived about one-half hour later and it took still another half hour to load it up with the cumbersome satellite uplink dish and other equipment.

Sconyers had planned to run the pool up to Quarry Heights by road, but the closure of the Bridge of the Americas across the canal and reports that Quarry Heights was under fire impelled a change in plan.

Instead, the pool was taken to Ft. Clayton, about 10 minutes away by helicopter. This is when it all began to go down hill as it dawned on the reporters that they were not moving to the scene of combat.

By 7 am, it was becoming clear at the Pentagon that the pool was immobilized. Taylor and Williams urged Sconyers in succeeding hours to get the pool to the action.

At no time, however, did Williams contact General Powell, the Joint Chiefs of Staff Chairman, for help in this situation. He should have done so as soon as he became aware of the problem.

Powell heard nothing about the pool's plight until Thursday afternoon, about 30 hours later.

"I thought everything went smoothly," Powell said. He said he "didn't have a single clue" the pool was bogged down until newsmen informed him.

Powell indicated he would have been prepared to act promptly if he had heard from Williams.

"Once it became clear that things were not going well, it should have been worked through command channels," the JCS Chairman said. "It never became a matter of discussion for me and General Thurman."

When the pool finally did get moving, Alexandrakos and Sconyers kept it in a single unit rather than splitting it to cover more of the story. Alexandrakos said the pool was kept together because of transportation limitations. It was split into two sections on the second day of the operation.

The first time the pool had a chance to get anywhere near any shooting was around 10 am when Sconyers managed to get a helicopter back and the group was flown to Ft. Amador, across the bay from Quarry Heights and the main part of Panama City.

Here is the way that Ken Merida of the Dallas Morning News described what the pool found there:

"Even at Ft. Amador, a military installation shared by the United States and Panama under the Panama Canal Treaties, the action was largely over. U.S. troops had repeatedly shelled the barracks of the Panamanian Defense Forces in the early morning hours when we were still on a military transport plane. All that was left to do was smoke out a few remaining Noriega loyalists, none of whom surrendered in our presence."

While at Ft. Amador, the poolers could see smoke rising from around the battered remains of the Commandancia in Panama City several miles away.

"We were told that because of continued sniper fire on the first day it was too dangerous for us to visit the neighborhood of Chorillo which housed another of Noriega's headquarters and was still burning from heavy shelling by U.S. troops," Merida said.

"It was also too dangerous, we were told, to take a helicopter tour of Panama City."

This issue of the pool's safety was a sore one. Some members of the pool felt it was being used as an excuse by escorts to divert the newsmen and women from hot military action.

Lieutenant Colonel Ned Longsworth, who was chief escort for the pool at Ft. Amador, acknowledged that "I may have been a little too protective at Ft. Amador." Longsworth claimed that, otherwise, safety was not invoked to prevent moving the pool to newsworthy sites.

But Kathy Lewis, reporter for the Houston Post, said "we were often told we could NOT go to a certain area because of concern about snipers or other threats to our safety."

As for the rejection of poolers' requests to be flown over the city, Longsworth said, "I wasn't going to put a helicopter pilot's life on the line to fly over the city when there still was fire."

Regardless, Longsworth said, "The pilots advised that they didn't want to fly over Panama City. They were still catching rounds. This was not for the safety of the pool. The pilots thought it would endanger their ship."

I strongly doubt that any news professional would expect members of the armed forces to risk their lives just for the purpose of getting reporters and photographers a story. But concern for safety of newsmen and women should never be used by the military as an excuse to seal off news personnel from the scene of fighting.

After-action reports prepared by members of the pool and interviews point up a number of other episodes which were especially galling to them.

Photographers and reporters were incensed when they were told they could not interview or take pictures of American wounded. This bar was ordered by Williams' office out of concern that pictures or identification of wounded might appear on TV or in print before next-of-kin were notified officially.

In this case I feel the bar was proper, to avoid the possibility of causing shock and pain to relatives who might not yet have been reached.

Later in the week, after notification of families was assured, wounded were televised at a military hospital in San Antonio, Texas.

Another frustration involving casualties is inexplicable.

In a meeting on the first night in Panama, pool photographers were turned aside by Colonel Sconyers when they sought to photograph caskets bearing men killed in action. The question of notification of next-of-kin did not apply in this case because the caskets were closed and bore no identification of the bodies inside.

Two pool photographers and a military escort quoted Sconyers as saying the caskets would be sent to the United States later in the week. The caskets showed up at Dover AFB in Delaware well before that time.

When asked about this, Sconyers said he did not remember any discussions with members of the pool about the caskets, but he conceded later that he may have had such an exchange with poolers. He noted things were in a pretty hectic state at that time.

Members of the pool were indignant when they were denied access to a place where Panamanian prisoners were being held. As Longsworth explained it, a young officer in charge refused to allow the pool to enter the prisoner detention area until he checked with his commander. Longsworth said he contacted Southern Command headquarters and finally received permission for the pool to take pictures of the detainees.

Still another confrontation between escort and pool occurred when Longsworth told photographers they could not photograph damaged helicopters at Howard AFB.

Here, Longsworth said he was carrying out an order by Air Force Brigadier General Robin Tarnow, commander of the 830th Air Division, who was concerned that photographers might inadvertantly take pictures of classified equipment on the field at the time.

Longsworth should have interceded for the photographers. Experience has shown, notably in the Persian Gulf, that photographers will refrain from picturing sensitive equipment if asked. It seems that such an agreement could have been reached with the photographers in this case and allowed them to take pictures of non-sensitive damaged helicopters.

Members of the pool resented what they regarded as special treatment accorded to ABC personality Sam Donaldson, who arrived with an entourage the day after the main attacks.

"When Sam Donaldson arrived, it was like the President had walked into the media center," said one military escort who shared the pool's feeling of resentment.

This officer said Sconyers was "given over basically to supporting Sam Donaldson."

Sconyers and his deputy, Lieutenant Colonel Bob Donnelly, made it clear they were unhappy at what they hinted was pressure from Washington to give Donaldson favored treatment.

It is self evident that there should never be any special treatment or favoritism for any outside newsmen or women at the expense of the pool.

-0-

"It was a nightmare," said Army Captain Barbara Summers.

"The faxing and refaxing operation was a nightmare," said the Houston Post's Kathy Lewis.

Both were describing their experiences, thousands of miles apart, in trying to get written pool reports from Panama to the Pentagon for distribution.

Summers was part of an undermanned crew at the Pentagon, grappling with a faulty fax machine and torturous telephone communications.

Lewis was a reporter serving with the media pool in Panama, harried by the same problems.

While TV and radio newsmen with the pool transmitted their reports without major difficulty, the newspaper, wire service and magazine reporters and still photographers ran into obstacle after obstacle.

The first obstacle arose Wednesday morning when the initial writing pool report was filed in Panama to the Pentagon. The fax machine in the Plans office was broken. As a result of this malfunction, the machine was cutting copy short at the margins.

Sergeant Rhueben Douthitt located a replacement, but then he and other staff members had difficulty reading the incoming material.

The Pentagon staffers then tried to phone the media center at Quarry Heights in Panama to clarify the copy. However, sometimes the calls were misdirected by the Quarry Heights switchboard and sometimes the phones in the media center went unanswered. It took as long as two hours to get a call through.

By this time, bureau chiefs from news organizations represented on the pool were calling the Pentagon demanding to know why they weren't getting the pool reports from the scene.

"Hours after the fact we discovered there had been transmission problems with our morning reports and hours after the late afternoon ones were sent, we learned the fax machines were cutting off large margins," Kathy Lewis said.

"We had to resend all of our dispatches," said Thompson of Time.

Facing these obstructions, reporters asked Colonel Alexandrakos for permission to depart from normal pool rules and dictate their reports by telephone to one of the wire services as a means of speeding up the distribution.

Members of the pool said that Alexandrakos refused permission until he could check with Washington. That caused further delay.

Bob Kearns of Reuters and Steven Komarow of the Associated Press took matters into their own hands and dictated by phone directly to their wire services.

Pool photographers suffered through painfully slow and frequently interrupted picture transmission by telephone line from Panama.

"The first day or two the phone line situation was next to impossible," said Tim Aubry, Reuters photographer.

As Aubry and UPI photographer Matt Mendelshon explained it, operators in Panama kept checking the phone lines periodically during transmission of pictures.

This caused a "hit" on the line resulting in the appearance of a black line across the picture. Therefore, the pictures had to be resent whenever this happened.

Aubry estimated it took about 10 hours to send six to eight photos. It should have taken about 10 minutes a picture.

Sconyers and his staff had arranged for only enough telephone lines to accommodate the pool.

Once other news personnel began pouring into the media center Thursday night, the pool had to scramble for lines.

"With the new arrivals, the task of securing a phone line...out was nearly impossible," Aubry said.

"It took up to an hour at times waiting for a phone line out to file our pictures."

Pool photographers complained that film material that was supposed to have been flown to the United States either arrived very late or not at all.

"There were no arrangements or priority given to the idea of transporting material out of Panama to Washington or New York," said Aubry.

"The first pool material shipped out on Thursday, including raw transparency film, service negatives and...clear negative film, did not arrive at its destination until Saturday."

Cynthia Johnson, Time photographer, told this story:

"Arrangements were supposedly made to send my Wednesday film out on a military aircraft headed for Dover Air Force Base (Delaware) on Thursday. We had a courier in place to transport the film to our lab when it arrived. The plane arrived, but the film wasn't on it. After much phoning back and forth in the middle of the night, my film was discovered in someone's in-box at Howard Air Force Base."

Sconyers should have anticipated a need for dedicated aircraft as a backup in the event that primary transmission means failed.

Instead, the only arrangement made was to try to send pool materials back to the States on planes already scheduled to carry cargo or passengers.

-0-

The problems back at the Pentagon in handling the print pool reports were aggravated by the fact that most of the small staff left behind by Alexandrakos was inexperienced in pool matters.

Although Alexandrakos knew Tuesday morning that the media pool might be sent to Panama, he failed to make sure that each of his staff knew what they were supposed to do when the copy began rolling in from Panama.

To have prepared his staff properly over the long term, Alexandrakos should have assigned specific tasks to each member and exercised the team periodically.

Marine Major Shelley Rogers and Captain Summers improvised. They organized themselves and two enlisted men into teams of two each so there would be around-the-clock coverage. This meant 12-hour shifts.

Rogers had additional responsibilities--she had to work in the Pentagon's Crisis Coordination Center handling messages and other tasks.

So she had to spread herself thin and this added to the burden on the other three.

Sergeant Douthitt was the only member of this small team who had experience with the pool. When he became aware Tuesday evening of what was about to happen, he pulled out a binder containing standard operating procedures developed in the past and gave it to Major Rogers. But it was too close to the event for a simple reading of the SOP to prepare sufficiently anybody who had not previously handled such responsibilities.

Examination of the SOP shows a total lack of any provisions for Pentagon handling of pool products other than print reports.

Apparently there has never been a requirement laid down by the Pentagon that organizations participating in the still photo activities of a pool must share their products with photo agencies outside the pool.

This is a loophole which must be closed. The pool must serve the entire news industry.

As long as the pool is an officially sponsored mechanism, the Defense Department must be prepared to make it work right.

Accordingly, I offer the following recommendations:

—The Secretary of Defense should issue a policy directive, to be circulated throughout the Department and the Armed Services, stating explicitly his official sponsorship of the media pool and requiring full support for it. That policy statement should make it clear to all that the pool must be given every assistance to report combat by U.S. troops from the start of operations.

—All operational plans drafted by the Joint Staff must have an annex spelling out measures to assure that the pool will move with the lead elements of U.S. forces and cover the earliest stages of operations. This principle should be incorporated in overall public affairs plans.

—A Deputy Assistant Secretary of Defense for Public Affairs should closely monitor development of operation-related public affairs plans to assure they fulfill all requirements for pool coverage. The Assistant Secretary of Defense for Public Affairs should review all such plans. In advance of military action, those plans should be briefed to the Secretary of Defense and the Chairman of the Joint Chiefs of Staff along with the operation plans.

Public affairs staff officers and key staff personnel representing policy offices, such as International Security Affairs, should be brought into the planning process at the very earliest stage. The practice of keeping key staff officers with high security clearances out of the planning process in order to limit access to sensitive information should be followed only sparingly and eliminated where possible.

—In the runup to a military operation, the Chairman of the Joint Chiefs of Staff should send out a message ordering all commanders to give full cooperation to the media pool and its escorts. This requirement should be spelled out unambiguously and should reach down through all the echelons in the chain of command. Such a message should make clear that necessary resources, such as helicopters, ground vehicles, communications equipment, etc., must be earmarked specifically for pool use, that the pool must have ready access to the earliest action and that the safety of the pool members must not be used as a reason to keep the pool from action.

—The ASD(PA) must be prepared to weigh in aggressively with the Secretary of Defense and the JCS Chairman where necessary to overcome any secrecy or other obstacles blocking prompt deployment of a pool to the scene of action.

—After a pool has been deployed, the ASD(PA) must be kept informed in a timely fashion of any hitches that may arise. He must be prepared to act immediately, to contact the JCS Chairman, the Joint Staff Director of Operations and other senior officers who can serve to break through any obstacles to the pool. The ASD(PA) should call on the Defense Secretary for help as needed.

—The ASD(PA) should study a proposal by several of the Panama poolers that future pools deploy in two sections. The first section would be very small and would include only reporters and photographers. The second section, coming later, would bring in supporting gear, such as satellite uplink equipment.

—The national media pool should never again be herded as a single unwieldy unit. It should be broken up after arriving at the scene of action to cover a wider spectrum of the story and then be reassembled periodically to share the reporting results.

—The pool should be exercised at least once during each quarterly rotation with airborne and other types of military units most likely to be sent on emergency combat missions.

—During deployments, there should be regular briefings for pool newsmen and newswomen by senior operations officers so the poolers will have an up-to-date and complete overview of the progress of an operation they are covering.

—There is an urgent need for restructuring of the organization which has the responsibility for handling pool reports sent to the Pentagon for processing and distribution. The ASD(PA) must assure that there is adequate staffing and enough essential equipment to handle the task. The Director of Plans, so long as he has this responsibility, should clearly assign contingency duties among his staff to ensure timely handling of reports from the pool. Staffers from the Administration Office, Community Relations and other divisions of OASD(PA) should be mobilized to help in such a task as needed.

—The ASD(PA) should give serious consideration to a suggestion by some of the pool members to create a new pool slot for an editor who would come to the Pentagon during a deployment to lend professional journalism help to the staff officers handling pool reports. Such a pool editor could edit copy, question content where indicated and help expedite distribution of the reports.

--The pool escorting system needs overhauling as well. There is no logical reason for the Washington-based escorts to be drawn from the top of the OASD(PA) Plans Division. The head of that division should remain in Washington to oversee getting out the pool products.

Pool escorts should be drawn from the most appropriate service, rather than limiting escort duty to officers of the Plans Division. The individual armed service public affairs offices should be required to assign military officers to the pool on a contingency basis. For example, if it's an Army operation, the escorts should be primarily Army officers. In the Panama deployment, the three Washington-based escorts wore Air Force and Navy uniforms in what was an overwhelmingly Army operation.

Escorts should deploy in field uniforms or draw them from field commands soon after arriving. The Panama pool escorts wore uniforms befitting a day behind the desk at the Pentagon and this, I found, had a jarring effect on the Army people with whom they dealt.

--The ASD(PA) should close a major gap in the current system by requiring all pool participant organizations--whether print, still photo, TV or radio--to share all pool products with all elements of the news industry. Pool participants must understand they represent the entire industry.

Any pool participant refusing to share with all legitimate requestors should be dropped from the pool and replaced by another organization that agrees to abide by time honored pool practices.

--There is merit in a suggestion by one of the pool photographers that participating news organizations share the cost of equipment, such as a portable dark room and a negative transmitter, which could be stored at Andrews AFB for ready access in a deployment. Other equipment essential for smooth transmission of pool products, such as satellite up-link gear, might also be acquired and stored in the same manner.

--All pool-assigned reporters and photographers, not only bureau chiefs, should attend quarterly Pentagon sessions where problems can be discussed and rules and responsibilities underscored.

--Public Affairs Officers from Unified Commands should meet periodically with pool-assigned reporters and photographers with whom they might have to work in some future crises.

APPENDIX D—EXHIBIT 3

U.S. Central Command Ground Rules for All Media—Version II
Operation Desert Shield
Early September 1990–January 15, 1991

USCENTCOM
~~████████~~ GROUND RULES ~~████████████~~
FOR OPERATION DESERT SHIELD

1. ~~████████████████████████████████~~
~~████████████~~ the following ground rules will be enforced for OPERATION DESERT SHIELD.

    A. The following categories of information are not releaseable:

        (1) Number of troops

        (2) Number of aircraft

        (3) Number of other equipment (e.g. artillery, tanks, radars, trucks, water "buffaloes," etc.)

        (4) Names of military installations/geographic locations of U.S. military units in Saudi Arabia

        (5) Information regarding future operations

        (6) Information concerning security precautions at military installations in Saudi Arabia

        (7) Names/hometowns of U.S. military personnel being interviewed, and names of Saudis being interviewed. Commanders of U.S. units being interviewed are excepted from this provision.

        (9) Photography that would show level of security at military installations in Saudi Arabia

        (10) Photography that would reveal the name or specific location of military forces or installations.

2. If you are not sure whether an action you will take will violate a ground rule, consult with your escort officer PRIOR TO TAKING THAT ACTION.

APPENDIX D—EXHIBIT 2

U.S. Central Command Ground Rules for All Media—Version I
Operation Desert Shield
Mid-August–Early September 1990

ADDITIONAL GROUND RULES FOR THE DOD NATIONAL MEDIA POOL
FOR OPERATION DESERT SHIELD

1. In addition to the standard DoD National Media pool ground rules, the following ground rules will be enforced for OPERATION DESERT SHIELD.

    A. The following categories of information are not releaseable:

        (1) Number of troops

        (2) Number of aircraft

        (3) Number of other equipment (e.g. artillery, tanks, radars, trucks, water "buffaloes," etc.)

        (4) Names of military installations/geographic locations of U.S. military units in Saudi Arabia

        (5) Information regarding future operations

        (6) Information concerning security precautions at military installations in Saudi Arabia

        (7) Names/hometowns of U.S. military personnel being interviewed, and names of Saudis being interviewed. Commanders of U.S. units being interviewed are excepted from this provision.

        (9) Photography that would show level of security at military installations in Saudi Arabia

        (10) Photography that would reveal the name or specific location of military forces or installations.

2. If you are not sure whether an action you will take will violate a ground rule, consult with your escort officer PRIOR TO TAKING THAT ACTION.

As of April 13, 1990

GROUND RULES

You have been selected to participate as a member of the DoD National Media Pool. The ground rules below will protect the security of the operation and the safety of the troops involved, while allowing you the greatest permissible freedom and access in covering the story as representatives of all U.S. media.

- Prior to your departure, do not tell anyone that the pool has been activated. This is absolutely essential to preserve security in the event of an actual contingency operation.

- You may not file stories or otherwise attempt to communicate with any individual about the operation until stories and all other information (from videotape, sound bites, photo cutlines, etc.) have been pooled with other pool members. This pooling may take place at a pool member meeting during or immediately following the operation. You will be expected to brief other pool members concerning your experiences. Detailed instructions on filing will be provided by your military escorts at an appropriate time.

- You must remain with the escort officers at all times, until released--and follow their instructions regarding your activities. These instructions are not intended to hinder your reporting and are given only to facilitate movement of the pool and ensure troop safety.

- Failure to follow these ground rules may result in your expulsion from the pool.

- Your participation in the pool indicates your understanding of these guidelines and your willingness to abide by them.

Additional ground rules developed by the news organizations within the pool are attached.

As of April 13, 1990

To: Members of the Pentagon News Media Pool

Re: Pool Operations

Representatives of the news organizations in the pool have adopted the following rules for pool operations:

1) The pool is a non-competitive pool. This means that all participants must share their reporting and photos on a timely basis.

Correspondents will share their pooled information at the scene of the operation. Photographers will make their film available by turning over their film to wire service participants.

2) Pool members should seek the widest possible coverage of the military operation. This will require pool members to assign themselves in an appropriate manner. If needed, pool members should draw straws or adopt some other method of allocating assignments.

3) The wire services undertake to transmit the newspaper pool's news report.

APPENDIX D—EXHIBIT 1

Defense Department National Media Pool Ground Rules
Operation Desert Shield
August 12–26, 1990

APPENDIX D

Media Ground Rules and Guidelines for
Operation Desert Shield and Operation Desert Storm

APPENDIX D—EXHIBIT 4

Pete Williams' Memorandum dated December 14, 1990
With Defense Department Contingency Plan for Media
Coverage of Hostilities, dated December 13, 1990

8. Media should be prepared to cover the high cost of visiting Saudi Arabia (such as $100 per night lodging, $30 per meal dining, ground transportation, telephone calls, etc.) CASH/RIYALS IS A MUST.

9. Interviews with military personnel entering/departing the Ministry of Defense or other public places will be coordinated in advance by the Joint Information Bureau. THERE WILL BE NO "AMBUSH" INTERVIEWS.

I CERTIFY THAT THE FOLLOWING INFORMATION IS TRUE AND CORRECT:

DATE: _____

NAME: _____

NAME OF NEXT OF KIN: _____
ADDRESS: _____
PHONE: (___) ___-____

MEDIA AFFILIATION: _____
MAILING ADDRESS: _____

PHONE: (___) ___-____/____
PASSPORT NUMBER AND COUNTRY OF ISSUE: _____
VISA EXPIRATION: _____
ADDRESS IN COUNTRY: _____

PHONE: _____

(JIB PERSONNEL WILL CHECK PICTURE ID'S)

I UNDERSTAND AND AGREE TO COMPLY WITH ALL PROVISIONS OF THE MEDIA GUIDELINES AND ANY ADDITIONAL INSTRUCTIONS THAT MY MEDIA ESCORT MAY PROVIDE:

SIGNATURE: _____

BADGE NUMBER: _____

MEDIA GROUND RULES

THE GROUND-RULES BELOW WILL PROTECT THE SECURITY AND THE SAFETY
OF THE TROOPS INVOLVED, WHILE ALLOWING YOU THE GREATEST
PERMISSIBLE FREEDOM AND ACCESS IN COVERING YOUR STORY.

1. All interviews with news media representatives will be "on
the record." Security at the source will be the policy.

2. All Navy embark stories will state that the report is coming
"FROM THE ARABIAN GULF, RED SEA or NORTH ARABIAN SEA." Stories
written in Saudi Arabia may be datelined, "EASTERN SAUDI ARABIA,
CENTRAL SAUDI ARABIA, etc. Stories from other participating
countries may be datelined from those countries only after their
participation is released by DoD. No specific locations will be
used when filing the stories.

3. You MUST remain with your military escort at all times, until
released, and follow their instructions regarding your
activities. These instructions are not intended to hinder your
reporting. They are only to facilitate troop movement, ensure
safety, and protect operational security.

4. The following categories of information are NOT releasable:

   (a) Number of troops
   (b) Number of aircraft
   (c) Numbers regarding other equipment (e.g. artillery,
       tanks, radars, trucks, water, etc.)
   (d) Names of military installations/specific geographic
       locations of U.S. military units in the CENTCOM Area of
       responsibility (AOR). (Unless specifically released
       by Department of Defense.)
   (e) Information regarding future operations.
   (f) Information concerning security precautions at military
       installations.
   (g) Photography that would show level of security at
       military installations, especially aerial and satellite
       photography.
   (h) Photography that would reveal the name or specific
       location of military forces or installations.
   (i) Rules of engagement details.
   (j) Information on intelligence collection activities to
       include targets, methods, results.
   (k) Information on in-progress operations against hostile
       targets.
   (l) Information on special units, unique operations
       methodology/tactical (air ops, angles of attack,
       speeds, etc.; naval tactical/evasive maneuvers, etc.)
   (m) Information identifying postponed or cancelled
       operations.
   (n) In case of operational necessity, additional specific
       guidelines may be necessary to protect tactical
       security.

5.- The following categories ARE releasable:

(a) Arrival of major U.S. units in CENTCOM AOR when officially announced by a U.S. spokesperson. Mode of travel (sea or air) and date of departure from home station.
(b) Approximate friendly force strength figures, after review by host nation government.
(c) Approximate friendly casualty and POW figures, by service.
(d) Approximate enemy casualty and POW figures for each action, operation.
(e) Non-sensitive, unclassified information regarding U.S. air, ground and sea operations (past and present).
(f) Friendly force size in an action or operation will be announced using general terms such as "multi-battalion", "naval task force", etc.
Specific force/unit identification/designation may be released when it has become public knowledge and no longer warrants security protection.
(g) Identification and location of military targets and objectives previously under attack.
(h) Generic origin of air operations such as "land" or "carrier based".
(i) Date/time/location of previous conventional military missions and actions as well as mission results.
(j) Types of ordnance expended will be released in general terms rather than specific amounts.
(k) Number of aerial combat or reconnaissance missions or sorties flown in theater or operational area.
(l) Type of forces involved (infantry, armor, Marines, Carrier Battle Group).
(m) Weather and climate conditions.
(n) Allied participation by type of operation (ships, aircraft, ground units, etc.) after approval of host nation government.
(o) Conventional operation nicknames.
(p) Names and hometowns of U.S. Military units/individuals may now be released.

6. If you are not sure whether an action you will take will violate a ground rule, consult with your escort officer PRIOR TO TAKING THAT ACTION

7. Media must carry and support any personal and professional gear they take with them, including protective cases for professional equipment, batteries, cables, converters, etc.

APPENDIX D—EXHIBIT 5

Pete Williams' Memorandum dated January 7, 1991
With Proposed Media Ground Rules and Guidelines dated
January 7, 1991
(These Ground Rules and Guidelines never were put into effect.)

(12) Information on special operations units, unique operations methodology or tactics, for example, air operations, angles of attack, and speeds; naval tactical or evasive maneuvers, etc.

(13) Information identifying postponed or cancelled operations.

(14) Information on missing or downed aircraft or missing ships, while search and rescue operations are planned or underway.

(15) Information on effectiveness of enemy camouflage, cover, deception, targeting, direct and indirect fire, intelligence collection, or security measures.

(16) Additional guidelines may be necessary to protect tactical security.

Casualty information

(1) Notification of the next of kin is extremely sensitive. By executive directive, next of kin of all military fatalities must be notified in person by an officer of the appropriate service.

(2) There have been instances in which next of kin have first learned of the death or wounding of a loved one through news media reports. If casualty photographs show a recognizable face, name tag, items of jewelry or other identifying feature before the casualty's next of kin have been notified, the anguish that sudden recognition at home can cause is out of proportion to the news value of the photograph or video. Although the casualty reporting and notification system works on a priority basis, correspondents are urged to keep this problem in mind when covering action in the field. Names of casualties whose next of kin have been notified can be verified by the joint information bureaus in Riyadh or Dhahran, the appropriate public affairs office, or the office of the Assistant Secretary of Defense (Public Affairs).

- end -

PROPOSED NEWS MEDIA LISTING FOR DOD CONTINGENCY AIRLIFT

MEDIA AFFILIATION	NUMBER OF SEATS
ABC-TV	10
CBS-TV	10
CNN	10
NBC-TV	10
NBC/ABC/CBS crews for local affiliates	6
AP	5
UPI	5
REUTERS	5
ABC RADIO	2
AP RADIO NETWORK	2
CBS RADIO	2
WESTWOOD RADIO	2
NATIONAL PUBLIC RADIO	2
UPI RADIO	1
UNISTAR RADIO	1
TIME	3
NEWSWEEK	3
U.S. NEWS AND WORLD REPORT	3
WASHINGTON POST	3
NEW YORK TIMES	3
LOS ANGELES TIMES	3
CHICAGO TRIBUNE	3
WALL STREET JOURNAL	3
KNIGHT-RIDDER	2
BOSTON GLOBE	2
GANNETT NEWS SERVICE	2
COX NEWSPAPERS	2
HEARST NEWSPAPERS	2
SAN FRANCISCO CHRONICLE	1
NEW YORK POST	1
NEWSDAY	1
CHRISTIAN SCIENCE MONITOR	1
BALTIMORE SUN	1
WASHINGTON TIMES	1
DALLAS MORNING NEWS	1
COPLEY NEWS SERVICE	1
NEWHOUSE NEWS SERVICE	1
SCRIPPS-HOWARD	1
MILWAUKEE JOURNAL	1
CAPITAL CITIES COMMUNICATIONS, INC.	1
ARMY-NAVY-AIR FORCE TIMES	1
TOTAL:	120

14 December

Operation Desert Shield
News media ground rules

All interviews with service members will be on the record. Security at the source is the policy. In the event of hostilities, media products will be subject to security review prior to release. Interviews with pilots and aircrew members are authorized upon completion of mission; however, release of information must conform to the ground rules stated below.

All Navy embark stories will state that the report is coming "from the Persian Gulf, Red Sea or North Arabian Sea." Stories written in Saudi Arabia may be datelined Riyadh, Dhahran, or other area by general geographical description, such as "Eastern Saudi Arabia." Stories from other participating countries may be datelined from those countries only after their participation is released by DoD.

You must remain with your military escort at all times, until released, and follow instructions regarding your activities. These instructions are intended only to facilitate troop movement, ensure safety, and maintain operational security.

You must be physically fit. If, in the opinion of the commander, you are unable to withstand the rigorous conditions required to operate with his forward-deployed forces, you will be medically evacuated out of the area.

You are not authorized to carry a personal weapon.

The following categories of information are releasable:

(1) Arrival of U.S. military units in the Central Command area of responsibility when officially announced. Mode of travel (sea or air), date of departure, and home station.

(2) Approximate friendly force strength figures in theatre.

(3) Approximate friendly casualty and POW figures by service.

(4) Confirmed figures of enemy personnel killed in action (KIA) or detained for each action or operation.

(5) Nonsensitive, unclassified information regarding U.S. air, ground, and sea operations, past and present.

(6) Size of friendly force participating in an action or operation will be disclosed using general terms such as "multi-battalion," "naval task force," etc. Specific force or unit identification may be released when it no longer warrants security protection.

(7) Identification and location of military targets and objectives previously under attack.

(8) Generic description of origin of air operations, such as "land" or "carrier-based."

(9) Date, time, or location of previous conventional military missions and actions as well as mission results.

(10) Types of ordnance expended, in general terms.

(11) Number of aerial combat or reconnaissance missions or sorties flown in theater or operational area.

(12) Type of forces involved (e.g., infantry, armor, Marines, carrier battle group).

(13) Weather and climate conditions.

(14) Allied participation by type of operation (ships, aircraft, ground units, etc.) after approval of host nation government.

(15) Conventional operation code names.

(16) Names and hometowns of U.S. military units or individuals.

The following categories of information are not releasable:

(1) Number of troops.

(2) Number of aircraft.

(3) Numbers regarding other equipment or critical supplies (e.g., artillery, tanks, landing craft, radars, trucks, water, etc.).

(4) Names of military installations or specific geographic locations of U.S. military units in the Central Command area of responsibility, unless specifically released by the Department of Defense.

(5) Information regarding future operations.

(6) Information regarding security precautions at military installations or encampments.

(7) Photography that would show level of security at military installations or encampments, especially aerial and satellite photography.

(8) Photography that would reveal the name or specific location of military units or installations.

(9) Rules of engagement details.

(10) Information on intelligence collection activities including targets, methods, and results.

(11) Information on operations underway against hostile targets.

Department of Defense
Contingency Plan for Media Coverage of Hostilities
Operation DESERT SHIELD

The objective of this plan is to ensure news media access to combat areas from the onset of hostilities, or as soon thereafter as possible, in Operation DESERT SHIELD. This is a three-phased plan for exercising and deploying rotating correspondent pools, aligned with front line forces to permit combat coverage.

Each pool would consist of eighteen news media personnel: three newspaper correspondents, two wire service correspondents, two three-member television crews, one radio correspondent, one wire service photographer, one newspaper photographer, one news magazine reporter, one news magazine photographer, one Saudi reporter and one third-country reporter. Membership in the pools would be drawn from news media personnel already in Saudi Arabia.

In Phase I of the plan, which would begin immediately, the first two pools would be formed by the Joint Information Bureau in Dhahran and randomly exercised at least once every two weeks to provide training for media participants and U.S. military personnel. These pools will always be exercised simultaneously to ensure that operational security is preserved. During Phase I, the pools would familiarize themselves with troops and equipment, cover activities in the areas to which the pools are sent, and exercise their ability to file news stories from the field.

Phase II would begin by deploying the pools when hostilities are imminent, putting them in place to cover the first stages of combat. If such prepositioning is not possible, the pools would be moved forward from Dhahran as quickly as possible to the immediate area of conflict. As soon as possible, additional pools would be deployed to expand the coverage. The size of these pools will be determined by the availability of transportation and other operational factors. These additional pools could be used to fill the gaps in coverage, if the conflict is spread over a wide area. Air Force, Navy, amphibious, and logisitical support units will be covered by additional smaller pools, which will be rotated to ensure continuous coverage.

Security review for all pool material would be performed at the source, where the information was gathered, and transmitted to the Joint Information Bureau at Dhahran, where it would then be available to journalists covering the operation. Ground rules would consist of those currently in effect.

Phase III would begin when open coverage is possible and would provide for unilateral coverage of activities. The pools would be disbanded and all media would operate independently, although under U.S. Central Command escort.

13 December 1990

ASSISTANT SECRETARY OF DEFENSE
WASHINGTON, D.C. 20301-1400

December 14, 1990

PUBLIC AFFAIRS

MEMORANDUM

To: Washington bureau chiefs of the Pentagon press corps

From: Pete Williams

Re: Plans for pools and flight for auxiliary staff in the event of hostilities in the Persian Gulf

Since the beginning of Operation Desert Shield I have met twice, at their initiative, with the bureau chiefs of several news organizations that are regular members of the Pentagon press corps. We discussed complaints from their correspondents in Saudi Arabia and the progress in refining a new plan for pool coverage in the event of hostilities in Saudi Arabia and the Persian Gulf. We also discussed a request from news organizations in the Pentagon press corps who cited difficulty in getting visas for staff and who accordingly wanted help in getting additional personnel to the region, should hostilities break out.

After the second meeting, on November 28th, I briefed Secretary Cheney and General Powell on a concept for combat pools, the result of a month of planning and discussions within the Pentagon and with military commanders in the Gulf. After making some suggestions, the Secretary and the Chairman approved the concept. I then briefed a representative of the Saudi government. Our staff has since been preparing the more detailed version of the pool concept that will become part of the overall military plan for the operation. That work has proceeded over the past week, while I was with the Secretary on his trip last week to NATO and Poland. A summary of the concept is attached. I am interested in your comments or questions.

The Secretary and the Chairman also approved the idea of sending a US military C-141 aircraft to Saudi Arabia, if hostilities were to break out, carrying supplemental news media personnel to help cover the story of combat, given that most news organizations have only very small staffs in Saudi Arabia now -- in many cases, only one correspondent. The objective is to help prevent the pool operation from breaking down through a lack of news media representatives necessary to make it work -- the editors, producers, technicians, writers, and pool coordinators who will be essential to successful pool operation.

This flight would be a one-way trip, transporting representatives of US news organizations who regularly cover the Pentagon. Space for cargo will be extremely limited: each passenger would be allowed one small suitcase. Equipment cases should be shipped separately. I solicit your comments on that list as well. The bureau chiefs who first suggested the idea said it was predicated on their inability to get more than one or two visas at a time from the government of Saudi Arabia. Should the visa picture open up, I suggest we readdress the need for the plane.

Thank you for your continued suggestions and comments.

ASSISTANT SECRETARY OF DEFENSE
WASHINGTON, D.C. 20301-1400

BLIC AFFAIRS

January 7, 1991

MEMORANDUM

To: Washington Bureau Chiefs of the Pentagon Press Corps

From: Pete Williams

Re: Ground rules and flight for auxiliary staff
in the event of hostilities in the Persian Gulf

Thank you for attending our meeting last Friday. As in the past, your comments were valuable and appreciated. I believe we share the common goal of working out a system under which information will be disseminated to the American people without jeopardizing operations or endangering the lives of U.S. service members.

The overwhelming view expressed during the meeting was that the ground rules should be brief and clear in order to be effective. We agree and have boiled them down to one page (copy attached). We adopted the suggestion many of you made and now list only that information which should not be revealed. The second page of the attachment contains guidelines to follow which are intended to meet the specific operational environment of the Persian Gulf.

You will note that we eliminated many of the earlier proposed ground rules, especially those which would have failed the critical test for combat ground rules: whether that information would jeopardize the operation, endanger friendly forces, or be of use to the enemy. As many of you noted, while every military operation has unique characteristics, past experience shows that reporters understand their heavy responsibility in covering combat. In the end, it is that professionalism upon which we will depend.

I am still working with the Saudi embassy to obtain visas for your people who may go over on the Air Force plane. As soon as I have the details worked out, I will pass them to you. In the mean time, we need the information listed below as soon as possible for the staff members you wish to send on the C-141.

    a. Name of news organization

    b. Full billing address of news organization

    c. Fax number of news organization

    d. Full name(s) of representative(s)

    e. Social security number(s)

f. Passport number(s)

g. Names and home, business, cellular (if applicable) and beeper phone numbers of two people (primary and backup) who will serve as your points of contact for activation of the flight

This information can be faxed to us at (703) 693-6853, attention: LCDR Gregg Hartung. You may verify receipt by calling (703) 693-1074.

Thank you for your continuing suggestions and comments.

7 JAN 91

OPERATION DESERT SHIELD
GROUND RULES

The following information should not be reported because its publication or broadcast could jeopardize operations and endanger lives:

(1) For U.S. or coalition units, specific numerical information on troop strength, aircraft, weapons systems, on-hand equipment, or supplies (e.g. artillery, tanks, radars, missiles, trucks, water), including amounts of ammunition or fuel moved by support units or on hand in combat units. Unit size may be described in general terms such as "company-size," "multi-battalion," "multi-division," "naval task force," and "carrier battle group." Number or amount of equipment and supplies may be described in general terms such as "large," "small," or "many."

(2) Any information that reveals details of future plans, operations, or strikes, including postponed or cancelled operations.

(3) Information or photography, including aerial and satellite pictures, that would reveal the specific location of military forces or show the level of security at military installations or encampments. Locations may be described as follows: all Navy embark stories can identify the ship upon which embarked as a dateline and will state that the report is coming "from the Persian Gulf," "Red Sea," or "North Arabian Sea." Stories written in Saudi Arabia may be datelined, "Eastern Saudi Arabia," "Near the Kuwaiti border," etc. For specific countries outside Saudi Arabia, stories will state that the report is coming from the Persian Gulf region unless DoD has publicly acknowledged participation by that country.

(4) Rules of engagement details.

(5) Information on intelligence collection activities, including targets, methods, and results.

(6) During an operation, specific information on friendly force troop movements, tactical deployments, and dispositions that would jeopardize operational security and lives. This would include unit designations, names of operations, and size of friendly forces involved, until released by CENTCOM.

(7) Identification of mission aircraft points of origin, other than as land or carrier based.

(8) Information on the effectiveness or ineffectiveness of enemy camouflage, cover, deception, targeting, direct and indirect fire, intelligence collection, or security measures.

(9) Specific identifying information on missing or downed aircraft or ships while search and rescue operations are planned or underway.

(10) Special operations forces' methods, unique equipment or tactics.

(11) Specific operating methods and tactics, (e.g., air ops angles of attack or speeds, or naval tactics and evasive maneuvers). General terms such as "low" or "fast" may be used.

(12) Information on operational or support vulnerabilities that could be used against U.S. forces, such as details of major battle damage or major personnel losses of specific U.S. or coalition units, until that information no longer provides tactical advantage to the enemy and is, therefore, released by CENTCOM. Damage and casualties may be described as "light," "moderate," or "heavy."

7 JAN 91

GUIDELINES FOR NEWS MEDIA

News media personnel must carry and support any personal and professional gear they take with them, including protective cases for professional equipment, batteries, cables, converters, etc.

Night Operations -- Light discipline restrictions will be followed. The only approved light source is a flashlight with a red lens. No visible light source, including flash or television lights, will be used when operating with forces at night unless specifically approved by the on-scene commander.

You must remain with your military escort at all times, until released, and follow their instructions regarding your activities. These instructions are not intended to hinder your reporting. They are intended to facilitate movement, ensure safety, and protect operational security.

For news media personnel participating in designated CENTCOM Media Pools:

(1) Upon registering with the JIB, news media should contact their respective pool coordinator for explanation of pool operations.

(2) If you are unable to withstand the rigorous conditions required to operate with the forward-deployed forces, you will be medically evacuated out of the area.

(3) Security at the source will be the policy. In the event of hostilites, pool products will be subject to security review prior to release to determine if they contain information that would jeopardize an operation or the security of U.S. or coalition forces. Material will not be withheld just because it is embarrassing or contains criticism. The public affairs officer on the scene will conduct the security review. However, if a conflict arises, the product will be expeditiously sent to JIB Dhahran for review by the JIB Director. If no agreement can be reached, the product will be expeditiously forwarded to OASD(PA) for review with the appropriate bureau chief.

Casualty information, because of concern of the notification of the next of kin, is extremely sensitive. By executive directive, next of kin of all military fatalities must be notified in person by a uniformed member of the appropriate service. There have been instances in which the next of kin have first learned of the death or wounding of a loved one through the news media. The problem is particularly difficult for visual media. Casualty photographs showing a recognizable face, name tag, or other identifying feature or item should not be used before the next of kin have been notified. The anguish that sudden recognition at home can cause far outweighs the news value of the photograph, film or videotape. Names of casualties whose next of kin have been notified can be verified through the JIB Dhahran.

PROPOSED NEWS MEDIA LISTING FOR DOD CONTINGENCY AIRLIFT

MEDIA AFFILIATION	NUMBER OF SEATS
ABC-TV	10
CBS-TV	10
CNN	10
NBC-TV	10
NBC/ABC/CBS crews for local affiliates	6
AP	5
UPI	5
REUTERS	5
ABC RADIO	2
AP RADIO NETWORK	2
CBS RADIO	2
WESTWOOD RADIO	2
NATIONAL PUBLIC RADIO	2
UPI RADIO	1
UNISTAR RADIO	1
VOICE OF AMERICA	1
TIME	3
NEWSWEEK	3
U.S. NEWS AND WORLD REPORT	3
BUSINESS WEEK	1
WASHINGTON POST	3
NEW YORK TIMES	3
LOS ANGELES TIMES	3
CHICAGO TRIBUNE	3
WALL STREET JOURNAL	3
KNIGHT-RIDDER	3
BOSTON GLOBE	2
GANNETT NEWS SERVICE	2
USA TODAY	2
COX NEWSPAPERS	2
HEARST NEWSPAPERS	2
SAN FRANCISCO CHRONICLE	1
NEW YORK POST	1
NEWSDAY	2
CHRISTIAN SCIENCE MONITOR	1
BALTIMORE SUN	1
WASHINGTON TIMES	1
DALLAS MORNING NEWS	1
COPLEY NEWS SERVICE	1
NEWHOUSE NEWS SERVICE	1
SCRIPPS-HOWARD	1
MILWAUKEE JOURNAL	1
CAPITAL CITIES COMMUNICATIONS, INC.	1
ARMY-NAVY-AIR FORCE TIMES	1

TOTAL: 126   4 January 1991

APPENDIX D—EXHIBIT 6

Pete Williams' Memorandum dated January 15, 1991
With Media Ground Rules and Guidelines dated
January 14, 1991
(Ground Rules and Guidelines were used for
Operation Desert Storm.)

ASSISTANT SECRETARY OF DEFENSE

WASHINGTON, D.C. 20301-1400

PUBLIC AFFAIRS

January 15, 1991

MEMORANDUM FOR WASHINGTON BUREAU CHIEFS OF THE PENTAGON PRESS CORPS

SUBJ: Ground rules and guidelines for correspondents in the event of hostilities in the Persian Gulf

Last Monday, I sent you copies of our revised ground rules for press coverage of combat operations and guidelines for correspondents that are intended to meet the specific operational environment of the Persian Gulf. I appreciate the comments I have received from some of you and understand your concerns, particularly with respect to security review and pooling in general. I also was pleased by the general consensus that the one-page version of the ground rules was an improvement.

The ground rules have been reviewed and approved with no major changes. They became effective today.

The guidelines were revised to comply with operational concerns in Saudi Arabia. We added a provision that media representatives will not be permitted to carry weapons, clarified the escort requirement, added a sentence giving medical personnel the authority to determine media guidelines at medical facilities, and deleted the sentence saying the JIB in Dhahran would verify next of kin notification on casualties. We also added a section, in response to many questions, which clarifies our policy on unilateral media coverage of the forward areas during the period when the pools are operational.

Last Saturday, I conducted a conference call with the majority of the CENTCOM public affairs officers, who were gathered in Riyadh and Dhahran, and discussed the ground rules and guidelines to ensure that the intent and purpose of the ground rules is clearly understood.

I appreciate your counsel and remain ready to discuss any problems or questions you may have.

Pete Williams
Assistant Secretary of Defense
(Public Affairs)

14 JAN 91

OPERATION DESERT SHIELD
GROUND RULES

The following information should not be reported because its publication or broadcast could jeopardize operations and endanger lives:

(1) For U.S. or coalition units, specific numerical information on troop strength, aircraft, weapons systems, on-hand equipment, or supplies (e.g., artillery, tanks, radars, missiles, trucks, water), including amounts of ammunition or fuel moved by or on hand in support and combat units. Unit size may be described in general terms such as "company-size," "multibattalion," "multidivision," "naval task force," and "carrier battle group." Number or amount of equipment and supplies may be described in general terms such as "large," "small," or "many."

(2) Any information that reveals details of future plans, operations, or strikes, including postponed or cancelled operations.

(3) Information, photography, and imagery that would reveal the specific location of military forces or show the level of security at military installations or encampments. Locations may be described as follows: all Navy embark stories can identify the ship upon which embarked as a dateline and will state that the report is coming from the "Persian Gulf," "Red Sea," or "North Arabian Sea." Stories written in Saudi Arabia may be datelined "Eastern Saudi Arabia," "Near the Kuwaiti border," etc. For specific countries outside Saudi Arabia, stories will state that the report is coming from the Persian Gulf region unless that country has acknowledged its participation.

(4) Rules of engagement details.

(5) Information on intelligence collection activities, including targets, methods, and results.

(6) During an operation, specific information on friendly force troop movements, tactical deployments, and dispositions that would jeopardize operational security or lives. This would include unit designations, names of operations, and size of friendly forces involved, until released by CENTCOM.

(7) Identification of mission aircraft points of origin, other than as land- or carrier-based.

(8) Information on the effectiveness or ineffectiveness of enemy camouflage, cover, deception, targeting, direct and indirect fire, intelligence collection, or security measures.

(9) Specific identifying information on missing or downed aircraft or ships while search and rescue operations are planned or underway.

(10) Special operations forces' methods, unique equipment or tactics.

(11) Specific operating methods and tactics, (e.g., air angles of attack or speeds, or naval tactics and evasive maneuvers). General terms such as "low" or "fast" may be used.

(12) Information on operational or support vulnerabilities that could be used against U.S. forces, such as details of major battle damage or major personnel losses of specific U.S. or coalition units, until that information no longer provides tactical advantage to the enemy and is, therefore, released by CENTCOM. Damage and casualties may be described as "light," "moderate," or "heavy."

14 JAN 91

GUIDELINES FOR NEWS MEDIA

News media personnel must carry and support any personal and professional gear they take with them, including protective cases for professional equipment, batteries, cables, converters, etc.

Night Operations -- Light discipline restrictions will be followed. The only approved light source is a flashlight with a red lens. No visible light source, including flash or television lights, will be used when operating with forces at night unless specifically approved by the on-scene commander.

Because of host-nation requirements, you must stay with your public affairs escort while on Saudi bases. At other U.S. tactical or field locations and encampments, a public affairs escort may be required because of security, safety, and mission requirements as determined by the host commander.

Casualty information, because of concern of the notification of the next of kin, is extremely sensitive. By executive directive, next of kin of all military fatalities must be notified in person by a uniformed member of the appropriate service. There have been instances in which the next of kin have first learned of the death or wounding of a loved one through the news media. The problem is particularly difficult for visual media. Casualty photographs showing a recognizable face, name tag, or other identifying feature or item should not be used before the next of kin have been notified. The anguish that sudden recognition at home can cause far outweighs the news value of the photograph, film or videotape. News coverage of casualties in medical centers will be in strict compliance with the instructions of doctors and medical officials.

To the extent that individuals in the news media seek access to the U.S. area of operation, the following rule applies: Prior to or upon commencement of hostilities, media pools will be established to provide initial combat coverage of U.S. forces. U.S. news media personnel present in Saudi Arabia will be given the opportunity to join CENTCOM media pools, providing they agree to pool their products. News media personnel who are not members of the official CENTCOM media pools will not be permitted into forward areas. Reporters are strongly discouraged from attempting to link up on their own with combat units. U.S. commanders will maintain extremely tight security throughout the operational area and will exclude from the area of operation all unauthorized individuals.

For news media personnel participating in designated CENTCOM Media Pools:

(1) Upon registering with the JIB, news media should contact their respective pool coordinator for an explanation of pool operations.

(2) In the event of hostilities, pool products will be the subject to review before release to determine if they contain sensitive information about military plans, capabilities, operations, or vulnerabilities (see attached ground rules) that would jeopardize the outcome of an operation or the safety of U.S. or coalition forces. Material will be examined solely for its conformance to the attached ground rules, not for its potential to express criticism or cause embarrassment. The public affairs escort officer on scene will review pool reports, discuss ground rule problems with the reporter, and in the limited circumstances when no agreement can be reached with a reporter about disputed materials, immediately send the disputed materials to JIB Dhahran for review by the JIB Director and the appropriate news media representative. If no agreement can be reached, the issue will be immediately forwarded to OASD(PA) for review with the appropriate bureau chief. The ultimate decision on publication will be made by the originating reporter's news organization.

(3) Correspondents may not carry a personal weapon.

Date Due
